In My Stride

Also by Jack P. Harland

Highland Journal
1. The Making of a Hillwalker

Highland Journal

2. In My Stride

Jack P. Harland

Matador
9 Priory Business Park,
Wistow Road, Kibworth Beauchamp,
Leicestershire. LE8 0RX
Tel: 0116 279 2299
Email: books@troubador.co.uk
Web: www.troubador.co.uk/matador
Twitter: @matadorbooks

ISBN 978 1838590 673

British Library Cataloguing in Publication Data.
A catalogue record for this book is available from the British Library.

Printed and bound by CPI Group (UK) Ltd, Croydon, CR0 4YY
Typeset in 12pt Minion Pro by Troubador Publishing Ltd, Leicester, UK

Matador is an imprint of Troubador Publishing Ltd

To Tom

Contents

Foreword

The sketch maps illustrating the walks in this journal should not be used for navigation, an Ordnance Survey map (or similar) should always be taken.

I have shared many happy days in the mountains with the best of friends and, with a few exceptions, have changed their names to protect their privacy.

Introduction

Children and dogs were put out into the fresh air and were allowed to roam in the 1950s and 60s. With my raggle taggle gang of friends and dogs I had adventures along and in the local burn where we caught sticklebacks, frogs and newts. The old trees of the wood tested our climbing skills and birds' nests were discovered. More exciting were the Red Hills, old colliery slag heaps where plant life was taking a hold and pale smoke rose from the clattering slopes; a strange and lonely place. Those early days did something irrevocable to my soul as, all these years later, I still love to roam.

I was ready for wider horizons when I joined the Boy Scouts at the age of eleven. My troop was particularly active, organising many short camps as well as long ones at Whitsun and in the summer holiday. The Lake District fells were not far away, so we loaded all of the equipment onto an open lorry then clambered on to our precarious perch. Snowdonia was too far away for the lorry, so we travelled along the railways in goods wagons or, if lucky, the guard's van. It was at these camps that I first experienced mountains. The tents were pitched on the last of the high pastures, at the foot of grey screes. I climbed the crags above and explored the windy ridges, thrilled by this new world.

I see now that these tough places were character-building. Once we missed a night's sleep, climbing a Welsh mountain instead. As we stumbled up the dark path we were encouraged by being told of the glorious sunrise that we would see from the summit. Those with some experience of such high places will already have guessed the outcome, clammy low cloud smothered everything and, shivering, we walked down again.

When running down a scree one day a friend slipped and suffered a deep gash in the bare arm he had put out to break his fall. Blood pumped out and I had to apply pressure to the wound for what seemed eternity before help arrived. I was terrified that his life would ebb away in a red stain on the matt grey shards of slate. Worse was to come.

A few years later, I finished an inadequate continental breakfast in a hostel high up in the Bavarian Alps then joined a straggling line of fellow Scouts to climb up to a high col. Our leader had decided to cross this then descend into an Austrian valley where we were booked into another hostel in a small village. He had ordered lunch there. It was hot work in the August sun, our nailed boots raising white dust from the track. High above the tree line, in a wilderness of giant rocks, we reached a tiny wooden hut which sheltered a soldier with a rifle. He checked our passports and we marched on through the boulder fields and snow patches. Well behind schedule, the senior Scouts consulted their exotic maps, realising, I would imagine, that they had misunderstood the scales.

It was after the early evening thunderstorm that things began to go badly wrong. Exhausted, hungry, dehydrated and soaked to the skin, one after another came to a halt and sat down. Some drank from puddles and this seemed to bring on violent bouts of diarrhoea. The adult leaders could walk no further and became confused and disorientated. The troop had disintegrated.

I saw the way ahead and followed the track down to the forest far below. The ranks of shadowy trees seemed endless and it was quite dark when I saw the lights of the village. At the hostel I used my few words of German and much sign language to raise the alarm. People ran up the cobbled streets and there was urgent shouting. Men began to gather at the hostel, some wearing lederhosen and some with feathers in their hats. I pointed to my stomach and a lady with an apron over her big bosom hurried inside, returning with a very large sandwich of black bread and spicy sausage. I often think that it was the best meal I have ever eaten.

The men began lighting long wax torches and one was offered to me. I looked puzzled. A grey-bearded man came close and used his own mixture of sign language and German, pointing first at me, then back up the way I had come. The horror of that moment still comes back to me at times, would my jelly legs be capable of carrying me all the way back up there?

It must have been the sandwich that got me back up that track. I refused to hold my torch until I had eaten every piece, much to the men's amusement. Then the line spread out, the torches dancing like fireflies in the pitch black. My sore legs made me think about my friends above the tree line. I was not physically stronger than many of them, so why was I the one who got down? I have never been able to answer that question. The rescuers yodelled, the sound echoing around the crags above. The Scouts knew that help was coming long before it arrived.

It is all a bit of a blur after that, but I do remember the bliss of sliding into the clean, thick cotton sheets the following morning and very briefly feeling that it was odd to be going to bed in daylight before falling into the deepest of sleeps.

The maxim, what doesn't kill you makes you stronger seemed to work for me. My attraction to hills and mountains was certainly not diminished. The biggest obstacle I faced was the competing demands of falling in love, building a career and being a father to four children. My first book begins when we started to holiday in North-west Scotland and I again had the freedom to roam the hills, now with my son. This second book begins after a move to Aberdeen, where I found a new walking companion and began to explore the big granite mountains at the headwaters of the Don and Dee.

30/12/07

Lochnagar and Conachcraig

Winter sun

I was filled with excitement as I prepared for my outing. It had been nearly nine months since I had been in the Highlands and I was thrilled at the prospect of my return. The Mountain Weather Information Service website predicted a ridge of high pressure and a fine day.

The months from that Good Friday on Bla Bheinn had been intense. Our new grandson Joe had arrived in the world and I had a new job. Pressure at work turned up to full and then got worse. We had to sell our house and buy a new one in Aberdeen. My youngest daughter had to sit her Higher exams and then start Sixth Year in a new school. My wife had to leave her friends and job. By Christmas we were exhausted but were settling into our new lives. The mountain I would climb at the end of all this should really have been special, so I chose much-loved Lochnagar.

Morag, one of my walking companions, was staying with her parents in Aberdeen, so I picked her up at 6.30 a.m. and we took the road to Deeside. Stags lined the single-track road down Glen Muick, their eyes red in the headlights. One stepped out in front of the car and I was pleased that I had been driving slowly enough to stop safely.

As we sorted out our gear, pale yellow streaks of light appeared in the dark sky. I was surprised to see so many cars and people, like us, getting ready for a day on the hills.

The dawn broke as we walked across the wide, flat floor of Glen Muick. Stags lined each side of the track, a fitting salute on the day I got back into my boots. As we left the

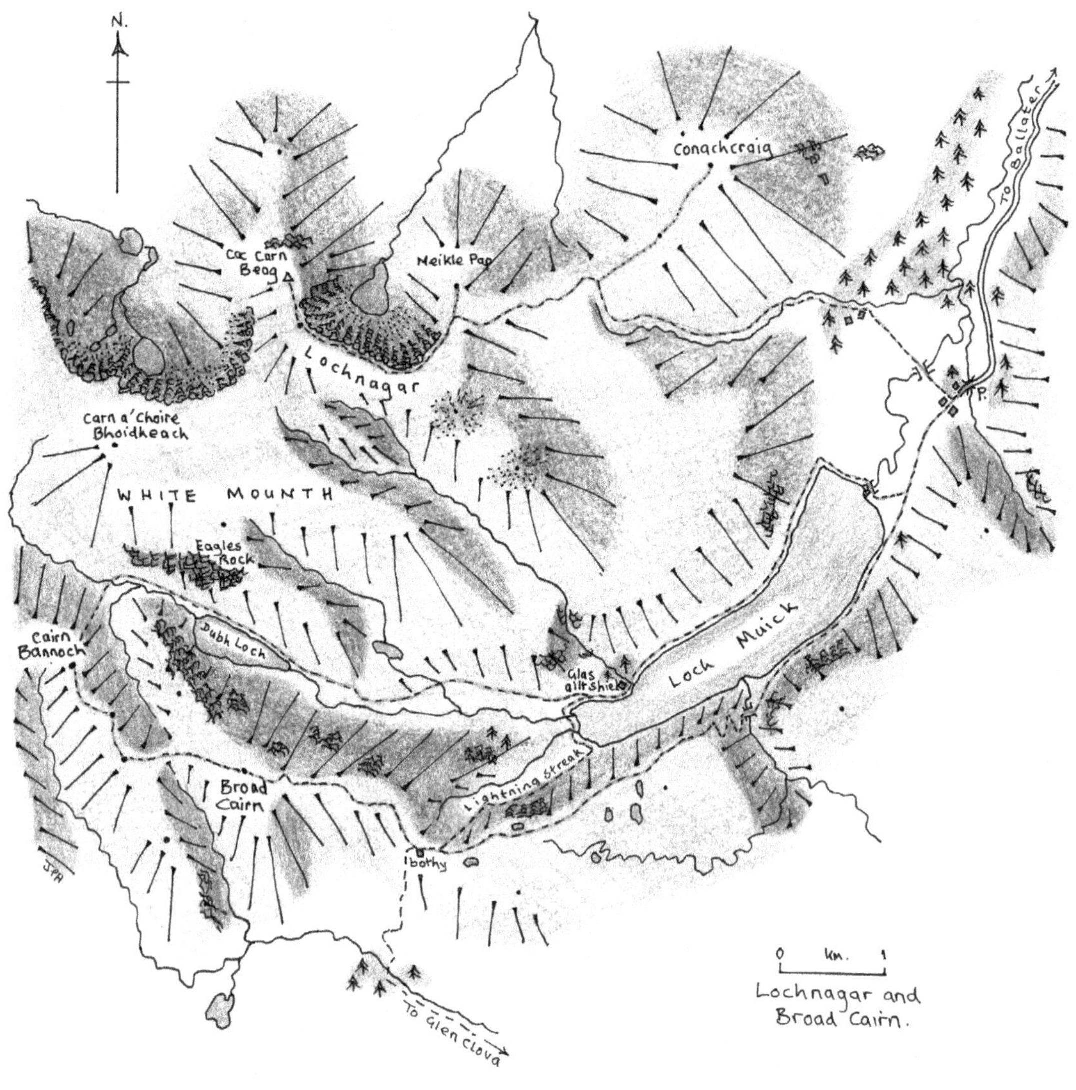

pinewoods on the west side of the glen and started climbing the track up the open hillside, the view ahead to the eastern outliers of Lochnagar showed that they were snow-capped; I was pleased that I had my crampons and ice axe with me. The rising sun coloured the snow rose pink, the summits beautiful against a dark blue sky and the air was filled with the robotic calls of Balmoral Forest's royal grouse.

We were soon at the high col between Meikle Pap, one of Lochnagar's Tops and the eastern flank of the main bulk of the mountain. It took a short scramble down the far side to get a good view of the giant corrie with its spectacular cliffs, Lochnagar's finest feature.

I suggested going up Meikle Pap where we could enjoy our breakfast with splendid views of the cliffs and summit tops. We gingerly climbed the granite tor which crowns this fine hill and from there picked out tiny figures far below, making their way up to one or other of the gullies. Morag showed me the Black Spout, the route she had used when she was taken to the mountain as a pupil. She assured me that it was easier than it looked, but I did not fancy spending such a perfect day in the cold gloom of the corrie. The sun was sparkling on the snows above and a high level walk around the scalloped cliff edge was more appealing.

We packed up our flasks, returned to the col and followed a steep but well-laid path up through the boulder scree and onto the wintry summit plateau. It was wonderful to be up there on such a day. We wandered from top to top and left the main path to find the cliff edge. Crossing the hard frozen snowfield, we came across a pair of ptarmigan. They were surprisingly tolerant of our presence and I photographed the male with his smart black eye stripe and larger red wattle as he posed on a rock.

As we walked on I commented that we had been lucky to see so much mountain wildlife on a day when dozens of hillwalkers, some with dogs, were on Lochnagar. We were climbing a steep slope at the time and above our heads, outlined against the azure sky, appeared a mountain hare. The sun was shining on his white winter coat and he looked very stylish as he posed for a while on an icy boulder like his neighbour, the ptarmigan.

The cliff edge had a track from which were dizzy views straight down the granite columns to the corrie floor below. We took our time, soaking in the spectacle and being careful not to stray onto the cornices.

At lunchtime we arrived at the summit, the strangely named Cac Carn Beag, or little shit cairn. This miniature mountain protrudes from the high plateau, crowned with a granite tor. We had to share it with a number of people and two dogs so we hunted for a quieter spot which was out of the cold breeze but still in the sun. There was a good place among the icy boulders on the west side. As we ate our sandwiches we easily picked out the features of the Cairngorms in the gin clear air. Their cover of snow helped to give sharp definition to the corries and ridges. Most spectacular of all was the Lairig Ghru, with Bod an Deamhain, Cairn Toul, Sgor an Lochain Uaine and Braeriach to the west and the massive bulk of Ben Macdui to the east. East again were Beinn a' Bhuird and Ben Avon, the granite tors on their broad summit ridges distinctive in that winter light. To the south-west lay the snow-covered plateau of the White Mounth (pronounced munth), cut by the graceful curves of arêtes, deep corries and steep-sided glens.

I was feeling on top of the world, both physically and metaphorically. Morag made the moment even better by producing a small bottle of Bowmore. I poured a drop into my steaming mug of tea and drank in the views along with the peaty fragrance of the malt.

On the way back we explored the cliff edge again, talking to the climbers and walkers we met. I stood a short distance down the last steep snow slope of the Black Spout and decided that, gloomy or not, this would be a great route for a future visit.

By this time, I could count over twenty walkers on the plateau, along with five dogs. As I was thinking that we were unlikely to see more wildlife a raven flew overhead, angrily complaining about these intruders into its high domain.

The steep path down to the col had been made treacherous by the many boots compacting the snow, which had then frozen. We got down safely but, ironically, Morag slipped on the ice on the gentler gradient of the path leading east from the col. She was lucky to walk away with nothing worse than a bruised leg.

At the foot of Conachcraig we were looking to see whether we had enough time to climb this Corbett and still get back to the car in daylight when we were visited by a snow bunting. It was a male in winter plumage, brilliant white beneath and pale brown above. As with others I have seen, this one seemed little concerned to be in the company of humans.

Male snow bunting
Lochnagar 30 December
2007.

Having decided that we did have enough time, we climbed briskly up to the granite tors which cap Conachcraig. Sitting comfortably on the westernmost tor, we had a snack and mugs of tea, looking back to Lochnagar. A blanket of cloud came from nowhere and we watched as it crawled up to the edge of the corrie cliffs and began, very slowly, to spill over onto the plateau. I felt sorry for all the walkers under that cold cloud, particularly as we sat in late afternoon sunshine, the sky above us once again winter dark blue.

On the way down to Glen Muick, we were stopped by a party of young people in their late teens or early twenties. They asked if this was the way to Lochnagar. I replied that it was indeed but there would not be enough daylight to get up, never mind back again. They smiled pleasantly, thanked me and then continued up the path towards the mountain.

Morag and I walked down through the pinewoods, across the floor of Glen Muick and back to the car in the gloaming. By the time we had taken off our boots it was dark. We had made the most of every moment of that day of winter sunshine.

16/2/08

Broad Cairn and Cairn Bannoch

Good company

James Murray, Captain in the Royal Signals in his younger days, had asked at work if I would like to go with him to the hills for a day and I had eagerly accepted the invitation. As a member of the Cairngorm Club, with experience of the Alps and other big ranges, he seemed likely to be an interesting companion. On his second round of the Munros, he was an ideal guide for these, the hills of his home ground.

We made an early start and the sky had the red and yellow of first light as we neared the car park at the head of Glen Muick. The hills were in deep shadow with black silhouettes of deer against the dawn colours.

As we walked along the track on the east side of Loch Muick, detouring around the sections which were hard ice, the sky lightened, with not a trace of cloud. The weather gods were smiling on us that day because not even the finest wisps of cirrus spoiled the blue.

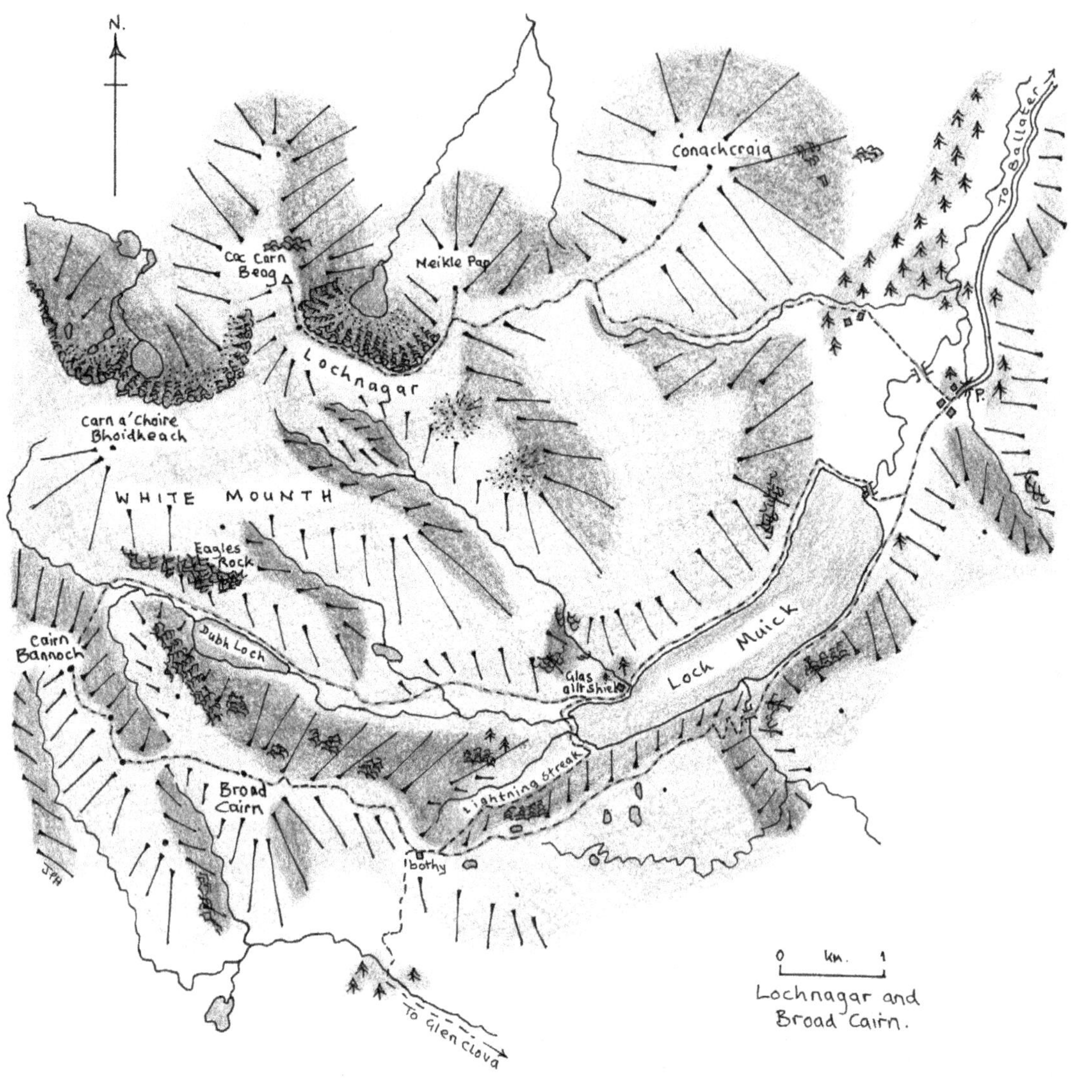

We warmed up as we followed the track up onto the plateau, stopping at the top to look down to Glas-allt Shiel, Queen Victoria's house on the shore of the loch. There was a gentle breeze but nothing disturbed the calm water below. It was like a mirror, perfectly reflecting the snow-capped peaks beyond. Ahead we could see our two Munros, with snow-streaked cliffs falling into the hanging valley of the Dubh Loch. The scene before us was coloured brown patched with white, the low-angled sun producing pockets of black shadow. The blue of the sky and loch made a startling contrast. A flock of bright yellow siskins flew up from the alders along the shore far below and performed acrobatics in perfect formation at our eye level. Perhaps they had flown up out of the shadow to enjoy the bright sun. When the light caught them they transformed into little gems.

We stopped for a hot drink and a second breakfast beside a little hut which serves as a rudimentary bothy then walked up through the boulder fields and hard frozen snow patches of Broad Cairn. A mountain hare in its winter white coat skipped ahead of us, covering the ground with great speed. It was the first of four we were to see up there.

The views from the summit were sharp and clear. In the south are the steep crags that line the walls of Glen Doll. Lochnagar's Cac Carn Beag is to the north and beyond rise the highest mountains of the Cairngorms, their brilliant white slopes drawing the eye on that winter's day.

From Broad Cairn we walked west to Cairn of Gowal and then north-west along the crest of a ridge to Cairn Bannoch, our second Munro. Both the Munro summits are granite tors, broken into blocks by the frost shattering of the periglacial era. We climbed a little way down from the summit cairn to be out of the breeze and ate our lunch in the warm sun.

Our intention then was to scramble down the steep slopes to the Allt an Dubh Loch but they were plastered with hard ice between the crags so we decided to descend further up the glen where the slopes were not so intimidating. Despite our detour, we had to put on crampons to get down. Near the bottom of the slope of smooth, hard ice we startled another mountain hare and watched as it ran straight up without ever slipping.

The walk down to the Dubh Loch was spectacular. The waterfall was a thousand icicles and the loch, frozen over, was like a sheet of steel in which was reflected the towering crags. It was a hard place of grey, bare rock, deep shadow, ice and the chaos of rock avalanches. The tall cliffs of the Eagle's Rock were lit by the afternoon sun. A pale moon hung in the blue sky above.

The path from this hidden valley led us back into the sun as we came down to Victoria's retreat on Loch Muick. It was sad to see this lovely property with its shutters closed. I suggested that it would be an ideal centre for outdoor pursuits and could improve the lives of many young people. James showed me the bothy adjacent to the rear of the big house, a facility maintained by the Balmoral Estate. Downstairs is a common room with a fire, candles, cooking facilities and benches. Upstairs is a room for spreading out sleeping mats.

As we left the woodland around the house two barking bull terriers bounded along the track to check us out. James, no dog lover, held one of his walking poles in a threatening manner and declared, "Come any closer and I'll ram this in your mouth," adding menacingly, "or perhaps another orifice if you're unlucky." The owners, hearing these remarks, quickly clipped their dogs back onto their leads.

There followed a delightful walk back along the shores of the loch, its waters sparkling in the late afternoon sun.

As we began our drive down the single track road the sun had dipped behind the hills and the colours were draining from Glen Muick.

We stopped at Ballater where we had been promised afternoon tea by Sheena, another new colleague. She had a friend with her and all were in high spirits. A perfect end, I reflected as I drank my second mug of tea, to a splendid day.

Siskins over Loch Muick
16/2/2008.

15/3/08

Carn an t-Sagairt Mor and Carn a' Choire Bhoidheach

A walk on the White Mounth

This trip to the White Mounth began with a knock on my office door one morning in early March. It was James Murray and he announced in his crisp, economical way that it was time for another walk. Deeply immersed in my new job, I was weary to my bones but knew that an outing would probably invigorate me.

The next weekend was one of strong winds and heavy snowfalls on the hills, so I got my gear sorted and crossed my fingers for calmer weather. By the following weekend I was even wearier, had torn a muscle in my shoulder and had a chest infection, but the forecast was good for the Saturday. I reasoned that I might as well be ill climbing mountains as in the house, so I saw James, telephoned Morag and had an early night.

My wife Jane was not pleased with me when I dragged myself out of bed at the crack of dawn next morning, pointing out that I had tossed and turned with a temperature which had left the sheets damp with my sweat. I cheerily suggested that the planned walk would either kill or cure me.

"My money is on the former," she replied.

I was glad that there was no traffic at that hour as I could not turn to look to the left, never mind behind. I parked outside James's house and he asked me inside while he gathered his gear. His home was a perfect reflection of his personality: dark wood; worn Persian rugs; heavily framed landscapes in dusky oils and an ancient grandfather clock in the hall.

At Morag's parents' house I introduced my companion and we stowed the gear in her car. My shoulder was not up to the drive along Deeside.

Less than an hour later we were looking across to Lochnagar and its neighbours, their brilliant white snow caps radiant in the early morning sunshine. Morag drove to Braemar then a mile or so south to Auchallater Farm. She parked by the bridge and we were soon walking on the track which follows the Callater Burn up the glen.

I plodded along behind the others, hoping that my shoulder would ease off with the exercise. My lungs felt hot and under capacity. The morning, however, was a joy. The hillsides still had their winter palette of browns and pale yellows. The sky above was the deepest blue with the occasional brilliant cumulus cloud. I stopped where the track crossed the burn on a wooden bridge to photograph the dark blue sparkling water. As we walked on I was pleased that James and Morag were getting on well. James does not trouble himself to be politically correct but Morag seemed to understand both this and his dry sense of humour.

We stopped at Lochcallater Lodge, sitting on the wooden benches to drink cups of hot tea. The sun was warm and there was hardly a breeze. The outlook over the loch and the steep, crag-lined corries of the upper glen was beautiful.

We visited the bothy before we left, finding it clean and well maintained. The interior seemed dark on that bright morning, with worn wooden benches, candle stubs and the smoky smell of countless fires.

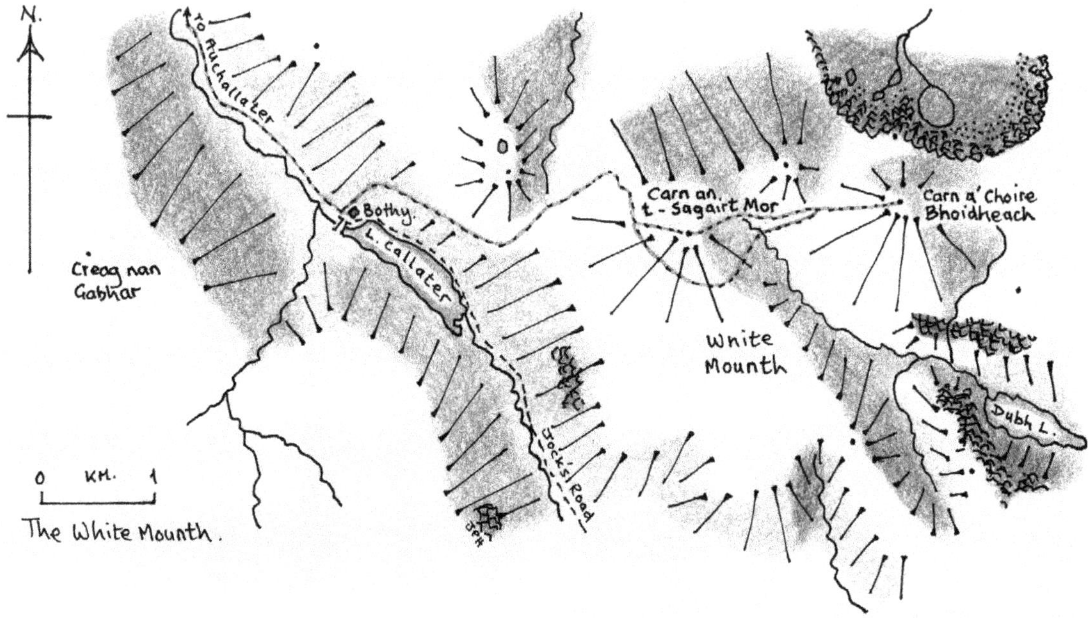

Our path climbed the north side of the glen, turning to run parallel to the loch, its shores 450 feet below. I stopped to get some air into my lungs, picking out the glacial features of the landscape. The loch is a classic ribbon loch, with Coire Loch Kander a hanging valley and the glen itself a perfect U-shaped valley with walls of exposed rock.

On we walked, the well-graded path now snow covered as it rounded Creag an Loch to take us to a high col with views over the big white mountains of the Cairngorms.

From the col we climbed the steep slopes of Carn an t-Sagairt Mor, our first Munro. We visited two cairns on the top, the northernmost built around the remains of a crashed aeroplane. We were now on the high snowfields of a group of rounded mountains dominated by Lochnagar. Together they make a rolling arctic plateau, the heart of which is the White Mounth. Striking landscape features are the cliff-walled corries on the edges of the plateau, rather than the mountains themselves. It is a big landscape. The snow had hidden the paths. There was not a living thing in sight. We dug our heels into the part frozen snow on the east side of the mountain and were quickly at the foot of its steep slopes.

Skirting Carn an t-Sagairt Beag, we then started on the long haul up the deep snow slopes of Carn a' Choire Bhoidheach, our second Munro. We were lucky that it was below freezing up there because the snow mostly bore our weight. I did not have the fitness for a climb where I sank up to my thighs at every step. Even so, it was a long and hard task for me to climb those slopes. At the top, James asked whether I wanted to go over to The Stuic and look down onto Loch nan Eun. I replied that coming this far was my dead strength and I would come back another day to explore.

On the summit we met two young men. They had been to Lochnagar and now this was their second Munro. They were clearly thrilled with their introduction to the Scottish mountains and told us they were looking forward to the next 282 Munros. I was glad for them that they had been so lucky with the weather, there are many days up there that might have brought a premature end to their Munro collecting ambitions. They wanted to go back via the Dubh Loch, so we pointed them in the right direction.

We dropped down below the summit on the west side of our mountain and dug shelves in the snow on which to sit and eat our lunch. I was too tired to have much conversation but pleased that I had overcome my lack of fitness to climb the two hills. I only remember one trip where I had more of a struggle and that was on a day of foul weather in Glen Dochart. On both occasions mental strength more than physical strength was needed to complete the walk.

The return across the pristine snowfields was wonderful. The low angle of the sun cast long shadows from each of us and I watched them move over the wind sculpted ripples and scallop shapes. To the south-east, the plateau fell away between tall cliffs and we could see two small specks, the young men heading for the frozen Dubh Loch.

15/3/8. On the White Mounth.
Looking S.E. towards
Creag an Dubh Loch.
JPH

We found the line of the path again and began to retrace our steps, stopping a number of times to watch mountain hares in their white coats and ptarmigan in their white winter plumage. As the path took us below the snowline, the arctic wildlife gave way to red grouse and we saw a group of stags moving fast down toward the shores of the loch.

I wished that I had a bike to ease the journey back from the lodge to the car and made a mental note to buy one in the Easter holiday. When I left my job in the Borders, my colleagues had presented me with a cheque and I had said at the time that their gift would buy me a mountain bike. I simply had not had the time to make the purchase.

We stopped at Sheena's flat in Ballater on the way home and again enjoyed her warm hospitality. There was delicious bread, moist and rich, and home-made scones stuffed with plump raisins, all washed down with mugs of tea. My body was suffused with the endorphin glow I get after a day on the hills, a feeling of well-being which managed to override my ailments. Sheena talked about a close friend who had won Big Brother. When James looked puzzled she explained that, "It was on one of those channels with adverts you know, the sort you never watch."

Postscript

It has been strange to write the above account, shortly after this adventure, from the house we rent for holidays in Whitby's Old Town. A busker with a strong voice accompanied by an accordion is singing sea shanties in the narrow street below. Herring gulls cry as they wheel in the wind above the chimney pots and the kipper smell from the smokehouse wafts in through the open window. The silent arctic wastes of the White Mounth are another world.

19/4/08

The Cairnwell, Carn Aosda and Carn a' Gheoidh

Spring in Glen Shee

As I drove to the Glenshee Ski Centre to meet Morag on that fine spring morning, I did not expect a great deal in terms of scenery. I had met hillwalkers who had talked of hillsides scarred by pistes, defiled by ski tows and littered with the debris of the skiing industry. They had also described the adjacent hills as "boring".

At Braemar, the road turned south into Glen Clunie. It narrowed, the fences on either side petered out and snow poles appeared as it slowly climbed to the watershed. All around was wilderness, the steep hills capped with snow.

I came upon the ski centre suddenly and could easily have driven past. I had imagined something much larger. Morag had parked outside the café, now closed for the summer, and was eating her Weetabix. There were no other vehicles.

Ten minutes later, we were climbing up the steep north-east side of The Cairnwell, following the line of a chairlift. At first the snow was soft and sugary but half way up it changed in character to a thin covering of fresh powder snow sitting on a sheet of compacted ice. We stopped to swap our walking poles for ice axes.

The top of the hill had a hut, two radio masts and an old wooden shelter buried inside an enormous cairn. To the north and east were ski tows and pistes, all radiating

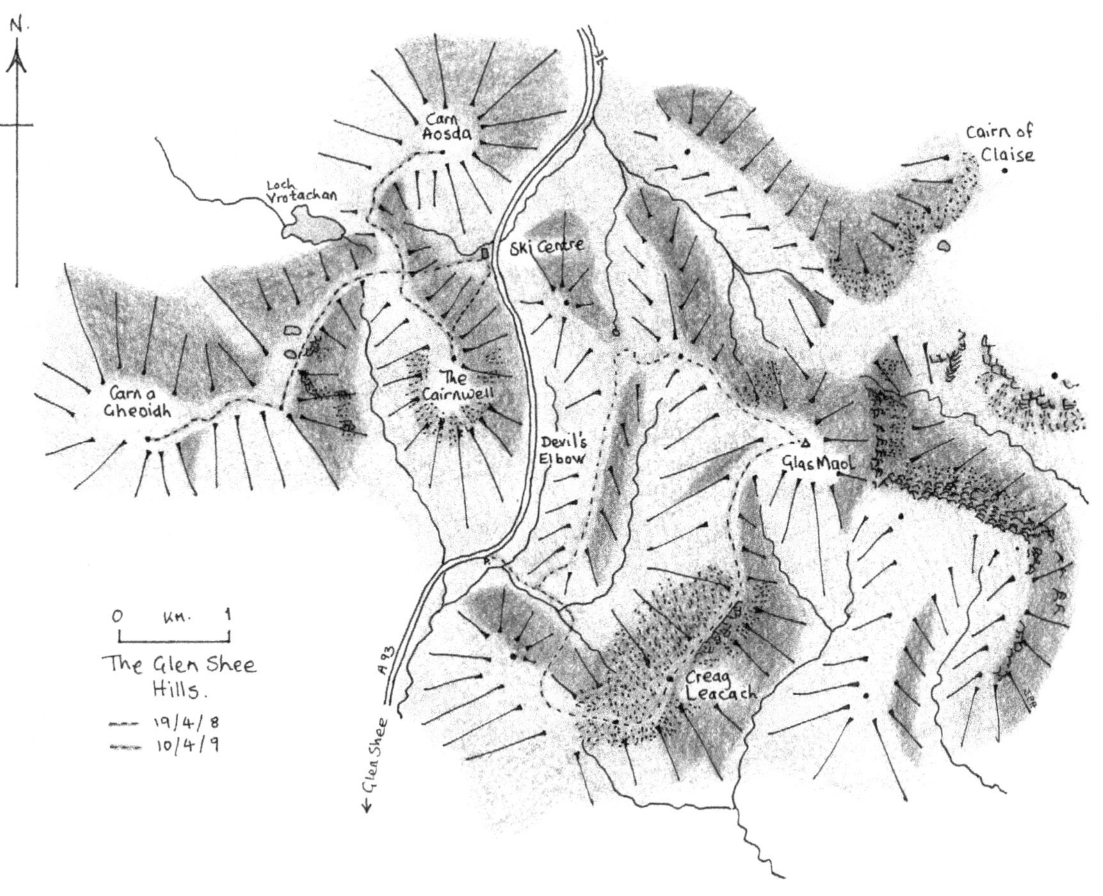

up from a small group of wooden buildings far below by the narrow road. In front of the largest building we could see our cars. All around were the snow-streaked hills, the White Mounth high above its neighbours, its snowfields incredibly bright in the morning sunshine. The infrastructure of the little resort seemed to blend into a landscape which completely dominated it.

We took a few steps from the shelter cairn and looked west. Here were rank after rank of wild hills. First the scallop shell corries of Glas Tulaichean, then the Beinn a' Ghlo mountains with Ben Alder and the Ben Lawers range beyond.

As we walked north from The Cairnwell along the ridge to Carn Aosda, snow fences and ski tows were always present ahead and down the steep slopes of the corrie to our right. To our left was the lovely Loch Vrotachan and a wide expanse of hill country. Rising above all else to the north were the snow-covered mountains of the high Cairngorms.

On top of Carn Aosda (pronounced carn oeshta), the aged mountain, we picked out Ben Avon, then Beinn a' Bhuird, then the high snowfields rising to Ben Macdui. After this was the deep notch of the Lairig Ghru with Bod an Daemon and Cairn Toul towering above on the west side. The north-east wind was very cold, however, so we retreated down the south-west slopes to sit among some boulders and eat our second breakfast.

With two Munros climbed, we set off for the third, Carn a' Gheoidh. It rose to the south-west on a long ridge which begins just south of the loch. Neither of us felt like hurrying on such a beautiful day, so we made our way over snow patches and across heather, stopping often to enjoy both scenery and wildlife. Loch Vrotachan was particularly attractive in the spring sunshine. Morag told me of the time she had come second here in a national Nordic skiing event.

I almost stood on a red grouse. It clattered up in alarm, upsetting three of its neighbours who did likewise. I think it was sunbathing and daydreaming of whatever a grouse daydreams. A few steps later, I stopped to look at the hind leg of a mountain hare. It was soft, with fresh blood. I wondered what had very recently torn its owner apart and concluded that it was more likely to have been an eagle than a fox, probably disturbed by us when we appeared, far away, on the skyline. Looking up, we noticed two (living) hares, then another, then another. It seemed a big enough population to feed an apex predator. The hares were losing the bright white of their winter coats and they had a pale yellow/beige tint. We were to see more of these very British animals on our walk, each alert and athletic as it ran to safety from these strange invaders of their mountain home.

We climbed up to the ridge and back onto extensive snowfields. In the areas where the snow had melted were pairs of dotterel. The density seemed too high for those patches of stunted heather and piles of loose rock. They needed a big thaw so that they could spread out into adequate territories.

The walk along the ridge was a delight. The cold wind was on our backs and I felt warmed and cheered by the bright April sun. The air was clear, we could see familiar hills in the far distance and it felt a privilege to be at the hub of so much beauty.

We climbed a final snow slope and walked to Carn a' Gheoidh's flat summit. The cold wind did not encourage us to linger so we took some photographs, agreed that the 360 degree panorama from this hill was marvellous, then turned to descend the way we had come.

On the south-facing slope of Carn nan Sac, sheltered from the wind, we stopped at a pile of rocks which were free of snow. There we ate a good lunch, discovering that we had both made peanut butter and honey pieces. Excellent hill food but I was grateful that I had mugs of steaming hot tea to wash it down. It was so pleasant that I could have dozed in the sun.

I shook off the sleepiness and climbed up to Carn nan Sac's cairn. We found ourselves perched on the top of plunging crags that curved before us to enclose a massive amphitheatre of a corrie. The masts and huts of The Cairnwell were tiny on the far side. The snowfields continued to the edge of the corrie where there was the remains of what would have been an impressive cornice. The higher parts of the east wall were also snow-covered but the snow had melted on the corrie's south and west-facing sides.

We stuck to the rim of the corrie, just back from the cornice, until we reached the col between The Cairnwell and Carn Aosda. Here we kicked steps in the hard packed snow and zig zagged down one of the deserted pistes. After 100 metres or so we were on the yellowed and flattened vegetation that had emerged in the April thaw. The springy surface took us back to the ski centre. This was still deserted. We sat on the steps in the afternoon sun, drinking the last mugs of tea from our flasks. It had been a perfect day, a calm respite from my working life and not at all what I had expected.

11/5/08

Derry Cairngorm

How not to climb the Devil's Point

Early on Sunday morning I travelled west along the road which follows the River Dee. I was to meet Morag at the Linn o' Dee car park and we were to head for the Devil's Point, a spectacular mountain rising steeply from the Lairig Ghru which neither of us had climbed. The plan was to use bikes and leave them at Derry Lodge, thus easing the strain of a lengthy day. A study of the map had revealed that all walks from the Dee into the Cairngorms to the north were long.

As I drove, I thought back to leaving my job in the Borders the previous autumn. My colleagues had clubbed together and I had found the time to spend their generous gift on a mountain bike. Shiny and new, it lay behind me in the car. The last time I had ridden a bike was 1969, so I was somewhat apprehensive.

The cloud was low and there were sporadic showers but the weather forecast had predicted that it would lift and, as the day progressed, the sun would break through. At Braemar, steep forested slopes rose up into the swirling cloud, a strangely Alpine scene. Beyond Inverey, a red squirrel flicked on to the road in front of the car and flicked back again in the nick of time. Three well-fed red deer stood by the roadside, their lower jaws grinding from side to side. Their heads turned to follow the car as it sped past.

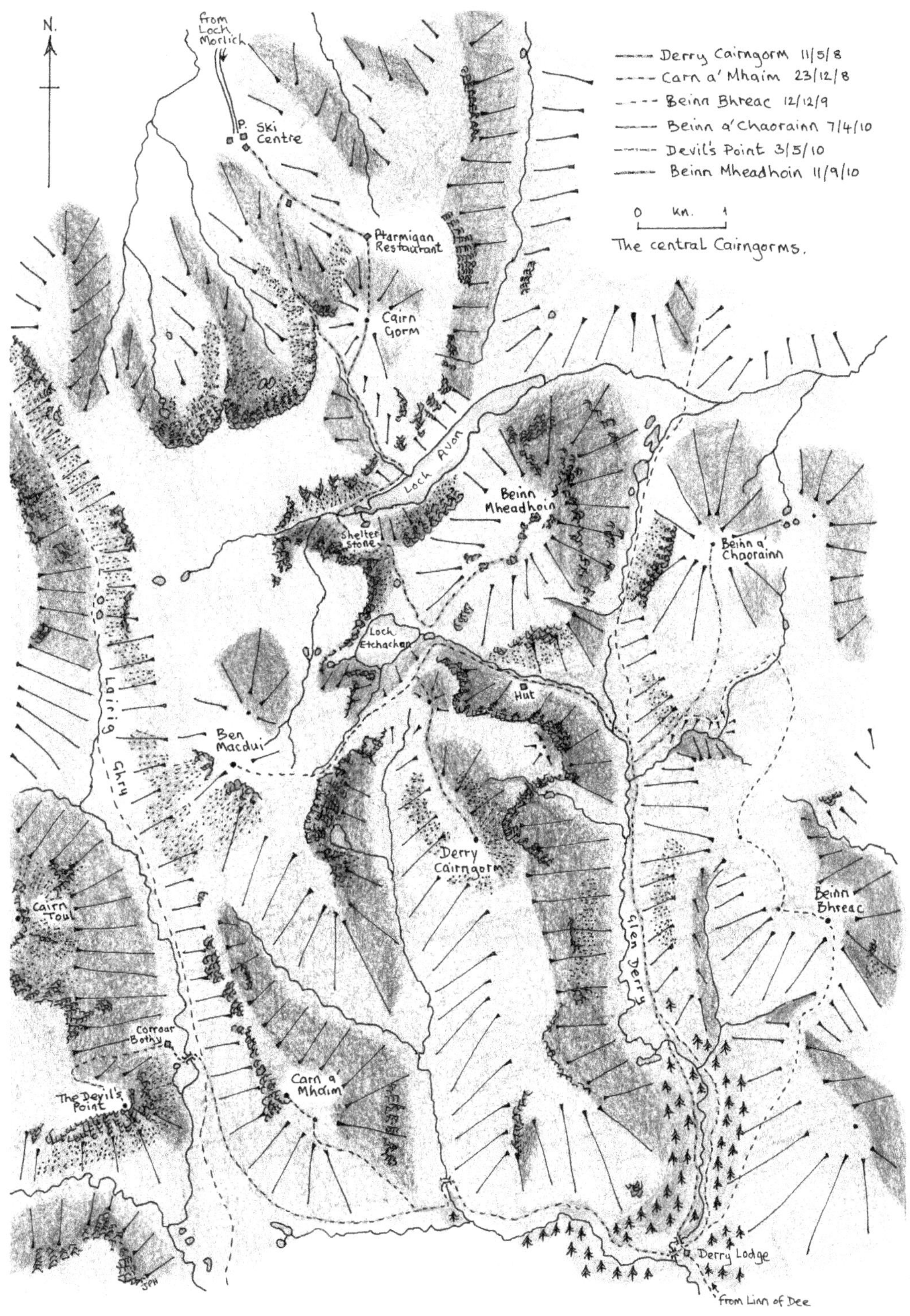

N.
From Loch Morlich
P.
Ski Centre
Ptarmigan Restaurant
Cairn Gorm
Loch Avon
Shelter Stone
Beinn Mheadhoin
Beinn a' Chaorainn
Loch Etchachan
Hut
Lairig Ghru
Ben Macdui
Derry Cairngorm
Cairn Toul
Glen Derry
Beinn Bhreac
Corrour Bothy
The Devil's Point
Carn a Mhaim
Derry Lodge
From Linn of Dee
Derry Cairngorm 11/5/8
Carn a' Mhaim 23/12/8
Beinn Bhreac 12/12/9
Beinn a' Chaorainn 7/4/10
Devil's Point 3/5/10
Beinn Mheadhoin 11/9/10
0 km. 1
The central Cairngorms.

At the car park, Morag was waiting. I lifted out the bike and, neither of us being disposed to waste a minute of our precious day, we were off. I found that "like riding a bike" was true, even though my steering was rather erratic.

Morag turned towards a narrow path studded with polished boulders which wound steeply up through the trees. "This is the way," she declared, "I remember taking it on past visits."

"I am not riding up there," I replied, so we rode back to the road and went the long way.

We bumped onto a rough Land Rover track which went up a steep bank beside the Lui Water. I had to stop twice as I had not got the hang of the gears. After the bank it was easier but I found that I could not relax. My full concentration was needed as I rattled along, trying to avoid outcropping rocks and keep up with my companion, who stopped at intervals for me.

At Derry Lodge I shouted for Morag to stop, telling her that this is where James had said we should leave the bikes. She was keen to go a distance further, however, and felt justified when we met three walkers crossing the bridge from the north bank. They described the track as perfect for a mountain bike for a good way yet.

I followed Morag as she carried her bike over the wooden footbridge and set off again, this time on a more challenging path. My bike bounced over tree roots, plunged down sudden banks and seemed precariously near long drops down to the river on my right. I was relieved when she decided that we had better leave the bikes and walk. We propped them up against an ancient Scots pine so that we could not miss them on the way back and set off on foot.

Two miles or so further on, I asked whether we were in the Lairig Ghru. The cloud was still low and I could not see enough landscape to relate our progress to my previous evening's cursory glimpse of the map.

"Have you done the Lairig Ghru before?" asked Morag.

"Only from Loch Morlich to the Pools of Dee." This was all new to me.

She stopped walking. "You know, this doesn't look familiar."

"Are we in Glen Derry?" I asked.

She was not sure, so we switched on our GPS sets to get a grid reference. This revealed that we were indeed in Glen Derry. Morag was annoyed as the Devil's Point was the only one of the Cairngorm Munros she had not climbed and she had been looking forward to it. I was annoyed with myself. A combination of assuming that my companion knew the ground well and trying not to fall off my bike had led me to follow like a sheep. She suggested going back to Derry Lodge and setting off for our original objective. My stomach, however, was telling me that it was already past lunchtime so I suggested that we walk up to the Hutchison Memorial Hut and, as we ate in its shelter, consider climbing Derry Cairngorm instead. This is what we did.

As soon as we started walking again the character of the glen changed. The path narrowed, the gradient steepened, we had to cross torrents on stepping stones and drifts of snow appeared on either side. We passed some huge boulders and there in front of us was a strange sight. A hut of Alpine character, its roof extending over a veranda, stood in a small circle of fluorescent green grass. This green was all the more startling in the context of the monochrome of the giant corrie in which it sat. Massive black crags rose up into the low cloud, snow filled the steep gullies and brown vegetation covered the moraine of the corrie floor.

I pulled back the heavy bolt on the door and stepped inside the hut. The wooden walls, floor and sleeping benches were clean and dry. A shrivelled and blackened human head hung by its grey pony tail on a hook.[1] It was a perfect place for lunch.

11/5/8
Hutchison Memorial Hut and Creagan a Choire Etchachan.

1 For those who worry about such things, we assumed that this macabre object was not a real head.

I was enjoying my peanut butter and honey sandwich when, looking out of the window, I spotted a party of four toiling up the glen in our direction. They were members of Aberdeen Hillwalking Club, intent on climbing Derry Cairngorm. They, unlike us, had taken the right path. Three of them gratefully collapsed onto the grass and began their lunch. They had little spare breath for conversation. The party leader, however, was as fresh as a daisy and full of good advice.

I told him that, as we had planned on climbing The Devil's Point, we only had Sheet 43 with us so would have to take a direct line of assault on our second choice Munro. I pointed to a snow-filled gully leading very steeply up to a narrow notch in the cliffs behind the hut. Any other route was out of the question as it was off the map. Our new friend spread out a computer printout map which covered the area to the north and showed us a much easier and safer way. This involved following the path out of the corrie up to Loch Etchachan, then what he described as a clear path south to Derry Cairngorm's summit. We could then either walk along the ridge back to Derry Lodge or return the way we had come. It was good advice and we decided to take it but a little voice in my head said that we had already shown ourselves to be shameful route finders and now we were **going off the map.**

As we talked, the cloud at last began to lift. The black crags behind the hut were shown to be considerably higher, ending in jagged teeth. This seemed a good moment to say farewell to our lunchtime company so we wished them well for the rest of their day and set off on the path again.

We crossed the stream on boulders and began climbing steeply up into a narrow pass, kicking steps in snow banks as the landscape became increasingly wintry. I stopped to pack Sheet 43 in my rucksack, it was no longer of use. We now had to rely on the quick study of our lunchtime friend's map and memory. One should never do this.

Despite having broken the Good Hillwalker's Code, we were rewarded with a fantastic sight at the top of the pass. The clouds were still lifting, revealing patches of pale blue sky. This blue was reflected in the still water of Little Loch Etchachan. Beyond lay the expanse of Loch Etchachan. Most was iced over but the section nearest to us was breaking into ice floes. The lochs sit in a deep bowl, lined with soaring crags, in the Cairngorm plateau. Winter had not left here, the steep slopes were still covered with a thick veneer of ice and snow. Shafts of sunlight lit the scene, a wild landscape sprinkled with diamond dust. We had walked from the bluebell pinewoods of a Highland spring to an outlier of the Arctic.

We followed the path as it climbed the south side of this giant corrie. It disappeared under snowfields, fresh falls having covered any trace of human footprints. I spotted a narrow track branching off on our left and heading, I was sure, for our Munro. Morag, however, thought that it was too near the pass and suggested that we continue on the main path for a while longer. I think that she wanted to prolong her stay in that pristine and beautiful place and cannot blame her for that.

Further up, a turquoise blue pool had formed at the front of a thick sheet of ice. Black rocks stood as islands in the meltwater. It was a perfect glacial scene.

The path had been following the floor of a broad gully containing a stream which ran down to the loch below. We passed the still, grey-blue waters of a lochan and the gully narrowed. The south-east slope had been eaten into by the spectacular headwall of the Glen Luibeg corrie. We stood on the top of this cliff, looking through a deep notch down the glen. Immediately below was a hanging corrie occupied by Lochan Uaine, jade green and thus satisfyingly living up to its name. What interested me more than the lochan was Derry Cairngorm, its massive bulk rising above the glen almost due east of our viewpoint. We had walked around the head of the corrie and had to backtrack to the path I had spotted earlier. It was not until much later that I traced our wanderings on the 1:25,000 map and realised that we could have added the summit of Ben Macdui to our tally with little extra effort, it was less than a kilometre from where we stood.

Our wanderings, however, were destined to continue for a while longer. We had no map to help us contour round the head of the corrie so went back to a point above Loch Etchachan where, in the absence of any track, we turned south.

We climbed (unnecessarily) the northern top of Derry Cairngorm. From its summit we could, at last, see a clear path leading up to the massive boulder field which capped our mountain. The remaining small patches of white cloud had sunk down into the deep glens cut into the Cairngorm plateau and above our heads the sky was brilliant blue. Visibility had steadily improved since we were at the hut, which was fortunate for mapless travellers in this remote land.

Lunch was finished on top of Derry Cairngorm, which turned out to be a fantastic viewpoint. The cloud was still moving in strange ways. To the south and east it had settled in the glens, with the highest ridges and tops like islands in a chalk white sea. To the west, a broad patch of sunlight lit up Lochan Uaine, perched high on its shelf on the towering backwall cliffs. I could see the notch where we had stood earlier that afternoon.

There was a brief debate about the route of our return journey. The ridge walk down to Derry Lodge was appealing, but we would then have to go north again up Glen Derry to find our bikes. We were also tired so decided to go back to Loch Etchachan, down the pass and home the way we had come.

The march south down the glen was a very different experience to our march north earlier in the day. We could see everything for a start and the afternoon sun warmed my weary body but the mind plays strange tricks when tired. This stretch seemed much longer than it had in the morning. I thought about my customary phone call to Jane to say that we were safe down, looked at my mobile phone and was surprised to find that it was six o' clock. I had no signal and, thinking of the long distance we still had to cover, hoped she would not start to worry. I stepped up my pace. If it was late evening before I could contact her, would she phone the police? If they informed the mountain rescue team, my note left at home had the Devil's Point as our objective. We were not that late, of course and were eating up the miles, so none of this was in the least likely but I was relieved to see the first of the trees.

The sun was low in the west and it lit up the red trunks of the ancient Scots pines. Mounds of little sticks marked the busy towns of wood ants. Tiny goldcrests flitted between the branches, their yellow crowns catching the sun like jewels. Through my weariness I knew that here, away from the worldly things that packed my life, I could find the peace and freedom I craved.

I was very pleased to see our bikes against that tree trunk. They made short work of those last miles to Derry Lodge and then back to the Linn o' Dee. To have had to walk this last stage after the many hard hours of our day would have tested my good humour.

At the car park I packed the bike and my rucksack in double quick time, said a hasty farewell to my stalwart companion and set off for Braemar. I stopped in the village to phone Jane, expecting her to say how worried she'd been but she cheerily asked if I'd enjoyed my day and when she could expect me for dinner.

Driving home through a Deeside of spring colours and long shadows, I realised that the top of my head, these days inadequately protected by hair, was sunburnt. I listed the day's mistakes:

- Forgetting to put on my hat;
- Not looking at the map and ending up in the wrong glen;
- Not checking the time once until 6.00 p.m.;
- Venturing into terra incognita without a map.

I told myself that I will try never to repeat them but they in no way spoiled what had been one of my best days in the mountains.

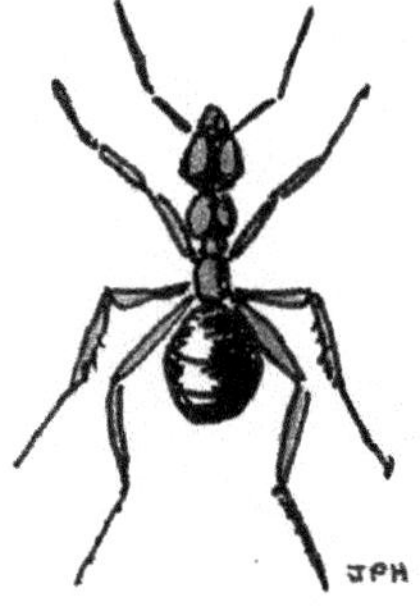

21/6/08

Ben Tirran

On The Goet with the Jolly Boys

The sun was low as I drove up Glen Prosen on Midsummer's Eve. The landscape was a dreamy mix of golden slopes and pools of dark green shadow. The torrential summer showers of the day had passed, leaving the sky and glen washed clean.

The old school in the calendar-pretty village has been converted to a bunkhouse and the Jolly Boys[2] were in residence for the weekend. The interior is finished in pine with a mezzanine and dark leather sofas. I had been away for eight months and everyone made me feel welcome.

The evening was warm in both senses of the word as Eric fed logs into the stove and I chatted, laughed and sipped a whisky as Ray and Struan lived up to tradition by touting for custom for their rival walks.

The following morning, that of the longest day of the year, was perfect, with not a trace of cloud in the sky. It seemed to take an age before everyone was ready but eventually we streamed down the path to the cars, passing Fionn snoring loudly in his sleeping bag on the lawn.

2 An anarchic group of Munro baggers from the Borders, known by readers of my first book.

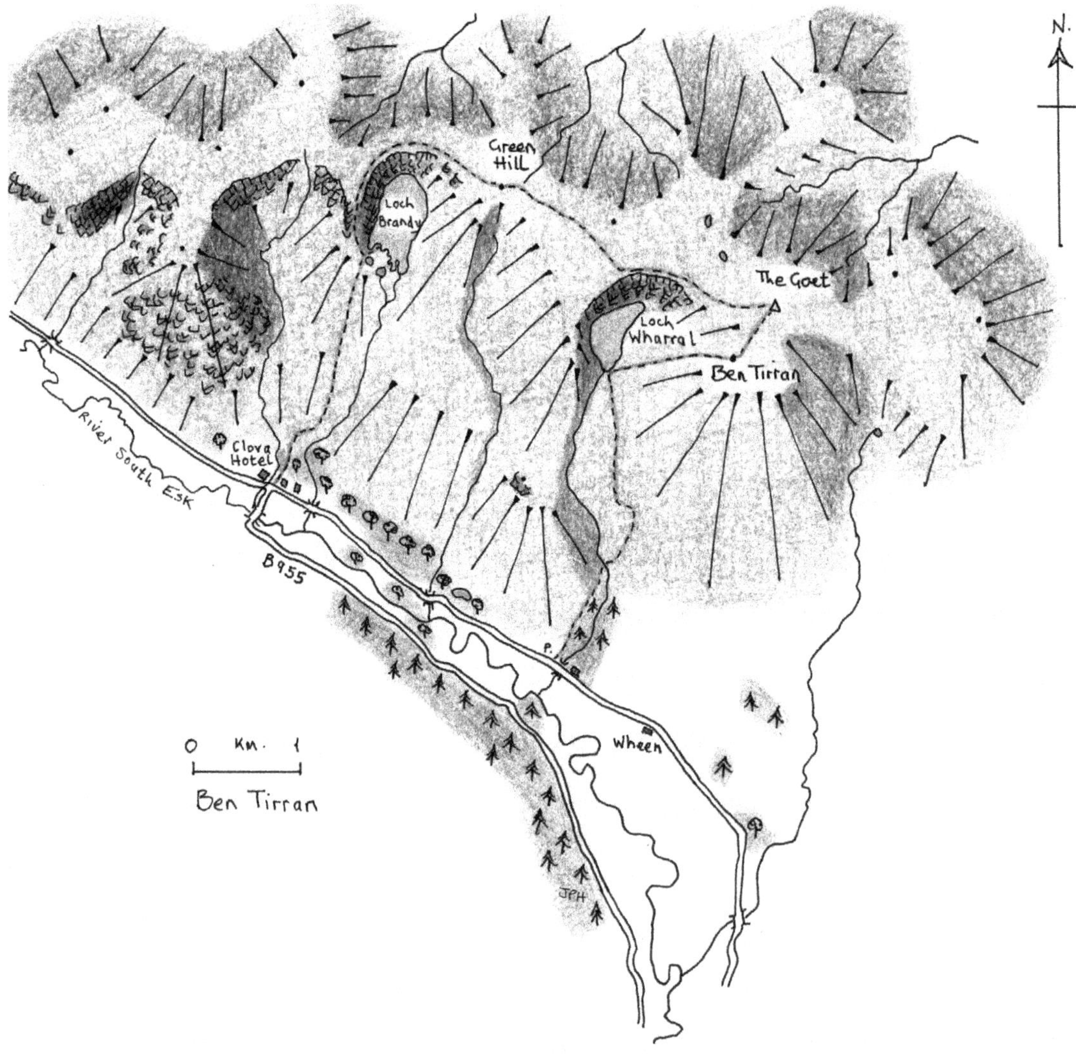

I had opted for the Ben Tirran walk which was Ray's choice. He had been waiting for his son to arrive with his girlfriend but they had failed to show. This left only four in our party, most had gone with Struan to climb the Munros of Mayar and Driesh. We drove up Glen Clova to Wheen, parked near the farm and followed the track up the steep hillside to Loch Wharral. A shelter with a panoramic view of the corrie provided a good place to have a second breakfast.

From the shelter we walked up the abrupt shoulder of Ben Tirran, the vegetation bone dry and crispy beneath our boots. The slope levelled off and we stopped to swap superlatives as we looked down the length of Glen Clova. Walking across the plateau towards the cairn we came across a small flock of dotterel. They trotted off to a safe distance, not overly concerned. From the cairn we walked to the summit of this Corbett, The Goet. No one could explain the odd spelling.

I noticed that the sun was now filtered through high level clouds, the precursors of the front which was heading towards us from the south. England was being drenched by heavy rain and it was coming our way. The wind picked up a little and I was glad of my jacket and hat.

Coming down from The Goet, we disturbed a pair of ptarmigan then stopped to look down into the crag-lined corrie of Loch Wharral. We walked north-west up to some lichen-crusted rocks on the flank of Green Hill. There we stopped to eat lunch while Ray went back to the vantage point on the top of the crags to see whether he could spot the two youngsters. Having failed in his mission, he returned to find that we were sprawled on the dry ground, having a nap.

The west side of Green Hill provided grand views of Loch Brandy and its crags so we stopped here to take photographs. The next stage was around the rim of the corrie, following a path which allowed us to look down the steep cliffs to the loch far below.

A massive slab of rock had recently come away from the back wall of the corrie and it did not look like it would take much disturbance to send the whole thing crashing down into the loch below. A wide crack ran parallel to the path. I was in front at that point and looking into the crack saw a young man dressed only in a tee shirt and shorts with a young woman, sheltering from the cool wind. I guessed rightly that they were the missing members of our little party. I thought it fortunate that it was such a fine day as I watched girlfriend Mini pick her way down the steep rocky path in pretty slip-on shoes with bows.

At the foot of the path we turned to go to the loch shore where it was sheltered and warm. A copper butterfly landed on my flask. A black headed gull paddled towards us and Ray broke a piece of cheese and guacamole roll for it. He talked of some sick individuals feeding gulls things like powdered instant meals and dried mustard powder, which caused the gull to explode in the air. My head filled with grisly images. More and more black headed gulls appeared. This was strange given that our gull was the sole resident on Loch Brandy when we arrived. Ray stood on the shore, pleased to be the focus of attention of this flock of hungry birds. They were beautiful, white and graceful against the sombre grey of the corrie cliffs. It was clear that the original gull was getting almost all the food. Perhaps being on its own territory made it more confident, aggressive and therefore stronger and more successful. It had soon consumed most of the cheese roll. I wondered whether it liked guacamole. I considered the size of its stomach and concluded that we might have our very own exploding gull spectacle over the still waters of the loch.

The path down ends at the Glen Clova Hotel. We sat on the benches in front of the main door, enjoying a drink while Ray's son took our driver back to retrieve her car. We talked to a mountaineer who had lost his leg in a motorbike accident at the age of 17. I have enormous respect for a person who could describe the problems of balance on a mountain bike and his frequent falls in such a matter-of-fact way. As he left us to join his friends at the bar, the familiar figure of Fionn appeared on his bike. He had cycled (and pushed) from Glen Prosen up to Driesh and then down to the hotel. He was hot, tired, suffering muscle cramps and complaining loudly. His first beer disappeared incredibly fast. He explained that his plan now was to cycle down Glen Clova then up Glen Prosen to the bunkhouse. He scorned our driver's offer of a lift, declaring himself a "purist" and then instantly changed his mind.

At regular intervals on the long drive back Fionn commented that he was lucky indeed to have met us as it would have been midnight before he would have crawled through the bunkhouse door. He had not worked out the distance involved, largely because he had no map.

At the widest part of Glen Clova we stopped to look at a large bird of prey wheeling in wide circles overhead. It was a golden eagle, primary feathers tipped upwards, never once flapping its wide wings. Its mate was gliding just below the cloud base on the east side of the glen.

Two of the Jolly Boys, Geraldine and Sharon, had a meal ready for us when we returned. We sat together at the long tables and tucked into lasagne, green salad, new potatoes, garlic bread and good red wine. Pudding was home-made cheesecake and steaming apple crumble, both topped with fresh cream. There was seconds for Fionn, Struan and others with big appetites. A true "triumph of a meal" in the tradition of Jean's legendary feeds at Glen Feshie.

The night that followed was full of laughter. Geraldine and Sharon pushed back the tables to make a dance floor and Charlie was DJ. Fionn showed a certain lack of sophistication as he grabbed his dance partner by the ankles and pulled her on her bottom across the mezzanine floor. Every so often he would lift one of the female "Boys" across his shoulder and run off with her shrieking into the night. When I went to bed in the small hours, I noticed that the rain was hammering on the roof.

It was still pouring down the next morning as I ran with my gear to the car. Fionn was in the same place on the lawn, sleeping like a baby.

12/7/08 - 17/7/08

Wester Ross

I drove up to Ullapool on a fine July day and checked in at the hostel. I was shown to the same room I had on my previous visit and chose the same bunk by the window with a view over Loch Broom.

Happy memories were triggered at every corner as I walked about the village. I was pleased to see a seal by the pier and expect that it was the same one. My companions arrived and as we ate together we discussed plans for the next four days, determined to make the most of them.

13/7/08

An Teallach: Sgurr Fiona and Bidein a' Ghlas Thuill

Lord Berkeley's Seat

The next morning we were up, breakfasted and gone before anyone else had stirred. The car was parked at Corrie Hallie and we walked along the public right of way which leads south into Dundonnell Forest. The turn off to Shenavall was clear, as was the turn off for Sail Liath, the southernmost of An Teallach's dozen summits. There had been good views of this complex of peaks, with cloud drifting away from the uppermost reaches.

We needed no excuse to stop on the south-east slopes of Sail Liath as the view to the south to the Fisherfield mountains was splendid. While we drank mugs of tea we agreed that the ridge walk from Beinn a' Chlaidheimh to Mullach Coire Mhic Fhearchair would have been perfect on a day like this. The cloud had lifted from all the summits and the sky was summer blue. Beinn Dearg Mor is a particularly fine mountain, its triple peaks rising above the dark waters of Loch na Sealga.

On the way up we had seen frogs among the cotton grass and orchids. Here were bristly hawkmoth caterpillars among a shorter vegetation which included dwarf juniper. A buzzard wheeled up from the shores of the loch far below.

On top of Sail Liath we got our first good view of the peaks of An Teallach. The air was cool and visibility perfect, with not a trace of cloud. We had long hoped for such a day on which to enjoy our time on this icon of the Highlands.

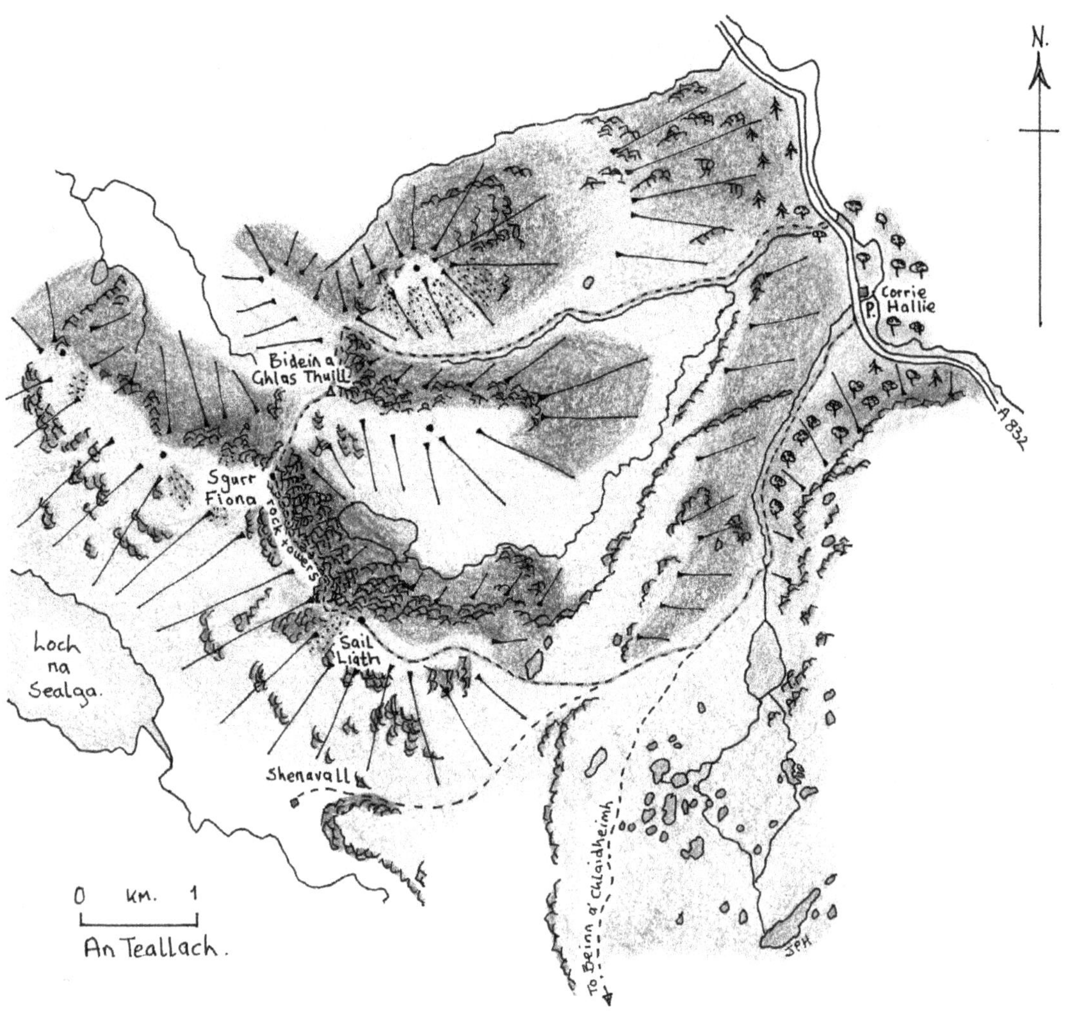

Sail Liath is capped with hard Cambrian quartzite but the series of tall pinnacles, ending with Sgurr Fiona, are all Precambrian Torridonian sandstone. This is horizontally bedded, with well-defined vertical joints. Weathering and erosion have combined to dislocate large blocks, resulting in the characteristic sheer cliffs and towers.

We scrambled down a very steep slope into a narrow notch in the ridge and before us was the first pinnacle. It was hard to find a way up on the south side as obvious routes ended in overhangs or were slippery with dripping water. On the west side we found a narrow, near vertical, chimney which was dry and had excellent holds. At the top, on the very crest of the ridge, we sat on a rock platform with wonderful views to eat some lunch.

Rested, we scrambled up to the top of the first pinnacle then slowly made our way along the crest of this serrated ridge, enjoying each of the towers. To look down from the overhanging platform at the top of Lord Berkeley's Seat requires a head for heights, I would not like to have done it on a day of strong wind.

On top of Sgurr Fiona, we sat down to enjoy a mug of tea and the view back along the dramatic series of summits we had scrambled over. An Teallach is more a range of peaks than a single mountain. A colony of ravens nest on the sandstone cliffs. We watched their aerial acrobatics and listened to their raucous calls echoing around the walls of the corrie below. Patches of snow had survived in shady gullies.

The descent of the north ridge of Sgurr Fiona opened up a new vista. Glas Mheall Liath has a white cap of quartzite and long white screes streak its steep slopes.

The climb up to Bidein a' Ghlas Thuill was straightforward. We shared the summit with a young black Labrador who had made light work of the climb up from Dundonnell House, his owner and two cheery girls. This is the best of all the viewpoints. I enjoyed the view to the north in particular, picking out the peculiar shapes of the mountains of Coigach and Inverpolly. Suilven seemed so near, I thought of walkers on its long ridge enjoying this perfect day.

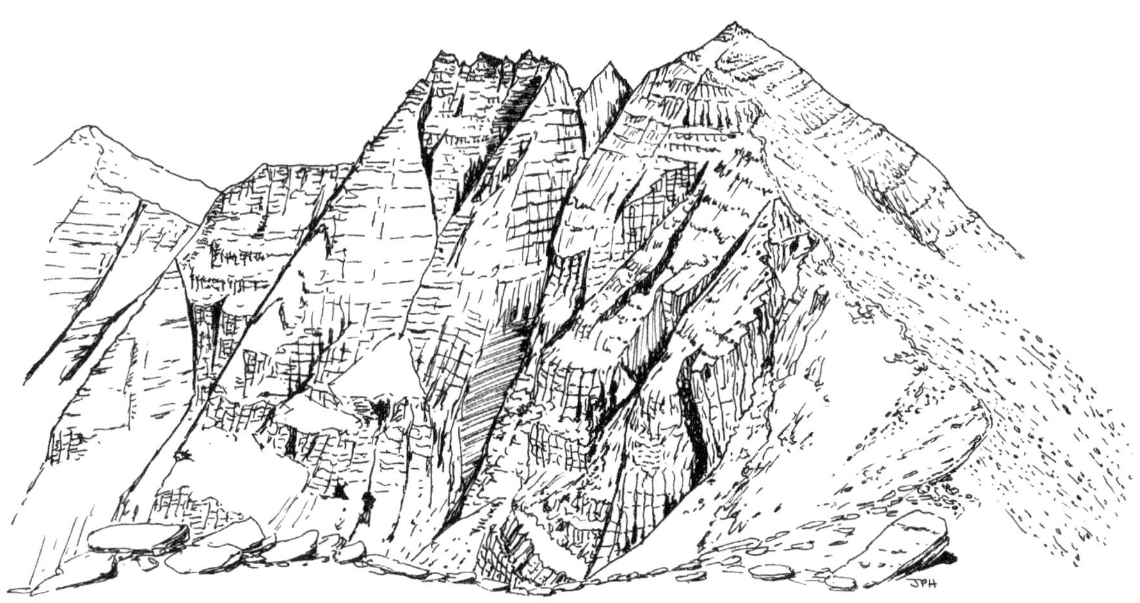

An Teallach 13/7/8
Sgurr Fiona from Bidein a' Ghlas Thuill.

It was sad to leave the summit. We scrambled down to the bealach between it and Glas Mheall Mor. From there we dropped steeply down into the east-facing corrie and followed the path which runs along the north side of the burn. The two girls followed behind, singing, in tune, all the verses of "Help!" by the Beatles. They were as fit as fleas so we stood aside to let them overtake.

It was a lovely walk out, past waterfalls, plunge pools and little gorges. It ended in a stand of old Scots pines but was marred by a jungle of rhododendrons near the road. These Himalayan intruders should have no place in this wonderful part of Scotland.

Back at the hostel we made friends with Chris, a German and Martina, a Czech. As neither could understand each other's native tongue, their relationship was conducted in English. We were joined by Ruth the pilgrim. She had come from her home in Vancouver to walk across Spain to San Diego de Compostella but had injured her knee. Pilgrimage abandoned, it had seemed a good idea to come to the Highlands before her planned two week retreat in a Buddhist monastery.

My wife, Jane, had made an enormous lasagne for us, the others made big bowls of Greek salad with feta cheese and black olives and two good bottles of red wine appeared. There was plenty to share with our new friends.

Later that evening, when glasses of Laphroaig had been poured, Chris talked about the German sense of humour and, strangely, The War. Ruth followed, telling us about her adventures in Spain. On one occasion she accepted a lift from a young man who took her up to the mountains where she could stay with his friends as long as she wanted to. Home was a circle of tepees and the first friend was a naked young man who stretched out his arms in welcome. "Don't look at his penis, don't look at his penis," was all she could think. She had become part of a Rainbow Gathering and felt somewhat out of place among all these nubile young people. After a night when, "The whole camp were at it, I got no sleep," she begged a ride back down to the Meseta.

14/7/08

Ben Wyvis

A battering on the mountain of terror

The forecast for the following day was not good. As it suggested that the further east one travelled the less severe the weather would be, we headed back along the Inverness road, intent on climbing Ben Wyvis, (wyevis by those, like me, who know no better; wivis by real hillwalking types and, according to the SMC, weevis by locals). Whatever the pronunciation, it is thought to mean mountain of terror.

I parked just beyond Garbat and we followed an excellent path up through forestry and on to the open hillside. Despite the forecast, I took off my waterproof trousers as it was so warm, a mistake as it turned out.

Cloud covered everything over 600 metres, so, just below that height, we stopped to have a mug of tea while we still had a panoramic view of the valley we had walked up and the cloud-capped Fannaichs beyond. At least I had the sense to put on my waterproof jacket before we walked into the cloud, crested the ridge and entered a different world.

A full gale whipped over from the south-west. It was impossible to walk in a straight line as the gusts blew us off the path. We paused in the shelter of An Cabar's cairn to draw breath then, heads down, we battled towards the summit cairn of Ben Wyvis. Curtains of cloud droplets crossed the top of the ridge in rapid succession, creating a strobe light

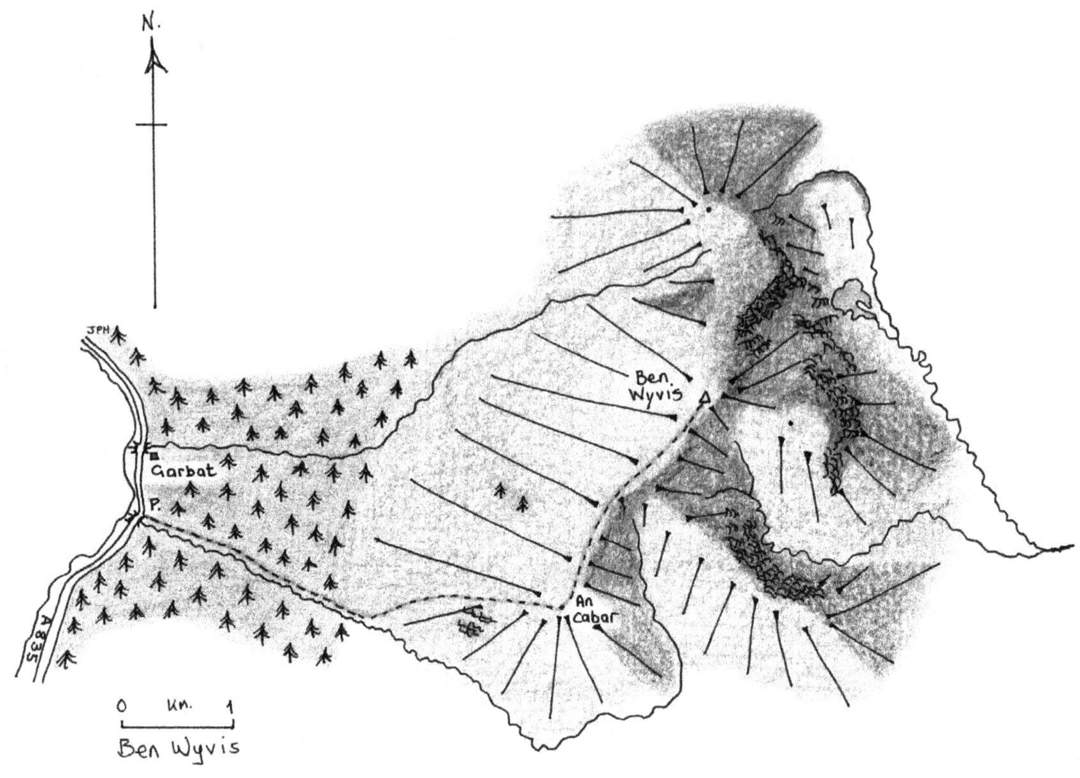

effect. We reached the cairn with its triangulation pillar and decided in two seconds to return the way we had come rather than walk further along the ridge to complete a circular route. It was not pleasant, I was already soaked to the skin and wanted off by the quickest and safest path. Once past the An Cabar cairn, we began to descend and got some protection from the full force of the wind. It was surprising how quickly I warmed up. By the time we had reached the break of slope in the lower reaches of the Bealach Mor, my trousers were bone dry.

It was long past time for lunch. We walked a little way from the path to a dry, stony patch where we sat in warm, gently moving air, listening to the peaceful sound of the trickling of a burn. It was the calm after the storm. I absorbed the minute detail of the surrounding heathers with their pink or white flowers. The seed heads of a fine selection of grasses swayed as the air moved. I counted 14 different flowers without getting to my feet. Cotton grass, bobbing peacefully in the breeze, carpeted the whole valley down to the tree line.

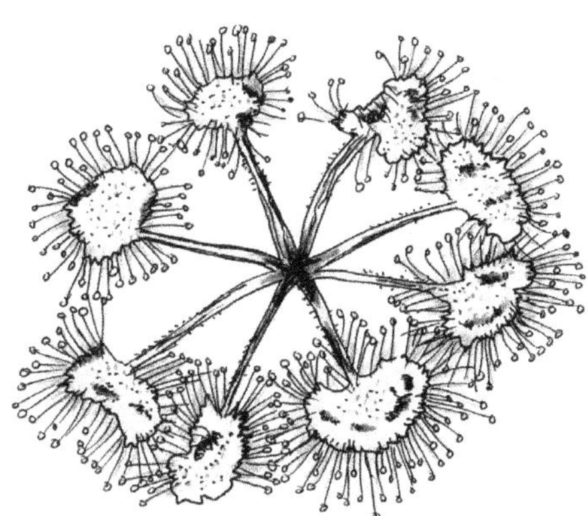

Ben Wyvis 14/7/8
Sundew with trapped insects.
JPH

Sundews grew on the banks of the little burn and I took a close-up photograph for my eldest grandson, Sam, who is interested in this sort of thing. I wandered over to look at some orchids; one was the dark pink northern marsh orchid, the other had deep pink spots on pale pink petals. I crushed some bog myrtle leaves to smell the eucalyptus scent. A black beetle marked with four orange lozenges on its wing case ambled by.

Relaxed, full and calm, we had a delightful walk back to the car, enjoying the afternoon sunshine.

That evening we walked with our new friends along Ullapool's waterfront to the Arch Inn. I tried their fish soup, which turned out to be more of a chowder, but it was packed with scallops, chunks of smoked salmon and other sea foods. Cheap, substantial, fishy and good. The waitress told us that, if I didn't mind two fish courses, they had herring landed on the pier that morning, so we ordered them next. The plates each had three large, sweet herrings baked in oatmeal, new potatoes and green vegetables. I had dipped into my energy account on that day's battle with the elements but it was soon well in credit again.

Later, in the common room, we talked to Albert from Barcelona, in Scotland for the first time and learning English from scratch. He told us that he "had to eat some haggis in a tea store."

15/7/08

Eididh nan Clach Geala

On the web of white stones

Very early next morning, Chris joined us for breakfast. His sleep had been disturbed by young Italians who had occupied the spare bunks in his room. "The girl above me moaned whenever I turned over, but not in an interesting way."

Not long after, the cars were left at Inverlael and we got on our bikes. As we cycled off, a lean man with a shaved head pulled his car into the parking space behind us. Three kilometres of forestry tracks further on, we had just locked the bikes together when he appeared with an adolescent black Labrador, having walked as fast as we had cycled. They both said hello and then shot off on the Beinn Dearg path. They were soon out of sight and we followed at a steadier pace. I came upon a frog that had been stood on, its leg still twitching. What bad luck to be on this rarely used thoroughfare and be hit by a speeding pedestrian.

It was warm as we walked up the sheltered Gleann na Squaib, the air clear and the sky dark blue above. A smell of honey drifted from the flowering heather. Dozens of red deer hinds and calves walked in single file in a line parallel to our path. They were pale beige rather than red. Two mature hinds brought up the rear and they shadowed us, not more than 40 metres away.

We turned off the main path to follow another which winds up to Lochan a' Chnapaich. I stopped to look south to the majestic cliff wall of Beinn Dearg's west ridge. Nearer the summit were large snow patches. I did not linger, however, because the blue sky was rapidly filling with grey clouds. A cold rain fell when we were at the corrie. We clambered under some large slabs to add a warm layer and then waterproof trousers and jackets. The forecast was not good and we wanted to be prepared for the worst. In our shelter we ate some hill food and sipped tea while watching sheets of rain cross the surface of the lochan.

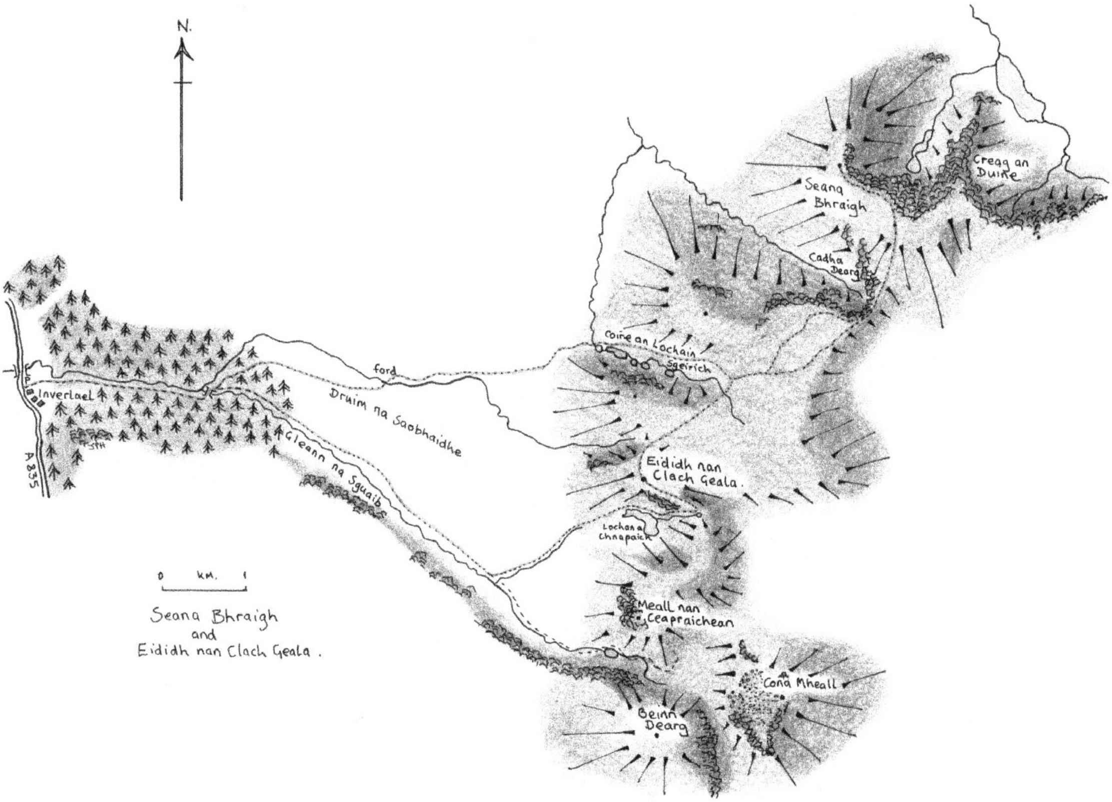

Resigned to a second day with no views from the top, we packed our flasks and trudged up to the bealach where, at a tiny lochan, the strong wind tore a hole in the cloud, the rain stopped and soon the sky was again blue.

The summit has a cap of large white angular boulders, many in lines down the slope and some in interlocking circles. These patterns were formed in periglacial times by freeze-thaw action and give the mountain its wonderful name, the web of the white stones. We scrambled over them to the summit, where we were again battered by strong wind. Retreating down the lee side to the shelter of a large outcrop, we had our lunch in pleasant sunshine. Rest over, we returned to the summit and crouched behind some huge quartzite blocks to enjoy fantastic views to the Fisherfield mountains, An Tealach, Loch Broom, the Inverpolly mountains and, within walking range on a better day, Seanna Bhraigh. I could see dark clouds rolling towards us from An Teallach and knew that our window of clear weather was closing.

Looking towards An Teallach
from the summit of
Eididh nan Clach Geala 15/7/8.

We wandered down to the head of Coire an Lochain Sgeirich where again we saw a large herd of deer, but this time they were stags. We took our time locating the path which leads west out of the corrie, enjoying the orchids and insectivorous plants growing between rock outcrops which seemed the very ribs of this ancient mountain. Just as we found the path the rain came down again and it continued, blown into our faces by the strong wind, as we marched down and out of the corrie.

Even in these conditions there was much beauty. Our walk took us past a string of lochans backed by massive cliffs on the south side of the corrie. It was a long way back. The path winds down Druim na Saobhaidhe from where we could see the end of the forestry where we had left the bikes. It was a fast ride downhill back to the cars.

Then it was off to a land stranger than any I have seen abroad and, insignificant among its mountains, the Torridon Youth Hostel. I was very impressed by this place. In the foyer was the latest weather forecast (not good), books, maps and displays of local geology, geomorphology and wildlife. There is a big kitchen, an airy dining room and a lounge which has a picture window with a splendid view of the mountains on the south side of Glen Torridon. The staff make the safety of walkers a priority, encouraging all groups to complete a route card. I made a big meal of spaghetti with Jane's home-made sauce while the others made us a Greek salad and produced enough Californian red wine to maintain our good health.

Eididh nan Clach Geala 15/7/8
Stags running over the skyline.

16/7/08

Maol Chean-dearg and Meall nan Ceapairean

Applecross oysters

I rose at six to the sound of a strong gale rattling heavy raindrops against the window which normally has such a fine view of Loch Torridon. "You're not going out in that?" enquired a sleepy voice. Its owner pulled his duvet over his head, adding, "You must be mad."

We started at Annat on the shore of the loch and took the old way to Coulags, following that well-made path to Loch an Eion at the foot of Maol Chean-dearg. Our route then branched off to follow a path running around the base of the mountain and into the corrie containing Loch Coire an Ruadh-staic. The rain stopped but cloud still hid the mountains above 600 metres. The corrie is beautiful, with Torridonian sandstone cliffs rising up to Maol Chean-dearg and white quartzite, sleek with the morning's rain, rising up to An Ruadh-stac. Torrents roared down the steep slopes and frogs were at every turn of the path. Pink orchids grew on the corrie floor and on the bealach dwarf juniper clung to the rocks. There was a stiff wind but, given that the bealach is a giant wind tunnel orientated north-east/south-west, the wind will roar across on many days. That is why these little trees, flattened to the ground, have occupied this ecological niche.

We were relaxed, did not consult the map (again, will I ever learn?) and wandered to the summit of Meall nan Ceapairean, thinking that this was the way to access the south-

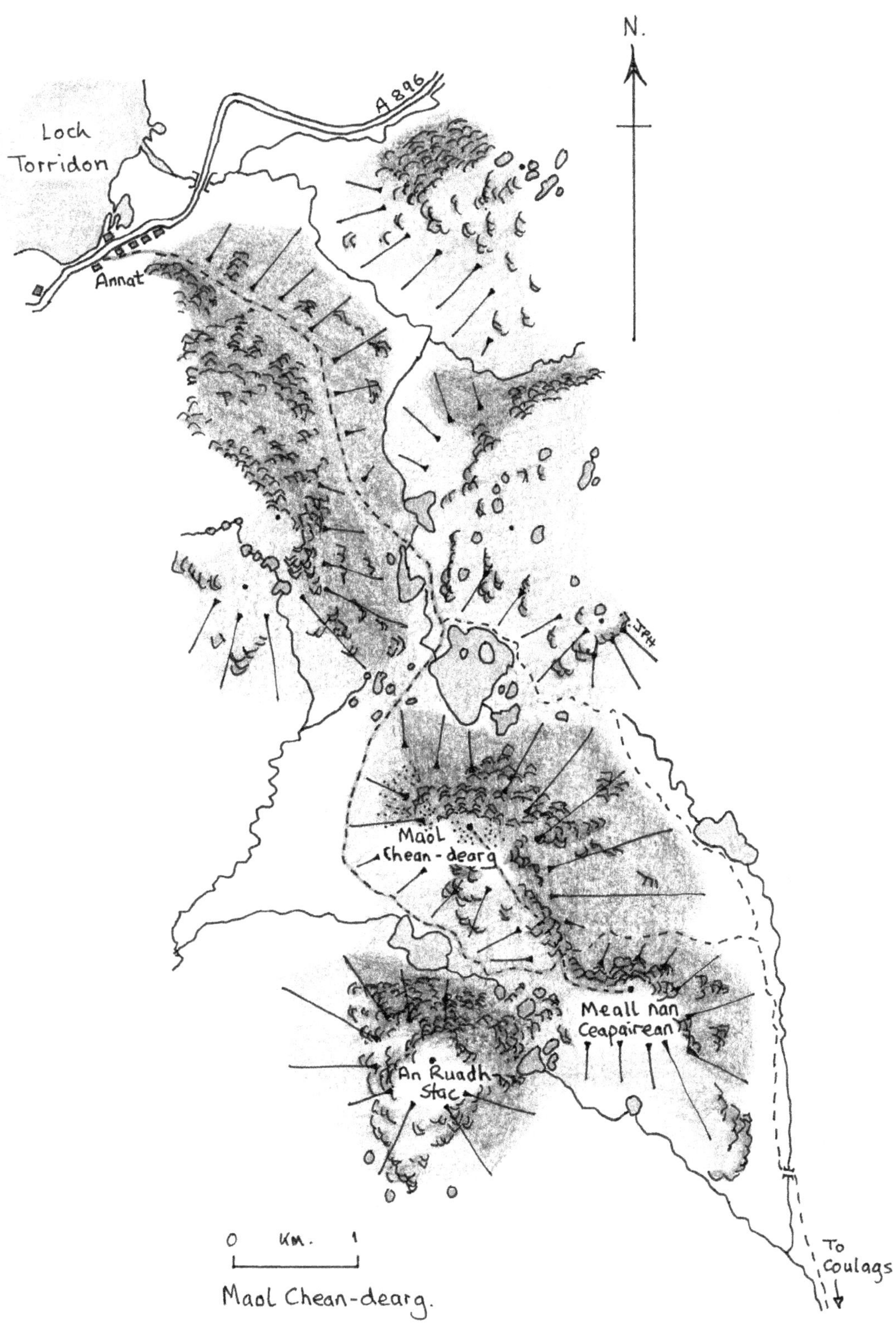

Maol Chean-dearg.

east ridge of our objective, Maol Chean-dearg. While we stood on the summit, the cloud lifted to about 750 metres and the ridge we wished to climb was revealed.

Up this steep ridge we went, into the cloud. It became increasingly rocky. We lost the path on boulder scree but used GPS, map and compass to locate it again.

At the top is an expanded cairn with alcoves all round, each designed to shelter up to three people, whatever the wind direction. We settled into the easternmost shelter and ate a well-earned lunch. The sun was visible through thin cloud and we had tantalising glimpses of Sgorr Ruadh to the east. This must be a five star viewpoint on a clear day and so, as with many previous Munros, I vowed to return.

On the way down three ptarmigan ran in front until they blended with the rocks. After 100 metres or so of descent, we emerged from under the white, swirling mist and in front was the handsome An Ruadh-stac, a giant tooth of quartzite, gleaming in shafts of sunlight pouring through holes in the thinning cloud cover.

Meadow Pipit
JPH

We drank the last of our tea on warm slabs above Loch Coire an Ruadh-staic, watching meadow pipits busily foraging on its shore, then returned to the Coulags path. Back at Annat, the sun was shining on Loch Torridon. The trip had taken nine hours.

At the hostel, the warden asked if we'd had a good day. "Great," I replied. While peeling off my wet boots, a couple in their 40s came in. The warden asked the same question. "Horrible," the man replied. The warden caught my eye.

Morag drove us to the local hotel. A sign declared 'Walkers welcome, we don't mind muddy boots'. She asked to see the menu but was told that, as there was a staff meeting, they would not comply with her request. None too pleased, she decided to drive us to Applecross and took the single-track road which hugs the coast. The sun shone, the sea sparkled, we were treated to wonderful views of Skye's mountains and her equilibrium was restored.

Torridon 16/7/8
stags by the Applecross road.

The Applecross Inn is an unpretentious place on the waterfront, looking out across the Inner Sound to Raasay and Skye. It was crowded but we were welcomed by a member of staff who assured us that he would find us a table and that we would be fed. I took to the place immediately. The menu was written on a blackboard, no frills. We had a plate of oysters each and then I chose sea bass from the catch of the day. This was roast whole and served with new potatoes and vegetables. Simple, fresh, delicious and a bargain.

We took the rollercoaster road over the Bealach na Ba on the return journey. At the bealach, it plunges down into the Coire na Ba in a series of steep hairpin bends. The drive was a memorable experience and would be frightening in winter conditions. At the bottom, we stopped a number of times to look at groups of red deer, hinds and calves separate from the groups of stags. They seemed little concerned by our presence and even went on grazing near the road when I left the car to photograph them. They put the finishing touch to a fantastic landscape, with stags on the ridges above the road, silhouetted against the violet sky of evening. Then it was back for mugs of tea and a glass of Caol Ila.

30/8/08

Beinn na Lap, Chno Dearg and Stob Coire Sgriodain

A mountain adventure which began with a railway journey.

Some people enjoy driving. I don't. The drive from Aberdeen to Tulloch Station on that Friday, however, was an exception. I left home at 6.00 p.m. and drove down the familiar Deeside road to Ballater. There I turned, for the first time, onto the Cock Bridge/Tomintoul road. Three bikers passed me, going south, and that was the only traffic I saw until I got to Speybridge. It was a beautiful evening and I drove slowly, enjoying the light of the low sun and the long shadows. The narrow road follows the sparkling River Gairn, winding through woods of birch, rowan and alder, and emerges on open moorland, with the rounded eastern outliers of the Cairngorms rising above. The lonely Corgarff Castle guards the foot of the high pass on which the ski centre is built. The road climbs to 640 metres, no wonder snow closes it so often. I enjoyed the big skies and the emptiness. My ears popped at the top.

The road from Grantown-on-Spey to Aviemore was, if anything, more beautiful that evening. The setting sun coloured the Cairngorms deep red and in the clear air I could pick out familiar corries, crags and ridges. The red mountains gradually darkened to a rich maroon until the weather gods snapped their fingers and the red was gone.

The last section of the road, from Newtonmore, I drove in the gloaming. Pale grey mists rose from Loch Laggan. There were no sharp edges any more. The mountains were subtle, cold, gloomy and exquisite. I arrived at the station as the night began. A rectangle of yellow light as the door opened made everything seem suddenly dark. Geraldine, Sharon and Claire each gave me a hug and then urged me inside, away from the midges.

I was in bed late and up early, thinking, as I made my porridge, about the need to sleep fast on these Jolly Boys weekends. The charming old station buildings have been converted to hostel accommodation, so we did not have far to go. We opened the door of the common room, which once had been the waiting room, and were on the platform.

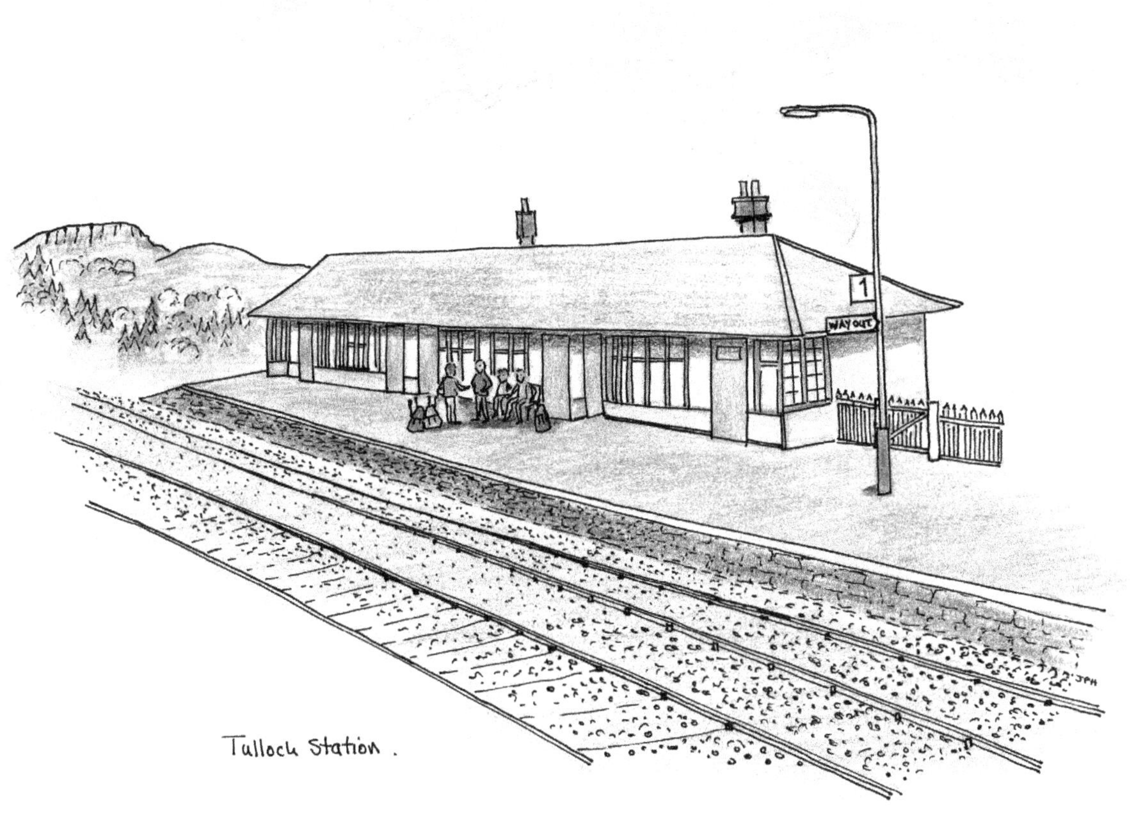

Tulloch Station.

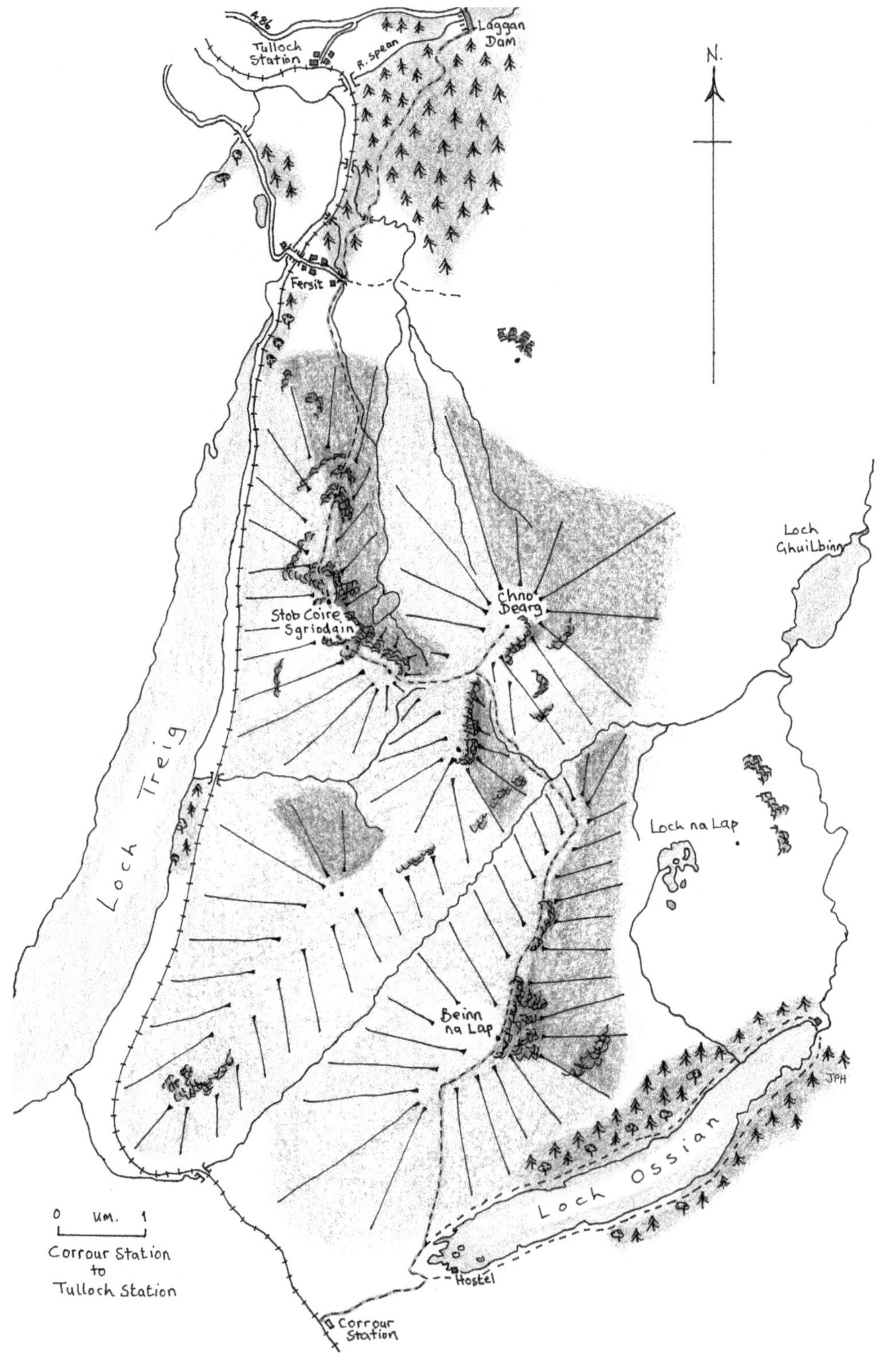

A86
Tulloch Station
R. Spean
Laggan Dam
N.
Fersit
Loch Ghuilbinn
Chno Dearg
Stob Coire Sgriodain
Loch Treig
Loch na Lap
Beinn na Lap
JPH
Loch Ossian
0 KM. 1
Corrour Station to Tulloch Station
Hostel
Corrour Station

The train was dead on time at 8.13 a.m. As it rolled into the station the driver changed the destination sign above his window to Glasgow Queen Street. The conductress was somewhat taken aback when twenty hillwalkers with bulky packs began to squeeze into the already full rear carriage. "You're not all paying separately?" she asked in a strong Glasgow accent. A single cost me £2.70.

The morning sun bathed the landscape in summer light. There was enough wind to create long parallel lines of turbulence on the otherwise flat blue surface of Loch Treig. Stob Coire Easain and Stob a' Choire Mheadhoin, both over 1100 metres, rose sheer from the far shore. The railway turned away from the loch to wind over bleak moorland and then, all too soon, the train pulled into Corrour Station.

We tumbled out onto the platform and I watched the train as it rattled away and receded into the wilderness. Above the chatter of my friends I was conscious of the quiet of this place. A lonely halt on a single track line. A place many miles from the nearest road. The distinctive nature and relative positions of the old buildings, as well as their setting, stirred memories. It was not until I was climbing up Ceann Caol Beinn na Lap and looked back that I realised the station had a frontier quality. It would hardly be out of place in a film set in the American West or Australian Outback of bygone years.

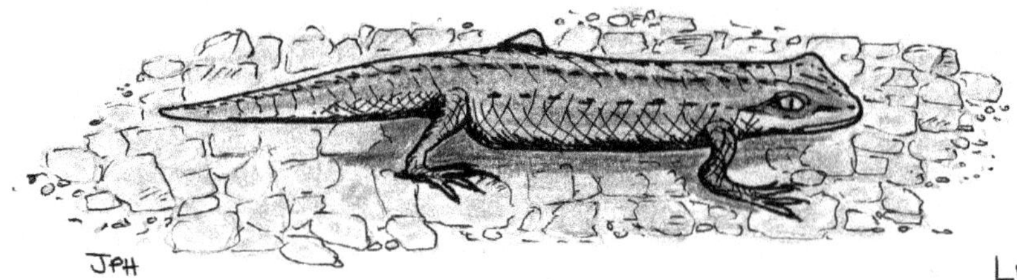

Lizard at Loch Ossian 30/8/8

Our crowd of walkers warmed up their leg muscles for the rigours ahead on the track which leads to Loch Ossian. I was chatting to Charlie at the rear of the party when I spotted a small lizard. I don't think that it had warmed up properly because, instead of flitting off before I could blink, it hung around and posed for close-up photos.

At the junction of paths by the head of the loch, we gathered to decide who was doing what. Geraldine, Sharon and Kenny opted for a walk around Loch Ossian. Morag and I invited others to join us on our planned route along three ridges, over three Munro summits and then walking back to Tulloch. We got looks of horror at the prospect but no other response. The rest, led by Ray and Struan, were off to climb Carn Dearg and Sgor Gaibhre, to the south-east of the loch. They had to make good time indeed as they had bought return tickets and needed to be back at Corrour Station by 3.00 p.m. Only free spirit Fionn was unaccounted for. No one was sure where he had slept and he was obviously set on doing his own thing once more.

Cloud now covered the sun and the mountain tops. The lower slopes of Beinn na Lap, our first objective, were warm, humid and perfect for midges. I paused briefly to gather bunches of bog myrtle and rubbed the eucalyptus smelling sap into my hair, on my face and other exposed skin. It had been some years since I had used chemical sprays like Skin So Soft and Jungle Formula. I found them far worse than the midges, especially when they mingled with sweat running down my forehead and stung my eyes. Nothing is better than bog myrtle and I do not find it unpleasant to rub on this natural protection. A person can, in any case, outwalk midges, even on steep slopes like the one we were ascending.

At about 700 metres we stopped for a last look back at Corrour Halt and Ossian, then we plunged into the cool, damp world of the cloud. We had climbed a clear path, briskly because of the midges, but this disappeared on the sparsely vegetated top of the ridge. So did the midges, which were no match for the stiff, chilly easterly wind. We turned right and kept to what we judged to be the crest of the ridge, steadily climbing with each step. The wind and cloud droplets rapidly lowered our body temperature so we stopped at a stone shelter which, on better days, would be the perfect place to drink tea, gazing down to Loch Ossian and the mountainous lands beyond. As we were putting on warm layers, a figure loomed out of the mist. He seemed anxious. "Have you seen the small lochan?" he enquired. When we replied that we had not, he sped off without another word. He was the sole person we were to see on the hills that day.

At the summit, we sat with our backs to the large cairn, in the lee of the wind, enjoying a hot drink and a second breakfast. We decided that we wanted to be on the Sron na Cloiche Sgoilte, so I set a bearing to be sure and off we went.

It was good walking but sticking to the path was not easy in such poor visibility. We needed the security of the compass. It was a relief when we began to emerge from the cloud at about 700 metres. We walked until we could see the landscape clearly then sat on a rock to check our position with GPS and map. Shafts of sunlight hit the surface of Loch Ghuilbinn below. It was interesting that we were facing Loch na Lap, feeling before we consulted the map that our way led in that general direction. Feelings, however, are not to be trusted. Our way led in the opposite direction. Again I took a bearing in case the cloud base lowered. Morag set her own compass and thus armed, we continued our journey.

We descended the steep side of the deep and spectacular Allt Feith Thuill valley. Halfway down I suggested that we stop at flat rocks to eat lunch. There would be little wind on the valley floor and, on such an overcast day, that meant midges.

I needed the energy from my peanut butter and honey sandwiches because it had been hard going to that point and the worst was to come. As I sipped from my steaming mug of tea I considered the valley from my high perch. It was unusual in that it was a steep angled V shape, rather than the ubiquitous U-shaped valleys of the Highlands. U-shaped because they have been carved by moving ice, with fluvio-glacial deposits creating the typical flat floors. This valley must have been eroded by a roaring meltwater torrent in a time when the area was a place of ice dammed lakes and decaying remnants of an ice sheet. The map shows the Allt Feith Thuill running north-east out of the valley and the Allt Luib Ruairidh running south-west out of the valley. These streams, running in opposite directions, are shown as joined in the middle. Looking down at the valley floor, there was no area of poor drainage that I could see that would mark the watershed. Running water occupied the entire valley floor. I wished I had time to explore and try to sort out the mystery and vowed, as I have done so often before, to come back when there is not so much pressure on my time.

A bright light made me look up from that intriguing valley, it was the mountains between Loch Treig and the Blackwater reservoir, clear of cloud and now bathed in pale, watery sunshine. Ahead, however, the upper regions of Chno Dearg were hidden in cloud which had a base of about 800 metres above sea level. This allowed us to see the hanging corrie between the Munro and its south-western Top, Meall Garbh. This was our route up.

Quickly descending to the valley floor, we crossed the stream where nature had provided stepping stones and began the hard climb, a relentless 300 metres. Just below the cloud we fixed our position and took a bearing for the summit. It was a relief to reach the ridge and see the slope level off. To add to our joy we found a path which clearly led to the cairn. It was a fickle thing (again), disappearing whenever there was a stony section or where boulder screes had to be climbed. Our compasses were our security and led us, without problem, to the summit. There we had a welcome mug of tea and finished our lunch before setting a bearing for the bealach between Meall Garbh and Stob Coire Sgriodain. On a clear day the path, I am sure, would be as plain as the nose on one's face, but on that day we took no chances. Coming off the ridge the wrong way at that stage, so far from the nearest road, would put a serious strain on our reserves of energy.

Emerging from the cloud at the bealach I took another bearing which would get us to the summit of Stob Coire Sgriodain, our third Munro of the day. It was at this point, now mid- afternoon, that the mood of the weather changed. The cloud thinned to broken patches which began to stream off the ridge in undulating ribbons. The ridge was revealed as an airy spine of bare rock. Loch Treig lay far below at the foot of a remarkably steep 600 metre slope. The long parallel lines of broken water caused by wind turbulence were still there but, strangely, it was nothing more than breezy on the crest of the ridge.

We walked the length of the ridge to Sron na Garbh-bheinne, scrambling up the contorted outcrops of mica schist, seamed with compressed bands of white quartz. Beyond was a panorama of mountain and loch. I stopped to stand and stare at the pattern of light and shade which produced so much contrast between adjacent peaks and glens. The light shifted as I watched, illuminating a mountain which shone out from its shaded neighbours before lighting up the next. Sunbeams created pools of gold on the shining levels of Loch Laggan.

It was with some reluctance that I left the high crags and followed the distant figure of Morag down a stream fed by Lochan Coire an Lochain. The lochan occupies the floor of the giant north-facing corrie between Chno Dearg and Stob Coire Sgriodain. Unusually, the stream splits into a number of channels as it meanders north across a wide expanse of moorland. We followed what appeared to be the largest channel. It provided us with a bonny walk, with waterfalls, plunge pools, sections of gorge and rowans, heavy with berries, clinging to the rocks.

At Fersit we consulted the map. The shortest way back to the hostel would be along the railway but this is not to be advised. Our choice was a forest track to the Laggan Dam, a tedious march at that stage of the day. One more bend and there was the welcome sight of our station, charming and trim with its green and white paintwork.

We were barely through the door when Alan and Belinda announced that dinner was ready. We sat in the dining room to enjoy their home cooking and listen to everyone's stories.

Full of good food and wine, we squashed into the waiting room. I had brought a bottle of Laphroaig from which I decided to have a nightcap and then retire. I had been up late the previous night and needed some sleep. It was, however, 2.30 a.m. before I got into my bunk, having experienced a remarkable night of juggling, magic tricks, massage and the sort of laughter that hurts.

14/10/08

Beinn a' Bhuird and Ben Avon

Two granite giants

October

A huge, yellow, autumnal full moon was slowly setting behind the hills as I drove James west past Braemar. A stag and hind forded the Dee and a pine marten rippled across the road in front. By the time Morag arrived and parked before the bridge at Allanaquoich, the sky to the east was barred with the pink and red of the dawn.

We pulled our bikes from the back of the cars and were soon cycling along the track up Glen Quoich. James led the way on his rickety old bike, a strangely old-fashioned figure. It was cold and clear, perfect conditions to enjoy the autumn colours of the birch and rowan, their bright yellow and orange stark against the dark green of the Scots pines. Autumn sounds too, as stags roared from their rutting grounds within this ancient, open forest. The track continued through a pebbly ford across the Allt an Dubh-ghlinne, the Quoich Water's western tributary. Here we left the bikes.

James took off his boots and waded across the river in stocking feet. Morag and I picked our way across on the largest boulders without getting our feet too wet. We were lucky that the rivers were so low, especially as there were three similar crossings to come. Our route may well be a serious proposition when they are in spate.

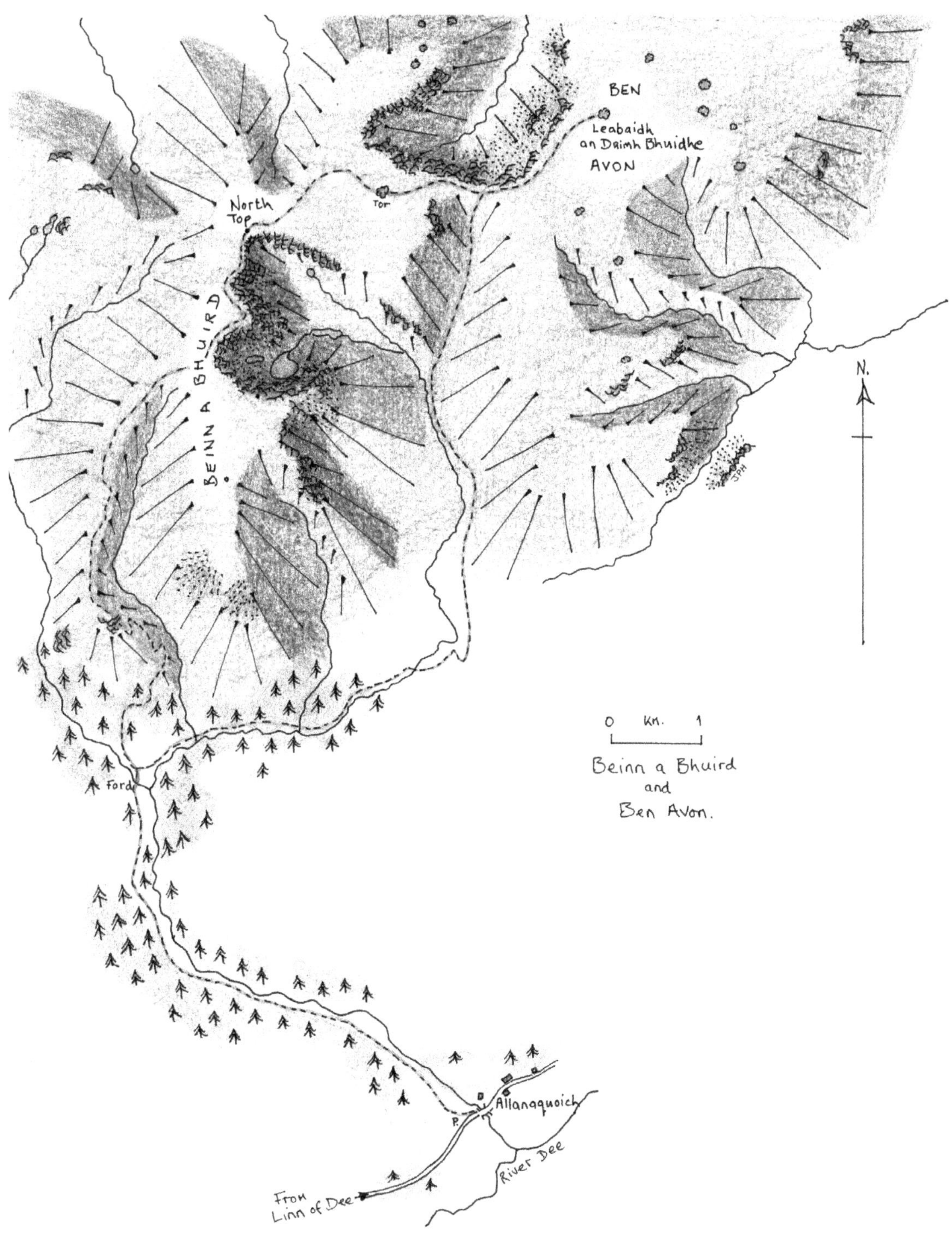
BEN
Leabaidh
an Daimh Bhuidhe
AVON
North
Top
Tor
BEINN A BHUIRD
N.
0 Km. 1
Beinn a Bhuird
and
Ben Avon.
Ford
Allanaquoich
River Dee
From
Linn of Dee
P.
JPH

We walked through a delightful wood of old pines where we met a National Trust warden. He told us that the bulldozed track up onto Beinn a' Bhuird had been restored and replaced by a narrow path. This we followed up onto the plateau. An iridescent black grouse shot from under our boots, shattering the silence of the morning. Higher on the path, three ptarmigan, their wings and heads already white in anticipation of their winter plumage, flew away, skimming the top of the short vegetation.

Once the steep climb eased off, we stopped for a mug of tea and a snack. It was an excellent vantage point, with views over a massive tract of wild country to the north, west and south. My gaze settled on the spectacular heart of the Cairngorms, north-west of our high seat, the craggy walls of Loch Avon and tor-studded ridges, already white with the first of the winter snow.

The summit of Beinn a' Bhuird is three square kilometres of sub-arctic plateau, its surface granite grit with sparse dwarf vegetation, mostly pale yellow on that day. James saw me looking at it and commented, "It's regrettable that there's a lack of large boulders as I ate a good portion of figs yesterday evening and fear I may need some privacy."

The slope had been gradually steepening but the climbing ended abruptly at the lip of the giant corrie containing the Dubh Lochan. The top of its plunging cliffs was marked by a cornice of fresh snow. I stopped to take a photograph and noticed that fine cloud was rolling in behind us and moving faster than we were walking. With the cloud came a light rain of the finest droplets, not much in itself but, when combined with temperatures little above freezing, it made us zip up our jackets and put on warm hats.

We stopped at the cairn which marks the North Top, the true summit, for lunch. It was a hasty affair and I was glad to be on the move again to get some heat into my numb fingers. Visibility was not good and it would have been easy to set off in the wrong direction on this broad section of the high plateau. James had his map displayed in a new map case so he took a bearing and off we tramped to the first feature of the mountain top, a granite tor.

I find granite a fascinating rock. It has large crystals of pink or creamy-grey feldspar, mixed with translucent quartz, sometimes with specs of dark biotite mica. The rock of the two mountains of this walk is granite, but with interesting variations. Some boulders and exposures have particularly large feldspar crystals, four or five centimetres long, this type is called porphyritic. One would think it just about indestructible, yet rainwater reacts with its minerals and gradually breaks it down. Granite has a structure of massive blocks separated by joint planes. When the rock is exposed at the surface the joint planes become lines of weakness, cracks to admit the water, and the granite begins to rot. Much of the weathered material in the Cairngorms was removed at the end of the last glacial period. A thawed, saturated surface layer became like a thick porridge and began to flow downhill in a series of ripples which can be seen on the mountainsides. In between the joint planes, the massive blocks of granite become rounded boulders, left high above the surface as tors as the weathered granite particles are gradually carried away down the slopes.

As we descended from the tor the cloud rolled away, leaving a rainbow over the eastern sky. The landscape revealed was truly grand. In the foreground the path zig zagged down to a high col separating Beinn a' Bhuird and Ben Avon and then zig zagged steeply up again. To the north the high plateau drops by precipitous cliffs into the deep bowl of the Garbh Coire. Ben Avon itself forms the eastern wall of this giant corrie, with the ridge of Stob an t-Sluichd, bristling with tors, forming the western wall.

The path to the summit plateau of Ben Avon was a slog but we stopped often to admire the changing views as we climbed higher and our perspective changed. Once the angle of slope eased, we could see the highest point of this huge mountain, a granite tor called Leabaidh an Daimh Bhuidhe, the bed of the yellow stag. It stands in a desert of granite grit in which struggle dwarf dry grass and brittle grey lichen among the pink granite boulders. The tallest points are two towers of granite blocks, Ben Avon's chimneys.

We scrambled over a lower part of the tor and left our rucksacks on the north side. It did not take us long to climb to the top of the westernmost chimney but my satisfaction was marred by looking at the easternmost because it looked higher. It was also narrower, with near vertical sides and would be a daunting prospect to climb. With this in his mind, I suspect, James lay down on our chimney's flat top and sighted the top of the other. He declared it no higher. I remained unconvinced and stated that I must attempt to climb the second of Ben Avon's lums as it seemed the higher. However daunting, honour was

at stake, so James said that he would accompany me. Morag, sensibly, opted out of this macho stuff and went to make a mug of tea.

The eastern tower was a challenge. As its rough surface bit into my soft hands I was reminded of the gabbro of the Cuillin. Our route involved some athletic contortions which, we agreed, took us out of our comfort zone. The top, however, was achieved but, sadly, seemed much the same height as the first chimney.

We returned, somewhat out of breath, to join Morag for tea and a second lunch. It was a lovely picnic spot. A black grouse called to warn his rivals, though I would not have thought that this detached piece of windswept Arctic would be much fought over. It looked and sounded like a blackcock to me but, if so, was an adventurer far from his home on the lower slopes.

The vista before us was strangely beautiful, a gently undulating plain of exposed dusky pink granite with sparse tufts of a tough yellow grass. At widely spaced intervals a tor stood resilient against the storms of the millennia, each a relic of a more ancient, higher land surface. I determined to return to Ben Avon on a fine day and walk the length of its north-east ridge from the Linn of Avon. This is a mountain that can not be explored, or properly enjoyed, in a hurry.

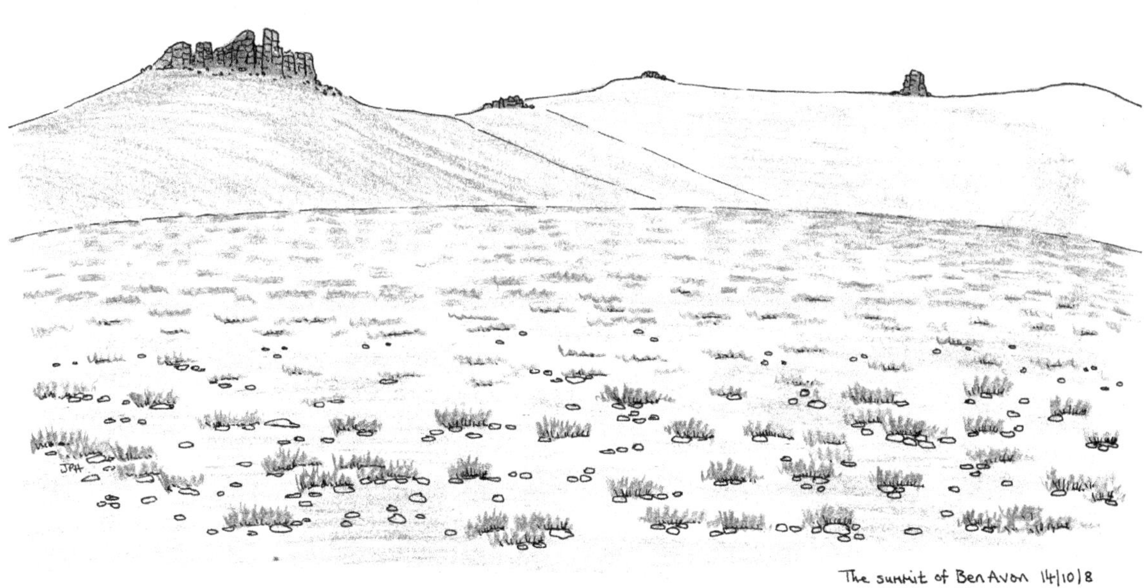

The summit of Ben Avon 14/10/8

Daylight, however, was not going to linger for us on this short October day, so we had to pack up and head back to the place we had left the bikes. I could not resist a few stops to gaze at this wild landscape and take photographs, dreaming of a return with a sketch pad and time to draw.

At the col between the two mountains we turned south, dropping down into the steep-sided valley of the Glas Allt Mor. After its confluence with the Allt Dearg, dramatic views opened up of Beinn a' Bhuird's massive corries to the west. These also merit a return visit.

Then began the long walkout. We turned west and made the first of three river crossings. Soon after, we entered an open forest of mature Scots pines. I was pleased to see that where ancient giants had crashed to the ground in one of the many storms that lash the Cairngorms they had been left in peace, adding to the biodiversity as they decay. Occasionally a birch, its leaves bright yellow with autumn colour, stood out like a flame against the deep red trunks and dark, sombre green of the pines. All that was missing was the saplings, without them this wonderful forest is doomed.

At the last ford I crossed on the tops of boulders, James waded. Morag told us how glad she was that we had brought the bikes. The track down Glen Quoich to the car is nearly six kilometres and it would have been a long, weary slog after such a big day. The cycle ride was delightful, with trees showing their best colour, stags roaring and a red squirrel wondering what sort of creatures we were. We got back to the cars in the gloaming after cycling and walking for nearly ten hours.

18/10/08

Mount Keen

In the rainbow

The weather forecast had been full of gloom. There were to be strong northerly winds and heavy wintry showers, with prolonged rain in the west. The best chance of clear spells was in the extreme east, so Morag and I decided to explore the land at the head of Glen Esk and take a chance. It was certainly a glorious early morning as I drove the long miles up this lovely Angus glen.

We set off on our bikes in good spirits, enjoying a detour around someone's back yard before we found the track again. Glen Esk ends where we left the cars, beyond that point it splits into two tributary glens, Glen Lee and Glen Mark. It was up the latter we went, cycling the three kilometres to the Queen's Well.

The bikes were left at a stand of pines beside the lonely old stone house called Glenmark. I was impressed by the scale of the landscape and the steep, bare crags on each side. Morag asked what I thought the house was used for but her question was answered by a ghillie leading a sturdy grey pony, saddled and ready for an expected deer carcass. No brightly coloured Gortex clothing for the ghillie, he wore a traditional flat cap and tweeds. His steady pace, aided by a tall walking stick, saw him quickly enter the shadowed, rock-walled gorge of the Water of Mark. We did not follow as our route wound up the east side of the glen, at first following the line of the Ladder Burn. It was an excellent track, one of the area's ancient drove roads which we could have followed all the way to Ballater in the north.

The hills of Glen Mark and Glen Lee.

Before long, the gradient slackened and we were on the high plateau of the Mounth, catching the strong, cold wind from the north-west. We turned off the drove road and followed a good path up the cone-shaped summit of Mount Keen. The very top is a granite tor on which sits an old triangulation pillar. Another, smaller, tor lies to the north and it was behind its substantial boulders that we took shelter to eat our lunch.

It was an interesting picnic spot, with views over 360 degrees and for many miles, visibility in the cold air being excellent. I picked out Bennachie in the north, the sea beyond Stonehaven in the east, the Angus hills to the south, Lochnagar in the west and, towering over all, Ben Avon in the north-west. Ben Avon was of particular interest as we had been on its summit tor only days before. From this vantage point it was a massive wall of rock, storm clouds settling on its summit and then spilling down before streaming on the powerful wind towards us. I huddled into my jacket and warmed my hands on my mug of tea. Only ragged remnants of Ben Avon's storm reached us, enough to make a perfect rainbow which bathed the summit of Mount Keen in stripes of purple, blue, green, yellow, orange and red light. We stared, transfixed, until the colours disappeared along with the tatters of cloud which rushed towards the sea.

Striding down from the summit we could see more dark cloud settling on the Cairngorm mountain tops but above us the sky was blue, the sun shone brightly, and so it

was to remain for the rest of the day. We had made a good choice of location for our walk. It was a slow return to the bikes as we often stopped to enjoy the dramatic landscape, particularly to the west along the Water of Mark. We considered detouring there and hunting for Balnamoon's Cave, but decided that this could wait for another day as we wanted to see the other tributary fork of Glen Esk.

The afternoon was now so balmy in this sheltered glen that I had to stop to remove my warm jacket. The bikes made short work of the journey back.

At the bridge we turned right into Glen Lee. A grim old castle stands at the point where the Waters of Lee and Mark join to become the Esk, its loopholes commanding the old road from Deeside to The Mearns. Not far beyond, we stopped to watch a mature stag as he made his way along the fringe of an open birch wood.

On again and we came to the wave-lapped shores of Loch Lee, steely blue on that fine day and filling the whole floor of the glen. To the west are steep crags, not unlike those in the upper reaches of Glen Mark, between which the Water of Lee runs down to feed the sparkling loch. Morag went to look at an old kirkyard and I lay down on a smooth, sun-warmed rock. The day was over but I felt that I had much more to explore in this corner of the Highlands.

23/12/08

Carn a' Mhaim

Midwinter in the Cairngorms

James slowed his car beyond Inverey to allow a group of hinds, pale ghosts in the headlights, to step off the road. They were not in a hurry. A little further on a young stag pranced along in front of us before tossing back his head and jumping up the bank.

As the dawn light seeped into the sky we lifted the bikes out of the car and attached ice axes to the rucksacks. Morag arrived in a flap, "My car spun right around on ice coming down from Glen Shee."

"Are you alright?" I asked.

"It gets worse," she replied, "I dislocated my jaw eating my breakfast croissant."

"Are you in pain?"

"I was, but it went back with a click."

We were soon cycling up Glen Lui, James setting a fast pace on his old bike. At one point, despite being last and struggling to keep up, I had to stop to look properly at the mountain we planned to climb, Carn a' Mhaim (va-eem). It rose up, directly ahead, a colossal dark mass, streaked with brilliant white snow and ice. The sky was deep pink, with the single cumulus cloud even deeper pink. It was going to be a fine day.

The bikes were left at Derry Lodge and we enjoyed a pleasant walk through the Scots pines of Glen Luibeg. The sky was now pale blue, a perfect backdrop for the dark green

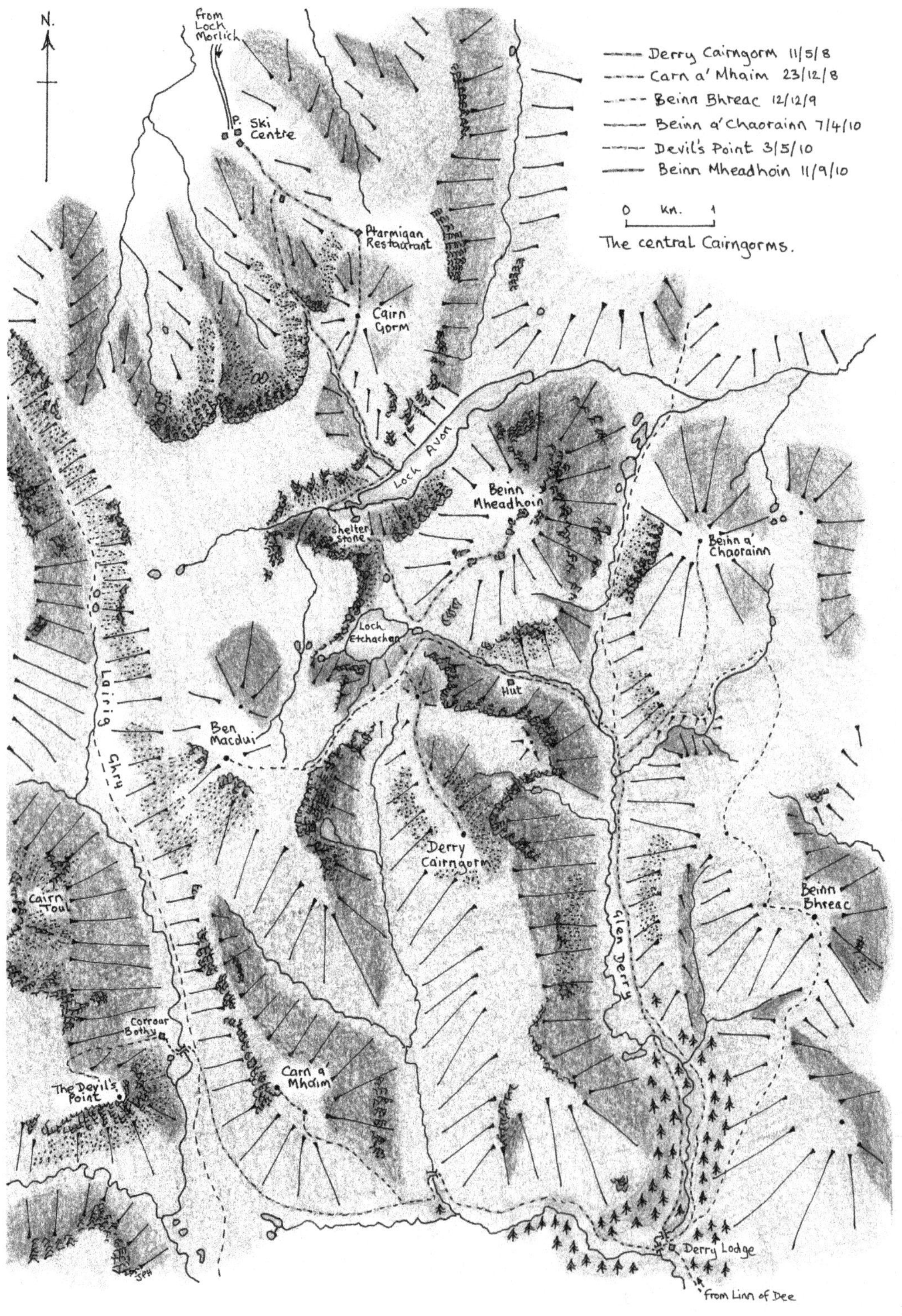
N.
from Loch Morlich
P. Ski Centre
Ptarmigan Restaurant
Cairn Gorm
Derry Cairngorm 11/5/8
Carn a' Mhaim 23/12/8
Beinn Bhreac 12/12/9
Beinn a'Chaorainn 7/4/10
Devil's Point 3/5/10
Beinn Mheadhoin 11/9/10
0 km. 1
The central Cairngorms.
Loch Avon
Beinn Mheadhoin
Shelter Stone
Beinn a' Chaorainn
Loch Etchachan
Hut
Lairig Ghru
Ben Macdui
Derry Cairngorm
Glen Derry
Cairn Toul
Beinn Bhreac
Corrour Bothy
Carn a Mhaim
The Devil's Point
Derry Lodge
From Linn of Dee

crowns of the trees. Once over the Luibeg Bridge we followed the track for less than a kilometre before branching off to the right along a narrow but well-made path. This climbed steeply up the blunt south-eastern end of Carn a' Mhaim.

There was not much conversation as we laboured up a demanding gradient, climbing over 300 metres. Again, James set a cracking pace. My heart was pounding and my knees were weak as we came up onto the crest of the ridge. Up there it was well below 0°C and the extensive snow patches were frozen as hard as rock; to avoid crossing them we tried to pick our way over the granite boulders.

I needed to sit down beneath the bare granite of the mountain's first summit, a massive tor which has fallen apart in a chaos of boulders. We broached our lunch boxes, my chunks of fruit cake giving me a much needed energy boost. I was soon on my feet again with my similarly revived companions.

We went round the west side of this first summit, walking carefully over the icy boulders. The pyramid of The Devil's Point appeared before us and then the wide panorama of the Lairig Ghru. The sky was a thin ice blue, with a white blanket of cloud about 100 metres thick sitting above the mountain tops in the far west. It was almost midday but the copper sun was near the horizon in the south.

Near the true summit were curious granite standing stones, like weathered ancient sculptures. James and Morag sat down at the cairn but I walked to each point of the compass, running out of adjectives as I described the views. All were spectacular but none more so than those to the north and west. My gaze moved north from The Devil's Point to Cairn Toul, Sgor an Lochain Uaine and then to the scalloped corries of Braeriach. I remembered sitting on the cliff edge above one of these corries in the summer of 2000, my boots in the remains of the winter's snow cornice. My son, Tom, had pointed out Carn a' Mhaim, remarking that it looked a great ridge walk. I had agreed and added that the views would be first-rate on a fine day. Eight and a half years later, here I was to discover how true those observations had been.

A bitter wind sprang up out of nowhere, giving a wind chill so severe that my camera battery packed in. I skidded back to the others and we agreed to drop down to the lee of the boulder crown to eat lunch.

Our high platform was a perfect spot, with a view that included Beinn a' Ghlo in the south-west and Lochnagar in the south-east. We were alone in this beautiful place and had barely seen a living thing since leaving the Linn o' Dee. There was a trace of warmth from the low sun, our shadows were long on the mountainside and all was serene.

Morag broke the silence to tell us that there had been an intruder in her big old house in the Borders.

"I keep an ice axe by my bed for that very reason," remarked James.

"Intruders would be making a big mistake entering your house."

The Devil's Point (L.), Cairn Toul (R.), From Carn á Mhaim.

"Yes," he agreed, adding, "and I keep a Malacca cane by my front door."

"Have you ever used it?" I asked.

"Only once," he replied, "when I chased a persistent Liberal Democrat candidate down my path."

As I have said, James set a demanding pace in the morning. As no one had died as a result, which would have thrown our timings, we were well ahead of schedule. We could therefore afford to take our time on the return to Derry Lodge and properly enjoy this delightful day. We stood for a while on the Luibeg Bridge, watching the burn rush around boulders the size of cars. A little later, we drank tea under the twisted branches of venerable Scots pines.

All too soon we were back on the bikes and James was way ahead as usual. Where the track runs alongside the Lui Water there was a pool of fresh blood. "It must have been a walker with a Liberal Democrat badge," I remarked. Morag considered this for a moment then observed that there was no body. "James would have had time to tip a body in the water," I replied. When we caught up with him he was on the bridge, looking down into the water, perhaps to check on the progress of the corpse.

"Why are you looking at my ice axe?" he asked.

"I'm just checking for blood."

"Oh," he said, "that's alright then."

We said goodbye to Morag and then drove down Deeside under a deep pink sky as the light began to fade. The winter darkness was cheered up by the twinkling Christmas decorations of houses near the road. Ballater was ablaze with fairy lights. We stopped there to have tea with Sheena. I had left my change of clothing and shoes in my car and was concerned about arriving in boots and a shirt that would have made its own way into the washing machine should I have peeled it off. "Don't worry," said James, "she's horsey so she won't mind." She did not mind, so she said, and we thawed out as we enjoyed her company and drank mugs of tea in her cosy sitting room.

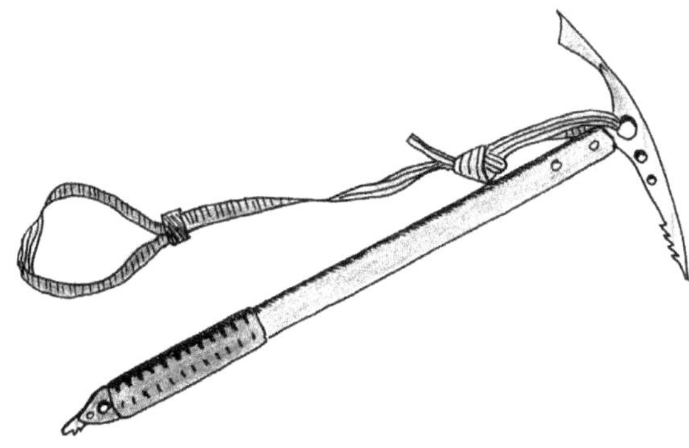

29/12/08

The An Socach Ridge

Arctic conditions

Snow blew onto the windscreen as James and I drove past Ballater and it snowed steadily as we turned south at Braemar to begin the drive up Glen Clunie. The dawn light was enough for us to see the snow-covered hills on either side of the road. Not another soul was abroad that winter morning.

I parked where the track from Baddoch Farm joins the old military road. We wrapped up well and set off at a brisk pace to get the circulation going. The farmhouse showed signs of being restored, but as a holiday cottage. Once over the stile the world of warm cars and centrally-heated houses was left behind and wilderness lay before us.

West of the farm the hanging Coire Chrid had a bright snow cornice, as did Coire Fhearneasg further up the glen. The tops of the hills were white, with wide streaks of snow down the slopes. A few inches of fresh snow lay on the track and it was still falling.

By the time we got to the eastern nose of the An Socach ridge, Socach Mor, the grey cloud was turning purple and brown with ragged tears through which we could see blue sky. Patches of bright winter sun began to dapple the mountain slopes.

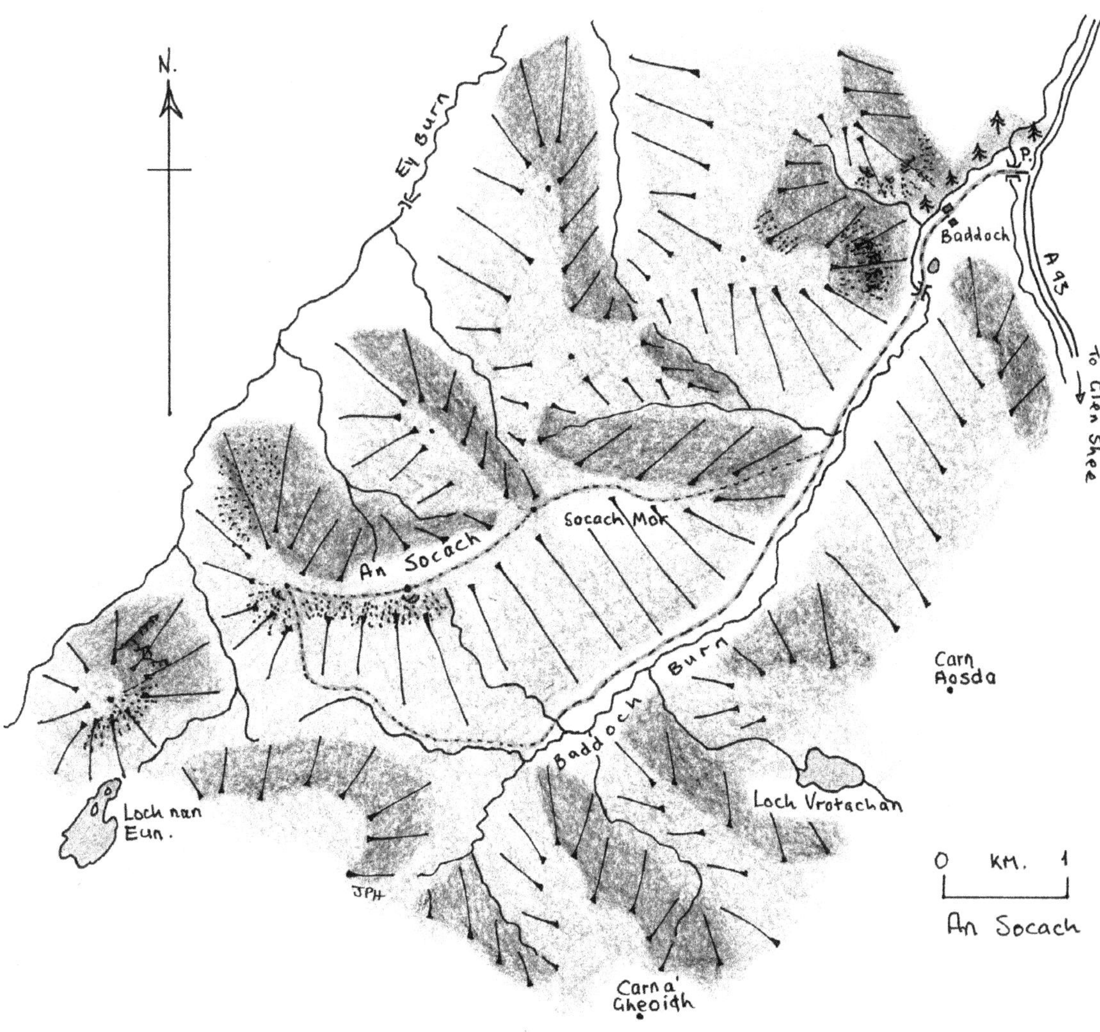

The falling powder snow had smothered the path to Socach Mor and was lying on top of slabs of hard ice, making the going slow. Within sight of this first summit we disturbed a group of four hinds and a calf. They looked in first class condition, fat with brown coats and pale beige rumps. As we stopped to admire them, we noticed three herds on the north side of Coire Fhearneasg, each leaving long trails through the snow. There were around 200 in all. We set off again, disturbing a small group of black grouse, the first of many we were to see that day. The sky to the north, above Glen Ey, had turned a beautiful patchwork of purple, pink and pale blue, with green along the skyline.

It was after Socach Mor's cairn that the hard work began. We began to climb steeply onto the high ridge, struggling against a bitter south-east wind. As the slope eased, we entered thin cloud and dry snow battered against my hood. The wind chill was painful and my fingers were numb, despite being protected by gloves inside winter mitts. Shards of ice, all orientated to the wind direction, grew from the sharp, frost-shattered rocks which carpet the crest of the ridge. It was time to put my head down and battle against the icy, hard pellets stinging my face. I wished that I'd packed my snow goggles.

The East Top is marked by a wind shelter, built using the surrounding litter of broken rocks. It was filled with snow and slick with ice, not in any way inviting us to sit in it.

The ridge is over three kilometres long and every metre was hard won. The western end is marked by another wind shelter which was also filled with snow. The tall cairn was so thickly iced over that it was difficult to see its stones beneath. It was no place to linger so we turned into the wind and began the steep and tricky descent down the southern slope. I could see the watershed between the Baddoch Burn and one of the headwaters of the Ey below, so I made for that area.

On the floor of the glen we were sheltered from the wind and could take stock. James was not convinced that we were at the head of the Baddoch Burn so I checked our position with my GPS. We were pleased to be in exactly the right place.

We walked down the burn until we found a sheltered spot to sit in the snow and have a well-earned lunch. As we looked up at the ridge we had struggled along, the cloud began to lift, leaving a line of turquoise sky behind the crest. Sunshine was breaking through the clouds behind us, making patches of golden light on the slopes. I sat in silence, warming my numb fingers on my mug of tea, soaking up this winter beauty.

Lunch over, we packed up and started off again, startling a white mountain hare which disappeared in a fleeting second, being so perfectly camouflaged. The walk out along the Baddoch Burn was a delight. The cloud continued to break up and sunlight dappled the monochrome patchwork sides of the hills. It had been a stern fight along the ridge in truly arctic conditions but we had both enjoyed it and felt exhilarated by the experience.

The short day was drawing to its close as we peeled off our boots at the car. The clouds were now pink and the shadows long. Not one vehicle passed by on the road. We had not seen a human being all that day.

10/4/09

Glas Maol and Creag Leacach

A Good Friday outing

The weather forecast would have discouraged most sensible walkers with its wind gusts up to 55 mph, wind chill of minus 11 degrees Celsius on the summits and periods of heavy precipitation throughout the day, but I needed an outing to the hills. I told James that he could expect three things, plenty of fresh air, good exercise and an opportunity to practice his mountain skills. He was, as ever, game.

The early morning drive up Deeside and Glen Clunie was sunny, the cloud just flirting with the highest tops. James declared that he thought we would get a good day after all, I had my doubts.

We parked in a lay-by about a kilometre past the Devil's Elbow and scrambled down the bank to cross the stream which runs parallel to the road. Then it was a steep pull up to a ridge with a wide track along its crest which led back up to the ski tows of the Glen Shee Ski Centre. It was a fine walk with good views, although white cloud swirled about the high tops. The wind was strong but, being in the south, was on our backs. Red grouse exploded from under our feet and although we jumped, our hearts stood the test and the walk did not end abruptly. Later, we stopped to admire a mountain hare, still with his white winter coat. As I looked more closely, I could see a blue sheen which spoke of spring.

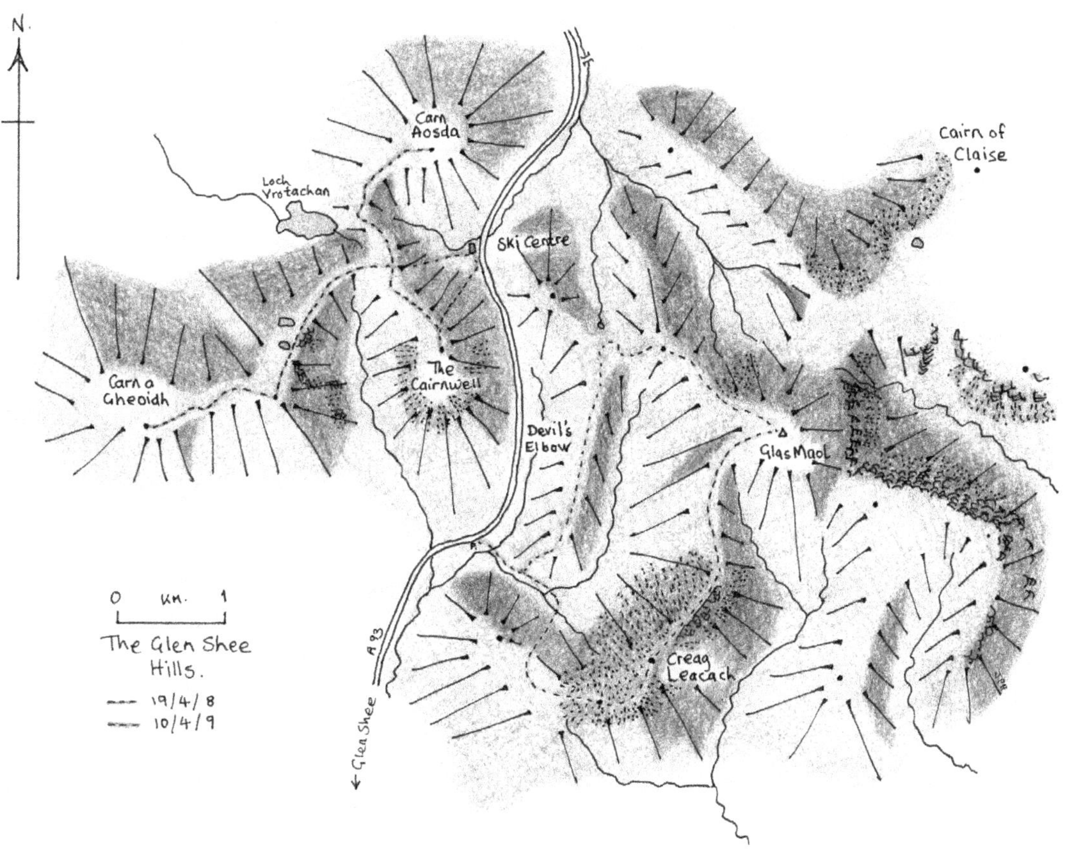

At the ski tows, we turned onto the path which leads east to Meall Odhar and entered the cloud. James noticed that a snow-covered bank was providing shelter so we sat down against it to eat a second breakfast while the wind howled in the ski tow wires above. He fiddled with his new GPS while I watched a meadow pipit, alarmed at these large intruders into its lonely world and making its shrill sipp sipp call. My drawing shows that these birds are visually unimpressive. Twitchers would group them with other LBJs – little brown jobbies. They impress me, however, in that they thrive on the inhospitable high ground and play an important role in mountain ecology. They are eaten by every hunter who can catch them, including hen harriers, sparrowhawks and peregrines, as well as mammals like weasels who raid their nests. As if all that wasn't tough enough for these resilient birds, their nests are also favoured by cuckoos. It's a hard life for some.

On the move again, we followed a well-used path up steep slopes to the summit plateau of Glas Maol. I know now that the views down into Caenlochan Glen and beyond over The Mounth are wonderful, but they were not revealed to us that day. We walked to the old triangulation pillar and the stone shelter cairn where we had a second stop for a hot drink. The walls of the shelter provided little defence against the cold wind. James commented that he had eaten lunch in more comfortable places. As he talked, a curtain of heavy rain was blown over the mountain top. This rudely interrupted our meal and we put on waterproofs.

Standing up, we could see that the sheets of rain blown on that strong south-easterly had further reduced visibility, so we each took a bearing to help us find the narrow ridge which led to our second Munro of the day. Compass in hand, we leaned forward into the wind and set off.

It was a strange descent from Glas Maol. The wide drifts of old snow seemed to merge with the thick, swirling mist. We were dropping down into a white void. James shouted, "In these conditions, it would be so easy to walk out onto a cornice." I thought of the crags a short distance to the east and put my trust in the compass to keep us away from them.

At the edge of one of the snowfields, a ptarmigan rose to fly at right angles to the strong wind. It must have decided that we were not worth the struggle as it landed a few metres away. After a few steps I looked back; the ptarmigan had disappeared, one more snow patch on the hill.

A stone dyke loomed out of the mist, this runs along the crest of the ridge and marks the county boundary between Angus and Perthshire. Along it we trudged, aware that the ridge was narrowing and of the steep drops on either side.

The terrain changed to exposed crags and boulder screes as we climbed up to Creag Leacach, the highest point on the ridge. We slowed down and placed each foot with care but, even so, the wet rocks were potentially dangerous. Perhaps because the tread on the soles of his new boots was not abraded enough to give a good grip, James slipped and landed heavily on the rocks. By the time I got to him he was on his feet, bruised but with nothing broken.

At the summit, we clambered down the crag on the west side where we could sit in the lee of the wind. The rain was lighter. We had a hot drink and consulted the map. A path led from our high perch directly down the mountainside in a line which would have taken us back to the start of the walk. The map showed that this would mean a steep descent over an extensive boulder scree, not a welcome prospect in those wet conditions. We finished our mugs and climbed back up to the path on the crest of the ridge, going south-west and then west. At the point where the old wall turned south-west again, we dropped down across the boulders to the col between the ridge and Meall Gorm, the big hill which sits above the Glen Shee road.

As we started to descend, we came out from under the cloud and could see the whole walk, a fine horseshoe around a deep and steep-sided glen occupied by a rushing torrent. Looking back to Creag Leacach, the scree slopes appeared steep and forbidding and we congratulated ourselves for not choosing the little path which led to them.

We were quickly down the steep slopes to the torrent but then had to follow a path on the north side, perched high above the narrow, rocky bed of the stream. This path was not cut into the hillside to provide a horizontal surface but was inclined down to the stream some distance below and passing boots had trampled the heather branches across it. At each step these slippery branches threatened to shoot the walker down the steep bank. I wondered how often the heather had taken its revenge.

At the place where we had crossed the stream at the start of the day the cloud was lifting, the views were splendid and it had stopped raining.

16/4/09

Carn an Tuirc, Cairn o' Claise, Tom Buidhe and The Tolmount

The Mounth in the mist

Six days after our last walk on the Mounth plateau, James and I were back. The weather forecast was again poor, with a strong, cold, easterly wind and low cloud. I told James that he could expect three things, plenty of fresh air, good exercise and an opportunity to practice his mountain skills.

"I think I'm having a déjà vu moment," he replied.

I parked by the new bridge over the Cairnwell Burn and we walked along the old military road to the 18th century bridge where we followed a path up the north side of the Allt a' Gharbh Choire. Carn an Tuirc, our first Munro, lay ahead, its summit hidden in pale cloud. Its steep sides were patched with three distinct colours; the brown of the over wintered taller vegetation, like blaeberry, the beige of the lichen and grasses and the grey of the boulder screes. To the south, the Garbh Choire, a massive amphitheatre cut into the Mounth plateau, had brilliant white snow cornices above its scree slopes. The path took us above a tree-lined gorge with rapids, massive rocks and clear pools on its narrow floor. A goosander drake took flight and we looked down on his distinctive black and white as he flew downstream. A big bird, almost the size of a goose.

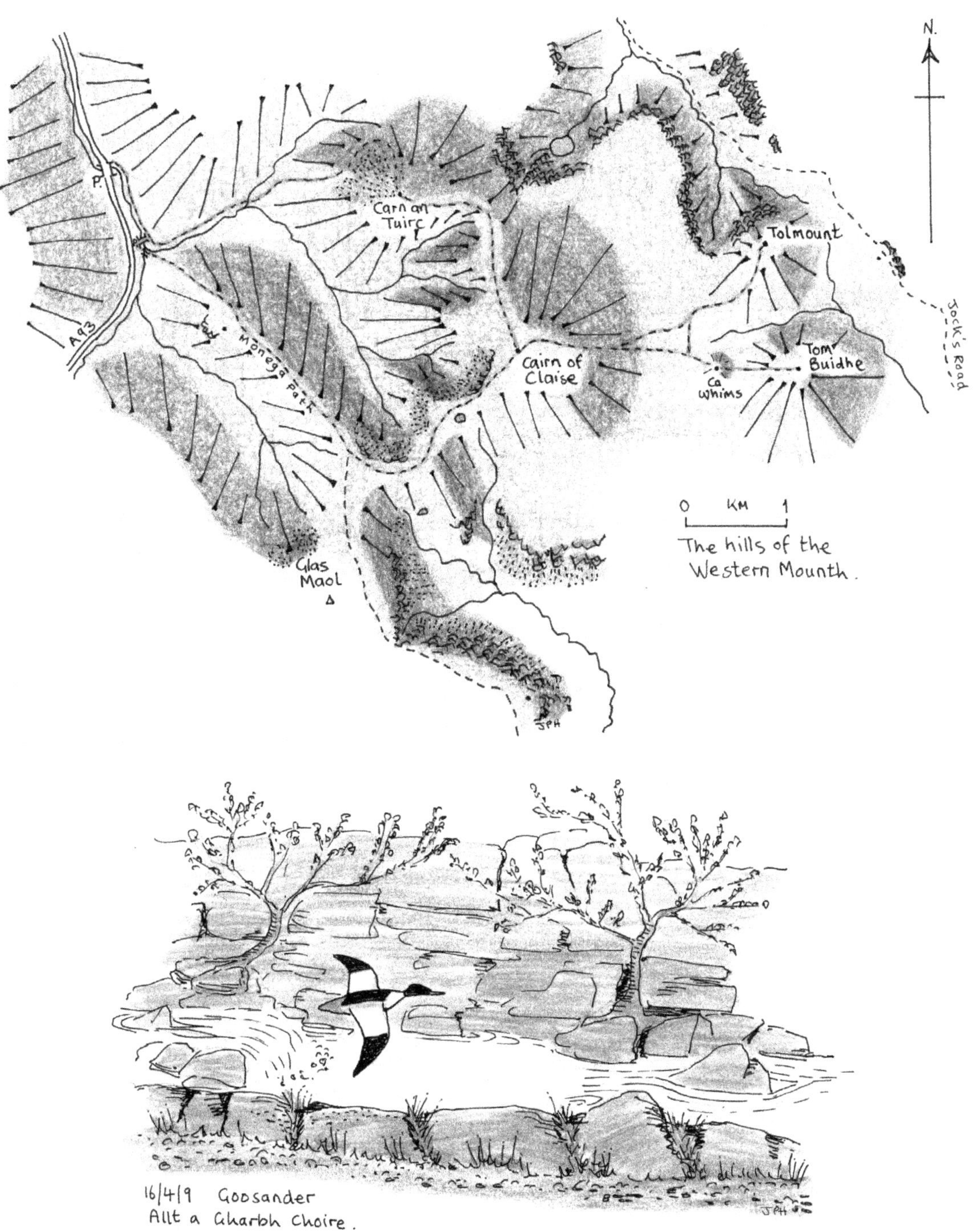
N.
P.
A93
Carn an Tuirc
Monega Path
Cairn of Claise
Tolmount
Tom Buidhe
Ca Whims
Jock's Road
Glas Maol
0 KM 1
The hills of the Western Mounth.
JPH
16/4/9 Goosander
Allt a Gharbh Choire.
JPH

There were patches of blue sky and the sun was making brief appearances through holes in the cloud. It was enough for a lizard, trying to get some warmth on the path. Pale brown from above, bright yellow with a black eye stripe from the side. We climbed some more of the path and then stopped to watch a grouse posing on a rock to our left. The red eyebrow comb was bright but the rest of its plumage was very dark, looking black at that distance. On again and my companion nearly stood on a large and handsome frog who was going down considerably quicker than we were going up. "It's my Alpine pace," said James when I compared the amphibian's progress to our own, but I suspect that he was simply as unfit as I was. We entered the cloud at about 850 metres and spent most of the day in its thick mist, not emerging until we were on the Monega Path and dropping down into the corrie again.

A path took us in zig zags up through the boulders which cap Carn an Tuirc. I drew my friend's attention to two ptarmigan on boulders just to his right. They had lost the white feathers on their backs and wings but were white on the lower breast and underneath. I remarked that only six days ago and a few kilometres away, we had seen a ptarmigan still completely white. Either the change in plumage happens very quickly or there is variation between birds in an area. We were to see another four ptarmigan that day, all like the first pair in their summer coats.

As we were discussing these high mountain birds we disturbed a mountain hare. It too had shed most of its white coat and the new coat had a clear blue sheen. I have heard them called blue hares before and, for the first time, could see why.

We got some shelter at the cairn on the top and had a hot drink. James took out his new GPS to check its reading against our map reference. We then set a bearing for the col above Coire Loch Kander and set off into the mist. Visibility remained very limited and it was clear that it was going to be a day to keep on the move.

At the col, we took another bearing, but a well-used path took us to just below the summit of Cairn o' Claise, the compass simply serving to reassure that we were on the right track, particularly when it forked. An old dyke follows the county boundary and leads to the tall cairn.

We stopped only to consult the map, deciding that we need only go due east for the next two kilometres before getting another GPS fix and climbing The Tolmount, our next Munro of the day. We reasoned that, on such popular hills, there was bound to be a path.

A path was, indeed, found and we followed it across the Mounth plateau. It was an eerie walk in such thick mist. We paused at the edge of each snowfield, hesitating to step into what appeared to be a white void. It was an act of faith to walk across with no horizon as a frame of reference. When we stopped to fix our position we realised that we were nearer to Tom Buidhe, the yellow hill, so we went over the knoll of Ca Whims and climbed up through boulders to the cairn which marked our third Munro of the day. The east wind was fierce up there so we dropped back down the path to find a sheltered spot for lunch. We found a natural bench above a snowfield and settled there to refuel. "I'm at a loss to explain why I'm enjoying this," commented James, "and, therefore, could not hope to give a convincing reason to any non-hillwalker among my friends and acquaintances."

As we had just been treated to some eccentric noises from a pair of ptarmigan who were sharing our picnic spot, I suggested that, whatever the conditions, there was always something unexpected to amuse or thrill. I pointed to the line of footprints coming towards us over the snow, "If we were to wait long enough, who knows what might loom out of the mist? The Mounth may have its own Grey Man."

We again consulted the map and decided to retrace our steps to just before the ground began to rise up to Ca Whims then turn due north, expecting to find a good path which would lead us to The Tolmount. This is what we did and we found the path climbing up through exposed rock. Just beneath the summit we came upon the remains of an old bothy, its rough boulder walls incorporating large outcropping rocks. Who lived in this strange little dwelling perched on a mountain top high above the cliffs of Glen Callater?

At the top we checked the map and, as we began the long walk back, used compasses to ensure we did not wander. The journey was more pleasant with the wind on our backs and we tramped happily over stunted vegetation and snowfields. The route took us around the rim of the Garbh Choire but the thick mist blocked any views.

When we arrived at the Monega Path, an old drove road to Glen Isla, we walked out from under the cloud. Ahead was the long ridge to Sron na Gaoithe, the path following its crest. To the north and east rose our first two mountains, each but a part of the wall of the great corrie. To our amusement, the cloud was beginning to lift from the tops and half the sky was blue. We decided to take our time walking down this fine ridge, enjoying the views we had been denied all day. It was a captivating place, teeming with life. Blue hares ran to either side, grouse stretched up their necks to keep a watchful eye and meadow pipits shot up into the air to make their shrill call.

At the foot of the ridge we crossed the sparkling burn by a footbridge and sat on the bank beside the old stone bridge to have a last hot drink. Our first two Munros, patched brown and beige, crowned and streaked with grey screes, were now free of cloud. We could follow our route in its wide sweep along the high rim of the Garbh Choire. "Not bad for an old man," said James as he sipped his cocoa.

"No, and I didn't do so badly myself," I replied.

3/5/09

Carn Bhac and Beinn Iutharn Mhor

A wild day on the Glen Ey hills

We had high hopes for the day as we cycled out of the car park at Inverey. It was not yet eight o' clock and little above freezing, but the sky was blue and the few clouds were white and high, far above the mountain summits. James wore his white sun hat.

This was my first visit to Glen Ey and it was lovely that spring morning. The Ey Burn shimmered in the sun as it meandered across the wide, flat floor of the glaciated valley. Pale grey screes lay in great fans down the steep sides. At the second wooden bridge I stopped to photograph Creag an Fhuathais, where the long northern ridge of An Socach has been truncated by the glacier which once filled the glen, leaving a dramatic cliff. James remembered our New Year walk on that complex mountain, when all was deep snow.

After this bridge the track turns to the south-west and the head of the glen appears, ringed by a group of tall hills. Rising above them all is the rocky Beinn Iutharn Mhor (byn yootharn vor), which means the big, sharp-edged mountain. The snow of its high ridges seemed to radiate its own light on that bright morning. The silence of the glen was broken by the sad, eerie call of a curlew, which glided away from us to land on a little pebbly beach on the inside of one of the river's meanders.

Carn Bhac & Beinn Iutharn Mhor.
Glas Tulaichean & Carn an Righ.

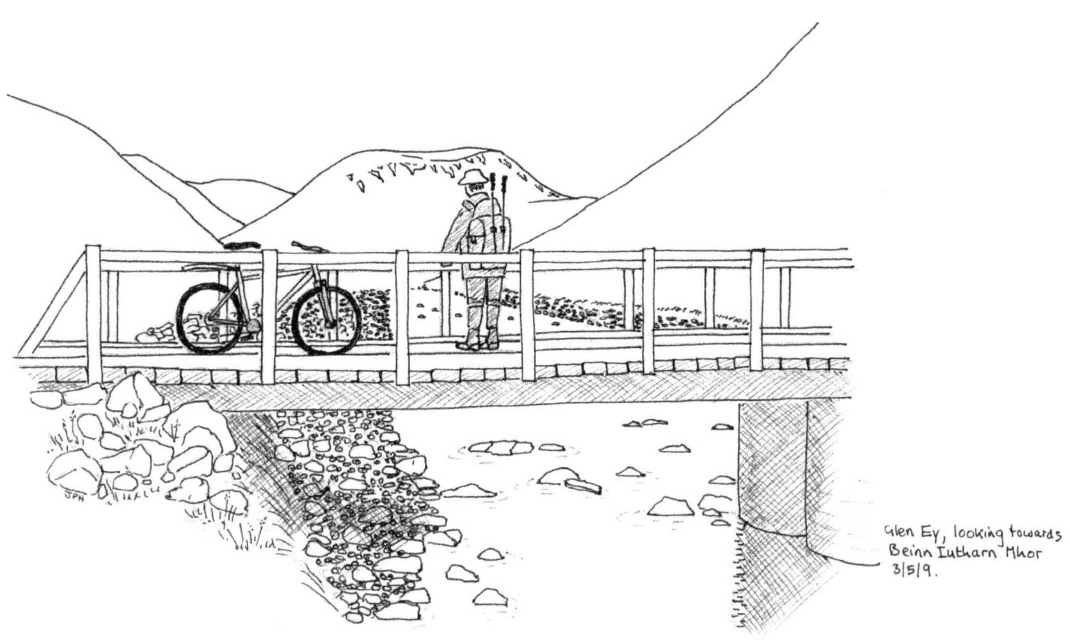

Everywhere was evidence of glaciation. There were mounds of moraine, kettle holes and huge boulders, dropped in jumbled piles as the ice decayed and melted. I stopped to photograph a perched block, a massive boulder precariously balanced on its small pedestal.

We rested at a third wooden bridge where James pointed to a stand of mature conifers ahead. "That's Altanour Lodge," he announced. I could see a stone gable among the trees. A common gull, startlingly white, regarded us with interest as it looked up from the river bank below.

The track wound among a chaos of car-sized boulders and ended at the crumbling ruin of Altanour. The old building stood on a sward of grass, watched over by a ring of dark fir trees. We pushed our bikes through the door, leaned them against a wall and spread out a map on the floor. "Underneath this floor is believed to be an old cellar, the only shelter left in the ruin," remarked James. Interested, I looked for an entrance but couldn't find one. Returning to the map, I suggested heading south to begin a clockwise round of the hills at the head of the glen, but James had learned to put waypoints into his GPS and had started with Carn Bhac, WNW of the lodge.

Beinn Iutharn Mhor from the ruin at Altanour. 3/5/9.

Carn Bhac was hidden behind the bulk of Carn Creagach, so we walked south-west then followed the Allt an Odhar which gave us a good line to our first Munro summit. As we climbed, we could see that the head of Glen Ey is a large basin, once full of the ice that fed the glacier, surrounded by steep-sided hills. Beinn Iutharn Mhor stood as a grey, scree-aproned wall, patched with snow and with a long cornice marking the rim of its north-west corrie.

As we had been admiring the hills to the south, we had not seen the squall as it swept over Carn Bhac towards us. In an instant we were in a whiteout, with snow blowing horizontally on a strong and icy north-west wind. We kept our backs to it and it soon blew past, the first of many such sudden showers on that day. I shook the crust of snow off my back and watched as the sun quickly melted it on the ground.

We resumed our walk up to the ridge and I noticed that the vegetation had a different character to that of the Cairngorms north of the Dee. There was a carpet of short yellow grass with much dry moss and blaeberry. Pink and purple flowers of tiny Alpines were everywhere. The schist rock of these hills seems to produce a more fertile soil than the acidic granite to the north.

Carn Bhac is a long ridge running north-east to south-west with three tops. The easternmost is the highest and, therefore, the Munro summit (even though my O.S. map names the middle top Carn Bhac). The hill has a cap of hard quartzite and the final section up to the cairn was over a scree of angular white blocks.

We had been climbing in the lee of the wind but now caught its full force. This was straight from the Arctic and the wind chill dropped the temperature to well below freezing. Despite the numbing cold, we stood there for some time, marvelling at the views all around. The air was particularly clear and features many miles distant were distinct and sharp. The prospect was one of an empty land, with no trace of house, road, radio mast or wind turbine. To the east stood Lochnagar, to the south Beinn Iutharn Mhor and Glas Tulaichean, to the south-west Beinn a' Ghlo and to the north the mountains of the central Cairngorms, all capped with fresh snow. As we watched, a blizzard struck the Monadh Mor and spilled down into the Lairig Ghru. Another rolled down Glen Derry and a third down Glen Quoich, the high hills between standing clear and in sunshine. We saw the same sort of thing all day whenever we were up on vantage points, blue sky, sunshine, high white cumulus clouds and always, somewhere, small but powerful snow showers.

The icy air drove us back down the slope we had just climbed so that we could sit out of the wind to have our second breakfast. A ptarmigan, perfectly camouflaged among the quartzite, flew up from beneath our feet. I watched its pointed white wings against the dark blue of the sky. Even with some shelter and the sun shining I was cold and was glad I had brought a flask.

The sub-zero temperature soon had us on our feet and back up onto the ridge. There we caught the full force of that cruel wind and by the time we were at the bealach between the summit and the central top we had put on all the winter clothing we carried in our rucksacks. Just in the nick of time as it happened, because the next squall struck, sending streaks of snow curving across the ridge. By the time we got to the cairn on the central top the whiteout was smothering the hills on the south side of Glen Ey. The view from there was perfect, particularly of Beinn a' Ghlo, which looked its very best. The snow-capped, pointed summit of Carn nan Gabhar as dramatic as an Alpine peak.

Looking south, our next Munro was a long, scree-covered cliff which made a shallow curve around a dramatic corrie, its lip supporting a substantial snow cornice. Between it and us, however, was a big tract of moorland and peat bog which had to be crossed. We could see no path, so we judged the line which would lose us least height and set off. Fifty metres down from the top we were in a different world. Sheltered from the wind and with the sun shining we had to stop and stow our winter layers again. We had just shouldered the rucksacks and taken our first step when we were hit by another snow shower, it was that sort of day. This was mercifully short and we watched as it travelled like a white wave to break on the slopes of An Socach and Beinn Iutharn Mhor.

The walk across the moorland was dry and good underfoot, with little heather. We entered an old peat bog where a mountain hare employed the tactic of sitting bolt upright and perfectly still to avoid our attentions. I think, like the ptarmigan, it was partly relying on good camouflage. It had not, though, remembered that it was still mostly white and was against the black wall of a peat hag.

We sat underneath the northern wall of our second Munro and ate some lunch in the sun. An examination of the map revealed that we had no choice but to scale the screes of this wall, a choice which promised hard work.

I looked down to my feet when we were half way up and could see between them the break of slope far below. I shouted to James to take care, a slip here would have dire consequences.

Relieved to be up, we found the first path since leaving the floor of the glen and followed this towards the summit. The wind howled over the crest of the ridge and I planted my feet wide to help prevent myself being blown over.

The path took us to the edge of a deep corrie with precipitous crags. A lochan occupies its base and a flowing, brilliant white snow cornice defined the top edge of its cradling walls. We followed the snow to the rocky summit where I saw that this was another mountain protected from rapid erosion by a hard quartzite cap.

The range of hills to the south and east tempted us to expand our walk but it was already late afternoon and we opted for prudence. Snow-capped Carn an Righ and Glas Tulaichean, along with the unusual Loch nan Eun, would wait for another day.

We decided to take the most direct route back to the bikes and began walking north-east along the crest of the mountain's curved backbone. It was a surprise and a relief to find a small path going down the steep nose at the end. I stopped to look down Glen Ey before I put my knees to the test. Altanour Lodge stood in a small green oasis among the browns and greys of this wild land.

Down again on the floor of the glen, we made our way to the river bank where we sat to rest. I had fought against the wind all along the ridge but down there I sat in shirt-sleeves, warmed by the westering sun. We were quiet, enjoying the soothing sounds of the fast-flowing water. It was crystal clear and had polished the rocks of its bed to show off their coloured bands of minerals. A skylark rose up to sing his joyous song, a song to tell all around that this was his territory. I understood perfectly, for this was a place about which one could sing one's heart out.

I was glad that we had the bikes for it was eight kilometres back to Inverey. It was mostly downhill and I could often freewheel, enjoying the pink early evening light on the glen. As we came to the trees a buzzard left its grouse supper by the side of the track and flapped lazily up into the branches.

20/6/09

Stob Ghabhar

A Midsummer walk across the Black Mount with the Jolly Boys

After work on Friday I drove from Aberdeen to Tyndrum. I was numb after an intense week and was barely conscious of the charms of Deeside. South of Braemar, as my car began to climb up to the Cairnwell, I became aware that it was a perfect evening. Ranks of massive rounded hills were framed against a pale, cloudless sky. Every detail of crag and boulder slope was sharp and black shadowed. I followed the road into Glen Shee and drove through perfect hill country, bathed in golden light. All was beautiful on that journey and the shadows gradually lengthened as I passed Pitlochry's sentinel, Ben Vrackie, a serene Loch Tay and the ice-scoured hills of Glen Dochart.

A quick dash through swirling clouds of midges and I burst into the By The Way Hostel to be met by old friends. On this 20th Jolly Boys' weekend I was given the warmest of welcomes, a glass of Glenmorangie was pushed into my hand and I was soon enjoying the chat and laughter. The celebrations were given added impetus as five of the original members, including Struan, Ray and Victor, were retiring from work the following week.

The traditional lobbying for the next day's walks had already begun. Ray's high level traverse of the Black Mount sounded a fine challenge and I happily signed up for that. Struan muttered darkly that Ray would never lead a mixed group the length of such a demanding

route, an accurate observation as it turned out. Fionn, busy boiling a concoction of dried fruit, onions and garlic, declared, "Everything sounds far too strenuous to me. I think I'll stay in my bed all day."

I drifted off to sleep hearing the shrieks of the die-hards who saw in the dawn before they too collapsed.

After breakfast we gathered in front of the hostel. Loud snoring from Fionn's room reassured us that he had survived the night. We took four cars to the White Corries and left two of them there. Cloud sat on the mountains but we comforted ourselves with a weather forecast predicting that it would lift around lunchtime. Struan led a group to the White Corries, another group started a low level walk onto Rannoch Moor and Ray ended up with a party of nine people who represented the full spectrum of hillwalking experience.

We parked at Victoria Bridge at the west end of Loch Tulla. The midges were waiting for their breakfast so I started walking with those who were ready. At Forest Lodge we turned left. Ray waited at the turning until the three in the rear could see him and then strode on to catch us up. When he looked back, they had not followed. He jogged back to the turning where, finding no sign, he jogged north along the West Highland Way, guessing they had gone that way. The five in the vanguard stopped at the old Glasgow University climbing hut. After some time, a red faced Ray appeared and told us that he had run for some distance north until he caught up with three people who, unfortunately, were not Jolly Boys. Where could the others be? The most obvious explanation was that they had, indeed, walked straight on up the West Highland Way, not having seen Ray at the turning. Ray had simply not run far enough. I walked back along the track and climbed a high bank. From my vantage point I saw three distant figures on our track. The moment I spotted them they turned and started walking back! I waved my arms and, thank goodness, one of them looked round and spotted my signal. As I walked to meet them I thought about the difficulties of leading such a diverse party. Struan's words of the night before came into my head and I began to doubt whether Ray's walk was possible. We had already wasted half the morning.

Reunited, we made good progress up into the narrow defile between Stob a' Choire Odhair and Stob Ghabhar. A small path branched off and plunged down to cross the Allt Toaig. Ray stopped on the bank. The water was running fast but there was a way across over boulders, some submerged. Given the lack of experience of some in the group, he decided to err on the side of caution and began a recce of the bank. The rest of us climbed back to use the main path. This second delay confirmed my doubts, our group would never complete the high level route to the White Corries that day. I was enjoying the company too much to care, however, and was happy whatever we might achieve.

We followed the path until we could see Stob Ghabhar's huge, crag-walled corrie with its lochan. A narrow but well-used path led steeply up through boulder screes and across slabs to bring us up to the crest of the Aonach Eagach ridge. Not the legendary notched ridge of Glen Coe, but its lesser known namesake.

The walk along the exposed rock of the narrow crest was interesting. I remembered the last time I clambered along it, when the mountain was under a deep cover of frozen snow, the lochan was solid and the corrie walls had thick, bulbous lobes of green ice. All was more benign on this summer day, with a patch of old snow near the summit the only reminder of winter.

As we followed the rim of the corrie headwall up to the cairn I realised that it was not just a snow cornice that made this potentially dangerous but in poor visibility there was little margin for error.

We ate our lunch on the summit but it was a hurried affair as Ray had booked a meal for us at eight o' clock at the hotel on Tyndrum's main street and he knew how far behind schedule we were. I was disappointed that we were in cloud, remembering the wonderful views on that winter walk here.

We set off down the broad crest of the Aonach Mor. Two ptarmigan in their summer coats trotted from the path, heads down, to miraculously disappear among the rocks and short vegetation, despite their white underparts. They triggered a conversation about other wildlife a hillwalker may find in the Highlands. On cue, two peaty brown frogs hopped in their ungainly way to escape being squashed under our big boots. They were the first of many mountaineering frogs we saw that day and, on lower ground, we were to see less common animals.

A ridge runs at right angles to the Aonach Mor and we followed that down to the Bealach Fuar-Chathaidh. I was in the lead at that point so I stopped to drink a cup of tea while I watched the others slowly clamber down the rocks. It was mid-afternoon and the clouds were beginning to lift, revealing a wild and dramatic mountain landscape.

Ray looked serious and called a pow wow. Some of the party were worse for wear and would not manage the climbing involved on the planned route over Clach Leathad, Creise and Meall a' Bhuiridh. The direct route south to the cars, over the bealach between Stob Ghabhar and Stob a' Choire Odhair was also ruled out on the grounds that there was too much climbing so it was decided to drop down to the flats of the River Bà below. The route along the Bà then south along the West Highland Way was thought longer than following that same route northward to the two cars left in the morning at the White Corries, so we decided to head north.

There were hundreds of pools and dozens of hurrying streams on the wide valley floor of the River Bà, an apparently perfect environment for amphibians, reptiles and insect life. I saw orange bellied newts in the dark brown pools and peaty frogs were everywhere. Twice I saw common lizards, out to sunbathe now that the cloud had cleared. I got too near one of them, making it turn and wriggle down a narrow tunnel in the tough yellow grass stems. Malachite green tiger beetles, sporting bright yellow spots, sparkled like jewels in the sun.

The flat lands had looked the ubiquitous camouflage mix of brown, beige and green but close up a carpet of richly varied plant life was revealed. The tallest plant was the aromatic bog myrtle, there were drifts of tiny forget-me-nots, dwarf marsh orchids, pink marsh woundwort and insect eating sundews as well as many more I could not name. I smiled to see a tiger beetle living up to its hard man reputation by clambering nonchalantly over a sundew, clearly too big a mouthful for the plant.

On the long distance footpath we turned left and wearily plodded on. Two women walked rapidly up and as they were overtaking us Victor asked, "Girls, where are you heading for?"

They looked surprised and curtly replied, "Fort William," before striding away. There was a debate about the reason for their surprised expressions, Ray suggesting that Victor's use of "girls" might have upset a contemporary woman. Victor looked somewhat crestfallen at this so I restored his good humour by suggesting that it had nothing to do with a possibly non-PC greeting, being rather that they were participating in a race along the West Highland Way and that they would, indeed, finish at Fort William that evening.

"The problem with that theory," declared Ray, "is that it's impossible to walk so far in one day." Two tall young men rapidly gained on us, one looked grim and determined but the second returned my smile and looked game for a chat. I learned from him that he and his friend were competing in the West Highland Way Race, 95 miles from start to finish, all done in one day and that the record for crossing the finishing line in Fort William was 13 hours. He encouraged me to get training and sign up for next year's race and then, with a cheery farewell, sped after his walking partner. I consulted my body and we agreed that I could inflict damage on it by walking 95 miles in one day; that I was long past my youthful prime and, finally, that I would shelve that particular idea.

Back at the cars, a still incredulous Ray declared, "We've been walking for nine hours and that was quite enough, thank you." It took a while for the footsore stragglers to arrive so I had time to have a last mug of tea while admiring Buachaille Etive Mor's Stob Dearg, beautifully lit and shadowed in the late afternoon sunlight.

Ray had booked the conservatory of the hotel in the heart of the village, where I was glad to discover that there was a self-service buffet of hot dishes. I started with a large helping of prawns and salmon in a tasty white sauce and finished with an equally large helping of slow-cooked venison casserole, accompanied by a glass of red wine. We swapped stories of the day and learned that everyone had enjoyed their chosen activity, none more than Fionn, who had sensibly slept until late afternoon, building up a truly colossal appetite.

Back at the hostel, Fionn used his surplus energy to host an epic of Sweaty Betty. The non-players chatted, joked and shared the various bottles we had brought. I had another glass of Victor's Glenmorangie while he tucked into my Laphroaig, a good arrangement as he declared the whisky excellent, downed a few glasses too many and got drunk enough to perform.

Victor

He got into the mood by reminiscing about his days as a Para. He had been taught songs in German, Russian and other languages. This was for use when approaching enemy checkpoints or when discovered behind enemy lines. He was to feign drunkenness, easy to imagine in his present state, and sing lustily in the appropriate foreign tongue, which he kindly demonstrated. This placed the enemy in a frozen state of indecision and allowed Victor to get near enough to dispatch them, which again he kindly demonstrated. His audience clearly appreciated this and, spurred on by success, he leapt onto a table and banged his head off a beam. This device secured the attention of all the Jolly Boys, even those locked into the fierce competitiveness of Sweaty Betty. Undaunted by the knock, he instructed his audience to join in the chorus and began a sad song about a well-hung Chihuahua. The Jolly Boys enjoyed this almost as much as Victor banging his head and it acted as a catalyst for Eric suddenly to stand up, give a crisp salute and recite his Boys' Brigade chant about fear and lemonade. This was followed by Bob's "The wee cock sparra sa'ron a barra..." and so it went on in its sweetly bizarre way until, one by one, in the small hours, the weary Jolly Boys headed for their beds.

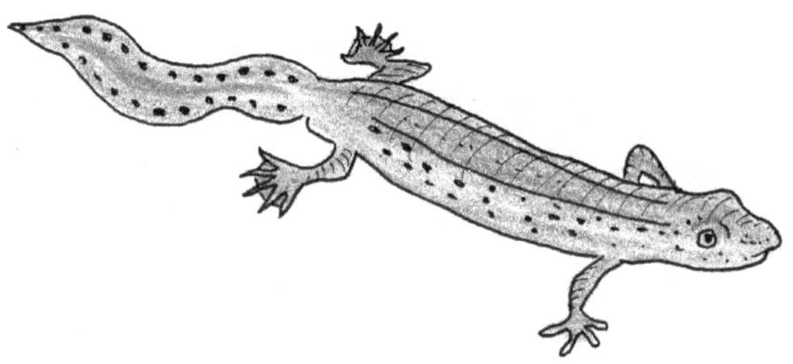

6/7/09 – 10/7/09

Luinne Bheinn, Meall Bhuidhe, Ladhar Bheinn and Roinn na Beinne

Knoydart

The mail boat Western Isles rocked with the swell as it left Mallaig's busy little harbour. I stood on deck with my son, Tom, his Kiwi fiancée, K and Morag. It would be strange to arrive at our accommodation without a car, but there are no roads to Knoydart. Our rucksacks lay in a pile covered by a tarpaulin to protect them from the rain. We tried the cabin but it was hot, stuffy and claustrophobic. It was better to get wet. A porpoise shot from the water and we watched as it overtook the boat. Dark mountains of polished rock rose from the sea.

I was looking for Inverie long before I saw it, a line of tiny white houses along the shore with steep forested mountain slopes rising straight from the back doors. The pointed summits of Knoydart's highest peaks made a serrated distant skyline.

The rain had stopped by the time the boat was tied up at the pier. Our rucksacks were thrown up to us and we walked through the village and along the shore to the bunkhouse where Izzie met us with a big smile. We had to watch where we stood as little froglets hopped about the floors. A jam jar by the door was labelled "froglet transportation unit". We spent ten minutes scooping up the disorientated little creatures but became more efficient as the week went on and we perfected our technique.

We ate in the Old Forge that evening. Britain's remotest pub is a memorable experience, its picture windows framing a living landscape of sea loch and mountain, with white yachts gently rocking at their moorings in the bay.

Back at the bunkhouse, we lit the wood stove in the common room and opened a bottle of Talisker. Tom tuned up his guitar and sang us his sad songs.

Morag and I were breakfasted and ready to walk before anyone else had stirred. We were to have an unexpected test of our navigation skills as it took us 30 minutes to get out of Inverie. At the end of one of a number of false tracks we stopped to admire a group of red deer stags grazing by the river. I took out the map and worked out that we needed to go back into the woods to find our path.

Once I knew that I was going the right way, I began to notice Inverie's unusual woods. This is warm temperate rain forest, sheltered by the enclosing mountain slopes, south-facing and enjoying frequent rainfall. So much rainfall that it is similar to the Amazon rainforest, both areas getting around 2,000 mm per year.[3] Bamboo and rhododendrons

3 Check the rainfall totals for Manaus and Fort William

grow among native species. The trees are smothered in dense, dripping mosses with epiphytic ferns growing out of the branches. A young conifer grew out of the thick branch of an old beech tree.

Morag talked about her recent trip to Mount Everest as we walked up Gleann an Dubh Lochain. I listened with interest but was glad I was here in this very different but no less special place. Alders grew along the banks of the meandering river and grey wagtails bobbed up and down on tiny rocky islands above the sparkling water. It was a fine morning but, being the North-west Highlands, it appeared to be raining further up the glen. A double rainbow, flanked by wide sunbeams, gave the place a 'Lost World' atmosphere, simultaneously eerie and beautiful.

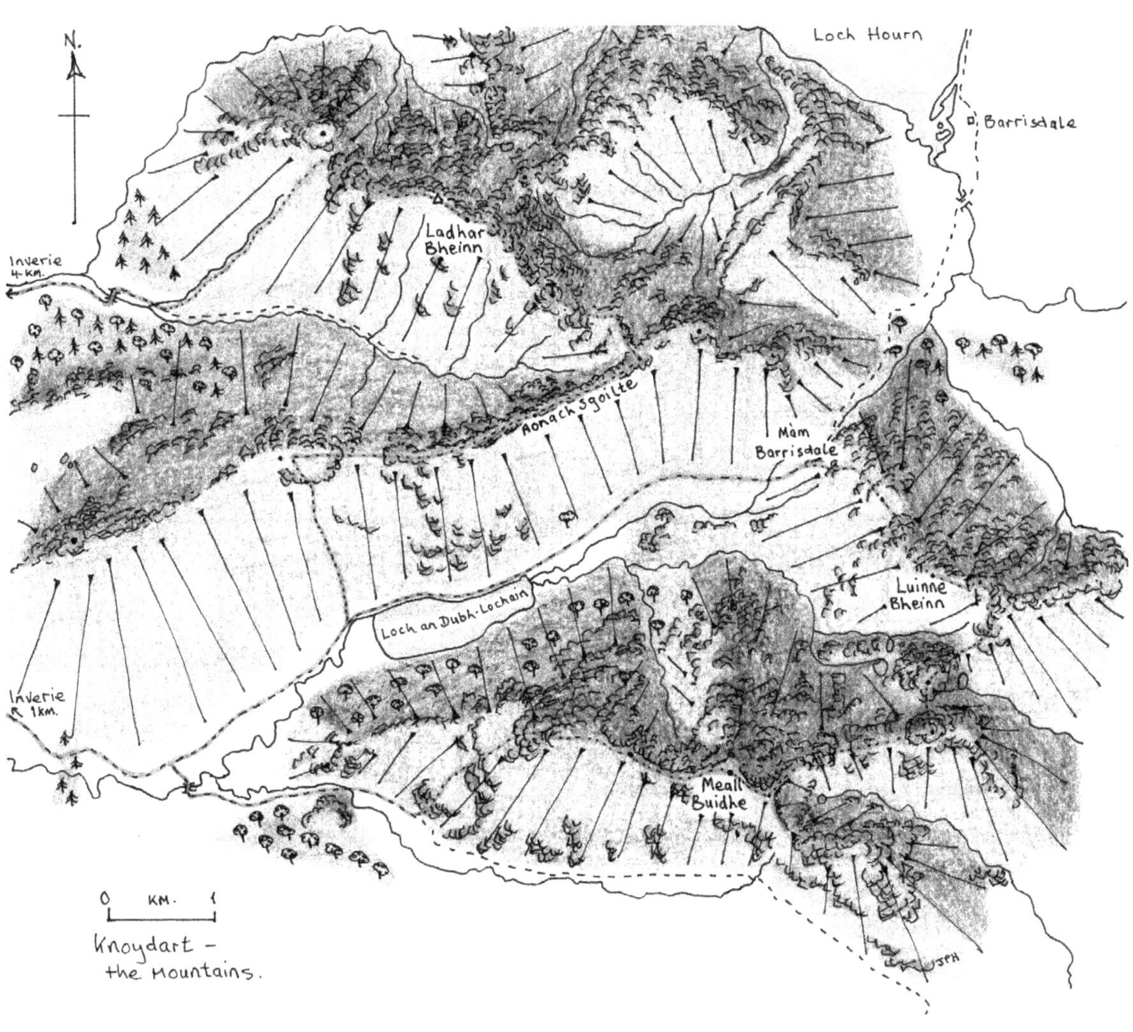

The vegetation was lush compared to the close-cropped, patchy plant cover of the Cairngorms where I had been walking of late. Among the many varieties of wild flowers were drifts of orchids, some pastel pink, spotted darker pink; some cream, spotted delicate pink and some lilac, spotted purple. Above these flowers danced butterflies, including coppers and a dark copper species with orange eyes on its wings. Little bright blue ones like flashing gems flitted across our path in pairs. Dark spotted frogs were everywhere and a similarly dark toad crawled along in our direction as we passed. The air was full of the shrill calls of wrens and meadow pipits. The wrens shot among the branches at the side of the track, stopping suddenly and flipping up their stubby little tails, not in the slightest shy of our presence.

Around a bend in the track, Loch an Dubh-Lochain came into view, a perfect foreground for the sharp peak of Luinne Bheinn which rose at the head of the glen. The loch was pristine, with turquoise water in the shallows and beaches of pale sand. The path began to climb and we were treated to the aerial acrobatics of large dragonflies, each iridescent blue/green with yellow hoops. Like the blue butterflies, the dragonflies came in twos and I counted nine pairs before the path crossed an old dry-stone bridge built into the steep mountainside. Morag had crossed it without noticing that it was a man-made structure, so weathered and overgrown had it become.

Beyond the bridge the path climbed steeply to the Màm Barrisdale pass. The vegetation became shorter and more sparse, the fertile glen was far below and we were in a high mountain land again. We stopped to fill our water bottles at a small waterfall by the path and surveyed the land to the south and south-east. Our route was plain and looked challenging, a high, rocky ridge walk over a series of sharp peaks in a grand arc around the craggy corrie at the head of the glen. At the pass we got our first shower of rain and put on our jackets while we ate a little and drank a mug of tea.

On the climb up onto Luinne Bheinn there were clear views nearly to the top but, as luck would have it, cloud streamed over the summit ridge just as we reached it. We came to a junction of ridges and knew that we should follow the southerly one. Morag had walked a little way down the obvious ridge but the GPS and compass showed that we should backtrack and go down the other one. As soon as we lost a little height we came out from under the cloud and before us was the Rough Bounds of Knoydart, a wilderness of exposed, ice-polished rock and sharp peaks.

We climbed up onto Meall Coire na Gaoithe 'n Ear, walking poles stowed as our hands were needed to scramble up the steep rock steps. The original bedding planes of these Moinian rocks, including Lewisian schist and gneiss, were bent into fantastic contorted waves when the rocks were forced deep below the earth's surface, heated and softened and subjected to massive pressures. We sat below a cliff patterned with these graceful undulations to eat our lunch while gazing out at the ancient geological landscape of the Rough Bounds.

It was a steep scramble down to a bealach above the giant, ice-smoothed knobs of bedrock at the head of the corrie. From there we climbed up to Meall Bhuide, the route always clear and with secure hand holds. As the ridge narrowed, monumental pointed blades of rock appeared, arranged one behind another. I felt as though I was walking up a monstrous fossil jawbone. At the first secure platform I stopped to take a photograph but, at that very moment, cloud streamed over the top. It appeared that we were doomed not to see the views from either of our Munro summits.

The blades of rock curved around a high hanging corrie and I picked my way around its edge then began the final climb to the summit. Just before the cairn, something ran over my boot. It was a fluffy ptarmigan chick. Another appeared, hurtling after its sibling, both going to my right. They nearly collided with three more, this time rushing to my left. A sixth chick appeared on my left and then the panic-stricken mother. All was confusion for a few brief seconds as she ran back and forth in front of my boots and then silence, the entire brood had disappeared among the rocks.

When Morag climbed up, we decided to continue west along the ridge. It was tough going as the northerly wind had grown strong and it was driving heavy showers across the crest. There were more ptarmigan but no chicks, which made them almost nonchalant about our presence. The crest of the ridge is sharply scalloped, its edge on that day clearly marked by white cloud boiling up from Gleann Meadail. To the north of this line, on our right, all was completely clear. The wind strengthened and another squall rushed towards us. We decided to drop south into the glen and began a long, steep, wet descent. Two groups of red deer hinds looked at us in disbelief, (which, I think, showed their intelligence), before lifting their knees and high stepping out of our way.

We arrived back at the bunkhouse tired and wet, our walk had taken 11 hours. Tom and K were in the kitchen, marinading their huge catch of mackerel and cleaning mussels. They had been fishing off the rocks on the seaward side of Eileen na Gàmhna. A young woman was helping out, it was Martina, the Czech we met the previous summer in Ullapool. Tom barbecued the fish and mussels in the yard outside while K and Martina put new potatoes, mixed vegetables and a bottle of wine on the table. It was a true feast. We all toasted the chefs and then retired to the common room where we lit the stove to dry out our wet boots and clothes. We drank tea and whisky and caught up with Martina's news, delivered in the unique accent she called "thickczech".

It was past 10 o' clock before we strolled down to the Old Forge. A large group of folk musicians, some local and some visitors, including Americans, were playing. Tom had brought his guitar and, Guinness in hand, went over to sit with them. We listened to their tunes for a while and then Tom was invited to perform. He has a strong, mellow voice, full of Celtic emotion. The pub went silent and, at the end, there was loud applause. Tom sang more songs and we made friends with Bob the B and B (aka Bob the Taxi, Bob the Boat etc.). He said that Tom could have free accommodation in his splendid wooden house if he was to play and sing. He also talked about his boat trip to Camusrory and Tarbet Bay the next day. I asked Tom and K if they would like to go and when they showed enthusiasm, I fixed it up.

Next morning, Morag and I were out of Inverie's woods and walking up towards Gleann an Dubh Lochain in 15 minutes. It was another fine morning. A dark toad looked at us and, unconcerned, continued his journey along the path. When Loch an Dubh-Lochain came into sight we left the path and began a long climb up the steep side of Stob an Uillt-fearna. It was hard work forcing a path through the patches of bracken but we stopped often to look at the world around us and at our feet. Morag called and pointed to a line of hinds on the skyline but I was distracted by a lizard, out to soak up the morning sun. A little further up the slope an orange-banded beetle caught my eye. I knelt down and saw that there were two squat sexton beetles[4] at the start of the process of butchering and burying a dead shrew. These useful creatures will have caught the smell of the carrion

Sexton beetles

4 Sexton beetles are also called burying beetles and there are dozens of species in Britain. Most are black but some, like the pair I describe, are marked with bright orange bands.

on the wind and hurried to the corpse through the heather and bracken. They will have been a male and female because the first beetle to arrive at the prize fights off later arrivals of the same sex. The pair I had found would mate, then might remove awkward bits like legs and tail before burying their treasure. The female lays eggs, feeds off the carcass and regurgitates food for her offspring until they are able to feed on it themselves. No decomposing corpses on the surface and nothing going to waste, the sexton beetle is a valuable creature and illustrates Nature at its efficient best.

We sat just below the summit of our hill and looked along the crest of the ridge we were to follow to the point where it joined Ladhar Bheinn's south-east arête. As I sipped hot tea, I looked north across the massive corrie to the summit of the mountain. Cloud streamed across it and then blew away in ragged shreds. I hoped that it would be clear for us when we were up there.

The sun came out properly as we began to make our way down to the Màm Suidheig. Up to then it had mostly been behind white cloud, now it blazed down. I put on my sun hat, too late as it turned out, as I was already burned. Along with the sun came blue sky and first class visibility. We stopped to admire the view of the previous day's walk, the tops completely clear of cloud.

The geology of the narrow ridge is unusual. Great upheavals in the earth's crust have folded the once horizontal beds of rock and they are now vertical. Subsequent erosion has removed whole slabs at a time, leaving many sheer faces and a dramatic landscape. Ahead was a great notch in the crest, as if a Celtic god had brought down his battle sword. At this point there are two parallel ridges, to me a clear explanation of the ridge's name, Aonach Sgoilte, which translates as the Split Ridge. As we drew nearer this became more impressive in scale, with the notch, aligned to a fault in the bedrock, becoming a narrow gorge with near vertical sides. The northernmost wall in particular is formed of a long series of rock blades. Into this narrow gorge I walked, with Morag close behind. We had to find a way over and around rocks that had fallen from the steep cliffs above. I felt tense and apprehensive. In the middle section there was a sudden booming roar which made me freeze. "Are you alright?" shouted Morag, "Has there been a rock fall?" But there was no dust or new debris. It was a strange phenomenon, as if the giant rock teeth were shouting at us. We moved fast and were relieved to climb out of that fearful place.

At first we climbed up, then down to a rocky col, then used hands and feet to climb up to the ridge again. I stopped on a ledge and looked back to take a photograph of the place of the shouting rocks. A dozen ravens flew over our heads, their harsh calls adding to the oddly sinister atmosphere.

The mood changed abruptly once we were on the narrow crest again. The sun hammered down and we stopped where we could lean back against smooth, warm rock to have a drink and eat some lunch. There were superb views of the previous day's route. Seen from this point, we could see what a huge walk it had been.

Making our way along the ridge again, we began to get tantalising views of Ladhar Bheinn. It was mostly clear but the top 20 metres seemed to attract a small white cloud which sat for a while, broke into streamers and then reformed.

Just before the ridge rose to Stob a' Chearcaille we turned to climb the south-east arête of our Munro. We stopped at the best viewpoints to look at the massive sweep of cliffs lining Coire Dhorrcail, which surely must be one of the most striking of the Highland corries. The narrow ridge leading to the summit is pinnacled, with a number of very steep sections. Walking poles stowed, it was time to use hands again. The final ascent was particularly steep, with sections of exposed scrambling.

For the third time in two days, the cloud came down to cover the Munro top. On the knife-edge summit a cold wind howled across so we hurried along it and soon began to descend, emerging from the cloud as we did so.

At the bealach between Coire na Diollaide and Coire Garbh we dropped a little down the south-western slope to get out of the wind and took a break on a high perch. The sun was blazing and I put on my hat again. It was quiet up there. The bare rock mountains fell into a deep blue sea. Eigg floated on it like a boat, its Sgurr the sail. The Cuillin of Rum, an exceptional mountain range, rose abruptly from the Hebridean waters. I finished my tea then we went steeply down to a stream where we filled our water bottles and began the long walk out.

11½ hours after leaving the bunkhouse we returned. Tom and K made us a welcome meal of pasta which we ate with red wine. I enjoyed the tale about their day out on Bob's boat. Tom was particularly taken with Frank, a local character who runs a hostel in a converted church in Tarbet Bay. Tarbet is almost as remote as Inverie. To get there one must be fit enough for a long walk across steep, rocky mountainsides on a rough and narrow path or arrive on a boat. Having done the latter, Tom played his guitar and sang which prompted Frank to get out his accordion. After the jam session, Frank told inappropriate jokes and Tom and K were well satisfied.

Full and weary, we retired to the common room for Talisker and tea. Tom had lit the stove and it was like a sauna, which was perfect after such a strenuous two days. We swapped photos of our adventures but when I came to the photo of the shouting rocks, it had not taken, there was only an "error" message on the screen.

Later that night, in the Old Forge, a local man played his bagpipes. Two local women danced and I felt like an extra in the cast of Brigadoon. The dancing, however, provoked an international incident. A Swedish couple got up to dance on the improvised

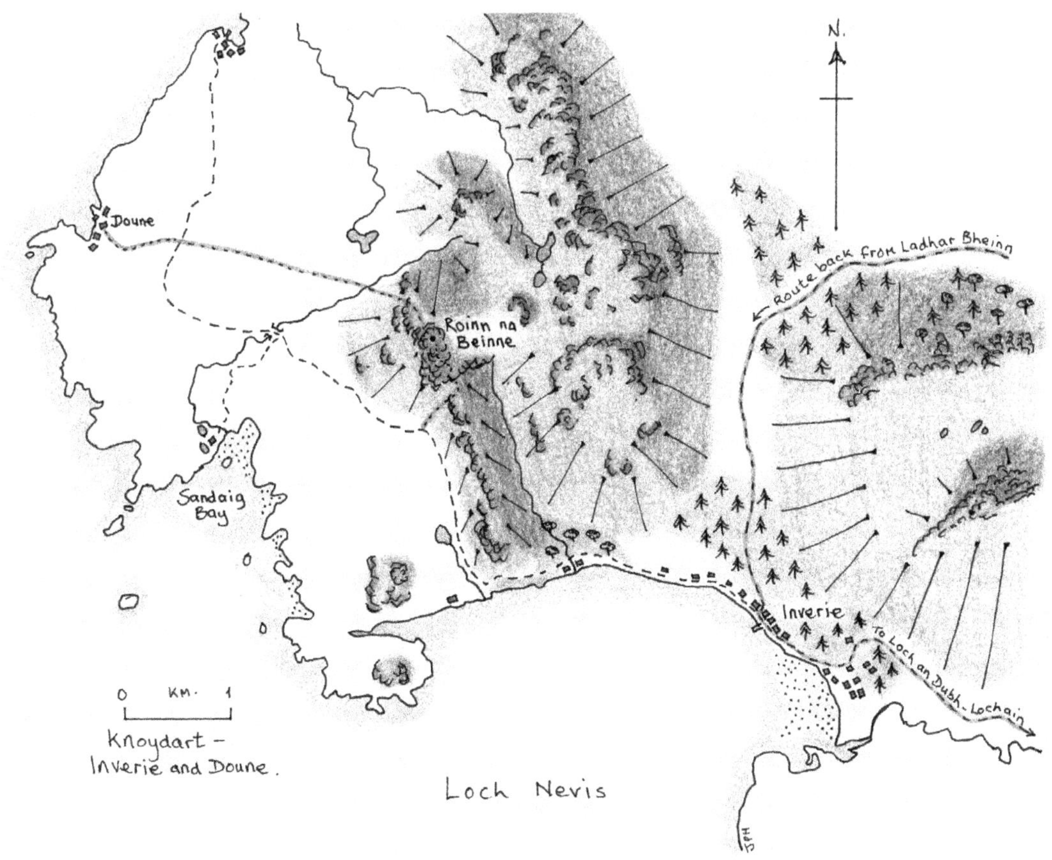

dancefloor and the man knocked over one of the local women. She sat with her leg on a stool and her ankle wrapped in ice while the Swedish couple made a diplomatic return to their yacht. To make things worse, I carelessly aired my opinion that Scottish bagpipes are not an instrument for a confined space, being more suited to places like battlefields. This upset both Morag, who has a daughter who plays the pipes and Tom, who loves all things related to Highland folk music. He was also worried that I might have been overheard and perhaps not survive the night. The piper, who told me later that he had overheard, took the heat out of the situation by switching to the softer, mellower, Irish pipes. On the way out I told him how much I had enjoyed his playing of them and he gave me a wink.

The following morning, we waited for Tom and K to waken and, when we eventually gave up, had a late start. We decided to climb Roinn na Beinne, the westernmost of Knoydart's hills. Martina had some books to return to Doune, so we decided to do both together. I left a note for the sleepers that we would look for them at Sandaig Bay on the way home.

In Inverie, Mark the Sculptor stopped his Land Rover and gave us a lift. Morag and I shared the back seat with his sad-eyed greyhound. I remarked that he must like Knoydart but he replied that he hated the place, then, with some passion, detailed the reasons why. He dropped us at the foot of our hill.

As we zig zagged upwards, I saw that, in contrast to the metamorphic schists and gneiss of the previous two days, this hill was of Torridonian sandstone. The near horizontal bedding and massive, blocky structure give the hill the same striking crags as many of the North-west's iconic mountains.

It was a perfect day of blue sky and sunshine. On top, however, there was a cold, northerly wind so we scrambled down a little on the south side to a sheltered, sun-warmed alcove where we ate a leisurely lunch listening to Martina's stories and enjoying perfect views of the bright Hebridean sea and its dark islands.

I took a bearing for Doune and we set off down the west slopes of the hill. The ground was dry and springy and the walking easy. Ahead, a white ferry left its ice-blue bay and moved silently into the dark channel. The mountains of Eigg, Rum and Skye rose sharply from the sea. Martina praised my bearing because it brought us to a wooden sign on which was written, "Doune here". It pointed to a footpath which led steeply down to the beach. No road goes to this place. Doune is from dun, or fort. The settlement would have been better known in the days when the Western Seaways were one of Europe's major transport and communication arteries and most of the continent had no roads.

What we found was a little bay of turquoise water and white sand. Half a dozen houses were strung around the beach and boats rocked gently at their moorings. Martina had been working at the little restaurant built on stilts above the beach. We climbed the stairs up to the balcony and she brought tea, coffee and cakes to enjoy in the warm sun. She talked about this special place. There were many tales, including the time a minke whale stranded. Its long bones leaned against the restaurant wall.

Rested and refreshed, we climbed up past the ancient dun to the cliffs and worked our way south around the little coves. We saw no one at all. Tom and K were at Sandaig Bay; they had been fishing and had a modest catch of mackerel. We walked back together.

We ate the mackerel with olives then went to the pub for a meal. I ate scallops followed by a glass of 18-year-old Lagavulin for pudding.

Back at the common room we sat around the stove. Steve from next door brought his guitars and played along to Tom's songs.

On the last morning the air was warm and the sky blue. I went for a walk along the beach then said goodbye to the friends we had made.

In the village, the smell of frying bacon drew us into the little café on the beach for a second breakfast. Then we sailed back on the Western Isles, porpoises following behind and a diamond sparkle on the crest of each wavelet. Looking back, Luinne Bheinn and Ladhar Bheinn were completely clear of cloud.

In Mallaig harbour a grey seal came half out of the water as he pushed up the side of the boat. “He likes to see who the passengers are,” said the skipper.

Then it was farewell to Morag and Martina and a day of perfect weather for our trip back to Aberdeen.

Two days later I went for prints of my photographs. All were fine apart from the one of the shouting rocks. That particular photograph, represented by an error message, sat stubbornly on the memory card, not even letting me delete it. I took everything to a camera shop where they had to reformat the card. “Very strange,” said the girl.

26/9/09 - 27/9/09

Buachaille Etive Mor: Stob Dearg and Stob na Broige • Carn a' Chlamain

The Jolly Boys at Weem

I stood in the yard of the bunkhouse at Weem and looked up at billions of stars, the prospect for the next day was good. Yellow light streamed from the windows of the common room.

It was great to put my feet up in front of the hot stove and be brought up to date with all the news. I was soon relaxed and enjoying the laughter and good company. Despite a forecast of excellent weather from Weem eastwards, but increasing cloud, wind and drizzle in the west, Struan announced that he fancied climbing Buachaille Etive Mor in Glen Coe. As Ray's rival walk was to Meall Chuaich, which I had done before, I nailed my colours to Struan's mast. Nick asked why we had chosen a bunkhouse in Weem if we were going to climb mountains in Glen Coe, particularly when there were a number of suitable places to stay on the doorstep of that place. This sort of question could only be asked by someone new to the ways of the old-timers. I tried to explain the tradition of eccentric behaviour but apparently failed, for his next question was, "And why would we travel west away from the good weather and into the poor weather?" Mugs of black tea and a tumbler of Laphroaig kept me going until the small hours, then it was time for a few hours of sleep to build up some energy for the rigours of the day, or so I thought.

The old-timers were enjoying the hard won freedom of retirement and were again measuring whisky by the bottle instead of by the glass. Raucous laughter and much banging about made deep sleep difficult. It seemed that I had only dropped off ten minutes ago when Victor came to the bedroom, a vapour trail of alcohol behind him. It was nearly five o' clock. I closed my eyes again but an urgent beep beep, beep beep, beep beep beep came from the direction of his bed. This continued, interspersed with expletives, beep beep "F...!" Beep beep beep "F...!" Beep beep "F...!" as Victor struggled to write a text on his new mobile phone. This went on, and on, and on, until I began to get out of bed, determined to do permanent damage to that beeping phone. At that moment, however, there was a great crash which shuddered through the bunkhouse and two seconds later Victor was snoring loudly. It was with some relief that I got up at six.

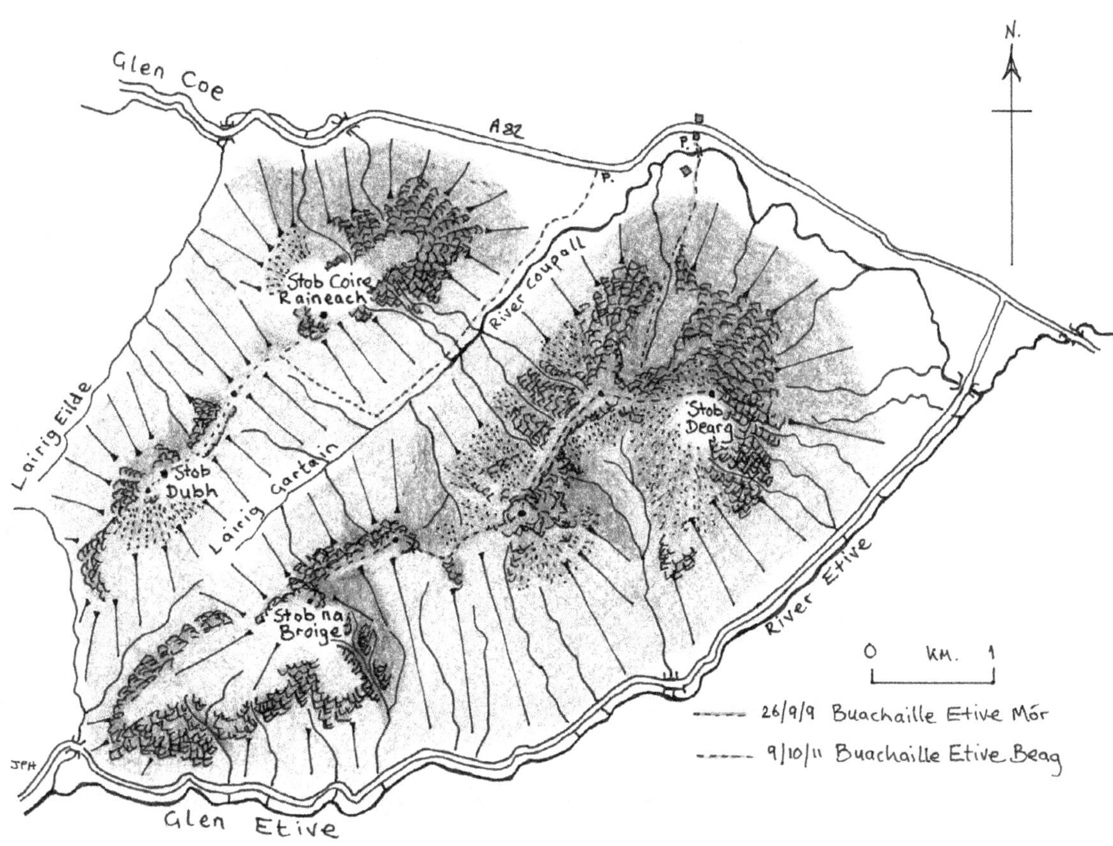

In the car park at Altnafeadh I looked up at Buachaille Etive Mor, the big herdsman of Etive, as I had done many times before. I had thought that I would have to climb it myself one day as hillwalking companions like Morag had all done it. It seemed ironic, therefore, that I was about to walk into Coire na Tulaich as a member of a party of ten.

The day was better than forecast, with a fast-moving stream of white cloud obscuring the top 200 metres of Stob Dearg every 30 seconds or so. I was going to climb the mountain I had admired on so many calendars. What towered before me was like an old friend, a true icon. "I suppose the way up is round the back?" asked Nick.

"No," I replied, "it's straight up there."

It was easier than it looks, a steady climb up a well-made path. We stopped before the last, steeper section with our backs to a crag to have some breakfast and a hot drink. We could see the Blackwater Dam and I thought about the tough men who built it using only hand tools. Far to the north, the sun was shining on the peaks of the Grey Corries, giving them a glint like polished steel.

The last section up to the notch at the head of the corrie was steep, calling for hands as well as feet and I was glad that the fine crystalline dyke rock was dry. Morag stumbled, cut her finger and her dark blood trickled down a smooth, coral coloured face.

On the top, we stepped into a strong wind and streaming cloud. I prepared myself for an uncomfortable struggle to Stob Dearg's summit and told myself that I would return to this mountain on a clear day so that I could see it at its very best. Once we started climbing, however, the wind, which was on our backs, did not seem too bad at all and the cloud began to break into thin white streamers, revealing the spectacle of Glen Coe to our left.

Not far from the summit I looked down onto white cloud and saw a perfect rainbow circle there. A black figure at its centre moved its arms up at exactly the same time as I moved mine; it was a Brocken spectre. I called the others, expecting it to disappear before they came, but it persisted and became even more intense. Only Morag and I had ever seen one before and most of the others had never heard of this phenomenon. "A person is lucky to see one once in a lifetime," declared Victor. The strong sun shining down behind us as we walked along the very crest of the ridge created perfect conditions and I became a black figure in the centre of a celestial halo. Each complete circle had the full spectrum of colour, bright against the dark floor of the glen far below. They persisted all the way to the top, quite stealing the show from the views framed in big rents in the cloud.

We came down a little from the summit and decided to find shelter in the lee of the west wind then eat lunch. Struan led the way onto a narrow ledge of slabs perched high above Stob Dearg's eastern cliffs. Some followed, others took one look and settled for something less exposed. I sat on the slab above Struan's, my boots over the edge of one of Buachaille Etive Mor's famous faces and felt this a perfect place for a picnic spot. The sun streamed down and the rock was warm to the touch. All cloud had gone from Stob Dearg and we watched as a party of helmeted climbers appeared, one by one, each triumphant, on the summit. Far below, Rannoch Moor stretched beyond the Kingshouse Hotel, its warm autumn colours studded with the bright blue of a hundred lochans. Victor, sitting on a slab above me, was strangely quiet. "Is it because you still have your hangover?"

"Hangovers I am used to," he replied, "vertigo I am not." And with that he cautiously made his way back up to the ridge.

Morag admitted that she felt the same, "The way the slabs slope down towards the cliff edge makes me feel insecure." I shouldered my rucksack and followed my friends but was sad to leave that spectacular seat. As I looked up to the summit again a raven, two metres above the cairn, rocked on the wind.

When we joined the others, all the conversation was about the Brocken spectres. Some had taken photographs and hoped they would come out. I thought that we had been very lucky indeed to see what we had seen but, as I walked down the ridge, the strange phenomenon appeared again on its canvas of white cloud. Although I was sure it would disappear if I made a move to photograph it, I took a few snaps with myself in the centre of the circular rainbow. At one point, a double rainbow appeared. I was somewhat surprised when, a few days later, my developed prints showed the Brocken spectres, sharp, clear and wonderful. After my experience with the shouting rocks, I had half expected these visions to be paranormal and impossible to photograph.

We walked along Buachaille Etive Mor's crest, heading for Stob na Broige, a straggled Indian file of bright orange, blue, green and red. Thin tatters of cloud streamed around the mountain peaks and then hurtled away over Rannoch Moor, revealing massive waves of frozen rock.

Cloud obscured our view down Glen Etive from Stob na Broige's summit but we emerged from under it as we descended and Buachaille Etive Mor's ridge was revealed, beautifully lit by the low angle of the sun. We made the most of our walk back along the spine of this well-loved mountain, enjoying the panorama of Glen Coe to the west.

The Adventurer's Escape
Weem. September
Weekend 2009.

The late September sun had set before we were back at Weem but there was enough warmth to sit out in the courtyard while we waited for Ray and Charlie to return with our orders from the Indian restaurant in Aberfeldy. No lover of carry-out food, I was pleasantly surprised at what a good dinner was provided, once the cartons had been tipped onto hot plates and the bottles of wine opened. Home baked apple pie and spice cake with fresh cream filled the last spaces of the hungry walkers.

I can not report on the late night activities as I retired not long past midnight, fell into an instant deep sleep and did not stir until I woke at seven o' clock.

A hasty breakfast, fond farewells and then I was driving on the deserted roads to Blair Atholl with Morag following. We parked in the Atholl Estate car park in Old Bridge of Tilt, mounted our bikes and cycled up the private road which follows the River Tilt.

It took about an hour to cycle the nine kilometres up to Forest Lodge. It was a fine, dry morning with cloud on the high tops but bright and clear below. The first section was wooded, with many splendid deciduous trees, all showing the yellows and golds of early autumn. As we pedalled further up the glen we came out from the trees and looked up at its steep walls, rising to bare, grey crags. We stopped twice to watch large herds of hinds, moving with incredible ease on such steep slopes.

Just past Forest Lodge, we left the bikes against a fence and started straight up the north-west side of the glen. It was hard work until we found the stalkers' path which is marked on the map. After that, it would be a matter of following this path to Carn a' Chlamain, the hill of the kite, our objective for the day.

High above the Tilt, our bikes too small to see, we stopped for mugs of tea. I ate a slab of fruit cake in the hope that it would give me a top-up of energy. Glen Tilt to the north-east looked impressive, a monument to the erosive forces of the Pleistocene Ice Age. Above its crags, the landscape was one of massive, heather clad, rounded hills, a clear contrast to the dramatically steep-sided bare rock mountains of Glen Coe in the west. Contrasting, neither poorer nor better, just different. These eastern hills of the Cairngorms area have their special character and this is fine walking country indeed.

Our break over, we followed the path to the head of the glen wall, where it changed direction to go west. Morag is habitually silent unless one of us spots something. This time it was mountain hares on rocky crags to our left. We saw about a dozen, all plump and healthy, their winter white coats spreading from their underparts upwards.

Carn a' Chlamain's cone of frost-shattered quartzite rocks appeared ahead and to the left of the path. We picked our way up to the cairn but the strong wind did not encourage us to linger there. Instead, we sat in the shelter of the crags where we had seen the hares to eat our lunch. The sun was visible behind the thin cloud, which was lifting from the tops.

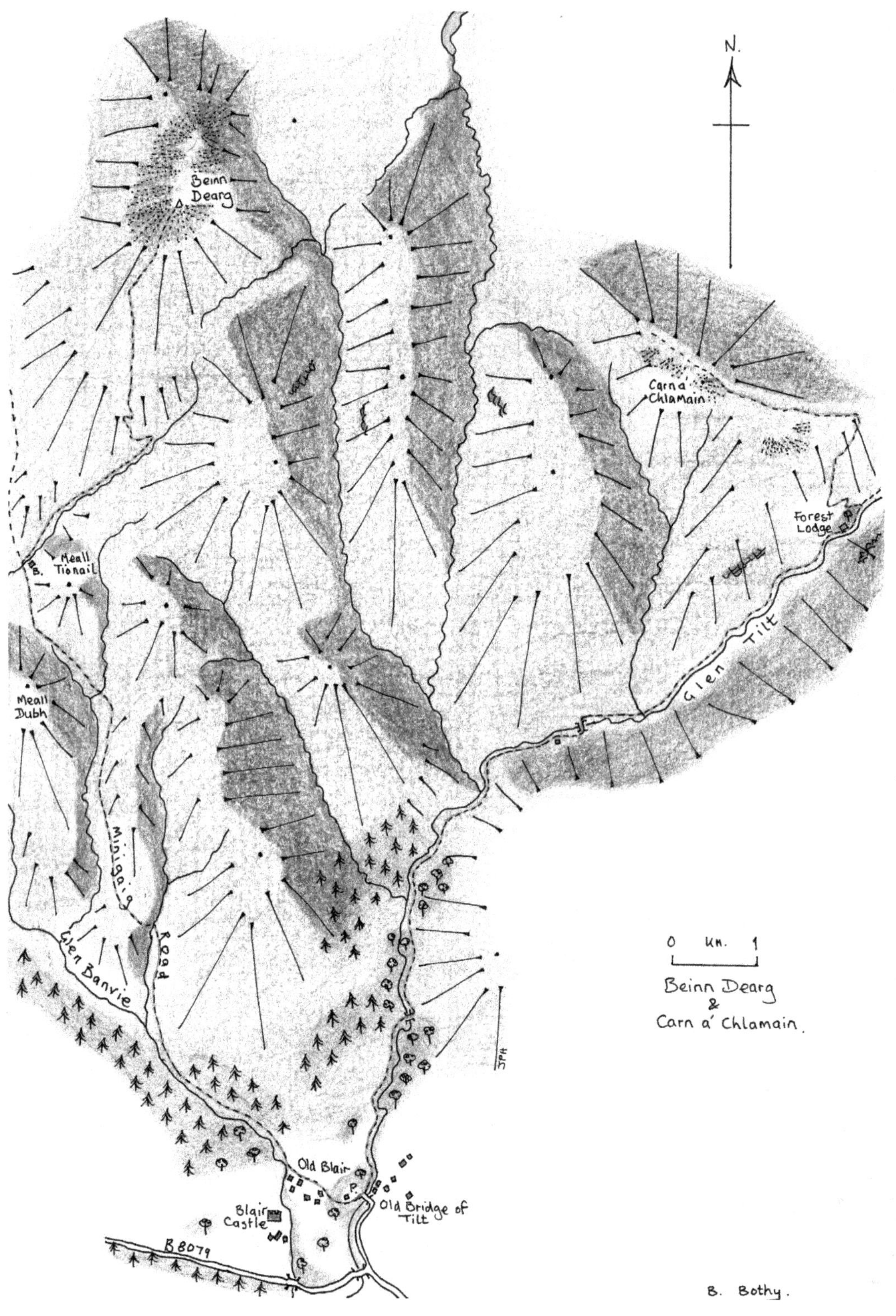
N.
Beinn Dearg
Carn a' Chlamain
Forest Lodge
Meall Tionail
B.
Meall Dubh
Minigaig
Road
Glen Banvie
Glen Tilt
Old Blair
P
Old Bridge of Tilt
Blair Castle
B8079
JPH
0 KM. 1
Beinn Dearg
&
Carn a' Chlamain.
B. Bothy.

We faced north, looking at rounded hill after rounded hill, seemingly repeated infinitely. I took out my map and noted that north of where we sat there was nothing man-made at all for the 25 kilometres or so of wild country to the map's edge.

On the way back, I stopped at the point where the old path gave me a view down into the deep and narrow defile of Glen Tilt. It was deserted. I stood for a while and, in my mind's eye, I saw the ghosts of hardy drovers, riders in heavy cloaks on urgent errands and Celtic warriors on nimble ponies, all using this ancient way.

After a rapid descent to the bikes we began the long return journey. Tiring, but so much better to me than weary miles of marching along the road.

12/10/09

Carn an Fhidhleir and An Sgarsoch

Into remote Glen Geldie

James, Morag and I set off from Linn o' Dee at nine o' clock on a fine autumn morning. We had our bikes because we had a long distance to cover to Geldie Lodge. Five minutes from the car park we heard the first stag roar and the roaring continued all day. My companions, both good cyclists, rode ahead.

After the White Bridge, I stopped at the side of the track to let an old green Land Rover past. It pulled up beside me and a purple-faced ghillie asked, somewhat abruptly, "Where are you two and the laddie going?" I told him, adding that, when he caught up, he would see that it was a strange sort of laddie. He asked me to climb Carn Ealar (the alternative name for Carn an Fhidhleir) first and, as this was our intention, it was an easy matter to agree. I watched as the Land Rover bumped and lurched along the stony track, wondering if he would trouble to look at Morag as he passed. He was the last person we saw that day.

There were twelve kilometres to be cycled along the rough track, interrupted by two swollen streams, one of which involved some precarious balancing on boulders while pushing our half submerged bikes over the slippery bed.

Faced with a wide and deep river crossing at the Geldie Burn, we decided to leave the bikes and wade across, our boots tied around our necks. It did not seem too cold at first but there was no feeling at all in my feet as I emerged on the south bank.

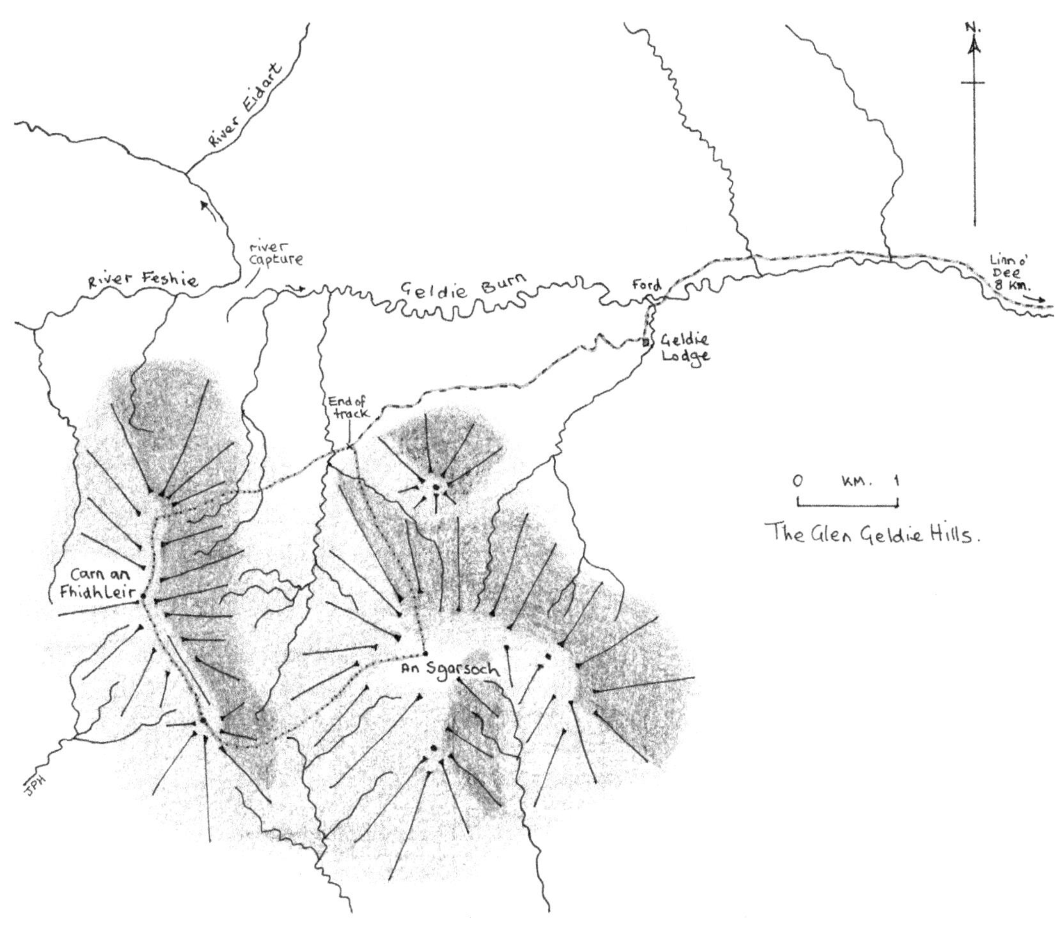

The Glen Geldie Hills.

Warm boots back on, we looked at the ruins of Geldie Lodge. An old shed still had four walls and a roof and could be used as a shelter.

We walked at a fast pace along a good path which led west, high above the Geldie Burn. Looking down to the meanders on the river flats, I spotted a large group of hinds in the centre of a bright green meadow. They all stood still, looking in the same direction. Following their gaze, I saw a mature stag running to meet another who was heading quickly towards the hinds. They met, then abruptly began a rapid parallel walk, heads up and antlers back. At the end of this the intruder ran back the way he had come and the champion stag threw back his head and roared. As I walked on I noticed another six stags on the slopes above this rutting green. They seemed agitated, running first this way and then that, some stopping to roar. Throughout it all, the hinds barely moved. Not one lowered her head to feed and all eyes were on the stags.

High pressure was building over the Highlands. It was calm, cool and crystal clear, with high white clouds in a pale blue sky and a sun which had lost its summer intensity.

Glen Geldie is on a massive scale, its slopes sweeping up to the Cairngorm Plateau in the north and to the remote hills we wished to climb in the south. The low-angled sun turned the autumn colours of the south-facing slopes of the Cairngorms into a rich Indian gold.

Where the track reached the bank of the Allt a' Chaorainn, we crossed and sat down for lunch. As I ate my sandwiches and sipped tea I looked up at the great bulk of the first Munro, it was formidable. Checking the map, I saw that we had 400 metres of steep slope to climb. James asked me to lead then inquired, "Full frontal?"

"Full frontal," I replied.

At first there seemed to be a narrow path through the tall heather and peat bog, but I soon lost it. There was an interesting section where a stream had cut into the black peat, revealing the white fossils of roots and stumps of the great trees which used to clothe the slopes of this mountain. Then the really hard work began.

I have too demanding a life to devote enough time to keeping 'hill fit', something of regret to me as I climbed metre after painful metre. I went at it like a machine, marvelling that my ribs managed to contain my leaping heart, half expecting it to crash through and land, throbbing, on the heather.

I noticed the heather change to dwarf heather and then to sparse tufts of yellow grass with dwarf juniper. Then there was more pale grey rock than vegetation and I realised that I was on the crest of the ridge. I could not see the others below, but could hear faint snatches of their conversation so I turned south along an intermittent path, heading for the summit.

Three ptarmigan ran before me, now mostly white but with enough specks of grey to give then surprising camouflage amongst the rocks. In a few weeks their plumage would be pure white, ready for the winter snow.

At the cairn I looked south to Carn a' Chlamain. I had stood on its cone of shattered quartzite rocks two weeks before with Morag. The others caught up and we picked out the long ridge of Beinn a' Ghlo to the south-east and the dissected plateau of the Cairngorms to the north. There was no wind to speak of and the air was cold and clear, giving perfect visibility. Even the distant Ben Alder hills were a sharp silhouette. The cairn is an interesting feature, being the meeting place of Inverness-shire, Aberdeenshire and Perthshire. Streams running down the east side of this mountain run into the Dee, on the south side into the Tay and on the west side into the Spey.

With the sun on our faces, we left the cairn to go south-east, heading for the bealach between the two Munros. The higher starting point made a difference and it seemed less of a challenge to climb up to the stony plateau which is the summit of An Sgarsoch, the place of the sharp rocks.

We sat in the shelter of a large and well-built cairn, its stone benches perfect as seats and for standing a flask. It was a lovely spot for afternoon tea, with the sun warming the rock of the mountain top and the glowing, golden Cairngorms a scenic marvel before us.

Our short rest over, we walked to the abrupt edge of the summit plateau. To the north-west lay the great notch of Glen Feshie, its river powerful enough to capture the headwaters of the Geldie Burn, the precise point of capture clear to see at the bottom of An Sgarsoch's long slope. The Geldie was a bigger river before this, certainly the major source of the Dee. Its valley would have been wide before the ice both deepened and widened it further. It lay before us now as a great trough, 10 kilometres across. The far side is the sub-arctic plateau of the Moine Mhor, bitten into by Coire Mharconaich. Rising above all was Braeriach, its east-facing corries corniced with fresh snow. The sun shone low in the sky in the west, spreading mellow light over this empty land.

I told the others to make straight for the notch made by the River Eidart, almost due north, which would bring us onto the path back to the ruined lodge. It was a fast descent, hopping over clumps of heather, peat bogs and crystal clear burns. On the path, I made a mug of tea with the last of my hot water while I waited for James and Morag. I sat quietly, at peace with myself and the world. Something made me turn around and there, less than 10 metres away, stood a line of nine hinds, all staring at me. We watched each other for a while and then I stood up. The hind at the head of the line turned her head to the front and led her sisters away, high stepping through the heather.

I turned back to the hill, there was no sign of my two friends. Had one of them turned an ankle? Were they lost? Was I lost? I felt a note to self coming on; it is easy to get lost in this wilderness, where human beings are incredibly difficult to see at any distance, so perhaps it is not a good idea to walk too far ahead of one's companions? I am not given to panic, preferring the application of logic. I reasoned;

1. these seasoned 'old hands' were unlikely to have damaged themselves on that descent
2. they would now be on this same track
3. they were not further west, i.e. having chosen to add distance to our long return journey
4. they must have come onto the track further to the east.

These points in my head, I cheerfully set off east along the track. Soon I spotted two tiny specks. I was surprised at how far ahead they were and sobered by the thought that they were about to disappear over a rise in the track, which they promptly did. Sobered but, of course, relieved.

James and Morag, meanwhile, were not having a good time. Had he been swallowed up by a peat bog? If we returned, would we have any chance of finding him? Should we alert the Braemar Mountain Rescue Team? Does he have the only key for the cable which he used to secure all three bikes? "Yes," I confirmed in answer to that last question, which made them turn suddenly, their expressions of relief identical. We are all too nice to have allowed this touching moment to have degenerated into even mere hints of blame. I immediately declared, "Mea culpa for getting too far ahead." Their riposte was that they had not followed the agreement to head for the notch made by the River Eidart.

James added, "I'm glad you're not a corpse to be preserved for centuries in a peat bog." Morag patted my head. We walked on in good fettle.

The Geldie Burn had not grown less icy but I consoled myself as I waded across with the thought that it was probably doing my abused leg muscles some good, like rugby players having an ice bath after a game. Then we cycled back to the cars in the gloaming. It seemed a long way but never did I even think of complaining, considering the alternative of a marathon walk out. We had maintained a relentless pace all day, yet the expedition had taken 9½ hours. This would be a test of endurance without bikes, a long mid-summer day for the fittest walkers. In the last of the light I freewheeled down to the public road with bats, stoking up on late insects, flitting alongside, reminding me that winter was not far away.

12/12/09

Beinn Bhreac

Dawn to dusk in the frozen Cairngorms

I drove down Aberdeen's Union Street at 6.30 a.m. on this cold winter morning; beyond the opulent blue and gold of the Christmas lights the sky was black. An hour later, streaks of pale pink announced the dawn as James and I motored west along Deeside. The sky turned Prussian blue and Lochnagar appeared against it, sharp and brilliant white.

We parked at the Linn o' Dee and cycled north to Derry Lodge. All was silent, ice-hard and the trees were frosted. The bikes were left against a bleached old stump in the ancient pinewood of Derry. We stood and looked north from this vantage point. Over the crowns of the Scots pines rose the steep sides of Glen Derry, streaked with pale grey screes, the upper slopes snow-covered. The icy crags of Derry Cairngorm rose above all else, every fine detail crystal clear in air so cold it was burning our lungs.

Our route up onto the plateau ran north-east through the trees, over rough ground. The going was hard at first, over tall heather and pale, broad-leaved grass, wilted under a crust of frost. Each old tree had its own character and all leaned over to the south, bending away from the deathly wind which spills off the high plateau and howls down the channel of the glen. The heather became shorter and the walking easier, much now over frozen peat bog.

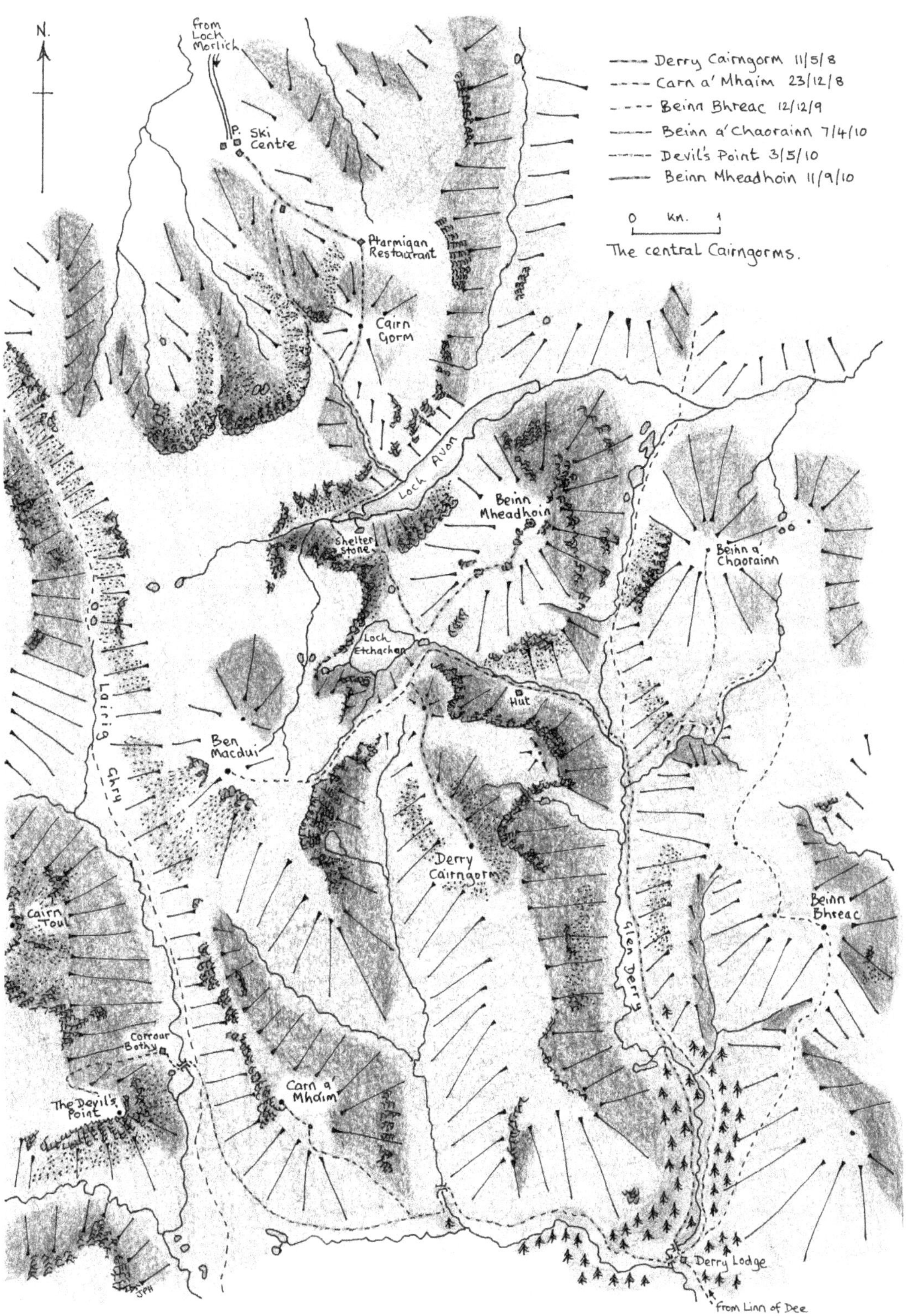
N.
from Loch Morlich
P.
Ski Centre
Ptarmigan Restaurant
Cairn Gorm
Loch Avon
Beinn Mheadhoin
Shelter Stone
Loch Etchachan
Hut
Ben Macdui
Lairig Ghru
Derry Cairngorm
Cairn Toul
Corrour Bothy
The Devil's Point
Carn a' Mhaim
Glen Derry
Beinn a' Chaorainn
Beinn Bhreac
Derry Lodge
from Linn of Dee
Derry Cairngorm 11/5/8
Carn a' Mhaim 23/12/8
Beinn Bhreac 12/12/9
Beinn a' Chaorainn 7/4/10
Devil's Point 3/5/10
Beinn Mheadhoin 11/9/10
0 km. 1
The central Cairngorms.

I stood under the spreading branches of the last tree, a 300 year old giant, and looked ahead. The slopes of Beinn Bhreac ("Ben Vreck") were a patchwork of grey scree, brown heather, beige grasses and white drifts of snow which presumably is why it has been named speckled hill. A thin blanket of cloud had settled on the highest ground.

James caught up and on we went, steadily gaining height. In the cloud, we were in an arctic world. The morning sun was a sharp white circle which gave no warmth. The larger streams were still flowing and we stopped a number of times to marvel at the ice sculptures on their margins. Those that made the most impression were the gothic ice hands, thrusting up through the hard ground, fingers clawing at the sky.

Higher again, snow covered most of the ground. Walking over the snowfields was a strange experience. All was monochrome, there was no shadow, no perspective, no normal frame of reference for eye and mind. We stumbled into hollows which had been impossible to see. Deep gullies which would have slowed our progress in summer conditions were easily crossed on frozen snow bridges.

The summit ground was a litter of granite boulders, each covered in wonderful feathery frost crystals. I stopped to look at the interlocking geometric patterns and do not remember ever having seen such large, well-defined shapes.

After visiting the summit cairn we dropped down through these frosted rocks to the north, to be out of the chill of the south-east wind while we ate some lunch. My honey and peanut butter pieces were frozen hard but hot tea helped them down. James asked whether I liked Sir Walter Scott and our conversation moved to Dickens and PG Wodehouse. It was time to pack up when my beard froze and I noticed that a lattice of frost crystals had grown over my Buffalo jacket.

With energy levels topped up, we walked to the West Top and then strode out over the snowfields to Craig Derry. The going was surprisingly good as the ground was so hard, so we pushed on north onto the Moine Bhealaidh, determined to have a good shot at climbing Beinn a' Chaorainn. We crossed the Glas Allt Mor and stood at the foot of this second Munro of the day. Here we checked the time and it was clear that we needed to turn back. It was only nine days to the winter solstice and the light would fade fast from 3.30 p.m.

We followed the Glas Allt Mor but it has cut a narrow gully into the side of Glen Derry and the exposed rock was dangerously slippery, so we climbed out and zig zagged down the steep wall of the glen.

On the path that we would follow back we sat down for a hot drink. A stream which crossed it was frozen over. I watched white tadpoles swimming in a line under the ice where the water was forcing its way just under the surface.

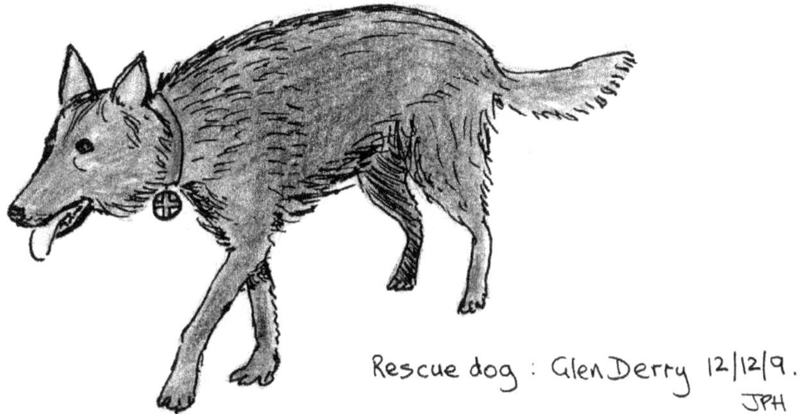

Striding down the path we were overtaken by a tall, thin young man with very long legs and an enormous stride, a physique made for eating up the miles in the mountains. With him was a black Alsatian dog. The young man stopped to chat, the first person we had seen that day. There was something about our fellow walker's face that I recognised and I remembered meeting him in the summer of 2003. I had been climbing down the massive blocks west of Cairn Toul's summit when he had overtaken me, this time with two collies. They were search and rescue dogs. I looked at the black dog and noticed a green cross on his collar, another one being trained. His owner told us that the dog had been rejected by the prison service as he was not aggressive enough. He had two rescues to his credit already. We watched man and dog lope off to join their mountain rescue colleagues at Derry Lodge. They were soon out of sight.

As we walked down the glen the cloud which had sat on the high tops for most of the day thinned. As the sun began to set, a suffused golden light gave its warm tone to the winter browns and tans, with streaks of silver marking the iced burns and dark green the first trees of the Wood of Derry.

In the wood again, among the long shadows, James noticed that a number of tree trunks were spiral. I wondered what force of nature had made these trees respond in that way.[5] At the bikes, we looked back up the glen to see that all the cloud had gone and the snow cap of Derry Cairngorm was flushed red by the setting sun.

---

5 I did some research on spiral tree trunks, learning that they are common in mountain trees. It was suggested that growing that way added strength. Other theories included lightning strikes which may result in a surviving tree growing in a twisted fashion. 'The Last Word', New Scientist Blogs, 30/1/08, has some interesting discussion. I remain, however, none the wiser, especially after noticing three trees with spiral trunks in my sheltered local park.

'he had a full white beard
and rosy cheeks.'
Glen Lui 12/12/9.
JPH

We cycled through a frozen land back to the Linn o' Dee. The trees were white with thick frost, giving off their own light in the gloaming. A stout figure was walking in the same direction up ahead. I turned as I passed to wish him a good evening and saw that he had a full white beard and rosy cheeks. Perfect in that Christmas card landscape.

It was dark when the car pulled out of the car park. We had covered 27 kilometres on this short winter day, 10 kilometres by bike. I was pleased that we had turned back when we did.

We stopped at Sheena's house in Ballater where I was revived by a glass of mulled punch, warm rock cakes with blue cheese and mugs of tea.

24/1/10

Morrone

In the deep midwinter

Heavy snow fell on the 18th December and more fell almost every day for the next three weeks. Temperatures were well below freezing so nothing melted. Roads were dangerous and travel was only for those with essential journeys. It was turning into the coldest winter since records began almost a century ago.

Our plans for a New Year walk in the Cairngorms scuppered, James and I walked from Donmouth to Balmedie and back along the beach. We saw three roe deer in the sand dunes but not a fellow human being for the entire day. The sky was savagely beautiful, the sea so wild that the beach was deep in briny foam and we were chased home by a blizzard.

It was a relief, therefore, to see a reasonable forecast later in the month and dust off the boots and rucksack. All was arranged for Sunday 24th but on the 23rd a deep little depression appeared in the North Sea off Aberdeen. Winds swirled counter-clockwise around it, dumping yet more snow on the Cairngorms overnight.

Snow was lying on the road after Ballater and more began to fall. Morag had called to say that she was stuck at the snow gates at Blairgowrie. She crawled her car up Glen Shee and down Glen Clunie, reaching Braemar just before James and I arrived, tense after a difficult drive.

I proposed a conference in the Fife Arms, so we sipped tea in front of the crackling fire and considered our options. I suggested leaving the cars parked in front of the hotel and a circular walk taking in Morrone, a Corbett rising south-west of the village. The

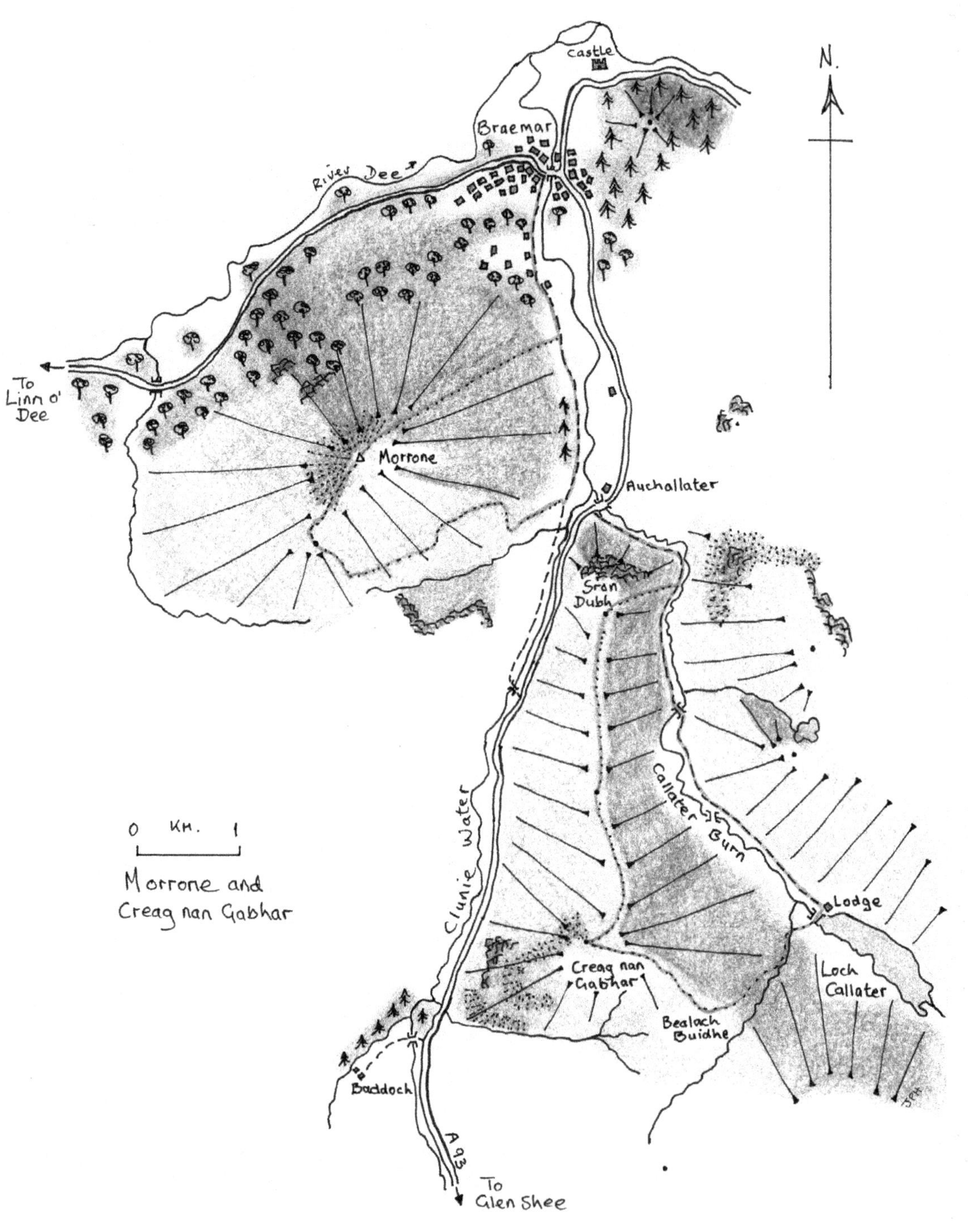
Castle
N.
Braemar
River Dee
To
Linn o'
Dee
Morrone
Auchallater
Sron
Dubh
Callater Burn
Clunie Water
0 KM. 1
Morrone and
Creag nan Gabhar
Lodge
Creag nan
Gabhar
Loch
Callater
Bealach
Buidhe
Baddoch
A93
To
Glen Shee

snow ploughs would hopefully have cleared the roads home by the time we returned. Morag, her heart set on high adventure in the northern Cairngorms, tried to hide her disappointment, but not very successfully. This is why, half an hour later, we were trying to coax our cars into the Linn o' Dee car park after nine kilometres of road which seriously tested our winter driving skills. Morag's Jaguar, however, refused to go any further or even backwards, instead sliding sideways alarmingly. As two stags looked on, her car was pushed back onto the road where she decided that, after all, Braemar was a good option and that we'd be best getting back there while there was still a chance.

We followed the narrow road along the Clunie Water, its banks piled high with ice floes as big as garden sheds. In the south was a small patch of mid blue sky.

West of Auchallater Farm, we turned onto a Land Rover track which followed a spur upwards to the rounded summit ridge. Over a hundred red deer, stags and hinds, kicked at the snow and pushed their heads down to get at the heather and coarse grasses below. They barely moved as we walked through the middle of the herd, to run away would be to use up precious energy.

As we climbed, the track disappeared completely under deep snow. The going became heavy, with James and I taking turns to make tracks. We stopped for a late breakfast, looking across Glen Clunie to the modest hills on the east side, transformed that day to mountain peaks by the snow.

It was considerably colder when we started again, prompting Morag to wear her huge, down-filled 'Everest mittens'. The snow was deeper and we entered the chill world of winter cloud. Snow began to fall more heavily, blown into our faces by a northerly wind. I was leading at the time and was having to strain my eyes. There was no difference between the white at my feet and the white ahead, it was a white-out.

white-out on Morrone,
24/1/10.
JPH

We stopped to fix our position and take a bearing. As there were no landmarks at all, a compass had to be held and we simply walked the way it pointed. There was considerable disorientation, it being impossible to see whether the next step would be up a slope or sharply down into a dip. We stopped again to put on goggles. These protected our eyes from the stinging pellets driven by a strengthening wind, but made no difference to the problems of seeing a way forward in these conditions.

As we approached a height south-west of the main summit, the slopes steepened and I had to check myself on the brink of sudden drops. Another bearing was taken and we turned to face north-east for the final pull to the top. Up on the ridge the snow was frozen hard, making the walking easier.

At the top we found the weather station and telecoms mast, along with their huts. All was plastered with frozen snow on top of plates of ice. The mast looked like a fantastic ice crystal, bristling with horizontal icicles. The wind had scoured a deep trough around the huts, walled in by a two metre 'cornice' with a delicately curled lip. The wind chill was so severe that the small area of exposed cheek under my goggles felt like it was burning. This detached fragment of the Arctic was no place to linger.

We went briskly downhill, compass in hand, sometimes breaking the icy crust and stumbling into deep drifts. Apart from one section where we had to pick a safe way along the top of a low crag which dropped into a gully, there were no landmarks, no rocks, nothing bar white.

After about 500 metres of descent, we emerged from under the cold cloud with its swirling pellets of snow and a monochrome Glen Clunie appeared before us. The snow became soft, my leg went deep into a drift and I slid downhill head first on my stomach, my teeth like a miniature snow plough. I sat up, spitting out snow, to find that my antics had provided the most satisfactory amusement for my friends.

Back on my feet, I watched some stags trying to get well away from these strange people descending from the cloud. They lacked their usual speed and grace, sinking up to their bellies in the deep drifts. Morag pointed towards that same patch of mid blue sky in the south and I looked up to see an eagle glide across.

On the river bank again I stopped beside the ice floes to watch a dipper in its smart black and white outfit, perched on a rock with the fast current swirling around.

Further on, I pointed out a flock of siskins, flitting in a synchronised, staccato way from branch to branch in the alders. These tiny yellow jewels would all stop and pose for a fraction of a second, flash off and do it again. It was a day of memorable sights but, for me, none better than the siskins.

The end was as the beginning, in the comfy chairs by the old stone hearth in the Fife Arms, where we drank tea in the glowing warmth of the log fire.

Tea in the Fife Arms.

13/2/10

Creag nan Gabhar

Winter at its very best

The freezing temperatures and snowstorms continued into February but a window of opportunity opened on Saturday 13th. The Mountain Weather Information Service indicated high pressure, negligible wind and temperatures only two or three degrees below zero. The downside was the predicted blanket of low cloud, white-out conditions in the snow showers and certainly no views from the Munro tops. As the roads looked like being ice and snow free, unusual for that winter, we decided that, on balance, we had the chance of a reasonable day.

James asked me what I had in mind and smiled when I traced a modest route to Loch Callater and back via the Corbett of Creag nan Gabhar. I reasoned that this would give us a better chance of being under the cloud base than if we climbed to Munro height. "Extraordinary," he declared, "I was going to suggest exactly the same myself!"

The snow cap of Lochnagar was radiant as we drove up the road to Braemar in the early morning, teasing us with the prospect of a better day than forecast.

We were early at Auchallater Farm for our rendezvous with Morag but she arrived one minute after us and five minutes after that we were striding up Glen Callater. The ground was frozen iron hard and the snow on the track was compacted to ice, which slowed our pace. We were in no hurry, however, our walk being only 10 kilometres and having the whole day before us.

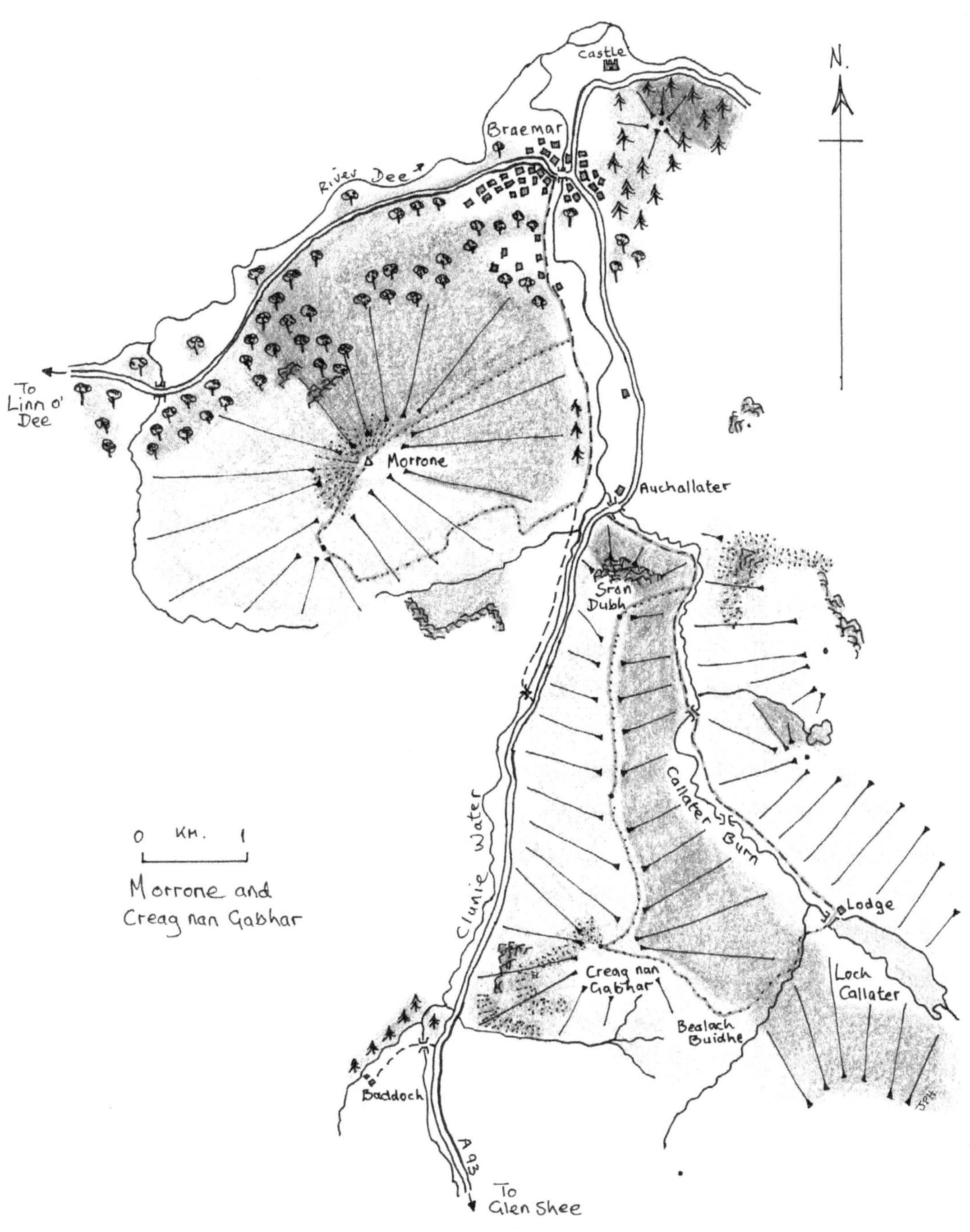
Castle
N.
Braemar
River Dee
To
Linn o'
Dee
Morrone
Auchallater
Sron
Dubh
Callater Burn
Clunie Water
0 KM. 1
Morrone and
Creag nan Gabhar
Lodge
Creag nan
Gabhar
Loch
Callater
Bealach
Buidhe
Baddoch
A93
To
Glen Shee

Morag pointed to the steep, snow-covered, east side of the glen and there at the top was a herd of red deer. They moved over the snow with ease and not one of these graceful beasts floundered in a drift, so it must have been frozen solid up there. Aware of us below, they filed to the skyline, silhouetted in a long, evenly spaced line against the bright morning sun.

As the track climbed, walking became easier because the previous night's snow lay fresh over every surface as a 10 centimetre blanket of powder. Not having to watch where I placed each step, I was free to enjoy my surroundings. The Callater Burn, glacial and crystal clear, swirled around a multitude of large boulders, all plastered with plates of ice. The river had cut through deep banks of snow, revealing clear layers which marked successive Cairngorm blizzards.

Climbing over large drifts, we came to Lochcallater Lodge. The windows of the bothy were running with condensation so I suggested that we would be best not tramping inside as there may be walkers sleeping late. Instead, we sat on an old bench against the wall of the lodge, facing south-east towards the loch.

It was silent and achingly beautiful. Four trees, every leaf gone, made a fine pattern of black branches against the spreading deep blue of the sky and the blue-tinged white of the snows. The loch, iced over, had a surface of drifts in gently rounded, frozen waves. Pale cloud lay above the heights of the Mounth, a strip of silver light, too strong to look at directly, marking the morning sun. It was a place to linger.

Our breakfasts eaten and steaming mugs of tea drunk, we explored the shores of the loch, finding the place where the Callater Burn bubbled up under pressure from beneath the thick crust of ice. We walked down the banks of the burn, already fast and powerful, watching the light flash from fantastically shaped icicles which grew down to the water surface. Two dippers, dapper in their black and white, bounced from rock to rock, stopping to bob up and down for us.

Crossing the bridge, we began the steady climb to the Bealach Buidhe, stopping often to look down at the frozen loch and the pristine white hills above. Here we disturbed the first of many mountain hares. Their white coats made them difficult to see against the snowfields unless they ran.

We had seen and heard red grouse since the start of the walk, mostly in pairs, but up on the bealach were more than I had ever seen in one place. This flock was almost indifferent to our slow progress up the long slope, merely trotting to one side to create the required minimum separation.

I had no desire to hurry and neither had my two companions. It was a rare treat to be able to truly savour the day. We stopped on a broad, south-facing slope of soft, powdery snow to have our lunch. The sun shone on us through a large window in the high, white cloud. Much of the sky to the west and east was now blue. I ate slowly, enjoying my peanut butter and honey pieces. Morag produced a pork pie from her characteristically well-stocked lunch box and James eyed it, licking his lips. "That's an awfully fine smell," he said, adding, "do you not like them?" I replied that my ageing digestion could no longer cope with such things. These days they seem to reconstitute themselves in my stomach and I can feel the pork pie for two or three days after making the mistake of eating one.

Warming my hands on a mug of tea, I looked south to Carn an Tuirc, the nearest Munro. Hillwalkers moving slowly up a snowfield were four tiny black specks. I watched them disappear into the cloud that covered the highest summits down to about 900 metres. I was glad that we had chosen a Corbett rather than a Munro and had been rewarded with a clear and sunny day.

We were reluctant to pack up and leave that perfect lunch spot but the prospect of a panoramic ridge walk made us shoulder the rucksacks again. The sun warmed my back as I kicked steps into the firm crust of snow that lay on the steepest slope of the day. The views from the summit cairn were wonderful. We picked out the deep glens of Quoich, Derry and the Lairig Ghru to the north, the high plateau blanketed in thick cloud. To the west were the crests of a succession of white ridges leading to the wilderness around the upper Feshie and the Geldie Burn. To the south the corries and crags clustered around The Cairnwell were black against the snowfields. Best of all was the Mounth to the east, completely cloud free and radiating white light in the low afternoon sun.

The remainder of the walk was slow, following the crest of the ridge, heading north for Sron Dubh, the black nose, overlooking Glen Clunie. We stopped often to look around and soak in this best of winter days, our long shadows black on the snow.

The day ended in the Fife Arms, with mugs of tea and shortbread. We sat by the crackling fire, dreaming of mountain days.

20/3/10

Glas Tulaichean and Carn an Righ

To the Hill of the King on the last day of winter

James and I arrived early at the turreted Dalmunzie Hotel so we ordered morning tea as the guests came sleepily down the wide staircase for breakfast. Our tea came in an old brass pot which stood on spindly legs and had a spout like a serpent about to strike. Morag turned up with a chest infection. "The day will either cure it or prove fatal," I suggested.

We walked into Glen Lochsie under a blue sky, the sun already warm on our backs. The previous week had seen the first change in the weather since winter began. Atlantic air had swept over the Highlands melting all the snow on the lower slopes and in the glens. It may have been winter's last morning according to the calendar, but it felt like long awaited spring.

We found the track bed of the old railway that used to convey shooting parties to the upper glen and made fast progress. Early primroses, relics of the ancient oak wood that would have grown here, flowered in ground just released from its cold winter blanket.

N.
From Inverey
Creag an Fhuathais
Carn Bhac
Altanour
An Socach
Beinn Iutharn Mhor
Loch nan Eun
Carn an Righ
Carn a Gheoidh
Glas Tulaichean
Glenlochsie Lodge
Ben Gulabin
Dalmunzie Hotel
0 KM. 1
Carn Bhac & Beinn Iutharn Mhor.
Glas Tulaichean & Carn an Righ.

Glenlochsie Lodge was sad, its roof timbers sagging, its windows unglazed and a gaping hole where the front door had been. It was the last building we were to see until we returned to the hotel many hours later.

We climbed steeply up onto the long southern spur of Glas Tulaichean and were soon trudging across snowfields. The reflection of light was dazzling and I wished that I had packed my sunglasses.

At 800 metres or so we stopped for a mug of tea and to look at the surrounding hills. Four young men, in widely spaced Indian file, gave us a wave as they moved fast towards the summit. Break over, we followed their tracks, stepping in their footprints in the soft snow to save energy. It was not a day for haste, however, and we stopped to take photographs of Beinn a' Ghlo to the west, a snow-capped range of mountains in itself. Morag and I talked to James about our last time on that mountain, when all was icy, still and crystal clear.

At the top, we talked to the young men. One said that he was from Derby, he was cold and shivering. The party leader was also English. He told us that he was a member of the local mountain rescue team.

I led the way on a northerly line down from the summit, this being gentler and, therefore, less at risk of an avalanche. We parted company from the four men before the

slope levelled out as they were to practice ice axe arrest. These were the last people we were to see until evening when we got back to the cars.

After crossing the infant Allt à Ghlinne Mhoir, I led the way west over snowfields covering a path which was marked on the map. It was heavy going breaking a trail in the deep snow, sometimes pitching forward as my leg plunged suddenly to thigh level. Exhausted, we stopped to eat lunch, looking south across the glen to the long white blade of Glas Tulaichean.

The climb up to Carn an Righ was steep. The wind had scoured away the snow at about 900 metres, revealing the mountain's cap of quartzite, broken by frost into large angular blocks. We picked a way across these, reached the summit plateau and walked to the cairn. It was shaped like a large chair. Morag flopped down onto its seat, her elbows resting on the massive stone arms. "If this is the hill of the king," I remarked, "you are the queen, sitting in state on your throne." The "raark, raark" of a raven broke the silence and the graceful bird floated up from below, wings stiff, primary feathers tilted upwards, riding a thermal current. Ravens have links with royalty and I wondered whether this one was one of a long line from the ravens who saw Malcolm, King of the Picts, rest beneath this mountain on his way from his palace at Blair Atholl to his hunting ground at Braemar.

James perched on one of the arms of the throne while I walked slowly around the cairn, stopping at each point of the compass to look at the wild land around. This mountain is a truly magnificent viewpoint. To the north is the gash of the Lairig Ghru, the dark pyramid of the Devil's Point growing from its western wall. Beyond, a glittering blanket of snow covered the high Cairngorms. Further west, pale grey streaks curving up into dark grey cloud marked snow showers. I watched as they moved over the hills and down into the glens, their lowest parts moving more slowly, seemingly dragging along the ground. The icefields of Beinn a' Ghlo sparkled, their brightness all the more startling against the dark smear which marked a snow shower, passing over the range from the north. An ominous dark snow cloud was racing towards us from the north-west, it was time to go.

The snow rattled off our backs but soon passed, leaving only a scatter of fine white cumulus clouds moving steadily across the cold blue sky. Three ptarmigan sprang up from the quartzite blocks, each with the first dark streaks of spring showing in their white plumage. They showed no fear of us, trotting along at our feet for a few minutes before veering away on some business of their own.

Back down into Gleann Mor, we carefully retraced our steps across the soft snow, heading for the bealach between Glas Tulaichean's north ridge and the hill marked 858 metres to the south of Loch nan Eun. On the last slope before the bealach was a pair of mountain hares, both pure white apart from the black tips of their ears. Like the ptarmigan, they showed little fear of this awkward and slow biped as he laboured across the snowfield.

We stopped in Glas Choire Bheag for afternoon tea, our way back beneath Creag Dallaig's cliffs clear before us. On our feet again, we had a tricky descent from the corrie, listening for the roaring of water beneath the snow and avoiding potentially dangerous snow bridges.

On the floor of Gleann Taitneach, we had to cross the river, which was swollen with melt water. Even using big boulders as stepping stones, the water swirled to just below my knee and I was glad of my gaiters.

It was a long walk down the glen, with flooding tributaries to wade across. The steep west-facing slopes and crags were bathed in a golden late afternoon light, enriching the greys, silvers, tans and browns of the hillsides. Back at the cars, James declared, "It's a good thing that you are driving as my legs are worn down to stumps." We had walked for nine and a half hours.

The inn at Spittal[6] of Glenshee provided a welcome respite before our respective journeys home. It had a relaxed atmosphere, with tired skiers and walkers sprawled on comfy sofas in front of the roaring fire. Over a good meal we discussed the day, agreeing that the gods of winter had smiled on us.

6 Spittal is an old word for a refuge or shelter for travellers and there has been one here for many centuries, providing rest and protection from hazards such as blizzards, caterans and wolves.

7/4/10

Beinn a' Chaorainn

An Easter walk to the hill of the rowan

Morag and I cycled from the Linn o' Dee on a perfect morning. There was not a scrap of cloud, there was no wind and the snow-covered mountains were sharp in the clear, cold air.

Just before the bridge over the Lui Water a deep snowdrift blocked the track. We pushed our bikes over it but soon had to dismount to cross another. Morag suggested that the bikes may have been a mistake but I was full of optimism. Once over the bridge, the track was clear to Derry Lodge.

We left our bikes there and took the eastern path through the old pines. Each stream we crossed was an adventure, so swollen were they with meltwater. Worse by far were the snowdrifts, which just bore our weight until one of us plunged a leg down through soft snow. This happened many times, making progress slow.

The scenery grew more grand as we walked into the upper glen. Derry Cairngorm was a perfect dome of snow, flashing in the sun. Its east corrie had a complete cornice around the rim and the smooth white of its bowl was broken by the debris of a large avalanche.

We stood below the corrie to plan our approach to Beinn a' Chaorainn, the hill of the rowan, our objective for the day. The most straightforward way was to follow the line

N.
from Loch Morlich
P. Ski Centre
Derry Cairngorm 11/5/8
Carn a' Mhaim 23/12/8
Beinn Bhreac 12/12/9
Beinn a' Chaorainn 7/4/10
Devil's Point 3/5/10
Beinn Mheadhoin 11/9/10
0 km. 1
The central Cairngorms.
Ptarmigan Restaurant
Cairn Gorm
Loch Avon
Beinn Mheadhoin
Shelter Stone
Beinn a' Chaorainn
Loch Etchachan
Hut
Ben Macdui
Lairig Ghru
Derry Cairngorm
Cairn Toul
Beinn Bhreac
Glen Derry
Corrour Bothy
The Devil's Point
Carn a' Mhaim
Derry Lodge
From Linn of Dee
JPH

of the path due north to the Lairig an Laoigh then turn to go north-east and attack the steep slopes. These were plastered with a considerable thickness of the recent wet snow, however, which lay on older, ice-hard snow. This layering is unstable and the possibility of a slab avalanche seemed very real. The eastern side of the glen where we stood was almost as steep but torrents of meltwater had exposed underlying deer grass, bleached pale beige, and patches of brown, brittle heather. These strips of vegetation could be followed to make a broken path to the top of the plateau, crossing only a few snowfields. Interestingly, the route would take us around the rim of the steep gully that James and I avoided last December.

We stopped on an island of newly exposed vegetation to eat a late breakfast and drink tea. The view had opened up into the north-west branch of the glen, walled with its tall black cliffs. The defile leading up to the lip of the corrie which holds Loch Etchachan was filled with deep snow and looked steeper than I remembered. It would have to have been ascended with great care.

We hit our first problem shortly after setting off again. I tried to cross a snowfield but the crust was frozen so hard I could not kick steps. Retreating, we detoured around it, using the islands of vegetation.

Once up on the plateau, things were easier. All was snow-covered apart from two tiny dark patches near the summit of Beinn a' Chaorainn. The snow was frozen hard but had just enough 'give' to make each step secure. There was a deep crack in the snow around the gully's break of slope and the whole of the northern wall seemed poised to slip down. We gave it a wide berth.

The walk to the final slope of our mountain was a memorable experience. All was sparkling snow, unmarked by any hillwalker's boots. It was completely silent, with barely a breath of wind. The sun warmed our backs and cast our shadows in front. To the left were the black cliffs, their couloirs choked with snow, of Derry Cairngorm and Ben Macdui. Beyond was the rim of the Garbh Coire, eaten into the sides of Braeriach. Above the granite crags were the snow-covered tops, over 4,000 feet high, and above again a perfect blue sky.

Shortly after beginning to climb the slope leading to the summit I stopped to look at a line of tracks made by a fox. It had crossed the plateau and the direction suggested that it was making for Glen Derry. I was impressed as these were the first tracks of any description I had seen up there and wondered why it had felt the need to cross these icy mountains. I remembered a similar line of fox tracks along the snowy crest of Beinn a' Bheithir, why do they follow these highest routes of all?

It was a hard slog up to the top and I was more than once grateful for the perfect snow conditions. An icy surface would have required crampons and ice axe and wading through softer snow would have been exhausting.

Near the top a powerful north-west wind had carved deep troughs in the snow with frozen waves up to a metre high. The convex sides of the waves sparkled so brightly that I was dazzled. The steep, concave sides were in blue shadow.

There was a magical transformation on the summit. I stepped off the snow and was suddenly in a three dimensional world of startling texture and colour. Rounded pink granite boulders made a perfect rock garden. Growing on the boulders and in the granite grit was soft, feathery, sage-coloured reindeer moss, lime green dwarf juniper and the densely packed stars of dwarf heather. I trod carefully so as not to damage any of these plants, conscious of their heroic struggle on top of this Cairngorm mountain.

The north side of the tall cairn was thick with ice but the granite on the south and west sides was dry in the sun. I found a flat surface for a seat and leaned back on the warm boulders. Morag arrived, wide-eyed over the views, particularly to the south-west towards Ben Macdui. We ate a leisurely lunch there, in no hurry to leave on such an unusually fine day.

The sun was in the west on our return journey, changing the pattern of light on the snow. The crags cast long, dark blue shadows. The sky became ice blue, with a band of yellow along the western horizon.

The old forest of Derry was still and quiet, the ancient fallen pines sad in the gloaming.

Our bikes were where we had left them at the lodge and it felt good as we set off to have the weight off my legs.

We were back at the Linn o' Dee exactly nine hours after setting off, we had not seen a fellow human being all day. I was weary but full of the peace of the day.

3/5/10

Bod an Deamhain

The Devil's Point

Our bank holiday plan was to climb The Devil's Point, the name being a Victorian euphemistic translation of Bod an Deamhain, the demon's penis. James was in high spirits as we drove through Braemar, having just accepted an early retirement package and knowing that his Antarctic dream could now become a reality.

There were four hinds by the road just past Inverey, dark brown at this time of year, survivors of a harsh winter that had killed unprecedented numbers of red deer.

As there was no sign of Morag in the Linn o' Dee car park, we took our time getting ready for the walk. A car appeared, its wheels throwing up gravel; it was our friend, last minute and in a flap. She had been slowed by a white-out around the ski centre at Glen Shee and she was talking fast, putting on her boots, sipping coffee and eating breakfast, all at the same time. Tissues fell from her pockets like snow. Off we cycled, Morag's breakfast lying forgotten on the roof of her car.

We sped down the track and bumped onto the bridge over the Lui Water. Morag was going fast when she turned round to adjust her mudguard, her wheel slipped off the wooden plank and she crashed to the ground in spectacular fashion, the momentum carrying her and the bike to the end of the bridge. I was relieved when she stood up, dusted herself down and began to straighten the handlebars. She was down but not out.

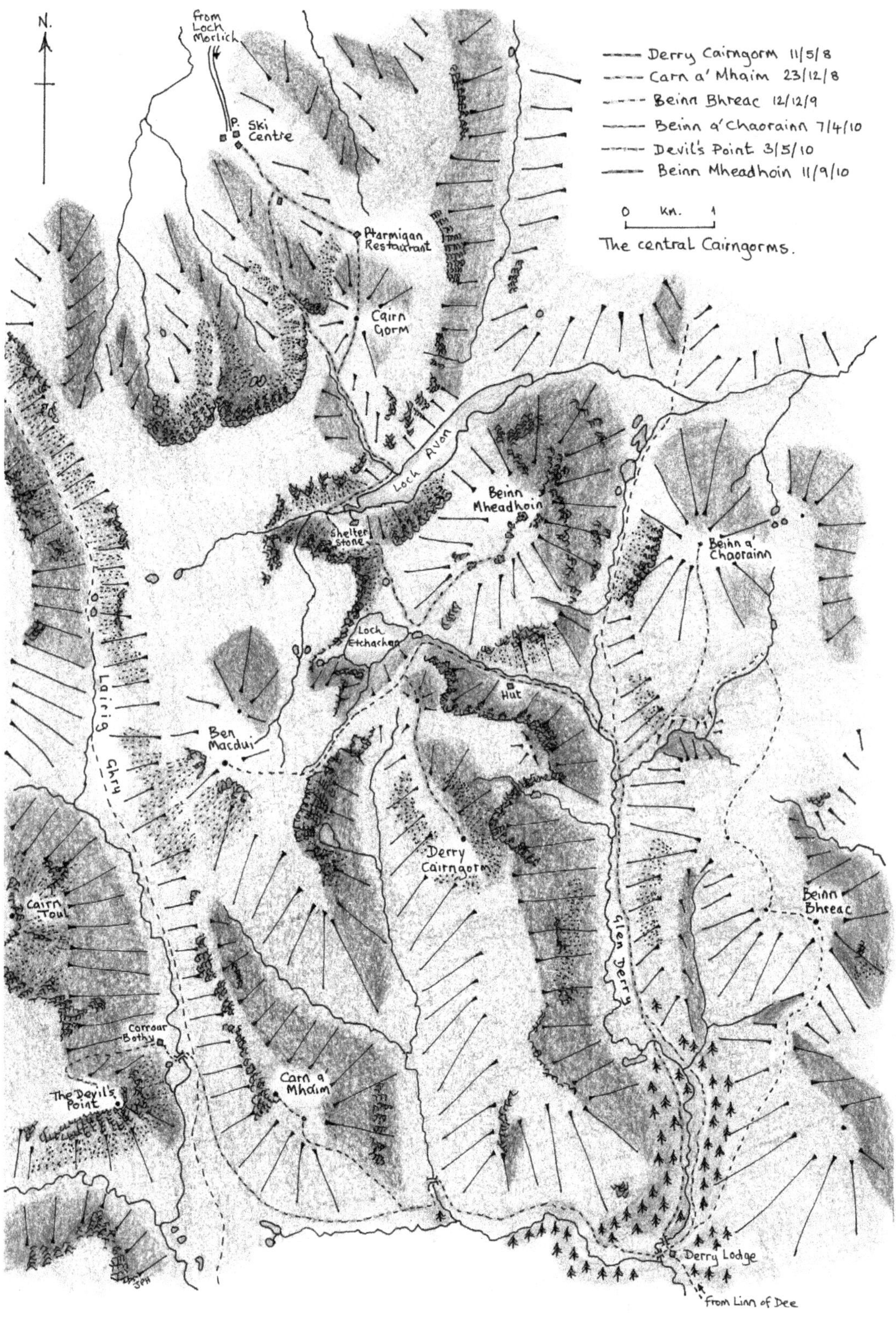
N.
From Loch Morlich
P. Ski Centre
Ptarmigan Restaurant
Cairn Gorm
Loch Avon
Shelter Stone
Beinn Mheadhoin
Beinn a' Chaorainn
Loch Etchachan
Hut
Lairig Ghru
Ben Macdui
Derry Cairngorm
Cairn Toul
Glen Derry
Beinn Bhreac
Corrour Bothy
The Devil's Point
Carn a' Mhaim
Derry Lodge
From Linn of Dee
Derry Cairngorm 11/5/8
Carn a' Mhaim 23/12/8
Beinn Bhreac 12/12/9
Beinn a' Chaorainn 7/4/10
Devil's Point 3/5/10
Beinn Mheadhoin 11/9/10
0 km. 1
The central Cairngorms.

The bikes were left at Derry Lodge and we followed a path through the mature Scots pines, snow on the high mountain tops generating brilliant light in the morning sun. Two skeins of geese high overhead flew steadily, pacing themselves at the beginning of their long journey to Iceland. Only birds were in the northern sky that morning, aeroplanes being grounded again to avoid the plume of ash streaming south from an Icelandic volcano.

The spectacle of the Lairig Ghru gradually unfolded as the path turned north. The west side of this deep, ice-cut trench through the Cairngorm plateau was illuminated by the strong May sun. Long streaks of snow followed the bottom of gullies running down from the white capped summits to end on the river flats by the Dee.

The river is joined by the Geusachan Burn, which flows from the glen of the same name, a tributary of the Lairig Ghru. Glen Geusachan, the glen of the little pine wood, is bare and lonely today. I stopped to look at its 1,000 foot walls of rock and listened to two curlews making their sad call.

The Devil's Point dominated everything, a steep and imposing pyramid of a mountain, black, then grey, then silver as the light changed from threatening, as snow-filled clouds hurried overhead, to glaring in the full sun. Beyond, a curved ridge led to the summit snowfields of Cairn Toul and Sgor an Lochain Uaine. Carn a' Mhaim towered above the path, wearing a dusting of fresh snow like icing sugar.

We came to an elegant little steel footbridge over the crystal clear Dee, on the other side of which was Corrour Bothy. It was dark inside after the bright sun, the single wood panelled room reeking of smoke. We ate a late breakfast there in the company of a lone walker who had camped overnight in temperatures below freezing. A notice instructed, 'Do not leave any foodstuffs, the mice have been getting worse'.

Behind the bothy is a steep path leading to the bealach between The Devil's Point and Cairn Toul. We kicked steps where snowfields blocked the way ahead.

On the plateau we walked across a desert of granite grit with a sparse scatter of dwarf heather and juniper. Patches of grey lichen looked dead. The angle of slope then increased and we scrambled up a granite boulder field to reach the summit cairn. There can be few finer viewpoints. I looked north into the Lairig Ghru, east beyond Carn a' Mhaim's snows to the high Cairngorms beyond, south into a great wilderness and west across the arctic terrain of Monadh Mor.

We dropped down to a ledge on the south side, perched above a cascade of bare cliffs. Here we were sheltered from the cold north wind. The long drop at our feet made one of the walls of Glen Geusachan, the other being the battlements of Bheinn Bhrotain. Perched high above the glen is the hidden corrie called Coire Cath nam Fionn, here the warrior Fingal and his band had to turn and fight for their lives. The rock platform was a perfect place for lunch. The sun shone and we stretched out our legs, drinking tea and discussing the wide sweep of lonely country before us, with no sign anywhere of a road, track or house. A ptarmigan, white on its wings and back but turning brown and grey, came to pose on a rock. Dark cloud shadows moved over the bright snowfields.

We lingered as long as we could but it is a long way back and all too soon we were up on the summit again. James took a photograph of the Lairig Ghru; seconds later a wall of white and dark grey began to roll down it towards us. We hurried down to the bealach but were caught by a fierce icy blast and stinging pellets of snow. This harried us down to Corrour.

The battering stopped as we arrived back at the bothy and we watched as the curtains of snow raced off to the south. The sun came out and illuminated Corrour bothy's luxury extension, the long drop. A steep flight of stone steps leads up to a little door and a throne fit for Fingal himself. I would be tempted to leave the door open and make the most of this loo with a view.

The walk out seemed longer but the scenery was beautiful and I was in the best company. We were glad of our bikes for the last stretch back to the cars, where Morag was reunited with her breakfast.

19/6/10

Beinn Dubhchraig, Ben Oss, Ben Lui and Beinn a' Chleibh

A dance on Beinn a' Chleibh

I left Aberdeen in the rush hour with high hopes for a fine walk the next day. Within ten minutes of the city boundary the traffic had disappeared and I was only to meet the occasional vehicle on my journey west. It was a golden evening of soft light and long, deep shadows.

The hostel at Tyndrum had been booked for the Jolly Boys. I entered to the shouts of welcome and warm smiles of my friends. There was a range of alcoholic beverages in industrial quantities, they had come prepared to party.

When the tables in the common room were solid with empty bottles, Cath quietened the banter and laughter to announce that potential walk leaders would each make a pitch. Nick began, describing a walk from Dalrigh in Strathfillan to climb Beinn Dubhchraig, Ben Oss, Ben Lui and Beinn a' Chleibh, crossing the River Lochy to the end point. The walk would take between 10 and 12 hours, there would be lots of ascent and departure time was to be 7.00 a.m.

Struan followed, "That's madness. That's two walks, not one. My walk will leave at 9.30ish, we'll climb one Munro, the name of which I can't pronounce and we'll be back in time for afternoon tea and scones."

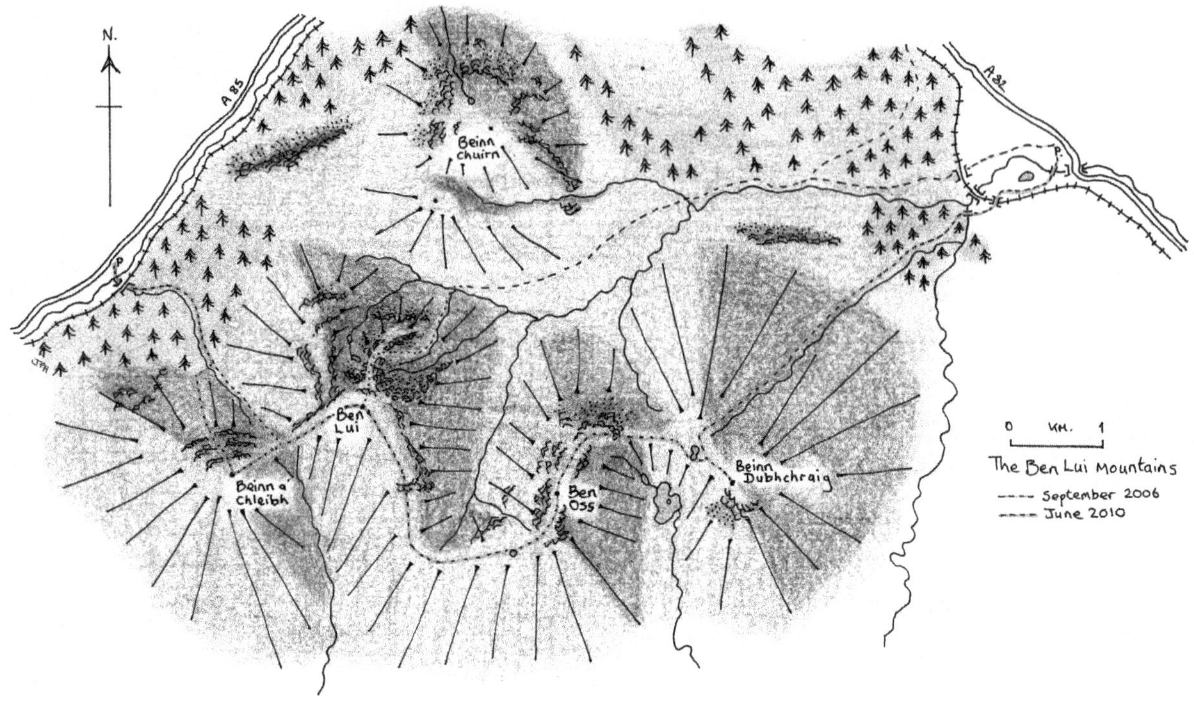

This was followed by a pitch for a low level walk along a stretch of the West Highland Way and one for a walk around Oban which seemed to have a nice lunch as its prime objective. Finally, someone asked Fionn. He was characteristically rebellious, "Get up at eleven; finish the bottles of Buckfast for breakfast; walk to the pub; walk back; vomit; fall asleep and wake up in time to go to the pub with everyone."

Nick only got three takers, Natasha, Morag and me.

I rose early, drove with Nick to the car park by the River Lochy and ran him back to the hostel to pick up the women. We left on schedule.

Nick was learning about mountain leadership and I was happy for him to navigate us across the river and up through the forest of native Scots pine to the open slopes of our first hill. It was warm work. There was to be no stopping until the top was reached and I found the slopes up to the little lochan a hard slog. The prospect of a cup of tea spurred me on. Beinn Dubhchraig's summit was a place to linger on such a perfect summer day. The sky was cloudless and there was a full panorama of the West Highlands. We enjoyed our time there, looking down at the deep blue fresh water of Loch Lomond and the deeper blue salt water of Loch Fyne.

Refreshed and rested, we retraced our steps and walked around the rim of the south-facing corrie which holds Loch Oss. As we scrambled down the steep slopes from the summit ridge a ptarmigan fluttered from just beneath our feet and soared away over the loch, its small white wings held as rigid as a glider's as it skimmed the dark water.

We were impatient with Ben Oss, leaving the path and going for what Nick described as "a full frontal attack." Legs were wobbly when the gradient eased on the top but we were elated when we got to the cairn where a check confirmed that we were well within our tight schedule. We had a second mug of tea on top of this, our second Munro and some lunch to top up our energy reserves. As we ate, we discussed the possibility of following the Allt Coire Laoigh and returning along the banks of the River Cononish, a sensible option for those with tired legs. None, however, were tempted. Natasha said that it would be a challenge for her but if she got to the last Munro she would dance on the summit.

Ben Lui from Ben Oss, 19/6/10.

The next stage was to walk around a wide horseshoe along the watershed between the Allt Coire Laoigh and streams running to the south. The climb up Ben Lui's south ridge was long and arduous on that day of shimmering heat. We stopped half way up for a rest, I was too shattered to take off my rucksack.

On my previous visit to the summit, it had been a grey and grim place in a world of swirling cloud. On this June day, however, there was not a trace of cloud and I swept my gaze from Loch Fyne to Loch Awe and then to Loch Etive. Beyond, sharp and clear, Ben More rose above the Isle of Mull. To the north were range after range of lonely mountains, with Ben Nevis easy to identify by its distinctive profile, head and hunched shoulders above the rest.

As we were sharing the summit on that sunny Saturday with at least a dozen people, we went a little down the south-west ridge to have the last of our hot tea and a second lunch. The prospect from our high seat was beautiful. Natasha said that it made her feel very tiny and insignificant. Once I'd revived a little I stood up to take a photograph of the others. I wanted a record of us on top of 'The Queen of the Highlands' with an unblemished blue sky. Three slim, attractive girls came down towards us and the one with blonde hair offered, in an unknown language, to photograph us all. She was charming and tried a number of shots before she was satisfied. As she took each one we became aware of the impact she was having on Nick, who had to remove his jacket due to a sudden rise in temperature. Morag and Natasha were merciless in teasing him.

Interestingly, as we descended the ridge on our way to Beinn a' Cleibh, we met more slim, toned and pretty girls toiling up to the summit. I stopped to chat to a true beauty with tiny shorts and long pale legs. Nick was silent, but when she moved on he quietly remarked, "What sights we've seen today. I suppose it's only going to be the fittest girls you'd meet up here."

Passing the bealach between Ben Lui and Beinn a' Cleibh, I suggested that we would have to backtrack to it for our descent. Nick insisted, however, that there was a way down the north face of the mountain.

At the summit, we lay on the warm, brittle vegetation. Natasha was weary but elated and remembered her intention to dance on this last mountain top. I offered to partner her but it was a gentle waltz rather than a jig, more suited to our tired legs.

On the northern edge of the summit plateau, we looked down a long, steep slope of bare crags separated by narrow grassy ledges. I asked Nick whether he was quite sure that we could get down it and he replied that this is what he had read. The women, sensibly, headed for the gentler gradient of the west spur, looking for a better route to the bottom. Nick and I began a long descent of the face, picking a way between the crags. There was no room for error. Once reunited on the edge of the forestry, we looked back at what was now revealed as a steep, craggy and challenging mountainside, unlike the straightforward track to the bealach, which could clearly be seen on the left. I congratulated Morag and Natasha on their common sense. At home later, reading the Scottish Mountaineering Club guide, I noted that the north face was described as, 'very steep and craggy, and no attempt should be made to ascend or descend (by it)'.

We followed a narrow path through the trees, waded the River Lochy and were at the car 10 hours and 20 minutes after leaving the last one.

The evening in the pub was everything expected on a Jolly Boys weekend. Some of the younger members had exposed too much skin for too long without sunscreen and were lobster red. It was like sitting next to a radiator. It did not seem to affect their appetite, though, as they had second, third and fourth helpings from the hot buffet.

Back at the hostel, Cath interrupted the chat and laughter to announce that someone had to phone the police as Fionn had not returned. Remembering his 'pitch' of the previous evening, I suggested looking in his room first. I had just taken a couple of steps when, on cue, our mercurial friend appeared at the door, dishevelled and sweat-soaked in his union flag shorts and fell running shoes. "Have I missed the pub?" he asked.

After a brief sleep I was up early and drove back to Aberdeen on a morning of sharp shadow, mirror smooth water and beauty everywhere.

6/7/10 - 8/7/10

An Socach, An Riabhachan, Sgurr na Lapaich, Carn nan Gobhar • Tom a' Choinich, Toll Creagach • Màm Sodhail, Carn Eige, Beinn Fhionnlaidh

The mountains above Loch Mullardoch and Glen Affric

James, Morag and I met at the old hostel in Drumnadrochit. We were given a friendly welcome by Yvan, a French student spending his summer holiday working there. Our fellow guests were young French, German, American and Danish nationals.

The setting of the village is strangely Alpine, with little fields on the valley floor, one with a solitary bull, another with one cow and calf. Beyond, pastureland clothed the steep slopes, with conifer woodland above and, above that, chalet style houses set in high meadows. All was bright in the strong sunlight.

At the nearest inn there was no welcome. We were told that a chef was missing and, anyway, there was no table. At The Fiddlers, we were greeted warmly and were quickly seated. The walls of this café bar were shelved and displayed hundreds of malt whiskies. The venison casserole was delicious.

The next morning was grey and damp. I drove us to the Loch Mullardoch dam; weathered, lichen-covered and not as incongruous as I expected. On the beach we met Carl Lawaerst, wearing wellington boots and a large camouflage jacket. An ancient rusty tractor was attached to an equally ancient motor launch. Mr Lawaerst started the tractor on his first attempt. Moss grew on the launch and there was a notice that anyone being transported by it did so entirely at their own risk. I was in the process of reassuring myself that it should, at a pinch, hold the three of us when a party of three from Northumberland hurried down from the dam. All seven people clambered aboard and our skipper steered the boat away from the beach. The boat was low in the water and I was relieved that the loch was only moderately choppy.

Mr Lawaerst is Danish. He bought the East Benula estate on the north shore of Loch Mullardoch many years ago but was about to retire as his wife wished to return to Denmark to be near to their grandchildren. He was clearly not entirely happy about this, describing his grandchildren as "very noisy". We would be one of the last parties to be taken up the loch. He told us that demand for his motor launch service used to be greater but he had observed that there have been far fewer people on the hills in recent years.

Cloud covered the tops but it was beginning to clear in places. Mr Lawaerst told stories of shooting deer as we watched a fine stag on the skyline above the north shore and a group of hinds grazing below.

Launching the boat on Loch Mullardoch 6/7/10.

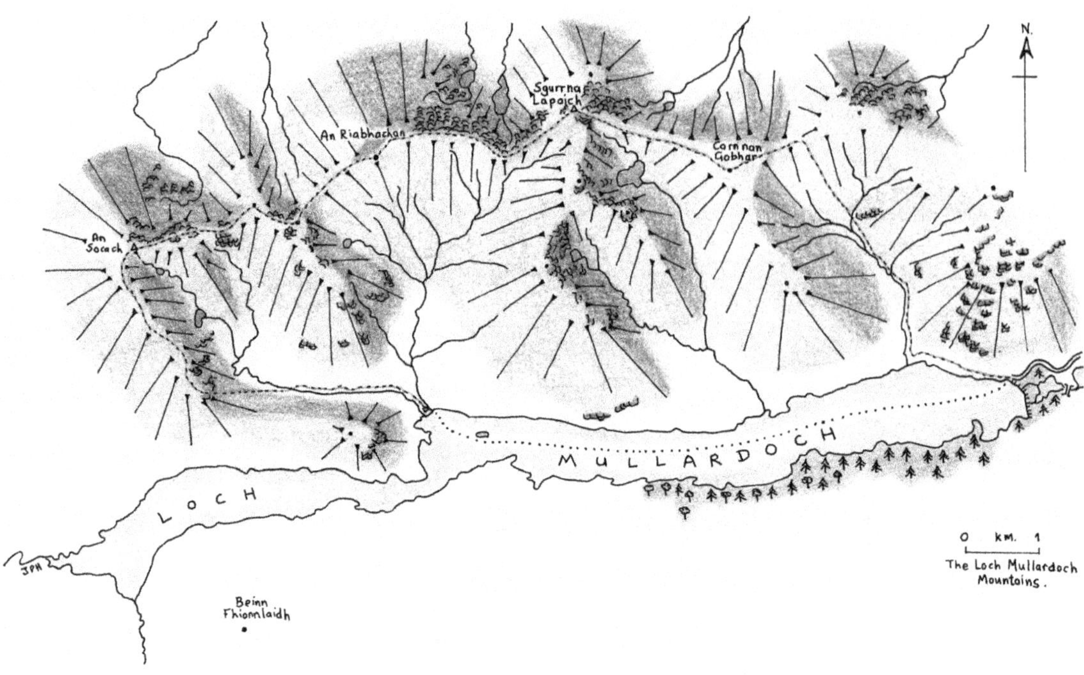

Later, we passed a large flock of wild goats, their long hair patched black, brown, beige, rust, cream and white. Wigeon flew past just above the water, distinctive with their ruddy necks. They were nesting on a small wooded island.

We landed on a little beach in a bay with a solitary and very lonely chalet. James commented on the remoteness of that place and the challenge we now faced in following our route back to the dam. He set off at a fast pace, picking a way across a large peat bog which, like a moat, blocked access to our first mountain. I stopped a few times to look at the black peat hag frogs, thriving in that perfect environment.

Wigeon, Loch Mullardoch.

The three Geordies were well ahead by now and they stayed that way, in sight but eventually more than 30 minutes in front. It was a steep climb up to An Socach's southern ridge and I found it hard. I was glad to stop and look at another frog, pale beige this time, well matched to the colour of the deer grass.

The cloud blew off the ridge as we reached its crest and we could see it curve before us to the summit. Steep slopes dropped to our right, down into a high hanging corrie with a little lochan. The lip of this led down to a second hanging corrie, also with a lochan and this in turn had a rocky lip above the main corrie with the peat bog on its floor. The wind was very strong and blew more cloud over us when we reached the summit cairn. James had arrived at the top before Morag and I, had eaten a sandwich and drunk a mug of hot chocolate, and was now getting cold. We had to eat and drink quickly and then we were off again, descending steep rocks to the bealach.

The climb up to An Riabhachan was a serious effort for me and Morag, too, was feeling the strain. All the cloud had dispersed by the time we reached the summit cairn. We needed a proper break but there was no time for lengthy stops on such a long and demanding mountain walk. I ate two of Morag's glucose tablets as we set off along An Riabhachan's narrow north-east ridge.

The ridge led to the rocky edge of a steep headwall. Its crags tumbled down to Coire Gnada, a corrie with two lochans, Loch Beag and Loch Mor. We scrambled down rock outcrops to a bealach, our third and highest mountain a massive feature ahead.

Willpower alone got me to the top of Sgurr na Lapaich, a fine pyramidal peak with five ridges running down from its summit, separating five deep corries. I interrupted my appreciation of the topography when I saw an ominous wall of dark grey cloud and rain rapidly approaching. It was time to put on waterproofs. I stood up to pull up my trousers and was returned to my sitting position rather roughly by the powerful wind which accompanied the rain. We struggled on from the summit. I was soaked, no waterproofs could cope with such driving rain. "I'm wet to my knickers," wailed Morag. Strangely, at this most extreme moment of the walk, I got into my stride at last and no longer felt that I was struggling to find the necessary energy.

We went down again and up again to Munro number four, Carn nan Gobhar, where the band of rain passed and the wind abated. The most straightforward return was now down to the bealach and then down into Coire an t-Sith. I suggested that we could climb Creag Dubh beyond the bealach as an extra but my companions suspected, quite rightly, that this was merely a joke.

The weather was now clear and it grew warmer as we descended into the corrie. It was heavy work until we reached the path and then we managed a remarkably good pace back to the dam considering what we had done that day.

We got back to the hostel at 8.00 p.m. While the others showered, I asked Yvan where the drying room was. Communication stalled but he led me to an outhouse with one very large and one standard sized tumble drier. He gave me an old-fashioned washing basket and said that he would deal with all our wet gear. I took him at his word and presented him with a sodden mountain of clothing.

When all were presentable we tried that inn again and again were given a cold reception, being informed that there would be no table until 9.30, even though there were a number of tables without reservation signs. Back at The Fiddlers, I was restored to good humour by tomato and lentil soup and a large plate of lamb and barley casserole.

We rounded off that full day by squashing onto one of the sofas in the hostel's sitting room and toasting in front of the glowing coal fire. We drank tea as our boots steamed and were in bed by 10.30.

Early next morning, I tracked down our dried clothing. Too late, Yvan had discovered a GPS device and an O.S. map in James's jacket but both appeared to have survived their ordeal. Morag remarked that most of the labels said 'do not tumble dry'. I did not care, being pleased that my boots and clothing were all bone dry and ready for another day.

Our destination was wooded Glen Affric. The sun was shining from a blue sky and at every bend in the road there was the sort of lovely vista that would set a landscape painter's pulse racing. We parked on the shore of Loch Beinn á Mheadhoin and walked up a sylvan side glen. When the track turned west we could see our first mountain, Tom á Choinich, ahead. It looked spectacular, with an abrupt, craggy end to its south-east ridge. "We're not going to climb up there, are we?" asked Morag. I assured her that the guide book advised following the path into the south-east corrie and from its floor a clear path led up onto the ridge, avoiding the crags. Not long after, we were scrambling up the crags, having missed the path into the corrie.

Determined to set a gentler pace than the previous day, we stopped half way up at a sun trap in the rocks. Here we had a proper rest, a snack and mugs of tea. With only two Munros to climb that day, the pressure was off. The mountain views to the south and west from our sheltered cove were impressive. Nearer at hand, the rock of these rugged crags had the dark and pale bands and swirling curves so characteristic of the gneiss of the North-west Highlands.

Once on top of the crags, we caught the wind on the ridge. We had decided on a clockwise circuit with this in mind, so that the wind would mostly be on our backs. The ridge was narrow, rocky and scalloped, an elegant curve up to the summit. Fifty metres along it, the wind picked up seriously and the walk suddenly became challenging. We touched the summit cairn and dropped down the east ridge, in the lee of the gale. Much of

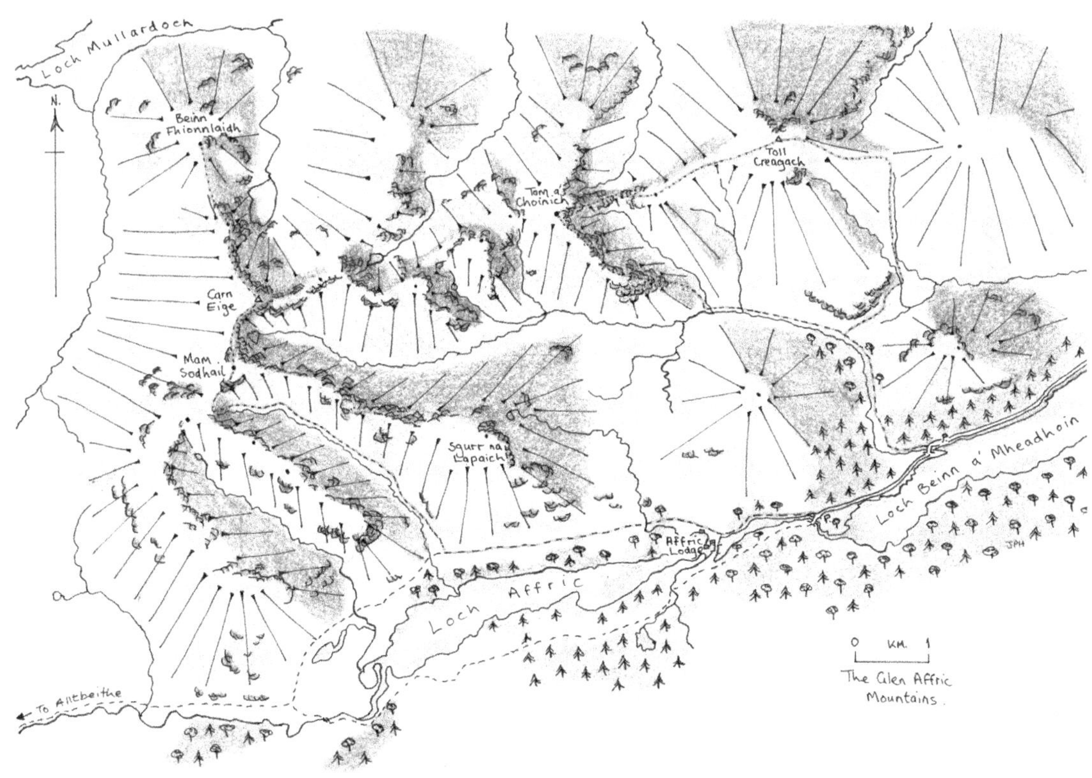

the afternoon that followed was like April, the sun was bright and the air clear and sharp. The strong, gusty wind brought showers which rolled over quickly and cloud shadows raced over the hillsides.

We found shelter in a hollow ringed by massive boulders, each with convoluted swirls of banded minerals. Here we ate lunch while watching two ravens show off their flying skills, using the wild wind to achieve incredible speeds.

Our second Munro, Toll Creagach, was a complete contrast to the first, being a big lump. It is made of different rock, more like quartzite, which had been eroded and weathered to create a more rounded profile than that of Tom á Choinich. It was also easier to climb as the wind did a good job of blowing us up to the top.

My initial plan had been to walk off along the crest of the south ridge but, bearing in mind the strong wind, I suggested going down the east ridge to the bealach and then dropping down into the lee of the south ridge instead. Steep slopes soon gave way to a gentler gradient and we crossed acres of waving bog cotton. Orange spotted mountain ringlets fluttered above a multitude of different flowers, including a profusion of pink bog orchids and large clumps of pink thrift.

It was warm out of the wind and the showers had been turned off for the day, so we stopped for tea. James lay back and nodded off. I lay back and watched small white clouds racing across a big blue sky. Too soon we had to go. We scrambled down a last steep, rocky slope and at the bottom found a good track. The walk back was delightful, with afternoon sun warming the glades of open woodland.

At The Fiddlers I enjoyed pea and ham soup and lightly smoked salmon on thick chowder with lots of fresh, crisp baguette. The day ended perfectly in the hostel's sitting room where two guitarists accompanied a mix of American country and Irish folk songs.

Early the following day we left the car at the last car park in the glen and followed the road along the north shore of Loch Affric. A fleet of white vans, a JCB, a large crane, other heavy equipment and an army of builders were at Glen Affric Lodge. A new, high fence surrounded the property, built right across the old path along by the loch. The new bridge under construction was already marked 'PRIVATE', as was everything else. A new path had been made for walkers along the outside of the fence, keeping them a safe distance from the lodge and its exclusive grounds. It was all sadly incongruous in this lovely glen.

We were soon past, however, and following a good path high above the loch. Clouds raced above the mountain tops and although there were small patches of blue between them, rain was on the wind. The path beside the Allt Coire Leachavie took us past a series of thundering waterfalls. We stopped beside one for tea and watched two groups of red deer hinds and calves grazing between the crags. There were around 50 of these agile and sure-footed animals. At all times some of the hinds watched us.

There was a zig zag path up the back wall of the corrie. We stopped beside a steep scree of large blocks to watch three adult ptarmigan with eight chicks. A male threw back his head at intervals and made a call like a hollow wooden rattle. They were in summer plumage, mottled grey like the rocks, and only when they fluttered their wings was there a flash of their winter white.

At the crest of the ridge we made our way through the old snow cornice and entered another world, a world of rock, toothed ridges, deep, dark, snow-filled corries and endless sky. In that sky were now large patches of blue, some mountains were brilliantly illuminated, some shadowed under dark cloud. The wind was strong but not too fierce. We walked north, climbing up to the summit of Màm Sodhail (pronounced mam sool).

Just before the summit, built into the ridge itself, was a strange dwelling. The roof had long gone, but the dry-stone walls had been well made. There was a hearth, a chimney and the remains of a fire hook and cast-iron pots. It was built as a bothy by the Ordnance Survey in the 1840s as this was the main triangulation point for the northern Highlands.

It was later used by estate ghillies as a lookout to keep walkers off the mountain and was mentioned by Sir Hugh Munro as something to be avoided.

The surveyors also built the massive hollow cairn which has well-laid cut stones like a small broch. The inside (which may still contain a visitors' log) can only be reached by climbing the walls. This was not for us though as, our energy blown, we sat at its foot and considered turning back. Tantalisingly, the fine pyramid of Beinn Fhionnlaidh did not look impossibly far off and Carn Eige looked so near…

On the bealach the wind became fierce and sleet began to rattle on our hoods. We were glad to hunker down in Carn Eige's shelter cairn where we ate as we watched the sleet blowing horizontally against a backdrop of black cloud. Fed up with peanut butter and honey, I ate corned beef sandwiches and salted peanuts which provided a surprisingly good alternative. Soaked and even more blown than on the last mountain, we were preparing to turn back when it cleared again. Sunshine illuminated Beinn Fhionnlaidh, one of the most inaccessible of all the Munros, and its steep cone looked quite near…

The cairn on Màm Sodhail, looking towards Beinn Fhionnlaidh, 8/7/10.

We began to scramble down the north ridge, looking into a substantial corrie, the floor of which holds a large, dark lochan. I was reaching for my camera when someone, somewhere, must have pressed a switch, immediately turning on howling wind and driving rain. I was soaked to my underwear by the time I got to the top of Beinn Fhionnlaidh. "I'm getting used to it," said Morag wearily. The someone, somewhere relented when we were up there and it cleared again. We looked down onto Loch Mullardoch and the little bay where the three of us had landed two days earlier. The whole of that walk was before us in a sweeping panorama and it looked big.

The journey back began. Wind, rain and sleet were switched on again and it was hard, hard work. We were re-climbing the two highest mountains west and north of the Great Glen. Collapsed in the shelter cairn on Carn Eige, I was too tired to eat. I swallowed a little water and two of Morag's glucose tablets, then it was back up to Màm Sodhail through the wind, rain and sleet.

On Màm Sodhail it cleared again and, tired as we were, we stood and stared at this beautiful mountain country. The ridge to Tom a' Choinich was spectacular against the rain-washed north-eastern sky and we agreed to return and enjoy scrambling over each of its many pinnacles.

Back down in Coire Leachavie, we stopped by a twin waterfall to eat. I watched some charming meadow pipits as I drank the last of my tea. They cocked their heads to look at us and I wondered what they were thinking about these strange creatures sprawled by the side of the booming water.

Then it was down again to sheltered Glen Affric with the warm sun on our backs. We walked through pools of sunlight and deep shadow. A cloud dropped a shower over the loch, making a perfect rainbow which marked the last of the rain. Our return was through a temperate rainforest dominated by an open canopy of old pines. It teemed with life: wild roses, ferns, birch, alder, rowan, grasses, and wild flowers. Eleven hours after leaving it, we were back at the car.

Well-fed after a visit to The Fiddlers, we returned to the hostel where three young men, two French and one Danish, played guitars and sang in English. This seemed to suit the international company and soon everyone joined in. It was a good end to our trip.

12/8/10

Bennachie

Gordon

In 2009, Gordon MacFarlane received Aberdeen City's Inspirational Adult of the Year Award. He was nominated for being a successful and well-respected teacher at Bridge of Don Academy but there was another consideration, he had been completely blind for many years. He was unfailingly cheerful and positive about his disability and certainly never let it interfere with any aspect of his very full life, which ranged from taking the stage to perform one of his tributes to Johnny Cash to making wedding videos.

When his beloved guide dog, Yulie, began to show signs of age, he began to consider retirement. Talking to him about this, his life and his plans, I asked if there was something special he would like to do. His quick reply took me by surprise, he would love to climb Bennachie. I was even more surprised to hear myself saying that I would take him up.

When my good friend James heard about this he immediately volunteered his services and I was much relieved, this was a two-man job. James took a characteristically military approach, making a reconnaissance of the hill and coming with a rope, which Gordon held. As Yulie was not able to accompany us, James reasoned that the rope would provide some security in lieu of the harness. I asked Gordon to link firmly onto my arm and maintained this arrangement for the rest of the walk.

James and I were Gordon's eyes. We described everything in detail, taking him around every rock in the path and helping him step over the many gullies.

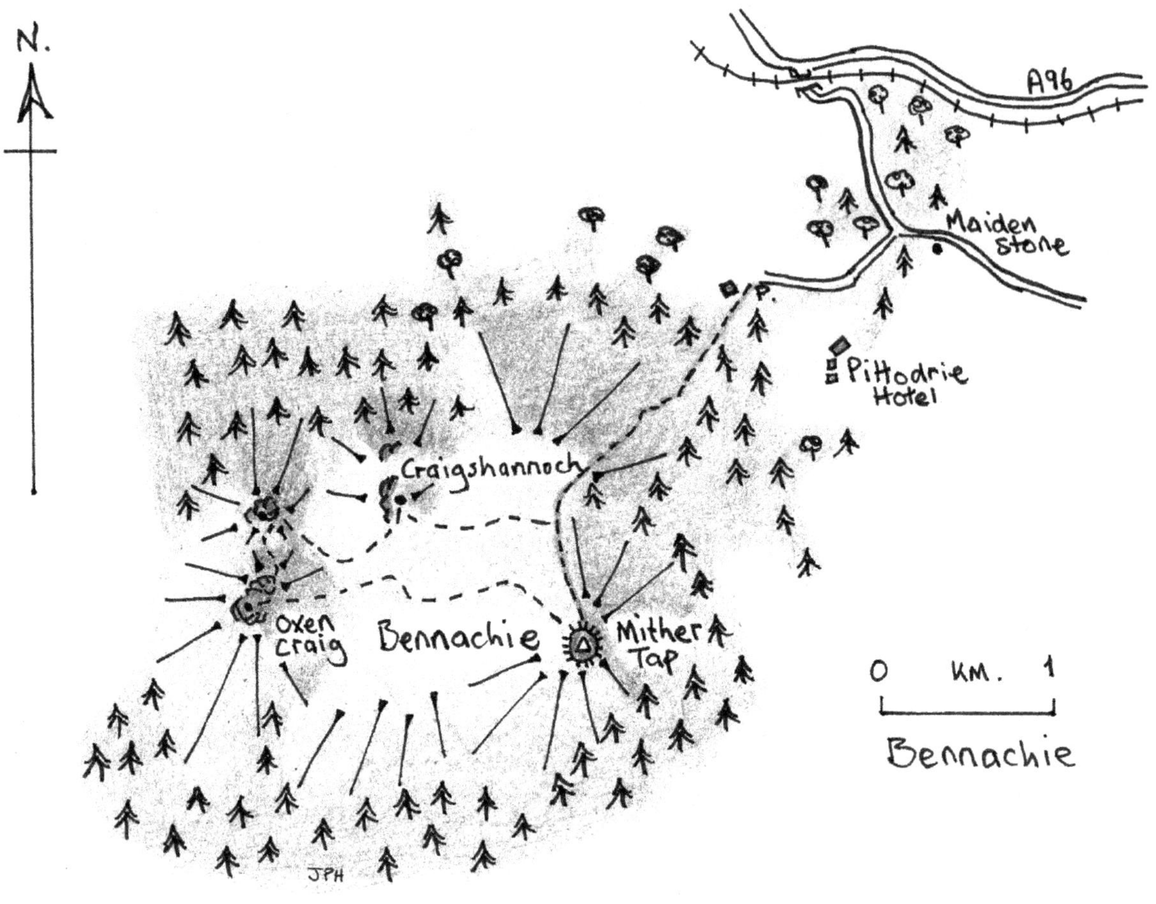

We were a cheery party, laughing at Gordon's awful jokes and worse puns. He had a small video camera attached to his shirt and, at intervals, would stop to film the climb, providing an idiosyncratic commentary.

We took the path from the north-east car park to the Mither Tap, so were sheltered from the strong wind. I knew, however, that we would catch it on the top. Cloud covered the highest reaches, which did not suit Gordon's video. As the ground steepened, the cloud blew away and the summit's dramatic granite tor was revealed. It looked a daunting task to help a blind man get to the top of it but James reassured us that only the very last 15 metres or so were going to be difficult.

The summit is guarded by a massive wall, a relic of what must have been an impressive Iron Age fort. We went through its long, narrow gateway, Gordon feeling the stone walls which are still vertical and over two metres high. Inside the fort the path

Gordon on Bennachie 12/8/10
JPH

twisted steeply up and around the tor, Gordon having to take big steps up the carefully laid granite boulders.

For the last section, he needed both hand and foot holds. We helped him place each one securely and, with a mixture of relief and elation, Gordon stood on the summit. The cloud returned and we were buffeted by the wind but it could not spoil the moment. Photographs were taken and Gordon produced a more sophisticated video camera on which was recorded his triumph.

It was a trickier proposition getting him down that last steep section but Gordon showed absolute confidence when we gave instructions.

We stayed high on the tor in the lee of the wind for a rest, a hot drink and a snack, savouring the successful outcome of our mission. As Gordon and James would both be officially retired four days after our ascent of Bennachie, Gordon asked James about his plans. James replied that he had already booked a trip to Indo-China and was thinking of going to Antarctica in January, adding that he was determined to spend his redundancy money quickly in case he was cheated out of it by premature death. Gordon, interested in Antarctica, asked why polar bears did not eat penguins, answering for us that it's because they can't get the wrappers off. On that note, one of the torrential downpours which had characterised the summer of 2010 fell onto us, soaking us to the skin.

The hot August sun came out as we walked down the path and we steamed dry. When I asked Gordon how he would follow this he replied, "By climbing a Munro of course."

11/9/10

Cairn Gorm and Beinn Mheadhoin

The Shelter Stone

On a fine early autumn evening I drove over the brown and golden hills on the Lecht road, which I had to myself. Little more than an hour later, I was parked outside The Laird's Bothy in Kingussie and was shaking Struan's hand. The little common room filled gradually during the evening until it was loud and warm with the chatter of friends who had shared many a happy weekend.

Plans were made for the next day and then the Jolly Boys got down to the business of unwinding after the working week. Cath reported with a shudder that the showers had clear glass doors. Geraldine pointed out that it was a ladies only room but this was no comfort to her. Struan suggested that she mustn't miss this opportunity to press her naked body provocatively on the glass and that he would carry up some chairs for spectators. "You needn't bother," replied Cath, "I'll be on the baby wipes all weekend." Later, as I fell asleep, I could hear the shouts and laughter of the diehards in the common room below.

Early next morning I looked out of the common room windows onto a gloomy garden saturated by a steady downpour. Inside a very wet sleeping bag in the middle of the lawn, dead to the world, lay Fionn.

I was joined by six bleary-eyed survivors of the night's jollity, including Nick, still working on his mountain leadership and Sophie, a young French woman experiencing the Jolly Boys for the first time, and we drove in two cars to the ski centre on the northern slopes of Cairn Gorm. We walked up a track which followed the raised line of the funicular railway. The rain seemed heavier. A dead ptarmigan lay on the side of the path, its white plumage radiant on that dark morning. At the restaurant a disconsolate Sophie announced, "My waterproof coat is not," adding, "and the rain is running down my skin." I thought of Struan and Ray who, when they were told that it was pouring down, had turned over in their warm beds and gone back to sleep. As we trudged up the straight, well-made path to the equally well-made summit cairn, the rain grew light and the wind blew away much of the dense lower cloud to reveal the sharp curves and sudden cliffs of the northern corries.

Once everyone had gathered at the cairn we set off in a southerly direction, heading for the notch where the Allt Coire Raibeirt leaves its corrie to descend abruptly in a chain of waterfalls to the loch shore far below. We were soon on the path which follows the stream that drains this hanging valley. Ahead was our first glimpse of the blue water of Loch Avon (loch aan), the dark mountains beyond capped by thin swirling cloud. Walking poles had to be stowed as we scrambled down the steep granite ledges. The hours of heavy rain had swollen the stream and its falls thundered and boomed, soaking us with fine spray. At the point where the steep angle of slope eased, we waded across the fast water and followed a rough path through and over large boulders that led down to the beach at the head of the loch.

On the white sands, rucksacks were dropped and everyone lay flat, it had been a relentless start to the walk. The sun was beginning to emerge from the thinning cloud and was shining on the lower reaches of the loch. The water near our resting place was dark blue, with clear, bright turquoise around the shores. Our beach was ringed with soaring crags, a broken crescent of rock rising in dark towers and deep gullies a precipitous 300 metres to the arctic plateau above. Hell's Lum Crag lived up to its name as the last trailing wisps of cloud rushed up it like chimney smoke.

At the foot of a near vertical cliff, part of the north-facing section of the crescent of crags, lay a tumbled pile of huge granite boulders, some estimated to weigh over a thousand tons. This was where I wanted to take our intrepid party. First we had to cross the stream which roared down the side of Hell's Lum Crag and entered the head of the loch. It was more a fast-flowing river, swollen like the waterfalls with the morning's rain. Nick and I picked a wide, stony section and waded quickly across. The others decided to go upstream to find a drier crossing place. A splash, accompanied by a squeal, seemed to be an indication that they were having limited success.

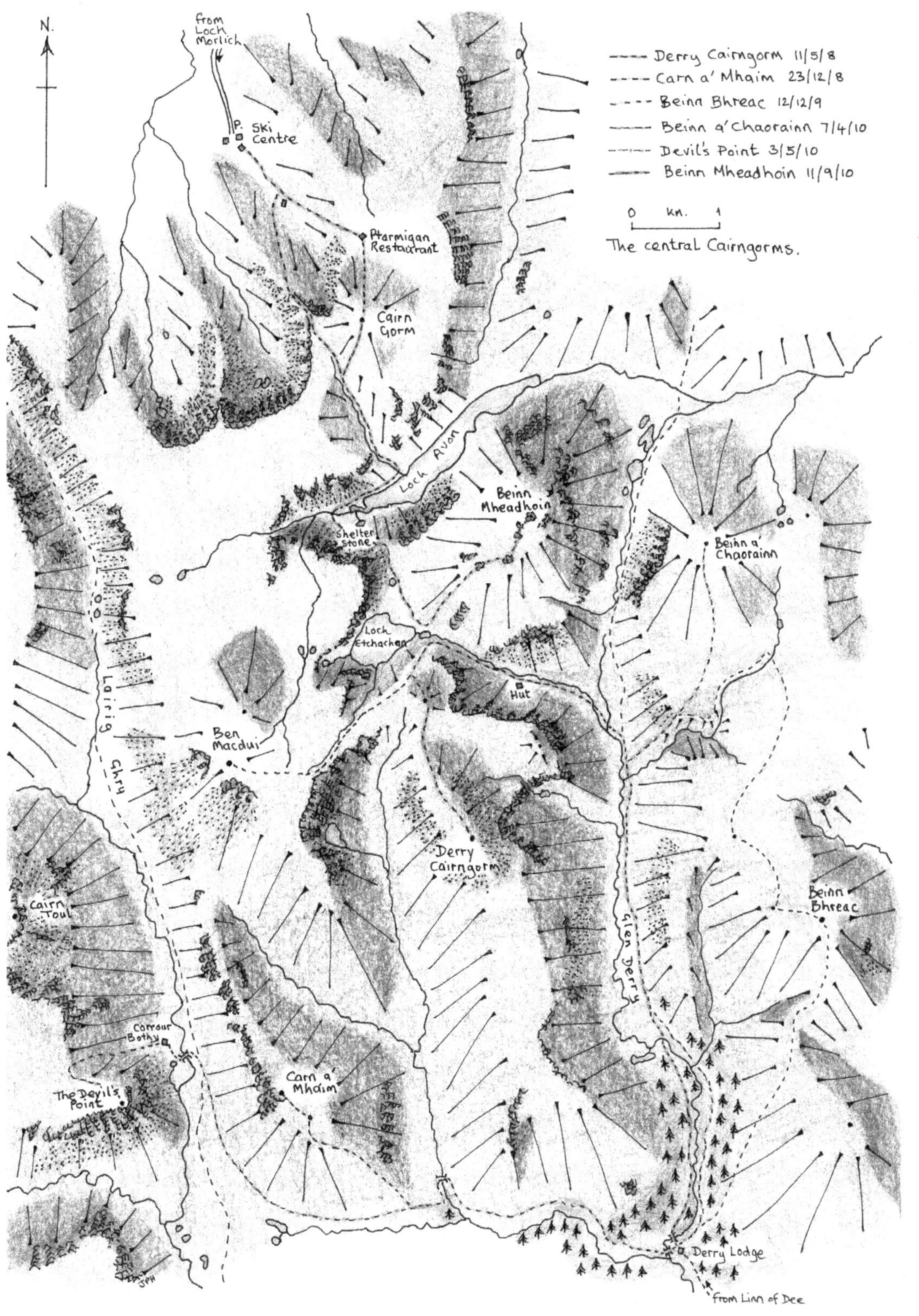
N.
from Loch Morlich
P. Ski Centre
Ptarmigan Restaurant
Cairn Gorm
Derry Cairngorm 11/5/8
Carn a' Mhaim 23/12/8
Beinn Bhreac 12/12/9
Beinn a' Chaorainn 7/4/10
Devil's Point 3/5/10
Beinn Mheadhoin 11/9/10
0 km. 1
The central Cairngorms.
Loch Avon
Beinn Mheadhoin
Shelter Stone
Beinn a' Chaorainn
Loch Etchachan
Hut
Lairig Ghru
Ben Macdui
Derry Cairngorm
Cairn Toul
Beinn Bhreac
Glen Derry
Corrour Bothy
Carn a' Mhaim
The Devil's Point
Derry Lodge
From Linn of Dee

I walked with Nick up to the big boulders. These had crashed down in a colossal rock fall long ago, some of the biggest coming to rest on smaller ones, thereby creating a space for a potential shelter underneath. I kept my eye on what appeared to be the largest, a massive, pale-coloured, rectangular boulder with a small cairn on its west end. Once there, I found a narrow passage, one wall of which was of carefully laid stones. I took my head torch from my rucksack, went down the passage and bent down to go through the dark entrance. Inside was a dry cave, perhaps big enough for a dozen people, with heavy plastic sheeting on its floor and candles scattered about. I found a box and took it out into the light. In the box was a bottle of juice, cereal bars, a hard covered notebook and pencils. It was the visitors' book of the Shelter Stone. This has been completed since 1924, with archives held in the Cairngorm Club in Aberdeen. I wrote a brief entry with our names and the date. I then took the candles I had brought from my rucksack, borrowed Nick's lighter and went back inside to light them.

The others began to arrive and I pointed out the passage. Each looked rather wary as they went towards the dark little entrance but shouted with surprise when they discovered the chamber with candlelight flickering on its walls and roof. Once they had all been in, I put out the candles and left them there.

We sat in the alcove by the entrance to eat lunch, looking out at Loch Avon and its dark walls veined with white ribbons of tumbling water. My companions asked me about the Shelter Stone and I told them that it has been a howff for a long time, long before the very first mountaineering club in Scotland, the Cairngorm Club, was founded there in 1887. I had read a number of accounts of it and had long wanted to make this pilgrimage.

The Shelter Stone 11/9/10.

Sophie, eating a most uncharacteristic hillwalker's lunch which included an avocado, asked about the mountain behind the Shelter Stone. I answered that this was Scotland's second highest, Ben Macdui. I told her of the Grey Man, a giant who chases people off the mountain, including those of a sober disposition and not known for telling fantastic stories, Professor Norman Collie for one. Nick needed no further encouragement, telling us his own curious story of the hillwalkers hit by a ball of lightning who had returned to Inverness with their hair completely white.

Lunch over, we found a narrow way between the big boulders. Rocks had been built up to fill gaps below two others, creating further refuges. I decided that I would like time to explore this place properly and that I would bring more candles and some matches to replenish the stocks of the Shelter Stone.

We climbed a steep path which leads to the gap between Carn Etchachan and Beinn Mheadhoin. At the top, it winds through a place of little lochans, flooded bog and sheets of slow moving water. It ended abruptly in places where the tops of large boulders stood above water. We jumped from one to the next. The pools here were strangely beautiful places of crystal clear water and a surprising number of aquatic plants, some lurid pale green, some so dark green as to be nearly black, others brown, purple and maroon. As we marvelled, a fat, pale brown frog slipped into the water, lazily kicked its long legs and glided in slow motion between the waving stems of this multi-coloured underwater forest.

Beinn Mheadhoin is a difficult mountain for hillwalkers, being nearly 4,000 feet high, remote from access points and protected on all sides by steep, crag-lined slopes. I guessed that the most likely place to find a path would be at Little Loch Etchachan, where the track we were following met that from Glen Derry and that from Ben Macdui. Loch Etchachan came into view and we stopped to watch the play of light on its waters, distorting the reflections of its encircling dark cliffs. At the outflow from the loch I was relieved to find a path which zig zagged along the top of granite crags to take us up onto our mountain.

Beinn Mheadhoin's summit is a long, undulating plateau of granite grit; a sub-arctic desert. The hardy vegetation consists of separate clumps of yellow deer grass which has rooted through the stone chips. There seemed little else but lichens. The half dozen high points of the plateau are capped by weathered granite tors, each quite fantastic in shape and different from its neighbours. These are the barns of Beinn Mheadhoin. I was in front of the party as I walked up to the first tor and surprised a mountain hare, its coat snow white. Although only early autumn, winter was not far away here.

I stopped at the biggest tor and checked with my GPS that this was indeed the highest point. I then walked around it to find the safest way up its steep sides. The wind had increased in strength as we walked along the ridge and it was just possible to stand on the top. The others arrived and I announced that this was as far as we were going, but if they wanted to be on the very summit they had to climb the tor. I pointed the way and then settled in a sheltered alcove in the granite to have a cup of tea and a snack. I heard screams above but they seemed to be the sort that would go with an unfamiliar climb up wet granite then being caught on the top by a fierce wind rather than the sort that would accompany someone falling off, so I was happily tucking into a sandwich when the others came to join me, pink cheeked and excited. As we sat squashed together, enjoying afternoon tea, the clouds tore apart and the sun streamed down on the wild landscape of the Lairig an Laoigh, Beinn a' Chaorainn and the deep trench of Glen Derry. All were in high spirits and we discussed possibilities for the return journey. Nick was in favour of a route which took in Ben Macdui and the path around the top of Coire an t-Sneachda's headwall.

I was getting concerned about the time, however, and as we set off the north-west wind gathered strength and howled over the mountain top, battering us with cold drops of rain. We needed off Beinn Mheadhoin and I led the party back down to Loch Etchachan at a relentless pace. Once down, I sat behind a boulder and was soon joined by Nick. I suggested that a combination of time, tiredness and uncertain weather pointed to the most direct return route, which was the way we had come. He heartily agreed, saying that his mind had been changed as he struggled back along the summit ridge. The others were happy with this.

No sooner had we started back along the path which would lead us to the beaches of Loch Avon again than the sun came out, both warming and cheering us. It was to stay out for the remainder of the day.

Loch Avon 11/9/10.

We took our time on the return journey, stopping again to look at the wonderful pools, illuminated beautifully by the afternoon sun, already quite low in the sky. As we descended, there were many stops to marvel at the patterns of light and shade on Loch Avon and its precipitous crags. The turquoise shallows seemed to give off their own light.

The lonely beaches provided the best viewpoints of the day. To stand on the spit of white sand looking along the length of the loch with the sun streaming over the top of the Shelter Stone Crag was to see Highland Scotland at its very best. It was hard to come away.

It was a tough climb up the waterfalls to get back to Coire Raibeirt and knees were sore going down the steep arête of Fiacaill a' Choire Chais, but the sun warmed our backs and we were all full of the joys of the day.

A hot shower, (I don't think anyone had the energy to press their body on the glass), a hot dinner in the Tipsy Laird and then an evening to swap stories about our various adventures brought to a close my hillwalking weekend.

No one stirred as I rose early on Sunday morning, ate a bowl of porridge and drove the deserted roads back to Aberdeen.

On the tor.

24/9/10

Beinn Dearg

First snow

In the car park at General Wade's graceful old bridge over the Tilt I discussed the weather forecast with James. A bitter wind straight from the Arctic with 50 miles per hour gusts on higher ground and the likelihood of snow showers. On the positive side, visibility between the showers was to be excellent and the afternoon was probably going to be better, with bright sun. "Hmm, I like a challenge," he concluded.

It was sheltered by the banks of the Tilt and we set off on our bikes in good spirits, along the rough road that runs on the east side of the Banvie Burn. This is the old Minigaig Road which goes from Blair Atholl to Kingussie. The cycling was relentlessly uphill, my heart banged against my ribcage and my lungs began to burn. I was glad to see James dismount and begin to push his bike up a particularly steep bank. At the top, we agreed that we needed to improve whatever muscles are used when riding mountain bikes. The autumn colours of the beech, rowan and birch trees were lovely but it was difficult to properly enjoy them with my blood hammering at my temples.

We left the woodland behind and followed the stony track as it climbed the hillside to leave Glen Banvie. At the top of a long slope stands a cairn to mark the spot where the blood of James's ancestors, (he is a Murray), was spilled in a fight with Simon Lovat's men. Ahead, a fierce looking shower galloped down from the high hills. The low morning sun generated a double rainbow against the billowing dark grey shower clouds. I considered

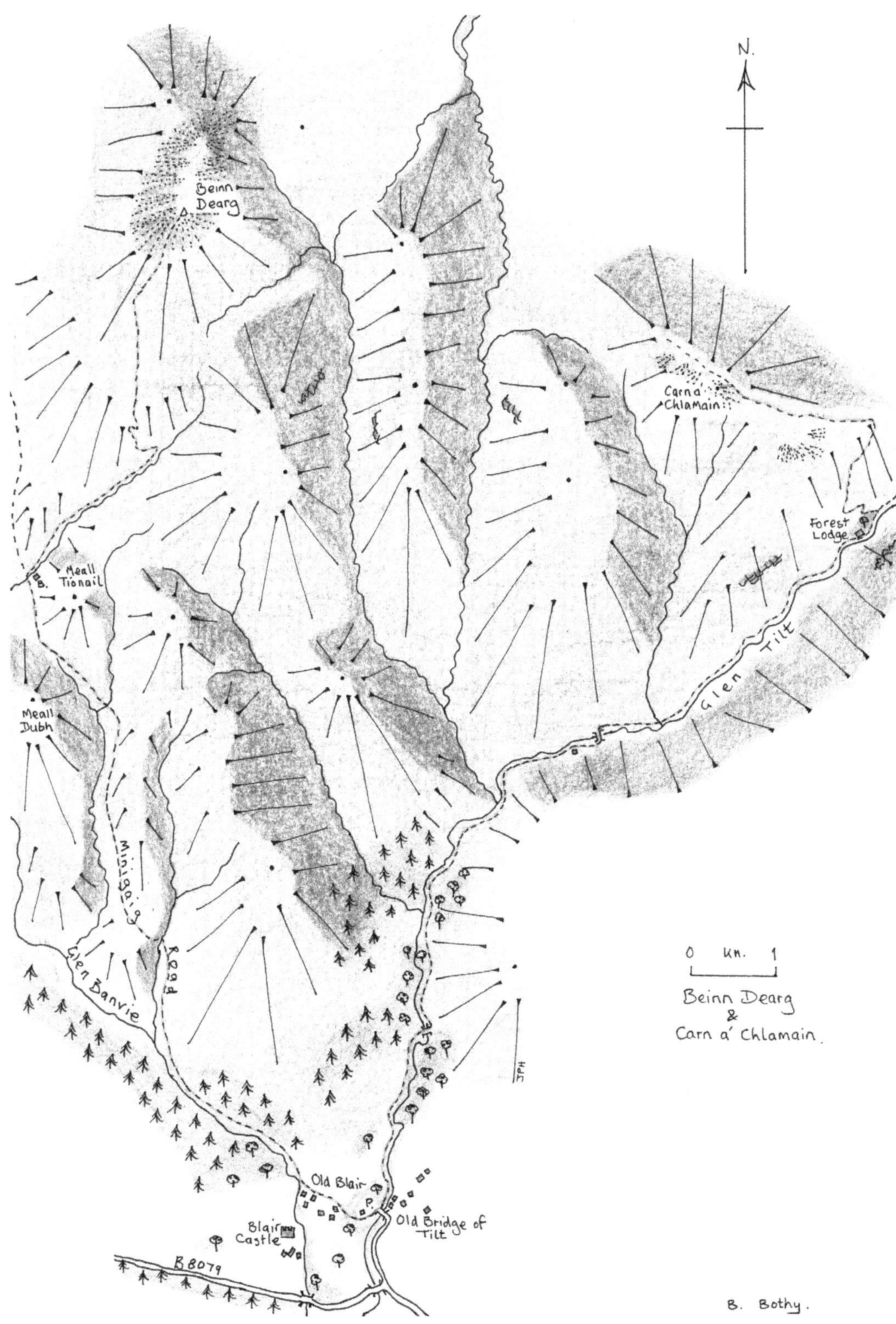
N.
Beinn Dearg
Carn a' Chlamain
Forest Lodge
Glen Tilt
Meall Tionail
B.
Meall Dubh
Minigaig
Road
Glen Banvie
Old Blair
P.
Old Bridge of Tilt
Blair Castle
B8079
0 km. 1
Beinn Dearg & Carn a' Chlamain.
JPH
B. Bothy.

photographing this marvel but quickly decided against on the grounds that I had barely enough energy to stand there holding my bike.

Leaving the cairn, we cycled towards the arch of the rainbow, the gradient of the track now tolerable. The honking of skeins of geese overhead showed that they were taking advantage of the north wind on their journey south from their Arctic breeding grounds. It was a relief to leave the bikes in the heather at the bealach between Meall Dubh and Meall Tionail. The track now went steeply downhill. At the bottom is the Allt Sheicheachan bothy, named after the stream beside which it was built. Far behind the bothy we could see the rocky peak of Beinn Dearg, our objective, about to be enveloped by another shower.

The bothy was tidy and clean, with stone flagged floors and robust wooden furnishings. A ladder led to an attic sleeping area. We sat in the main room to have an early lunch and a cup of tea. Sun streamed through the back window. On the wall opposite the hearth was an octagonal looking glass, a framed ink drawing of the bothy, a framed coloured drawing of Corrour bothy and a plastic coated map of the area.

Allt Sheicheachan bothy.
Beinn Dearg beyond.
24/9/10.

Now recovered from our uphill cycling, we set off cheerily up the Allt Sheicheachan. I told James that I felt extra pleasure in striding along this track in the Forest of Atholl, given the history of conflict over the right of the ordinary man and woman to walk here at all. I love the words of Sir Douglas Maclagan[7], written after the Battle of Glen Tilt to commemorate victory over the Duke of Athole and his ghillies (Murrays to a man).

It's justice and it's public richt.
We'll pass Glen Tilt afore the nicht.
For Dukes shall we
Care a'e bawbee?
The road's as free
To you and me
As to his Grace himself, man.

As we got higher up the stream the walls of the defile narrowed and steepened. The wind blew cold and strong into our faces, which is probably why the hind went on drinking from the stream, front legs splayed out, oblivious to our presence. She looked up and froze, giving us a precious second or two to observe her perfect condition after a summer of good grazing. Then she climbed the steep side of the gully in a series of graceful bounds. On top, she stopped and looked down at us, her coat red against the blue sky.

The path then climbed up to Beinn Dearg's south-west ridge. We were still sheltered from the worst of the wind but knew what to expect. It hit us like an ice storm. We sat down to pull on waterproof trousers as that north wind cut through clothing like a cold knife. We had no sooner stood up than a fierce squall rolled down the ridge and over us, spraying us with sharp-edged fragments of ice. It was a struggle to keep walking. "Is this where we turn back?" shouted James, but we kept going.

Just at the point where I thought we might well have to consider James's question, the squall passed, sweeping the ridge we had toiled up with its icy shrapnel. Ahead, the pointed summit of Beinn Dearg appeared, not far away. We climbed over the weathered granite boulders and crunched over the granite grit between them. The rock was interesting, with a particularly high proportion of large pink feldspar crystals, it being this that gives the mountain its name, the big red hill. Lichen grew over the outcrops and boulders, pale grey, jade green, near black and off-white. This last seemed to dominate.

---

7 The lines are from 'The Battle Of Glentilt (1847)' and were written by Professor Sir Douglas Maclagan, 1812-1900. It was a professor of botany, a contemporary of the author, out to collect specimens with his party, who stood up to the Duke and his men.

We caught the full force of the wind on the top and quickly sat down behind a shelter wall which has been built around the old triangulation pillar. James declared that he was hungry so we decided to eat the remains of our lunch, wind or no wind. As we ate, the sky darkened again and this time flakes of snow hurried down to settle on the mountain top. I watched them build up and then melt on my sandwich, the first snow of the season.

Lunch finished, we stood up and, with perfect timing, the grey snow clouds rushed away south. Strong sun shone on our faces and most of the sky was blue. We were in the centre of a great wilderness, a hundred square miles of lonely hill and mountain. To the north-east Carn an Fhidhleir and An Sgarsoch stood high above the surrounding hills. We remembered our long walk into this empty country to climb them and wading across the cold Geldie Burn. In the south-east rose the rocky ridge of Beinn a' Ghlo, with Ben Vrackie, a hill we had admired as we drove around its base the previous day, behind.

The walk back was a delight. The wind was on our backs, the sun on our faces and the world looked beautiful. The steep hillsides were russet and Indian gold and the waters of the glen floors flashed silver.

We stopped at the bothy for a last cup of tea, enjoying the afternoon sun streaming in the front window and the open door. Then we set off to find the bikes.

It was with some trepidation that I mounted the saddle again but my body and rucksack acted as a sail and the north wind sent me shooting down the track. James was already a speck in the distance. It wasn't until I returned the eight kilometres or so down the track without the need to pedal, hands on the brake levers to slow the breakneck speed, that I fully appreciated how relentless that morning struggle, uphill and against a powerful wind, had been. It was the quickest return journey from a mountain walk that either of us had ever made.

We stopped on the way back to eat at an old inn. The sign proudly announced, 'new Scottish owners, new menu'. The walls inside were hung with Scottish-themed items like weaponry and antlers. Among them, incongruously, was a splendidly horned bison head. The young Polish waiter brought knives and forks, closely wrapped in paper napkins, the corners of which had been dampened and stuck down. We chatted as we waited for our meal and I idly picked up my cutlery. "Look at this," I remarked to James, "someone's licked the corner of this napkin and stuck it down."

The waiter, collecting glasses across the room, overheard my quip and shot across, earnestly assuring us, "No one has spit on the napkins." I tried to explain that it was only my strange sense of humour but felt guilty that I had spoken loudly enough for him to hear. James was highly amused. When the meal arrived, the beef was the toughest either of us had ever encountered. I suggested that no beef cattle could ever have produced such a meat and that whatever animal it was, it was very old indeed. Looking up to the horned head upon the wall I declared that I had solved the mystery, we were eating bison, perhaps the last that ever roamed the Highlands, and its very head had been saved as a decoration. Unfortunately, the young waiter had been clearing plates from a table behind me and he appeared again, this time to assure us that we had been served beef and not bison. James seemed to choke at this point.

So it was a day of mixed fortunes, beautiful views in crystal-clear air, but tired leg and jaw muscles. I shall certainly never eat bison again.

6/11/10

Beinn Eunaich and Beinn a' Chochuill

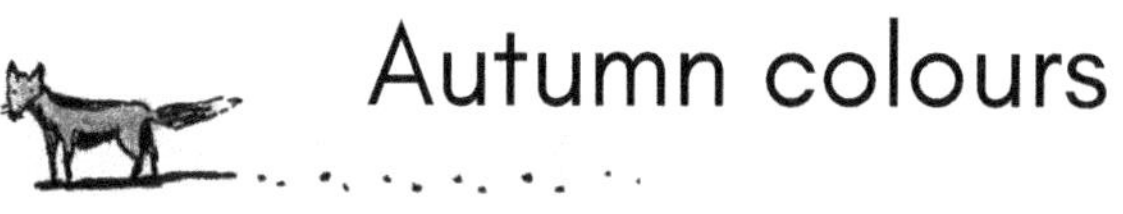

Autumn colours

There was a new moon on November 5th. I drove past Aberdeen's last street lamp and into a black night. Each village and town on my route was an oasis of light, Braemar, Pitlochry, Aberfeldy, Kenmore, Killin, Crianlarich, Tyndrum, each seen from far off spurting brilliant colours into the night sky. Outside the hostel at Tyndrum my breath clouded in the cold air when I stepped out of my warm car. The fireworks had stopped and above was the spectacle of the stars, a dust of diamonds swept in broad ribbons from horizon to horizon.

The common room was occupied by members of the Moray Mountaineering Club. I said hi and dropped my gear. A fierce buzzing came from the electric toothbrush in my washbag. "Don't even try to explain," said an amused spectator, "we're all liberal-minded here."

One of the members was canine, a little black and tan terrier bitch. I was 'in between dogs' and at the 'we're never going to have another one' stage and deliberately referred to her as "it", but she did have the most winning eyes.

Morag and I were parked near Castles Farm at the head of Loch Awe by 7.30 next morning. It was still and cold, with little patches of mist low to the ground and thin cloud

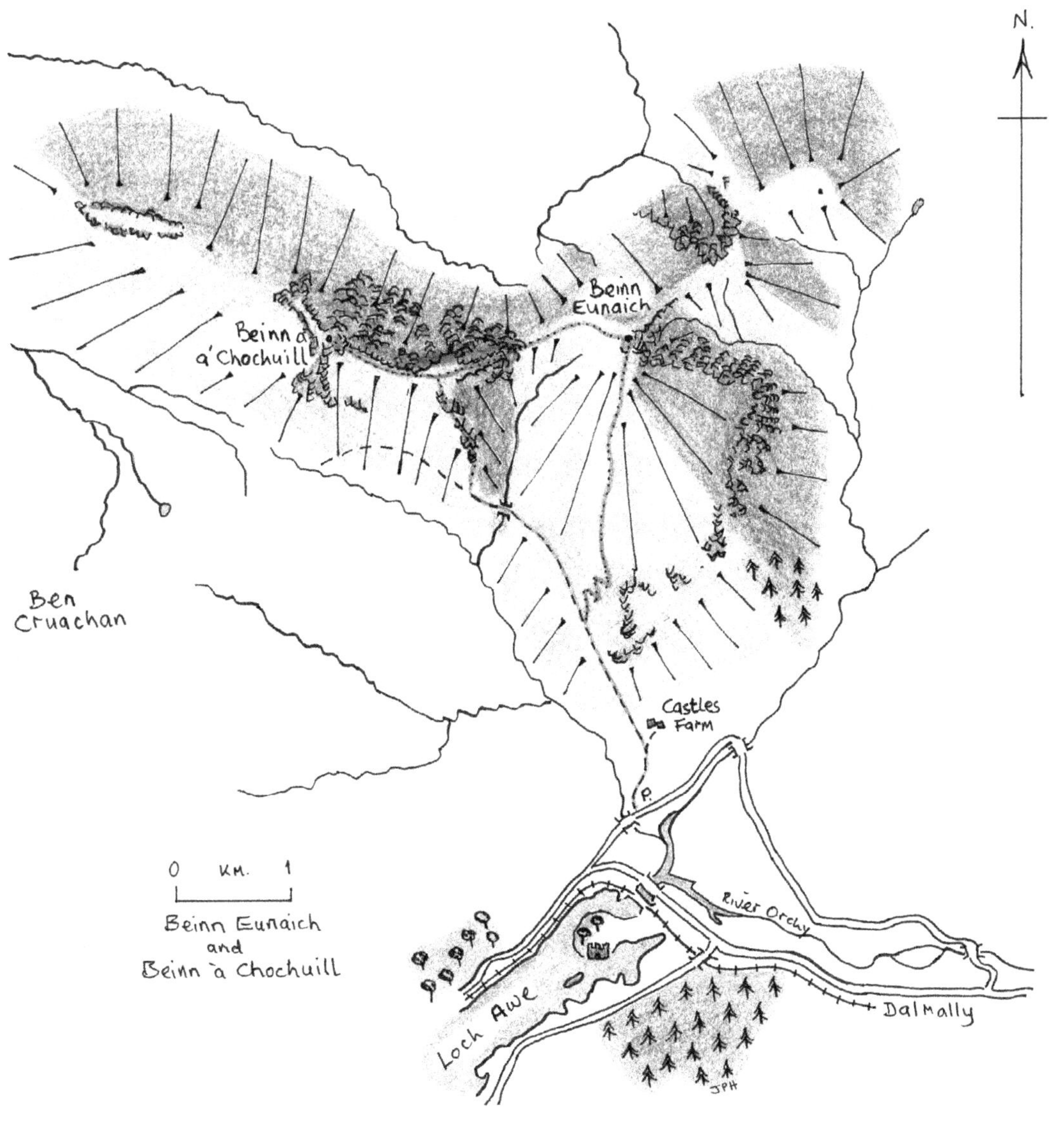

sitting on all the high tops. Not long risen above the hills, the sun had not cut through the high cloud but diffused sunlight lit the slopes before us. Browns, yellows, copper, beige, khaki, rust, maroon; mellow autumn colours all mingled into a subtle, coherent, beautiful whole. A large herd of Highland cattle stood on and near the path, their palette of colours perfectly complementing those of the mountainsides.

We stopped for some breakfast on the craggy south-east spur of Beinn a' Chochuill, just before entering the cloud. I looked out on a mysterious world where there were mushrooms of dense white mist. Loch Awe was bright silver in a broad arc of sunlight which slowly moved to illuminate different patches of the shores.

Meal over, we stepped up into the fine, dancing water droplets of the thin cloud and were soon crossing the snowline. Each blade of grass had become a perfect needle of ice. On the crest of the ridge all was peace and silence. We followed a line of fox prints in the snow which led westwards to the summit. This is made of pink granite, giving the mountain its name, which means red cowl.

It was too cold to stop, so we retraced our steps and walked back along the ridge, the visibility good enough for us to see a considerable distance down the steep drops on either side.

We stopped for lunch just beyond the bealach and before the final steep slope up to the top of Beinn Eunaich. My corned beef and pickle sandwiches were cold and unappetising but the mug of steaming tea was most welcome. It was well below freezing, so we were soon packed up and climbing again.

There were no views from the summit but just below it, as we began to walk down the long south ridge, they opened up. The cloud and mist was lifting, vertical columns streaming up from the glen like white smoke. To the south were patches of gold light and brilliant emerald meadows lit by wide sunbeams. At the end of a narrow peninsula which points down the length of Loch Awe stands the ruins of Kilchurn Castle, dark against the metallic sparkle of the water. Sunlight breaking through the cloud lit a hill to the west, molten orange among the muted tones of its neighbours.

Back down on the path, a buzzard ponderously flapped its wide wings as it rose from among the Highland cattle. We passed a pond where 30 mallard drakes, all in perfect team colours, gave an impression of a crowd of football supporters, out for a good time on that Saturday afternoon.

I drove Morag back to pick up her car in Tyndrum where we had welcome bowls of soup in the café before we began our journeys home.

The mature trees of Loch Tay, Aberfeldy and the Pitlochry area are one of the natural wonders of the British Isles at this time of year. I stopped the car to enjoy their splendid colours, the leaves reflecting the red sun as it sank in the west. There were many species, but the beeches wore the autumn crown.

In the last of the light, my car laboured on the long slope up Glen Shee. I was surprised to see the hills completely white with snow. I left the little pool of light that was the ski centre and drove into another black night.

Loch Awe from Beinn Eunaich
6/11/10
JPH

12/2/11

The abandoned farmsteads of Abergeldie

The road was quiet on that February morning as we drove to Balmoral. James asked how long it was since I had damaged my back. It was three months to the day.

A gale had blown the roofing felt from my shed so I stripped off the remains of the old and fixed a heavy duty new cover by hammering in dozens of felt nails. Under the eaves I had to twist back and knock in the nails above my head. The hammer grew so heavy that I had to talk sternly to myself in order to continue. The next day I was overcome with pain.

My doctor informed me that I had a prolapsed disc and primary nerve damage. I was to rest completely and a decision would be made at the year end as to whether to refer me to an orthopaedic surgeon who would open up my back. I had no more than a 50% chance of avoiding an operation. I was visibly upset at the prospect of losing my fitness and having a long period of exile from the mountains. The doctor assured me that, if I followed his instructions, I would be able to function properly again. Despite his positive prognosis, I was not happy. He put his arm around my shoulder and said, "Poor bugger."

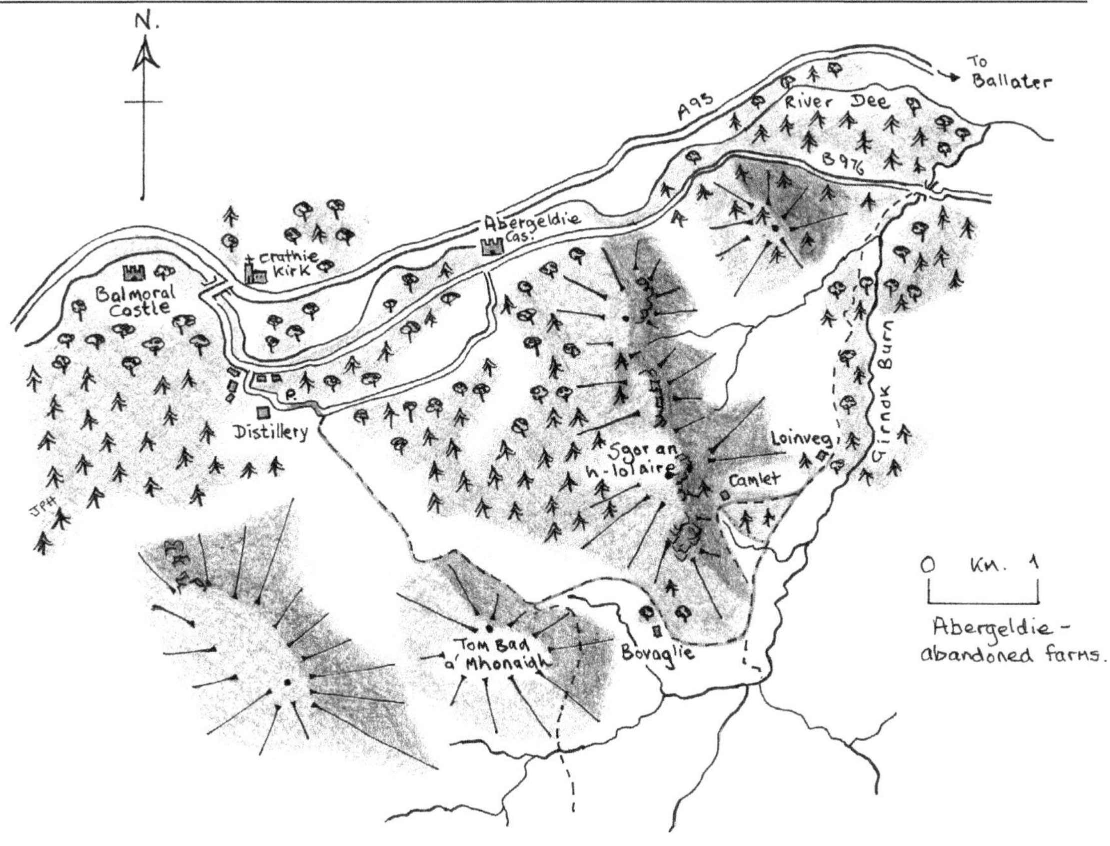

On my return visit he decided that, as I had shown signs of recovery, he would not yet refer me to a surgeon. I was to step up walking and cycling but be aware that I will always have weakness there and potential for another episode. He advised me never again to lift heavy weights and if I was ever to even contemplate D.I.Y., "You should engage the services of one of those Polish chaps."

The car was parked outside the Royal Balmoral Distillery and we walked south-east to Tom Bad a' Mhonaidh. There was snow on the track, it was uphill and James walks fast, so I had to concentrate on my stride and try not to limp too much. My left leg had been weakened by the sciatica that had resulted from the damaged disc and the toes on my left foot were still numb and tingling. By the time I got to the top of that gentle brae I was hot and breathing fast, but I knew that my back and legs were functioning again so felt good. I noticed the weather for the first time, it was overcast, still, cold and dry.

We followed the track east to a wood of Scots pine and a mixture of deciduous trees. On the far side was Bovaglie. The substantial farmhouse looked like it had been built in the inter-war period but was now boarded up. James had been there ten years previously and he led me to the back where a door opened to the bathroom and into the house. It was sad to walk through the empty rooms. The dark red and green tiles of the fireplaces still gleamed and ash lay in the cold hearths. The big barns were built around a wide loading bay for carts. In one barn were two old threshing machines, once worked by a steam engine. Outside was a sheep dip. It was easy to picture the farm alive and productive. Down a slope were the remains of black houses, a clear sign that farming has been practiced here for centuries. We sat on an ancient wall and ate some lunch, agreeing that the latest farmstead looked like it had been abandoned in the 1960s.

James went to look at some gnarled old trees, their tops snapped off by storms. They were rather dismal on that gloomy winter day, their crooked limbs like human arms with long twiggy fingers reaching towards their curious visitor.

We followed the track around the hillside as it twisted north. Ahead was a wood in which we could see the roofs of buildings. This was Camlet, a second abandoned farmstead. Walking along the side of the wood, we found an overgrown track to the house. It was a south-facing cottage which stood in front of a derelict byre and other outbuildings. Outside was a gas cooker of a type used in the 1960s. The front door was missing. The carpets had been removed from the floors revealing a lining of newspapers, one with an article about a Beatles' concert. James and I clumped up the wooden stairs and discovered a nesting box for barn owls. A hole under the eaves provided a suitable passage for them.

A drystone wall at the front of the cottage made a good seat. It was brighter and we could see the position of the sun through the cloud. James looked thoughtful, "I wonder why the farms have been abandoned? I'm sure that the E.U. will be to blame."

"Whatever part the E.U. had to play," I replied, "it's not sustainable to move food to our country from far flung corners of the world, so this land will be cultivated again one day."

It was a pleasant spot to finish our lunch. I asked whether James had enjoyed his recent snow-shoeing holiday in Austria. "That's a sore point," he replied, "I seemed to upset people one evening when we were given wax torches and joined the torch-bearing residents of the town as they marched through the streets. I merely remarked that it was like a Nuremberg rally."

Lunch eaten, we followed the path through the wood to regain the main track. Our next stop was Loinveg, the third abandoned farmstead. This, like the others, was sheltered by a small wood. Its Scots pine trees were planted to take the sting out of south-westerlies as they rampaged along the side of the hill. The granite built farmhouse was in better condition than the others, the boards nailed over doors and windows all still secure. We explored the outhouses and remains of the barn. It had been roofed when James last saw it but the slates had been salvaged since then, leading to a collapse of the timbers. In the debris was an old threshing machine like the big one at Bovaglie and the decaying skeleton of a sawmill.

Further up the slope were the overgrown walls of old black houses, similar to those at Bovaglie and showing again that this place had been farmed for many generations.

The best feature of the site was the two venerable ash trees, both with their tops snapped off long ago in a mountain storm, the tops, now moss and lichen covered, lying where they fell. The trees were a hoary grey/green. They looked as if they were host to a large colony of brown bats, all hanging sound asleep. Close up, the bats were revealed to be clusters of ash keys, waiting to be scattered by the spring gales. I stopped to look at the lichen growing on the branches. There were nine different types on one branch alone, from jade green hanging tassels to bright orange encrustations.

Walking back, I remarked that it had been a strangely sombre day, marked by a tangible sadness in the ruins of what had been busy farming communities. A sadness reflected in the bearded and broken old trees.

I suggested that we stop for a last cup of tea near the top of the brae above Bovaglie. We faced south and it was clear that the cloud was thinning and lifting. First the steep, snow-streaked slopes of Conachcraig were revealed, then its narrow top. White vapours boiled upwards from Lochnagar's corrie, stained the blue sky, then melted away. It was a curtain being slowly raised. Lochnagar itself appeared, blindingly white as its icy cap caught the rays of the low winter sun. The mood of the day changed, gloomy thoughts melting away with the cloud. That's where I want to be I thought, looking at those gleaming snowfields.

I limped terribly for the next few days and had strange pains in my ribcage, but they went away and I was no worse. It was worth the discomfort and more to know that I could walk in hill country and, with patience and care, would be climbing Scotland's mountains once more.

26/3/11

Broad Cairn

The end of winter

I parked at Spittal of Glenmuick on that dreich March morning. The overcast sky seemed to have sucked the colours from the land, so much so that the cock chaffinch hopping round my boots seemed startlingly bright. I wondered out loud where Morag was and while James was commenting on her reliability, she drove into the car park, reliable as ever. As I greeted her it occurred to me that I had not seen her since the week before I injured my back, I had missed a whole winter season on the mountains.

Chatting happily, we strode along the track which runs along the south-east shore of Loch Muick. Morag was first to spot a large herd of deer a short distance away on the hillside. They were pale beige rather than red, something I have noted before at this time of year. They were in remarkably good condition, suggesting that December's relentless snows had been countered by the relatively mild and often sunny weather in the early weeks of 2011. High above them a buzzard rose from rocky ground with a few slow, powerful wingbeats then hung, rocking gently, in a rising current of air.

James had walked this same route with a friend the previous Saturday. There were deep drifts of snow then and where the path zig zags up to the Mounth plateau his left leg had gone through a snow crust. As he plunged down to his crotch, his right leg twisted and ligaments were torn in his knee. He was collected enough to fill a plastic carrier bag with snow and apply this ice pack to the damaged area. It had prevented any swelling,

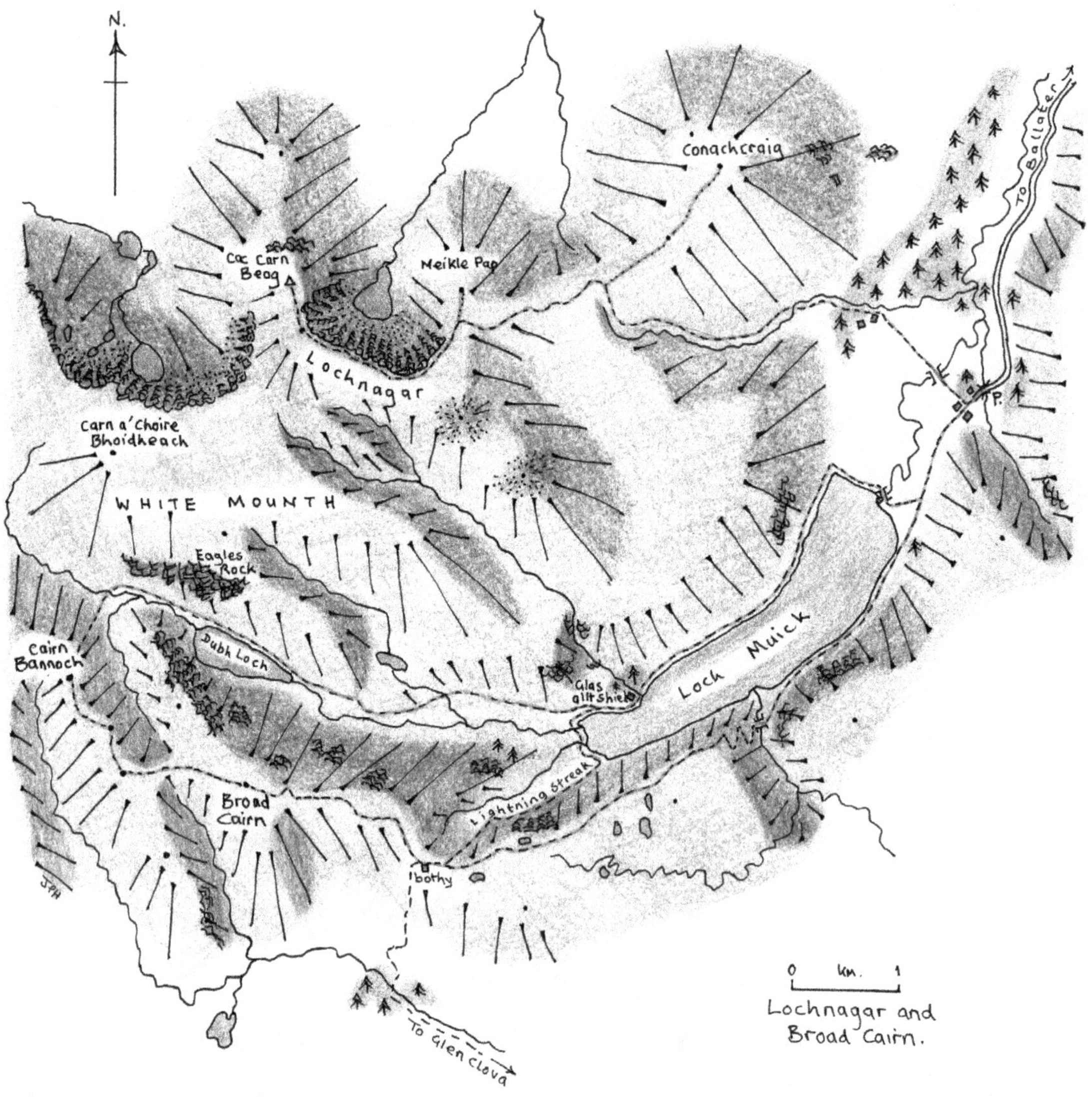

but the walk had to be aborted. While James was limping back, I was on Bennachie. I had been concerned that I might spoil our walk so had tried myself out by completing a round of the tops, walking mostly on snow. It took me four hours and I was stiff and sore afterwards, but there were no lasting ill effects. All this was too much for Morag, "What am I thinking, hanging out with two old crocks?"

There were still drifts at the zig zags but James noted with relief that they had shrunk down in the sunshine of the intervening week. We made our way across them with great care, however, doing what we could to avoid another jolt. At the top we entered the cold, wet cloud that sat on the Mounth.

The path was now at a height of 600 metres and mostly blocked by drifts which slowed our progress. Red grouse fluttered up from heather which was black after months under snow. Their plumage was a very dark red, almost black, so they were impossible to see unless they were spooked into rising. We stopped at the little bothy at the junction of our route and the path going south to the head of Glen Clova. A bench on the north wall provided shelter from the cold wind and fine rain and there we sat to eat some early lunch and enjoy a hot drink from our flasks.

The next stage was a steady climb across alternating patches of weathered granite boulders and spreads of coarse granite grit, these being separated by deep snowdrifts. The southerly wind had been blowing rain into my left side since the top of the zig zags, my trousers were wet and I began to feel cold water trickling down my leg. On the rocky summit of Broad Cairn James talked enthusiastically about the views but, as there were none, I sheltered behind the outcrop, removed my wet gaiters and pulled on waterproof trousers. Just in the nick of time, I thought, as the water had begun to soak my left sock and would soon have filled the boot. Properly shielded from the weather, I returned to the summit for a moment, thrilled to be on a Munro once more.

We retraced our steps on the way down, the old crocks taking it slowly. When my left leg broke through a frozen crust and plunged down into the soft snow beneath, it jolted my back. My companions were concerned but I was sanguine about it, reasoning that I needed to test it out if I was to be active in the mountains again.

A little past the bothy we took the path known as the Lightning Streak, cut into the steep side wall of Corrie Chash. The going was fine until we came upon steeply banked-up snow. One slip and we would hurtle down to the corrie floor, 100 metres below. Walking poles were stowed and replaced with ice axes as we gingerly crossed. After the snow we

came out from under the cloud and Loch Muick appeared in front of us as a vertical silver blue cliff. As we descended, this optical illusion faded and the surface of the loch became reassuringly horizontal.

We sat on the charming little beach at the head of the loch to finish our lunch. The cloud sat on the high Mounth behind us but scattered patches of golden sunlight patterned the hillsides.

On the home straight now, we visited the lovely pinewood which shelters Glas-allt-Shiel, the summerhouse built for Queen Victoria. At the loch shore, we watched a goldeneye duck and drake until they paddled to hide behind a little island. The bothy had a candle burning on the mantle shelf. It was dry, clean and smelled of wood smoke, a perfect shelter for hillwalkers caught in what local folk call coarse weather.

Our expedition ended with a pleasant walk along the path that follows the shore. A winter flood had scoured away one of the two piers supporting the wooden bridge over the River Muick at the outflow from the loch, which left the walkway dropping alarmingly at that point. James archly suggested that Morag should go over to test it and it proved perfectly safe. As we walked the last stretch to the car park a curlew gave its sad cry and flew slowly down the river.

14/4/11

Sgor na h-Ulaidh

A navigational error leads us to the treasure mountain

It was dark when James, Morag and I met at the hostel in Tyndrum. We made mugs of tea, spread out our maps and discussed plans for the morning. If the sky was clear of clouds and it looked likely to stay dry, we would climb Sron na Creise and spend the day high up on the ridges of the Black Mount. If it was damp but looked like it might possibly clear up, we would leave a car in Glen Coe and walk south to Sgor na h-Ulaidh. If it was wet and misty, we would climb Beinn Fhionnlaidh from Glen Etive, where we would be sheltered by forest for half the route. Satisfied with our plans A, B and C, we retired to bed. We were destined to follow none of them.

Early next morning we looked out on a scene of grey mist with water dripping from the branches and agreed that Glen Etive would be our destination. Rannoch Moor was in a rather grim mood, rain pattered on the windscreen, the mist revealed only mysterious black crags of otherwise hidden hills and the front of a car which had run off the road before us was sinking slowly in the bog. Driving along the single track road down Glen Etive, our field of vision was limited to the land near the river. We passed an unusual method of crossing this obstacle; a person could haul himself/herself across in a wooden box attached to four cables. There were groups of grazing red deer, unconcerned by the passing car. Some groups were exclusively made up of stags, others of hinds. Their coats were dark brown with large beige rump patches.

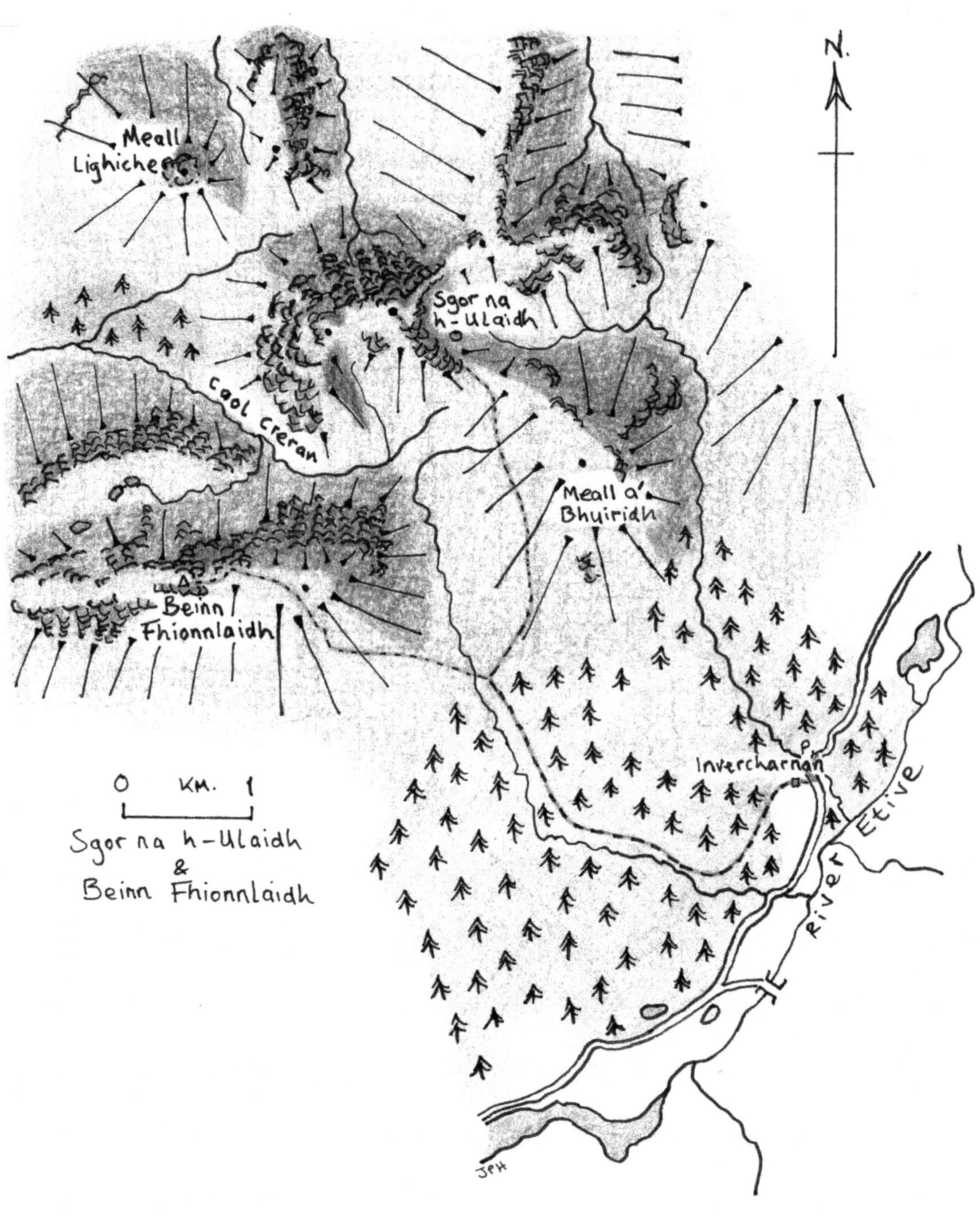
N.
Meall Lighiche
Sgor na h-Ulaidh
Caol Creran
Meall a' Bhuiridh
Beinn Fhionnlaidh
Invercharnan
River Etive
0 KM. 1
Sgor na h-Ulaidh
&
Beinn Fhionnlaidh
JPH

At Invercharnan we put on waterproof trousers and walked past the house to get access to the forest track, ignoring the 'dogs on the loose' notice. Near the northern edge of the trees the track turns sharply to the right and here a short path leads to the open hill. The path beyond was like a sponge but its line was clear and we happily splashed along it. Happily that is until the mist lifted somewhat, revealing the rocky base of what was obviously a mountain to our left. I remembered the map from the previous night and that it showed that Beinn Fhionnlaidh should appear ahead and to the right of the path. I called to my companions who had walked on and suggested that it was time for map, compass and, probably, GPS. James and I produced these items, James going for a GPS grid reference first. When we checked this with the map, I simply did not believe it. I switched mine on and it produced a contradictory reference, with more than a kilometre difference. The situation resolved itself, however, when the figures on the GPS belonging to James began to change rapidly until they came in line with mine. This, more importantly, was where we had worked out we were likely to be in the old-fashioned way. It was either backtrack to the forest to find the path we should have followed or march on to climb Sgor na h-Ulaidh instead. Considering that we would be unlikely to see anything from the top anyway, we opted to march on. Or rather squelch on. The ground was soft and the going was heavy, with sturdy dark brown frogs everywhere.

We kept on until we reached the bealach between Meall a' Bhuiridh (pronounced "voory", the hill of the roaring) and Sgor na h-Ulaidh (pronounced "hooly", the treasure mountain). The ground had become easier, with clumps of deer grass and patches of bog giving way to rock. Here we stopped for an early lunch and a hot drink. As we sat, the mist teased us by showing us the steep, craggy ridge which leads to the Bealach Fhionnghaill, Bidean nam Bian's narrow south ridge beyond. Above us, the wet black slabs we would have to climb looked forbiddingly steep.

James led the way, zig zagging up and around the crags, finding us a route with the minimum of scrambling. Even using our hands, however, it was a tense business as the angles were so steep and everything wet and slippery. On the top, it was so calm that we sat comfortably beside the cairn, eating more lunch and sipping hot tea.

The descent to the bealach was better than we feared, although I dislodged a rock which clattered down and smashed into James's hand far below. Sore, but no broken fingers. I wished we had thought to bring our climbing helmets.

We must have passed the test set by the weather gods because the cloud base steadily rose as we walked south from the bealach. The first feature to emerge was the rock-walled gorge of Caol Creran between Sgor na h-Ulaidh and Beinn Fhionnlaidh. Then the ridge of Beinn Fhionnlaidh itself was revealed, crowned with three sharp summits, tall and

In the forest.

impregnable from the north. I wished that I had longer to sketch it. To the south-east, across the forest, stood the shapely peak of Meall Tarsuinn, flanked by its two massive neighbours. Far to the south, the snowfields of Ben Starav were still capped with cloud. As I walked, I dreamed of clear days and fine walking along these high ridges before me.

In the forest, I noticed that there were strange mounds beside the path, thatched with bleached deer grass which overhung dark entrances. I half expected to see a stove pipe chimney poking through the roof and wondered who might live there.

The drive back up Glen Etive was spectacular, particularly where Buachaille Etive Beag and Buachaille Etive Mor rose above the bridge at Dalness. I decided that it was from this direction I would climb them one day. Rannoch Moor was in a completely different mood, with its lochs sparkling in the sun and its surrounding rim of mountains golden in the afternoon light. We ate together in an old haunt, the bar of the Clachan Cottage Hotel, looking over Loch Earn, and made plans for our return to climb the rugged mountains we had seen as we walked back from Sgor na h-Ulaidh.

29/4/11

Creise and Meall a' Bhuiridh

Prince William marries Catherine and James celebrates his 60th birthday with us

The day began with James opening his present and card and blowing out the six candles I had lit on a small fruit cake, one for each decade of his busy and active life. Morag had trumped my cake with a big home-made one covered in lemon icing, which was cut into large slices for the hill.

We had travelled to the hostel at Tyndrum the night before so that we could make the most of the extra holiday granted for the wedding of Prince William and Catherine.

Leaving early, we found the road empty and were soon making good progress across Rannoch Moor, which was tinder dry after days of sunshine and desiccating wind.

Our car was the only one in the White Corries car park when we crunched off westward across dried-out peat hags. We stopped at the tip of Creag Dhubh, our long shadows pointing towards the massive bulk of Buachaille Etive Mor. I thought of the thousands of climbs on its Rannoch Wall, many ending in triumph, some in tragedy. On that morning it looked benign, lit by a strong sun and framed by a perfect pale blue sky.

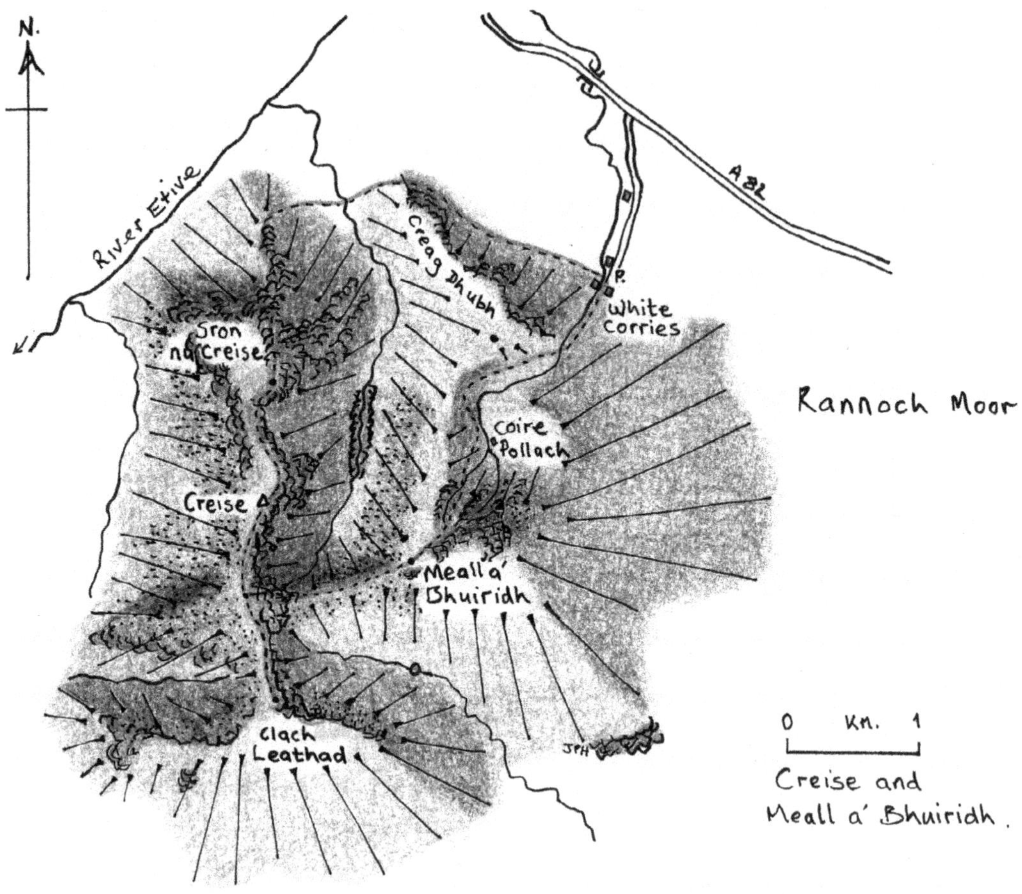

The Allt Càm Ghleann was low, so crossing it was easy. We stopped for a mug of tea on the northern tip of Sron na Creise, the nose of Creise. Climbing this feature to get up onto the ridge is described in the SMC guide to the Munros as 'more mountaineering than hillwalking', so I had been waiting for a day when the rock would be dry before suggesting it.

It was tough. Every foothold and handhold was vital and there was no distracting chatter. James declared, "I do not like this at all, it's far too exposed," adding, "but it's certainly too late to go back now." Morag decided not to look down, which was a sensible precaution for someone nervous of long drops, this one seeming not far off perpendicular.

She was, of course, elated once on the top, having faced the challenge in a stout-hearted fashion. There was a stiff wind, but not enough to spoil things in any way. The views took my breath away, particularly across the River Etive to the wild mountains of Glen Coe. A raven sailed up to eye level, the epitome of aerial grace, a true master of that east wind.

Nervous energy had made us hungry, so we sat behind one of the boulders and ate some early lunch.

The walk south along the crest of the three kilometre ridge was splendid. Not many hillwalkers will have been as fortunate as we were that day on Creise. We stopped often to point out mountains from Ben Cruachan in the south to Ben Nevis and Carn Mor Dearg in the north.

The mountain is made of banded quartzite and I was interested in slabs with clear ripple marks which had survived the metamorphism of what had been an archaic, water-lain sandstone.

As we climbed to the highest point of the ridge, a ptarmigan flew across our path and landed in the boulders ahead. It was almost completely white, which, on this penultimate day of April, seemed late to be keeping winter plumage. As I was thinking about this, a second ptarmigan ran over rocks not far from the first, this, however, had the mottled grey summer feathers and only its breast was white.

We dropped a short distance down the western slope of the ridge underneath the summit. Out of the wind, warmed by the spring sun, we enjoyed the rest of our lunch and a truly spectacular panorama of mountain wilderness. James, licking the lemon icing from his fingers, said, "I can't think of a more perfect way to spend my birthday."

A cairn marked the place where a track plunged down the craggy east side of Creise to a high bealach on the narrow ridge leading up to Meall a' Bhuiridh, our second Munro of the day. We walked past it, however, having decided to complete the whole of the Creise ridge to Clach Leathad, a high Top once regarded as the summit. It was well worth the effort for the fine views south to Stob Ghabhar and east across Rannoch Moor's blue lochans to the mountain wall of Beinn Achaladair.

Retracing our footsteps, we were soon scrambling down onto the ridge which connected our two Munros. We started to climb up to Meall a' Bhuiridh, pronounced voory, which means the hill of the roaring, the roaring being the voice of the stags in the rut. Orange/pink bands of rock ran at right angles across the line of the ridge, marking where ancient igneous activity had produced felsite dykes which had cut through the quartzite rock of the mountain.

Our way down was underneath the ski tows and chair lifts, firstly to Coire Pollach and then to our starting point. It was very steep and, particularly in the upper section, characterised by large rock outcrops. I expressed surprise that people ski over this very rough ground but Morag assured me that the snow regularly becomes so deep that the rock teeth are well buried.

The following day was to see thrills of a different sort as mountain bikers converged here from all over the country to compete. The race was simple, get bikes to the top of the mountain and then ride down as fast as you can. Given the steepness of the ground, the patches of old, icy snow and the random scatter of rock outcrops, it would certainly have been exciting. "We should drive back to Aberdeen to get our bikes and return through the night so that we can take part," I suggested to James.

"I would love to," he replied, "but feel that our mature years and experience would give us an unfair advantage over the young riders."

The walk had taken eight hours and we were well satisfied with the day as we motored back across Rannoch Moor, which was bathed in the honeyed light of the late afternoon. We noticed a tall plume of smoke up ahead and this grew more dramatic as we drove nearer. A huge area of heather, scrub and young trees was burning beside the road on the approach to Bridge of Orchy. The tinder-dry vegetation had caught alight and fire crews battled the flames, hindered by a gusty wind. Thick black smoke billowed over the road and tall red and yellow flames shot up from the verge. Morag calmly drove past, but it was a close thing. I found out later that fires had started all over the country that day and, in Torridon, hillwalkers in danger of being overtaken by a rapidly advancing wall of flame had to be evacuated by rescue helicopter.

We enjoyed a good meal in the Clachan Cottage Hotel in Lochearnhead that evening, which included home-made tomato soup, black pudding and mashed potato. I raised my glass to the royal couple, thanking them for being the reason for my extra day off work. "In a time when other countries are tearing themselves apart, we British are focused on a traditional state wedding," commented James, adding, with that mischievous expression I have come to know well, "Going abroad only confirms my worst suspicions about foreigners."

28/5/11

Beinn Narnain and The Cobbler

A wild day in the Arrochar Alps

...Gusts up to 80 mph on the tops...Heavy sleet, snow and hail showers... Severe wind chill...Risk of lightning...Near Clyde sea lochs, gusts not likely to be quite as strong.

I read out the mountain weather forecast in the comfortable sitting room of Crianlarich's Youth Hostel. Outside, there was little light left in the day and rain rattled on the window panes. After a long pause, Morag's response was, "Not good then." I suggested changing our plans for the morning and going south to the head of Loch Long.

The car park at Arrochar bore witness to this spell of stormy weather, a tree lay on its side and bladderwrack marked where a storm surge had combined with a high tide to flood the area. I hoped that my car would be there when I returned. We had decided to climb Beinn Narnain and then The Cobbler, so we crossed the road and followed the new track which zig zagged up through the coniferous forest. It was sheltered and warm, the many songbirds and a solitary cuckoo making it feel very much like late spring, but we knew what to expect when we left the trees.

N.
The Arrochar Alps.
Loch Sloy
Ben Vorlich
Loch Lomond
Ben Vane
Power Station
Beinn Ime
Beinn Luibhean
Rest and be thankful
Beinn Narnain
The Cobbler
Narnain Boulders
Arrochar
0 KM. 1
Loch Long
JPH

Out in the open, the well-made track followed the Allt a' Bhalachain. The gusty wind slowed us down but we were still in the lee of the Cobbler/Narnain/A' Chrois ridge, so it was not too difficult. We kept stopping to look at the mountain views; cloud covered the tops one minute and was blown off the next when the sun flooded the land and all was sharp and clear. The jagged crown of The Cobbler, straight ahead, stole the show.

The first shower to hit us began with snow and ended with hail, which stung our faces. We struggled through it to the Narnain Boulders and gratefully sat on the dry rocks under the huge overhang of the most easterly of these. Here we decided to have some early lunch and a cup of tea until the hail, which was screaming past horizontally, had passed. This boulder is massive, with a scalloped recess protected by the overhang which provided perfect shelter from westerly weather. It is made of folded schist, as are the many others littering the mountain slopes.

The shower stopped abruptly and we watched it roll quickly down to Loch Long and over the hill to Loch Lomond. Two young men, dripping wet, came to join us. They had very recently discovered the joys of hillwalking and were full of the wonder of it. This was the second outing for one of them, his first being the Aonach Eagach in Glen Coe! They asked us which path was best to get them up onto The Cobbler and how one got to the top. We warned them to be careful not to get blown off the summit pinnacle.

Standing by the second boulder, more massive even than the first, we watched the young men race ahead, eager for adventure. Then we followed, through more showers of snow and hail, climbing up to the Bealach a' Mhaim, the central axis of four of the Arrochar mountains. Here there is no shelter and we had to lean forward into the gale until we gratefully turned our backs to it at the path up Beinn Narnain.

The wind hurried us up slopes which are at first grassy and later rockier. There is a boulder field to cross just before the summit. The sun came out through a tear in the clouds and billions of sparkles flashed from the mica in the rock. Many boulders had their patterns accentuated by bands of white quartz, folded in tight waves like the golden mica schist above and below.

At the summit cairn a raven flashed by at incredible speed and shot down the mountain's eastern cliffs where it would get protection from potentially damaging gusts. We followed it as quickly as we could, climbing down a steep gully to the foot of the tall cliffs that guard the summit. At the base of these cliffs is a jumble of colossal boulders. We picked our way carefully across them to find one which gave us good shelter and some warmth from the strong sun which was revealed in an increasingly blue sky. A lichen-carpeted ledge served as a seat on which we ate the remainder of our lunch, staring up at small white clouds racing by.

Restored somewhat, we climbed back up the gully, prepared to battle the elements again. At the top, we turned east to look at the picturesque view dominated by Ben Lomond then put our faces into the gale and struggled across the summit plateau. Going down through the boulder field we were stopped in our tracks by a squall of hail driven by a hurricane-force wind. There was no alternative but to find a large boulder and sit behind it. It ended as abruptly as it had begun, its tail rattling over the mountain top. Morag told me that my right eye was now red, blood vessels having been broken by the impact of the small bullets of hail.

Back down at the bealach, we decided to explore the broken ridge of The Cobbler, despite the wild weather. My previous visit had been nine years ago, so this was my first experience of the new path with its well-laid rock steps. Morag disapproved, saying that the path detracted from the wild nature of the mountain. Given the intense pressure on this accessible and popular feature, however, I am much happier with what is a well-engineered and aesthetically pleasing path than the alternative, which would be an ugly erosion scar.

On the middle top, I left my rucksack and stepped across the fractured boulders to the eye in the rock wall one climbs through to access the pillar of rock which is The Cobbler's daunting summit. The wind was now so fast, however, that I could not even step across the last space between the boulders, much less attempt to remain on the small polished surface at the top of the pillar. It was an easy decision to retreat, I had climbed that pillar before and wished to live long enough to climb it again.

We dropped down from the summit ridge to get out of the roaring wind and sheltered at the base of a tall, overhanging cliff, in a place of jagged rock and a chaos of enormous angular boulders. Here we finished our provisions, drank hot tea and caught our breath.

The way back was a joy. The sky was now blue with little white clouds hurtling eastwards. We stopped often to look at the surrounding mountains, planning future walks. After the bealach, the wind was on our backs and in the lee of The Cobbler our progress was much easier. Once in the trees, I became overheated but was too tired to take off my waterproof jacket and trousers. This was just as well as a torrential shower rolled over from nowhere and I would have been soaked to the skin. The shower turned into a prolonged downpour, driven across the forest by the wind. It persisted while I drove to Lochearnhead where we stopped again at the Clachan Cottage Hotel, ready for a hot meal in the welcoming bar.

4/7/11 - 7/7/11

An Gearanach • Stob Ban • Sgurr Choinnich Mor • Ben Nevis

Good fortune to all who pass this way

We drove into the courtyard of the Grey Corries Lodge and were met by Ronaldo. As it was such a hot day, we wanted to put our perishables into a fridge. We told him that we would pick up the key to our room later as Tom wanted to make the most of the perfect weather by climbing a mountain and K was looking forward to her first Munro.

I parked the car in the last car park in Glen Nevis and watched a flock of chaffinches as I put on my boots. K put out her hand and twice a chaffinch perched on it to see if there were crumbs on offer.

I had chosen our route and the mountain, An Gearanach, with care as we only had an afternoon and I wanted something impressive for my son and daughter-in-law. There could hardly have been a finer approach than the Nevis Gorge. The river rushed along its smoothed and polished course between house-sized boulders and sunlight dappled the path under the branches of the trees. As I walked I was aware of feeling that I was leaving behind the tensions and cares I had been carrying. Then, abruptly, we emerged from

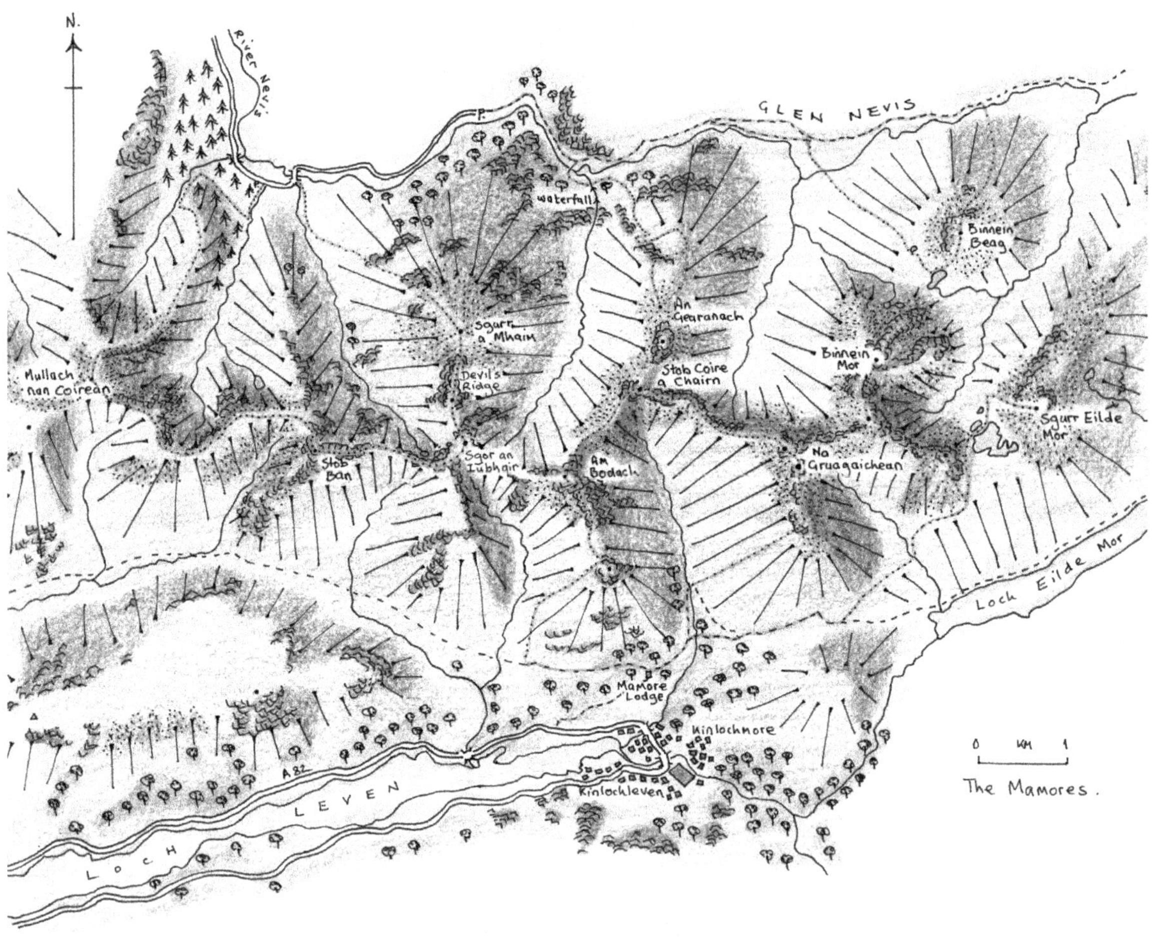

under the trees of the narrow gorge into the brilliant light of the Steall Meadows. The green was so bright that it seemed to radiate its own light. The diamond-sparkled River Nevis flowed crystal clear over a bed of multi-coloured polished pebbles. The meadows are walled by steeply stacked crags, their lower slopes clothed in native woodland. Tumbling dramatically down the rock sides of An Gearanach, the Steall Waterfall completes one of the most picturesque landscapes of the British Isles. Striding across the meadow grasses, heading for the river, I felt my spirit lift and thought, as I often do in the mountains, that I was entering another world.

K and Tom were not expecting the cable bridge over the River Nevis, one cable on which to place one's feet like a tightrope walker and two cables above for one's hands. Across and dry, we made our way to the foot of the waterfall and crossed the stream on boulders, shouting directions over the booming of the water above.

Once on the path which leads up into Coire Chadha Chaoruinn we rested on some rocks and looked back over the meadows to the gorge while we ate some lunch. Tom asked me to point out the way up onto the mountain and expressed surprise at what seemed an impossibly steep approach. I assured him that the path was reported to be a good one in its upper section but noted that his normally extremely healthy appetite seemed somewhat subdued as he gazed upwards.

It was warm. K led the way, stepping up the path as effortlessly as a young hind. I followed at a sedate Alpine pace and Tom brought up the rear, sweating profusely and stopping frequently to consume large amounts of water. He started counting 100 paces then collapsing. Colourful language seemed to help his progress. At one stop he asked what the name of this ****** mountain meant and K was most amused when I replied, "The complainer." On top of the false summit, Tom advised us that he may cough up his lungs. The final fitness score was girls 1, boys 0. At the summit cairn, I shook K's hand and congratulated her on climbing her first Munro. Tom lay on his back, past complaining.

There was hardly a breath of wind apart from gentle up-draughts of warm air from the glen below. I poured a cup of tea and answered K's questions about the surrounding mountains. There was a perfect view of the Carn Mor Dearg Arête making its graceful curve up onto the stern crags of Ben Nevis. Beyond rose the Grey Corries, an objective in the days ahead. The last peak of that range has a classic pointed mountain shape and is tipped with white, as if snow covered. This is Stob Ban, which I hoped to climb the next day.

Brown frogs hopped off the path as we descended. I wondered how they coped with the dryness in this rocky upper section of the mountain. I suppose that they only needed some shade and it would not be long before the next downpour.

Further down, a young hind was grazing on the path. We stopped to photograph her, commenting that it was hardly worth it at that distance. We approached quietly, she looked up and instead of springing away, calmly returned to her grazing. We walked nearer and nearer until she was no more than 10 metres away and we sat down to watch her. Close-up photographs were taken then we noticed her companion, a little above, standing on a crag. Her glossy brown coat, delicate legs, graceful neck and neat little head made her look like a model, posing on the skyline with a backdrop of perfect blue sky. She curved her neck back and pointed her elegant nose upwards, striking a pose for our cameras. I have never come across deer so little concerned about the presence of human beings and will treasure my photographs as I do not expect to get such good ones again.

I covered the ground more quickly than Tom and K as I descended into balmy Glen Nevis and stopped to wait for them, sitting on the path with my legs splayed out, looking down onto Steall Meadows. A pale golden frog, its skin marked with black spots, hopped into the space between my legs. It stopped, looked up at me and decided to stay there to keep me company, a patient subject for a quick sketch.

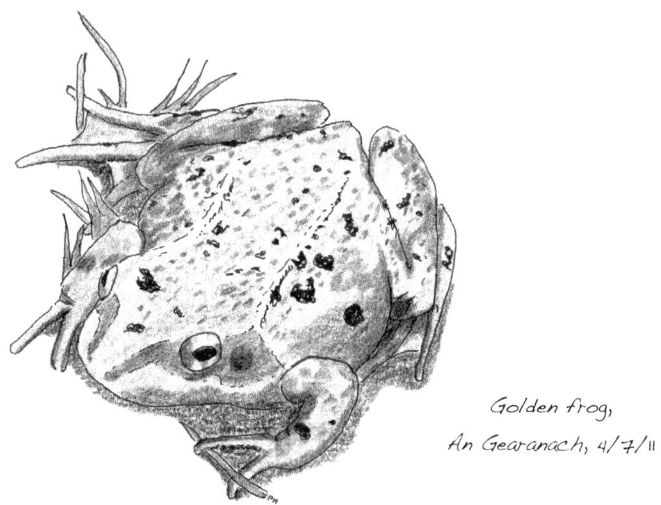

Golden frog,
An Gearanach, 4/7/11

We found a wide stretch of the river where it ran over rounded pebbles and stones and managed to cross without getting our feet too wet. Then it was a brisk walk back through the gorge to the car.

Morag was sitting reading in the sunny courtyard of the lodge when we returned. We ate well in the Roybridge Hotel that evening and despite the long day, managed a pub crawl of the village. The other pub in Roybridge is the Stronlossit Hotel where there was a good welcome and a nice pot of tea.

Tom and K were on the hunt for mackerel the next day, so Morag and I drove to Spean Bridge and then back along the south side of the river to what we thought was the road end. We parked at the bridge half a kilometre west of Corriechoille. There followed a long, long walk on the old drove road that goes over the Lairig Leacach. The weather forecast was awful but it was warm and clear, with cloud high above the Munro tops. A dark figure stood watching us from the top of a brae as we approached. I felt his eyes on me and it was

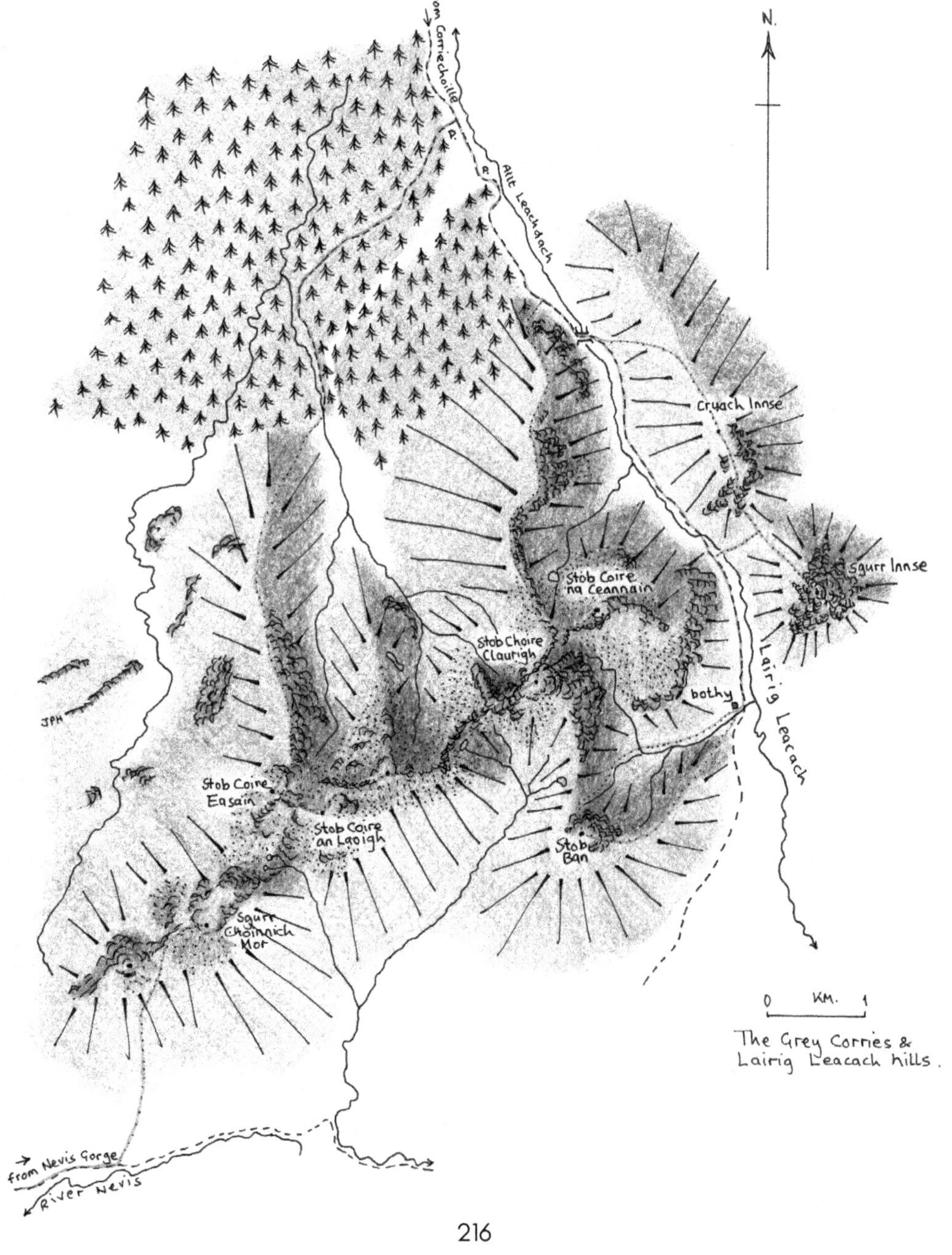

a disturbing moment. He turned out to be John McIntosh, the Wee Minister, carved from cedar. His mission was to wish good fortune to all who pass this way.

Most of the morning was gone when we reached the little bothy with its single window, nestled in a bank at the foot of Stob Ban. We opened the old door with its 1930s graffiti and were met by the smoky smell of the ancient cast iron stove. There we ate a much needed lunch then recorded our presence in the visitors' log.

We followed the path up the north side of the Allt a' Chuil Choirean and climbed steadily into the Coire Claurigh. It was sheltered and warm, with iridescent blue damsel flies dancing in pairs above the pink orchids. Dark brown dippers had a nest under a boulder in a tiny stream and I watched them pop in with beaks full of insects then out again having fed their brood. Higher up, the slope steepened and we moved onto rock and scree. Walking poles became a hindrance, we lost the path and began using our hands.

There was a very steep final ascent up pale quartzite scree. The rock characterises the uppermost section of this cone-shaped mountain and gives it its name, Stob Ban meaning white peak. On the small summit area we sat leaning against the cairn, drinking tea.

The day was perfectly clear and we were able to plan a future route up onto Stob Choire Claurigh and then west along the central ridge of the Grey Corries.

To make a circular walk, we dropped steeply down onto Stob Ban's north-east ridge and were soon back at the bothy for a second lunch. The rest was vital as we had a long, long walk out.

The peace of this remote place was interrupted by excited shouts as two mountain bikers careered down the bank and tried to get across the stream dry. One of them succeeded. They were young Belgian men, Lycra clad, slim and healthy looking. The one with the best command of English had been to the Highlands the year before and had fallen in love with it. His friend was here for the first time and was wide-eyed about it all, telling us that he had travelled widely but had not found anywhere more beautiful than this. I found myself agreeing with him as we waved them off to continue their adventure.

My body was showing clear signs of fatigue by the time we got to the point where the old tramway crossed the track. There we met a retired estate stalker. He wore a shirt, tie, tweed jacket, tweed breeches and deerstalker. I mentioned the Wee Minister and he told us the story. The original had been a fine stone sculpture brought along the tramway and set up at the top of the same bank. One Monday morning three women telephoned the estate factor, asked where the figure was and how they could see it. He was in a bad mood, lost his temper, slammed down the phone and instructed estate workers to take a

sledgehammer to the statue and break it up. The current Wee Minister is a replacement and has a box for donations to the local mountain rescue team.

The old stalker told us that he had been on all the surrounding hills bar Ben Nevis, "Because there are only tourists up there and shooting one of those could well have been a mistake." Finally, he told us that we could park where we stood chatting, which would have saved a lot of time and wear on our tired bodies.

Back at the lodge, Tom and K returned after their fishing expedition to Arisaig with a good haul of mackerel and salmon. They prepared and cooked it for us on a barbecue in the courtyard and served it with salad, boiled potatoes and pots of strong tea.

In the hotel bar that evening, Tom declared that we would have a pool competition. He and K would take on me and Morag. Andy, a boy on a bonding fishing holiday with his father, would play three wild card shots per team. This was Morag's first pool game and my second. Tom had been playing and as K had played many times he was confident of victory. The prize was to be special coffees in the Stronlossit Hotel. In my only other pool game I had played against Tom, who was described as having "a touch like an elephant". Things had improved, but not significantly. It was all to play for. We began to benefit from Tom's errors and judicious use of our eleven-year-old as a wild card. In the end, Tom potted black and white and we had the victory. He demanded a rematch for the next evening.

Rain hammered down. Brown frothy torrents hurtled through the Nevis Gorge. The Steall Waterfall was double the size it had been two days before and we would have been swept away had we tried to cross the river at the place we had skipped across on that day.

The heavy rain battering the bog myrtle of the Steall Meadows had created an air redolent with that distinctive peppermint/eucalyptus smell. We looked up to the high, craggy shoulder of Ben Nevis to see a golden eagle. It flapped its huge, square-ended wings in slow motion to settle on its eyrie.

The path into Glen Nevis was a river but we soon left it to begin a long traverse across spongy bog to Sgurr Choinnich Mor[8]. This is the most westerly of the Grey Corries and is greener, a fact reflected in the name of the mountain. At each step our boots sank into the saturated ground and the wind blew heavy rain into our faces. Despite this, there were memorable moments. The rain clouds were oddly high and we had a perfect view of the precipitous east face of Aonach Beag and Aonach Mor as we climbed. The many frogs here were dark brown, with sharp yellow and black markings. We were downwind of two young stags, who threw back their antlered heads and high stepped over the ridge ahead.

In those conditions, it took us the whole morning to get onto the bealach before the

8 See map of Grey Corries on page 216.

summit. I was expecting a buffeting as bealachs normally act as wind tunnels but it was surprisingly calm, our mountain providing shelter from the east wind. As we toiled up to the top, I stopped a few times to look at the beautiful pink quartzite, distinctive to this part of Glen Nevis. After a short rest on the top, we returned to the bealach where we leaned against a pink outcrop and ate our lunch. It had stopped raining and we enjoyed a splendid view of the Great Glen.

On the way down we saw a group of hinds and calves. They got spooked but instead of running away they ran towards us, following one of their tracks in single file. There were 36 hinds, all in good condition and four pale beige calves. They had no sooner gone than Morag nearly stood on a tawny owl. The owl rose calmly from under a clump of deer grass and sailed silently away over the boiling waters of the Nevis.

Back at the lodge, when making a pot of tea, I met a Danish mother and her teenage daughter. The daughter was simply a younger version of her mother, tall, slim, long-limbed, with natural blonde hair and honey brown skin. The mother had excellent English and I enjoyed hearing of her experience of Edinburgh. Her daughter was shy and silent. Mother said that she would have liked a not too strenuous walk that could be done in training shoes that would give a good impression of the Highlands. I went for the 1:25,000 map of the Ben Nevis area and spread it out on a kitchen table. It had a magical effect on the daughter, who came over to join her mother and seemed to absorb every detail of the walk I suggested through the Nevis Gorge to the Steall Waterfall. I invited them to play pool with us in the hotel bar but the mother was uncertain about taking her daughter into such a dubious place.

We had no qualms, however, and ordered dinner from Ronaldo. He served us hillwalkers' portions of hot soup with bread then bangers and mash with vegetables, roast potatoes and gravy. The pool game that followed saw Tom displaying oddly compulsive behaviours which included putting cue chalk between his thumb and first finger. It was won on the last ball by Tom playing Andy as a wild card.

Over teas and coffees in the Stronlossit Hotel, Tom decided that the next day's decider would have a prize of smoked salmon.

Tom and K wanted to climb Ben Nevis. The rain that had been hammering on the roof of the hostel and on the car roof as we drove stopped abruptly when we arrived at the car park. White cloud streamed up from the glen floor like smoke. It was very warm and humid and we were soon running with sweat.

There were excellent views which lasted until we reached the snowfield just below the summit. As we crossed it the cloud came down and torrential rain fell, driven by a powerful wind. We were soaked before we could put on our waterproofs. The rain turned to hail.

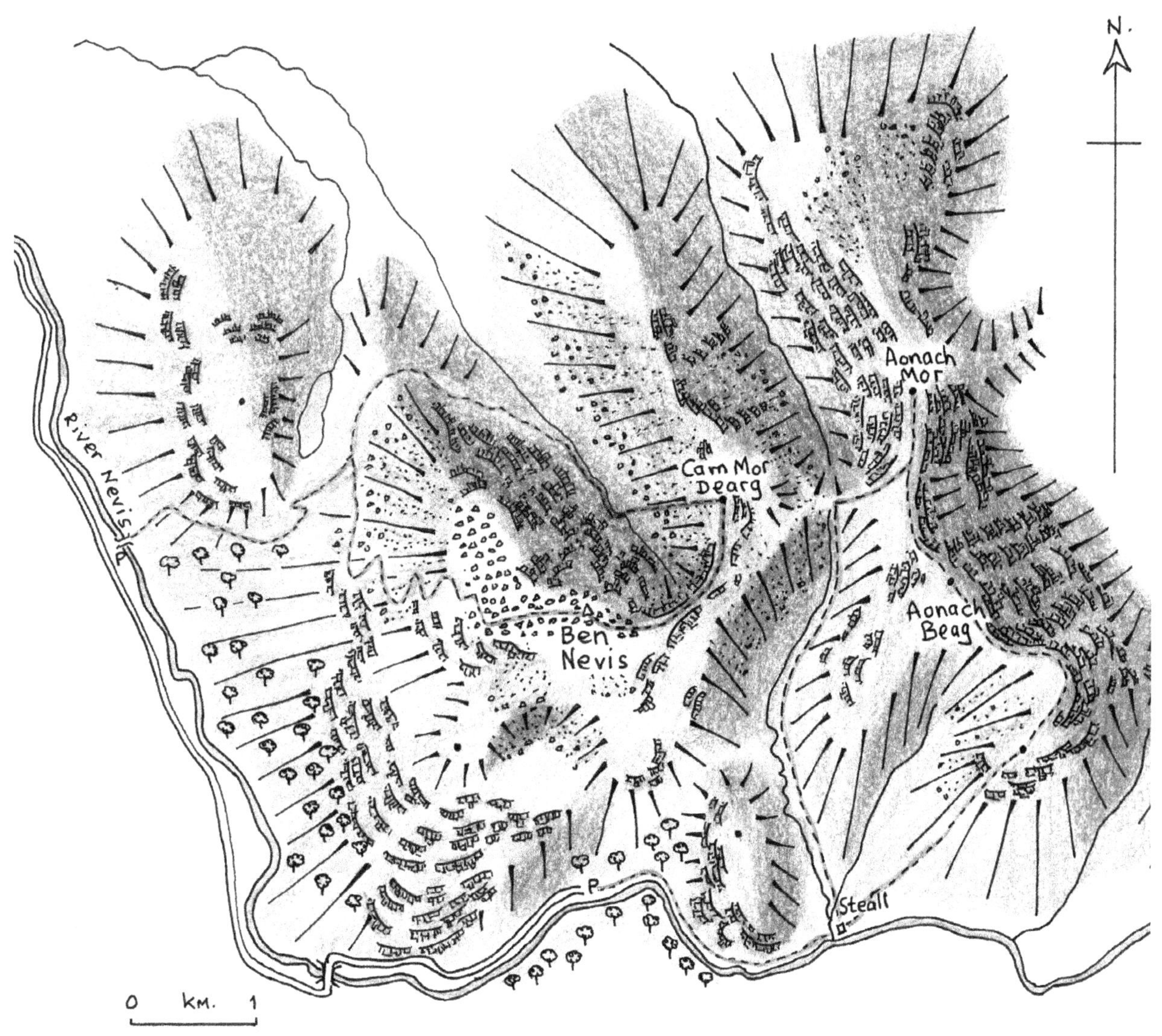

The Ben Nevis area.

We climbed up into the survival hut and struggled into extra clothing. As we ate lunch, K told us that she was shocked by the arctic conditions on the top of this mountain, particularly as it is climbed by so many ill-clad and ill-prepared tourists. She was cold and wet and Tom seemed even colder so we abandoned plans to cross the arête to Carn Mor Dearg and began a brisk walk down to warm up.

7/7/11
Survival hut
Ben Nevis.

We were soon out of the cloud, the sun came out and steam rose from rocks on the path. Views opened up over the Mamores and the fantastic mountains of Glen Coe beyond. Two ravens used the powerful up-draughts to show off their flying skills.

At the bottom, we went into the Ben Nevis Inn and ordered juice, water, teas and coffees. The south gable is filled with a beautiful picture window with a view down Glen Nevis, verdant and sunlit on this occasion. A guitar, fiddle and banjo hung on the wall for evening entertainment. We agreed to return one day to this hospitable hillwalkers' pub.

We ate at the Roybridge Hotel again that evening. As we had come to expect, the food was good in quality, value and quantity. I ate tomato and basil soup then a large portion of home-made lasagne with mashed potatoes, roast potatoes, broccoli, carrots, peas and a salad with vinaigrette dressing.

Tom decided that we would play blackjack as the decider. We had four packs of local smoked salmon and would play four hands, one lot of salmon going to each victor. Tom was very tense, declaring, "I'm playing a tactical game." Despite his undoubted skill, K won the first hand, I won the second, K won the third, then, much to everyone's relief, Tom won the last.

I took Tom and K up to Coigach on the last day of my holiday, a day of blue sky with every detail of the landscape sharp and clear in the sun. Driving down the most beautiful road in the world was, as Tom remarked, "Like coming home." Each hill had its memories and stories; Ben Mor Coigach, The Fiddler, Cul Beag, Stac Pollaidh. Cul Mor and Suilven appeared to the north, with Canisp and Quinag beyond.

We drove down to Badentarbat Bay and stopped to look at the serene and inviting Summer Isles. Then we passed the long strips of land going from the roadside houses down to the shore, with their small black cattle. Next, the little white cottage of our family holidays and finally the new campsite on the water's edge down from the An Fuarnan Bar. I left them setting up their tent, both with big smiles at the prospect of a week in this idyllic place.

9/8/11

Beinn Fhionnlaidh

A peaceful corner of our troubled world

We were getting used to the unseasonably cool, blustery and wet summer weather and I was not optimistic about our prospects for the second week of August when we had beds booked for a night in the By The Way Hostel in Tyndrum. The weather gods were to smile on us, however, as a ridge of high pressure with dry and settled conditions, although only lasting 24 hours, was forecast for the very day we had booked. The rest of the week was to be cold and particularly wet, with flood warnings.

James and I left Aberdeen before 7.00am and were parked at Invercharnan by 10.30am. We put on our boots, shouldered our rucksacks and were soon striding up through Glenetive Forest, Beinn Fhionnlaidh (Ben Finlay) our objective.

From the floor of the glen and for the entire walk up through the forest we saw mountain ringlet butterflies, very dark, glossy brown with striking dark orange markings on the wings. If butterflies are a sign of the health of the environment, all is fine in Glen Etive.

We emerged from the forest into brilliant sunshine and a sharp, cool, clear air, a perfect day to climb a Munro. The path led up towards a rock-walled gully on the southern flank

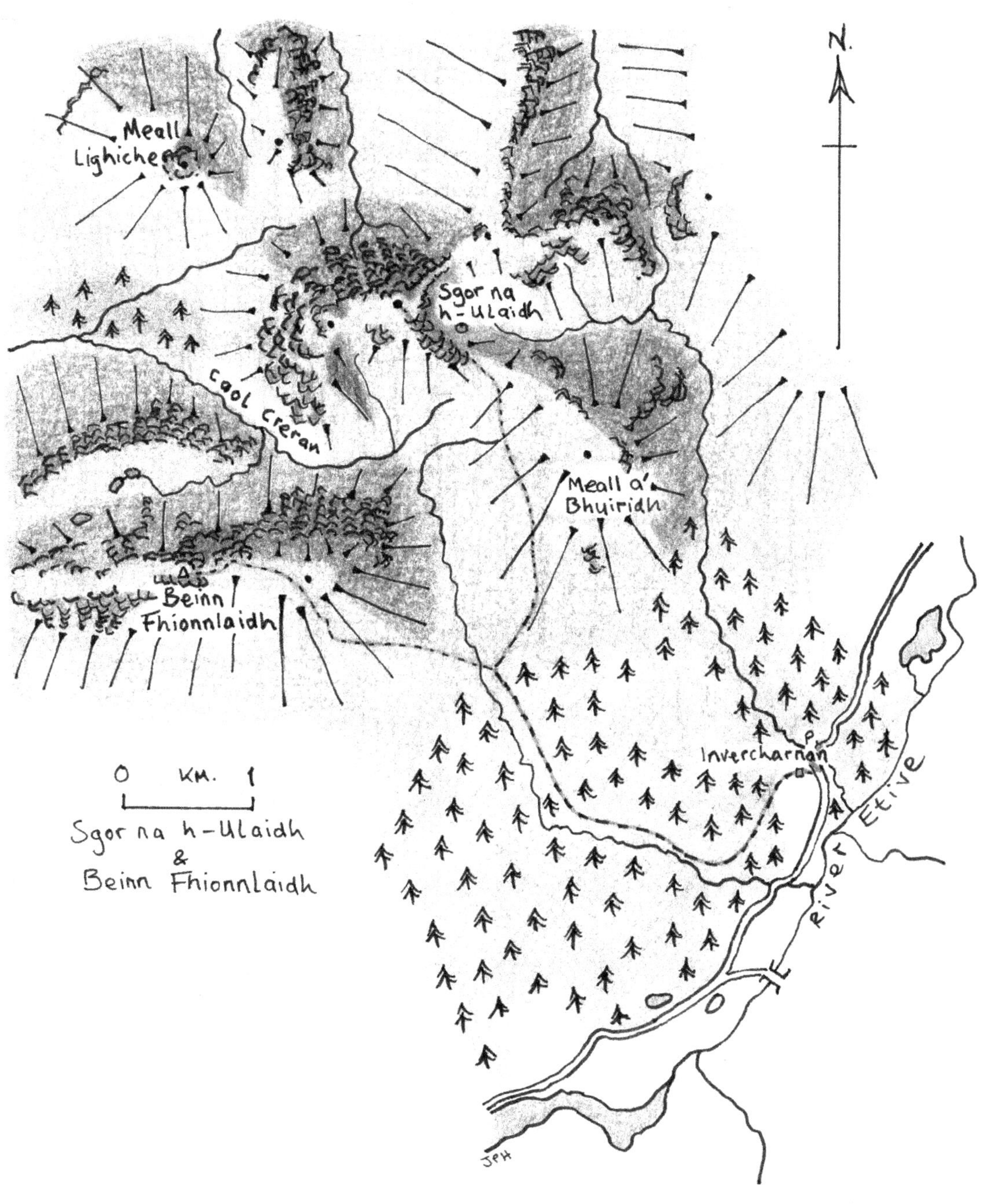
N.
Meall Lighiche
Sgor na h-Ulaidh
Caol Creran
Meall a' Bhuiridh
Beinn Fhionnlaidh
Inverchamnan
River Etive
0 KM. 1
Sgor na h-Ulaidh & Beinn Fhionnlaidh
JPH

of the mountain. We stopped just before it and sat on rocks to enjoy a cup of tea and a bite to eat. The views to the south-east of the Ben Starav group of mountains were superb. The orange spotted butterflies fluttered around us and all was well with this peaceful corner of our troubled world.

We climbed high up the north side of the gully across outcrops of schist and quartzite rock and I suggested stopping for lunch just before we got to the summit ridge, fearing that the north-west wind might make it uncomfortable up there. The views had opened up and we could see the azure waters of Loch Etive, Loch Creran, the Firth of Lorne and the dark green mountains of Mull beyond. Even at that height there were two intrepid ringlet butterflies.

On the ridge we stopped and agreed that we had rarely enjoyed a perfect 360° panorama in such particularly clear air. A white cloud sat stubbornly on top of Ben Nevis to yet again frustrate all the walkers hoping for a view from the top. It was the mountains of Glen Coe, however, that stole the show. From Beinn a' Bheithir in the west to Buachaille Etive Mor in the east, this is true mountain country, with precipitous slopes plunging down into dark shadow from summit after summit. It was good to see Sgor na h-Ulaidh beyond the deep defile of Caol Creran, as we had seen so little of it when we had climbed it with Morag in April.

I had been wrong about the wind. As we walked west along the ridge, the wind was so light that the silence was tangible. We progressed slowly, often stopping, enjoying every moment of this walk.

There were two rock steps to climb up before the summit cairn. Once there, we walked to each point of the compass, thrilled to be on top of one of the best viewpoints in the Highlands on such a perfect day. "I will store all this up," said James, "and the memory will cheer me up on grey days in the future."

We sat down for a last cup of tea and a snack, more to make the moment last than for sustenance and were joined by a young man from the REME, wide-eyed and pleased to

[9]

share his enthusiasm for the Scottish mountains with us. He told us he was to be posted to Afghanistan and I sincerely hope that he returned in one piece to enjoy many more Highland days. We left him poring over his maps, identifying the dozens of peaks he planned to climb and walked slowly back along the ridge.

It was a steep descent back into the world of little dark butterflies. Just before the forest we stopped to look at the largest lizard I have seen in the Highlands. It was either pregnant or had been feeding especially well, or both. It tried to use its little limbs to help it escape into a clump of thick grass but, although they whirred around quickly enough, they were pretty ineffective. It wriggled like a slow worm, however, and this propelled it to safety.

The ringlet butterflies added charm and colour to our walk back down the forest ride but they were outclassed by the iridescent blue dragonflies we encountered near the glen floor. We stopped to admire these amazing creatures with their incredible agility and manoeuvrability, a perfect design, unchanged by evolution for the last 300 million years.

9 Four months earlier, on the way back from climbing Sgor na h-Ulaidh, I had made this rough sketch of Beinn Fhionnlaidh. As outlined in this chapter, James and I scaled it from the other side to that shown.

That evening, well-fed and relaxed in the armchairs of the hostel, we shared a pot of tea and chatted to two West Highland Way walkers. One came from the Manchester area and he told us that he was frightened about what he would find on his return. The building where he worked had been locked up early but if it was torched by the rioters he would be out of a job. The talk was of the riots in London, Birmingham and other English cities over the last days. James was characteristically forthright in his views, saying, "It should make our political leaders wake up and realise that we have a problem. Decent, hard-working citizens feel intimidated. They need police back on the streets and the law to protect them." No one disagreed.

As we drove home next morning through torrential rain, I thought of the burning buildings, the looting and the violence. James broke the silence by saying, "Wasn't yesterday simply splendid? What a wonderful country we live in."

"Yes," I agreed, "and you and I and the good majority of people are going to keep it that way."

9/10/11

Stob Dubh and Stob Coire Raineach

Buachaille Etive Beag

It had been a tense drive from Aberdeen that dark, rainy, autumn evening as parts of the road were flooded. I was relieved to see the yellow light of the hostel's windows. We were staying at Tyndrum again and Morag had just arrived.

She had brought splendid photographs of her trip to the Okavango Delta and the Kalahari Desert. I listened to her enthusiastic commentary as she turned the pages of the albums and as I drifted off to sleep that night my head was full of images of vast salt pans, strange, isolated baobab trees and the drama of African wildlife.

It was still dark when I was woken in the morning by rain rattling on the window. At breakfast a German girl, explaining that it had rained heavily on every day of her visit to the Highlands, asked me if it was always like this. I replied that it was not but she looked sceptical.

Rannoch Moor looked desolate and bleak as the light came into the sky. Glen Coe was a gothic vision of black mountains and swirling cloud. I drove into a small parking area beside the road and switched off the engine. The wind blew sheets of rain onto the car. As it was a westerly, I had suggested following the Lairig Gartain path which runs along the River Coupall. This would allow us to climb up onto Buachaille Etive Beag sheltered

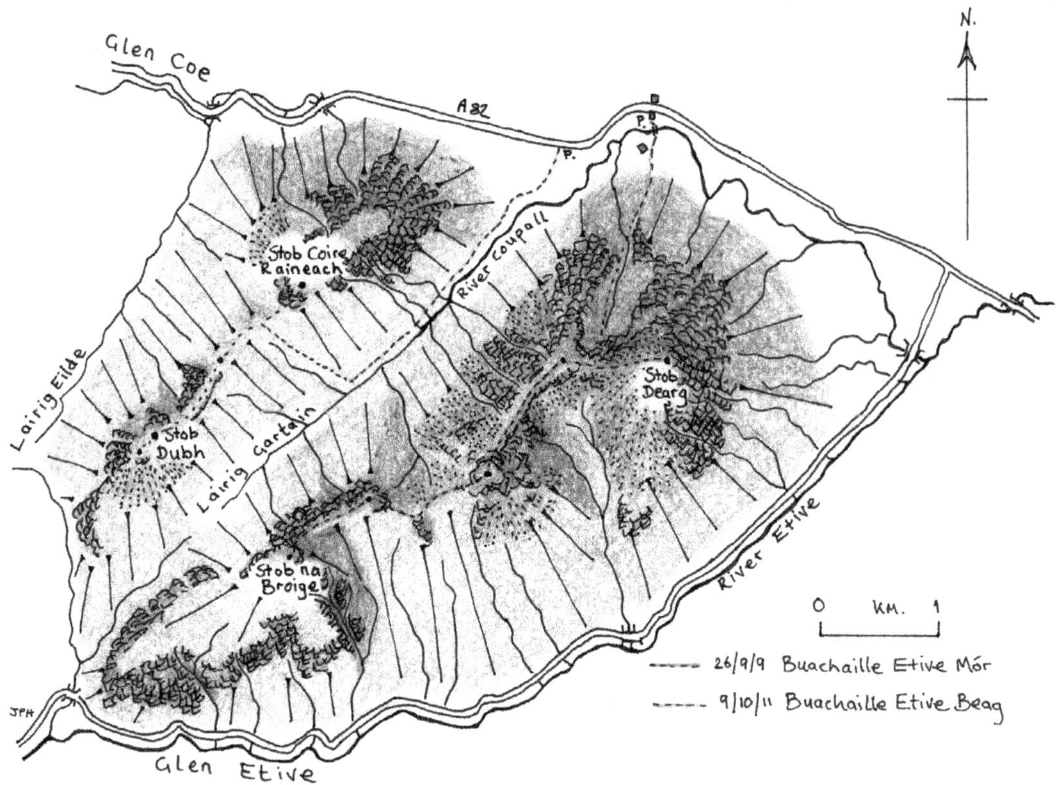

from the worst of the gusts. We pulled on our waterproofs and left the comfort of the car.

Our first challenge was to cross a tributary of the River Coupall. This would normally be unremarkable but the week's heavy rain had swollen it to a torrent. Even using the large stepping stones, the water swirled around our calves. I was glad of my walking poles which helped keep me steady.

This is a dramatic place. On our left soared the dripping dark cliffs of Buachaille Etive Mor, the big herdsman of Etive and on our right the opposing cliffs of Buachaille Etive Beag, the little herdsman. White cloud streamed over the mountain tops, sometimes lifting, sometimes billowing down towards us. A roaring echoed in the glen, the autumn rut had begun.

A path branched off to the left and twisted down to the river. We could see it on the far bank and that it climbed steeply up onto Buachaille Etive Mor. The route would, however, have been impossible on that day as the river was a thundering creamy torrent. There would have been tragic consequences for anyone trying to cross.

We stopped a little further on to watch a mature stag in his prime with his harem of hinds. Two rival stags stood a short way along the slope and a little below and two more ran in short bursts back and forth across the slope above. Some hinds detached from the main group became nervous when these latter two approached and ran to join the others. The dominant stag lifted his head, tipped back his antlers and gave out a mighty roar which stopped his four rivals in their tracks.

Buachaille Etive Beag has an obvious bealach. A stream runs straight down from it to the river below and a narrow path hugs its north bank. We followed this, stopping to watch an impressive volume of water cascade down a stepped series of waterfalls and rush across wide, polished slabs of rock which tilted steeply downhill.

Morag suggested sitting on rocks just under the crest of the ridge so that we could enjoy a sheltered snack and cup of tea before facing the buffeting of the wind. The rain was much lighter now and the cloud was tantalisingly near to lifting from the mountain tops. I watched two damsel flies, the male holding on to the female's neck with claspers at the end of his abdomen, the female twisting round to receive his sperm. This mating embrace made an opalescent blue heart. Why, I wondered, were they mating so high up on a mountain in October?

On the bealach, the wind was WSW so, being good Calvinists, we turned to face it and get the hardest climb over first. The path grew steeper and the buffeting became stronger.

Buachaille Etive Beag
9/10/11.

The last part was on exposed rock. At the cairn, I had to announce to my disappointed companion that this was only a high point on the ridge, the true summit being the best part of a kilometre further along. Extreme care was needed on the next, very narrow section. Drops to left and right were severe, there was no shelter and we had to anticipate every wild gust of wind. I was grateful that this exposed part of the ridge did not last long and we were soon climbing steeply up a path which snaked through the rock outcrops of Stob Dubh. We went on a little further than the Munro summit to the last cairn, from where we could look into the tunnel that was Glen Etive, roofed by racing cloud.

The moment we turned to go back north-east the cloud lifted. We watched as frenzied white streamers raced up from the Lairig Eilde, curved over the crest of the ridge then tore away east. Buachaille Etive Beag was revealed as a high, knife-edged ridge between two deep, rock-walled glens.

We enjoyed our walk back along the stony crest and at the bealach decided to climb Stob Coire Raineach before eating lunch. The ascent was steep through boulder scree and rock outcrops. The ferocious blasts of wind nearly knocked us off our feet. I think that we used twice the energy we would have needed on a calm day. On top, we dropped down a little to the north-east and sat down to recover. I shared some glucose tablets with Morag to give our blood sugar levels a much needed top-up. The views were wonderful, of mountain studded Glen Coe and, best of all, of the vast waste of Rannoch Moor. Here there were patches of Indian gold where the sun was breaking through the cloud.

Our descent was rapid and before long we were sitting below the bealach in the lee of the wind, looking down to the River Coupall far below. Being in the shallow gully of the stream we had followed up, the skyline on each side was not far away. A stag and two hinds appeared against the sky to our right and they stood quietly watching us eating our lunch. I thought of the kudu and springbok that Morag had seen and was glad that our native deer still roam the Highlands.

As we walked out, the cloud lifted from all the summits and the classic mountain profiles of Glen Coe towered above us. Mine was the only vehicle in the car park, potential hillwalkers and sightseers must have heard the rain rattling off their windows and decided to roll over in their warm beds and enjoy a Sunday morning lie in.

We stopped in Tyndrum for a bowl of soup and a mug of tea before driving home, glowing with that combination of fresh air and wellbeing that comes from a day in the mountains.

5/11/11

Sgor Mor

A perfect autumn walk

Deeside was more beautiful than I had ever seen it. The sun had just risen above the mountain tops, turning the coppery brown beech leaves to rose gold. Each tree cast a long black shadow over the glittering carpet of frost and the river was hidden beneath a blanket of brilliant white mist.

I parked at the Linn o' Dee and walked briskly with James along the track which follows the north bank of the river. Once out of the trees and into the morning sun we felt its warmth and eased our pace.

At the White Bridge we sat by the clear, dark blue water to have a snack and a hot drink. I enjoy hearing about my companion's adventures, this time it involved cooking sausages on the flame vents at Chimaera.

Our next stop was the Chest of Dee. Here the river crosses bands of rock harder than the surrounding Moinian schists. It roars over stepped falls and through a narrow channel with vertical walls. At the foot of this little gorge is a clear, deep pool. We could see pale igneous dykes running across its floor, part of the reason why this point has resisted the erosive power of the Dee.

Not long after, we left the track to follow the course of a tributary stream which tumbles down a series of falls, hurrying to join the river below. High above the flats of the Dee we crossed the stream above a particularly fine waterfall and climbed more steeply

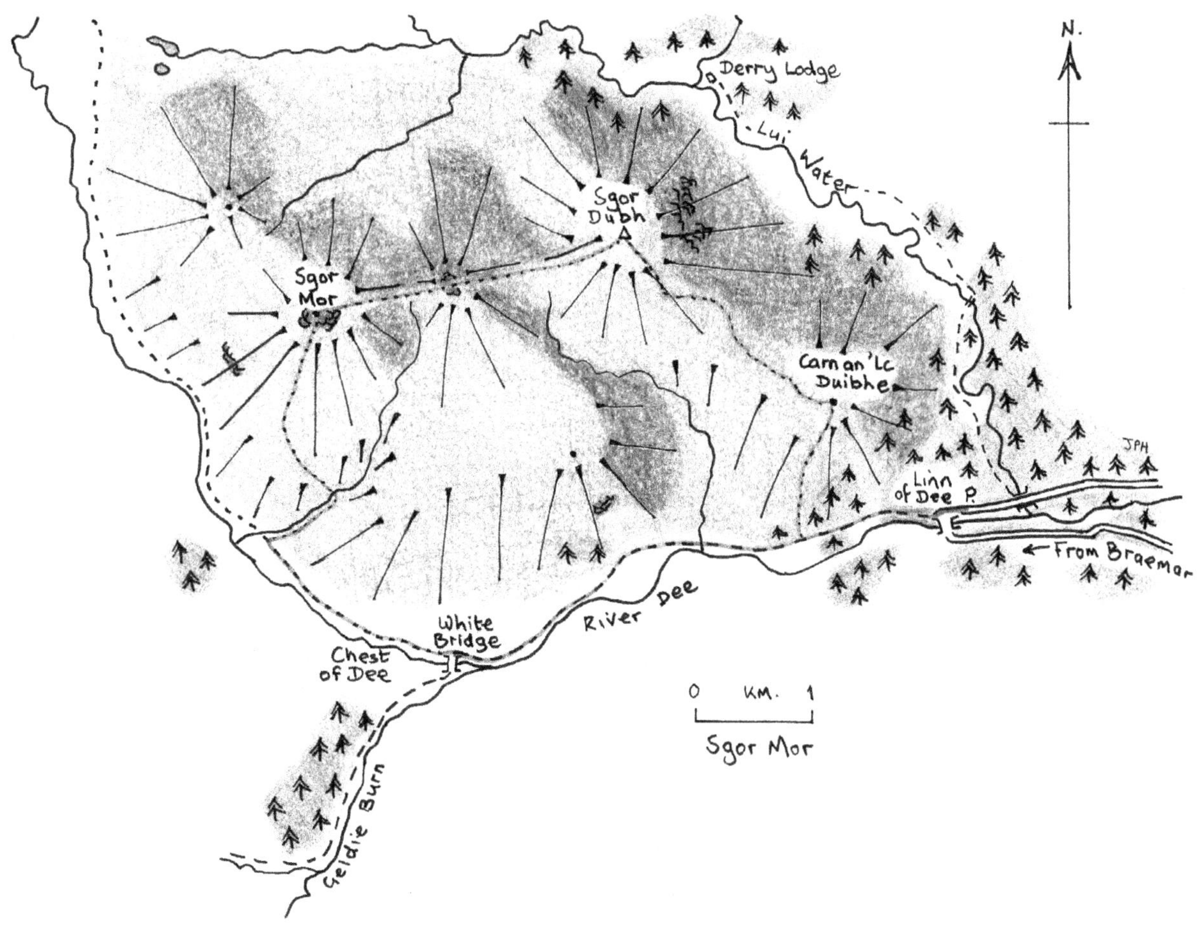

up Sgor Mor's south shoulder. The rock that outcropped through the heather was now granite. Soon the heather gave way to a shorter, sub-arctic vegetation of dwarf willow, dwarf juniper, blaeberry, crowberry, mosses and lichens.

I pointed to the skyline above which here is dominated by a granite tor. Six stags, stock still, were looking at us. Three of them broke away and trotted down across the lowest part of the tor. One suddenly lowered his antlers and punched them into the flank of the stag in front. The victim had seen it coming and was twisting back to connect with his assailant's antlers but was too late. James and I heard the thump and felt the shock.

The stags melted away as we made our slow progress upwards. When I looked up again, there were six hinds against the skyline, stock still, looking at us. We watched them until they trotted away, following the line of the stags.

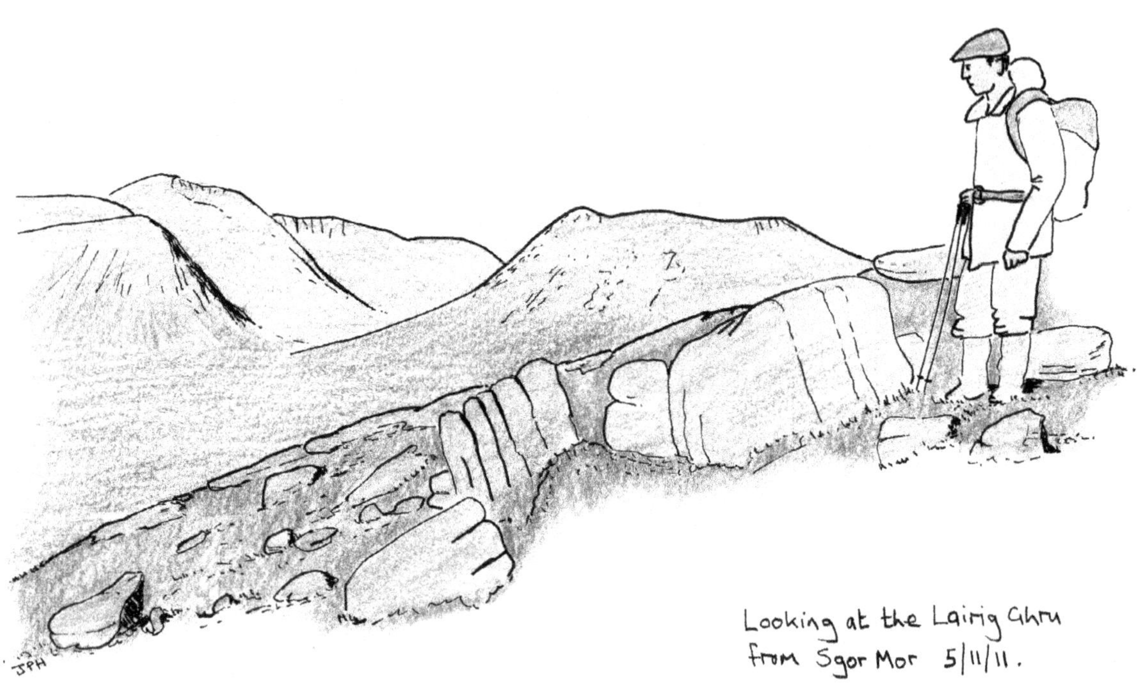

Looking at the Lairig Ghru
from Sgor Mor 5/11/11.

On top of the low tor we stood to catch our breath and take in the wide panorama of the Cairngorms, bathed in a strong light which enriched the autumn colours.

The next kilometre up to the summit of Sgor Mor was delightful. The walking was easy on grit, patches of dwarf vegetation and huge, rounded outcrops of granite. On our left rose the massive bulk of Beinn Bhrotain, separated from us by the deep trench of the Lairig Ghru. Snow lay in depressions that gave protection from the low-angled rays of the sun.

On the top of the Corbett the view to the north was worth all the effort put in to get there.

"Awesome," said James.

"Strange choice of adjective for a man who still refers to his radio as 'the wireless.'"

"I'm trying to be more up to date," he replied.

Although just above freezing there was barely any wind and the sun made it pleasant enough to sit there and eat our lunch. We looked north, remarking that The Devil's Point and Carn a' Mhaim, although Munros, were dwarfed by the giants beyond, Cairn Toul, Braeriach and Ben Macdui. Directly ahead lay the deep and narrow Glen Luibeg, with the scree-skirted Derry Cairngorm rising at its head. To the north-east were the cream coloured screes of Beinn a' Bhuird, bright as snow in that sharp light. We looked forward to many more happy days once I was retired and could go into the hills more than as an occasional treat. Routes were planned and challenges to take us into our old age were agreed. When we stood up, our thin shadows stretched far before us.

On the high ridge to Sgor Dubh we stopped at the next granite tor to look at a group of circular depressions cut into the upper surface of the rock. The SMC guide to the Corbetts describes 'a slab with a fine circular pothole scoured out by wind blast'. There was a group of these features, not one, and I remarked to James that I could not understand how these could have been created by wind. The circles were too perfect, the smoothly polished sides of the depressions were at perfect right angles to the surface and the circular base of each was perfectly flat. They were like man-made, straight-sided bowls and each was filled with clear water. The water would be a near permanent feature up there. If not man-made, I would look to running water as the force creating them but their position on the very crest of a high ridge makes me wonder about the source. If created under a massive ice sheet by some trick of rushing meltwater, why did every one look machine-made? Potholes in a river bed are not anything like as symmetrical. Also, if created long ago, why do the polished sides and sharp edges look like they were made merely months or, at best, years ago? Surely the angles would have softened over the millennia?

That high walk across the tops of a series of low tors along the granite ridge was a hillwalker's dream. The surface is a detached piece of the Arctic with irregular patches of dwarf vegetation growing through the coarse grit. The low sun lit the screes and corries of the big mountains across Glen Luibeg to the north and the long black shadows made the ridges and crags stand out in sharp relief.

At the Ordnance Survey triangulation pillar on Sgor Dubh, James remarked that he was sad to turn south-east for the last leg of the walk. We stayed on the highest ground until we came to Carn an 'lc Duibhe. Here the ground fell steeply down again to the Dee. We sat on sun-warmed rocks at the top of the slope to have a hot drink and enjoy the autumn colours of the forest below. Then we went down through long heather to the first trees, ancient Scots pines. The late afternoon sun lit the trunks, bringing out the red colour and accentuating the rugged texture of the bark by filling each fissure with shadow. My whole hand fitted into these fissures, which makes that bark the roughest I have seen.

I drove to Ballater where we stopped in the last of the light to call on Sheena. We were warmly welcomed and brought mugs of tea and hot scones while we told the story of our day.

10/12/11

Carn na Drochaide

A winter walk in the Cairngorms

December came in like an angry lion, with black ice; road accidents; freezing temperatures; hurricane force winds; power lines down; lorries blown over; buildings damaged; trees uprooted and blizzards. James, Morag and I decided to go for a walk on the 10th. The weather forecast promised a brief lull in the wild conditions, feeling as cold as minus 17° Celsius on the hill tops but largely cloud free and clear.

We followed the River Dee as we drove west, a full orange moon hanging in the sky directly ahead. The black sky turned deep purple and then the dawn light revealed a succession of Christmas card scenes, white hoar frost on the tree branches and cottages with snow-covered roofs. The white road ahead had black tracks where vehicles had passed before us. "Steady as she goes," said James, the driver. A golden halo above the high snows of Lochnagar announced that the sun was up to the south.

The entrance to the Invercauld Estate car park was blocked by a fallen tree but a forester invited us to park next to the estate buildings. It was minus 7° Celsius, still and frozen.

On the ancient right of way to Gleann an t-Slugain we walked past 200-year-old Scots pines knocked over by the wind. Some were snapped in half, some blown down, roots and all. Estate roads were blocked, power lines dragged down and there was a smell of resin in the air.

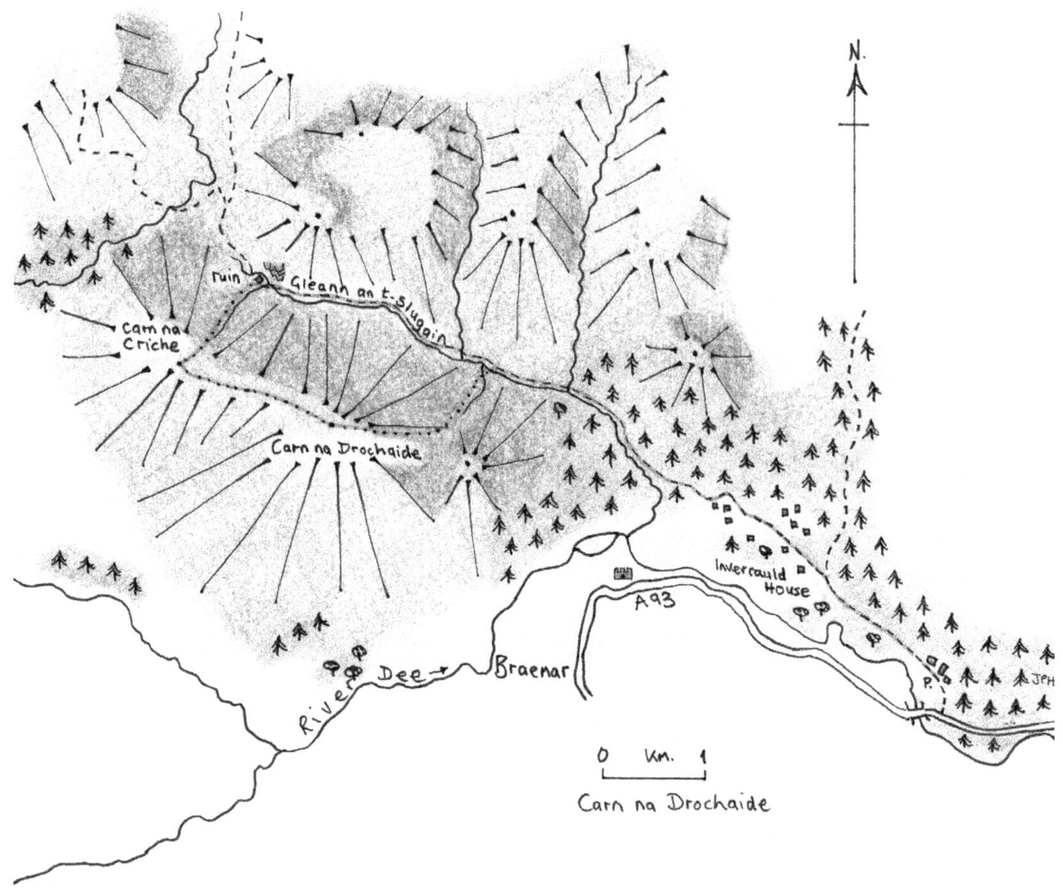

A thick cover of dry, granular snow lay over ice. We walked out of the pine forest and saw that the glen sides had an open woodland of hardy birch. They became more scattered and then the steep sides were white and bare. Drifts across the path slowed us down.

The glen narrowed between abrupt walls and outcrops of a dark, cream-spotted rock. We stopped to look at a ruin and agreed that it was a strange place to build a house. It was in deep shadow and deathly cold. Beinn a' Bhuird, nearly 4,000 feet high, rose above the glen ahead, caught by the low sun and brilliant white. I tried to take a photograph but the cold had got into the camera's battery.

We rested there and ate an early lunch. I had barely finished my cup of tea when it was time to get moving again. The brief stop had been enough to allow the intense cold to chill our bodies and numb our fingers.

It was hard work climbing up to Carn na Criche. There was an ice crust about five centimetres thick, not quite enough to bear the weight of a person. Each step broke

through to the soft snow beneath. In places there were drifts and here the snow came over our knees. It seemed a long time before we climbed out of the shadow of the glen and saw the copper sun low in the sky ahead. We walked up onto the ridge, each step easy now on the hard frozen ground, our enormously long shadows stretching back the way we had come.

At Carn na Drochaide's cairn there was an encircling panorama of pristine snow-covered mountains. Those to the west glittered in the sunlight, giving the impression that they were made of ice. There were peculiar horizontal bands of colour in the sky, with an apricot horizon to the west and green above Lochnagar in the east. The wind was moderate but the wind chill severe.

We dropped down from the summit and had a picnic in the snow, bathed in cold sunlight and perched above the shadowed glen below. It was a brief affair, however, as we rapidly lost body heat.

I led the way steeply down through a succession of drifts, following a frozen stream. On the floor of the glen was a hare. A line from The Eve of St Agnes by Keats came into my mind, 'The hare limp'd trembling through the frozen grass', but this was a Scottish mountain hare with a thick white coat. He shot off with never a hint of a tremble, perfectly at home in this frigid land.

Crossing the streams was a challenge as each rock above the surface had a thick, smooth cap of ice.

Back in the forest, a hind, crossing the track in front, skidded on the ice. A stag saw us and high-stepped deeper into the trees, his antlers thrown back.

At the end of the walk we met a forester with his spaniel. He told us that hundreds of trees had been blown down on the estate.

It was dark when we reached the Inver Hotel. We sat around the crackling wood fire, warming our chilled bodies and sipping tea. Our host, a large, well-spoken gentleman, brought us hot scones and made us feel most welcome. We thanked him for his hospitality and set off home, the orange full moon ahead.

4/1/12

Morven

A hard New Year walk

James and I left Aberdeen early on that cold, dark morning. We talked about the previous day's storm, the latest in a series surging across the country at the start of winter. Wind speeds of over 100 miles per hour were recorded in Edinburgh, chimneys were toppled and homes were without power. My youngest daughter, trying to return home after the New Year, had her train turned back before Newcastle-upon-Tyne. Scotland was cut off to rail travellers.

By the time we turned onto the Deeside road the sky was dark red along the eastern horizon. It made me think of the old rhyme, 'Red sky in the morning, shepherds' warning'. The forecast was somewhat uncertain. Would the snow sweeping across the country from the west reach us? Would the wind speed be low enough to make walking on the high ground possible? One thing was certain, the weather conditions were to deteriorate from afternoon onwards.

The hill we had chosen was Morven, the big hill, a Corbett 2,862 feet/872 metres high. We decided to start on the main road at Tullich on the grounds that all other approaches involving narrow minor roads might well be blocked should the snow come early. Our route had 16 kilometres of walking with 2,230 feet/672 metres of ascent, a pleasant hill walk in calm, dry summer conditions but something much more demanding in winter.

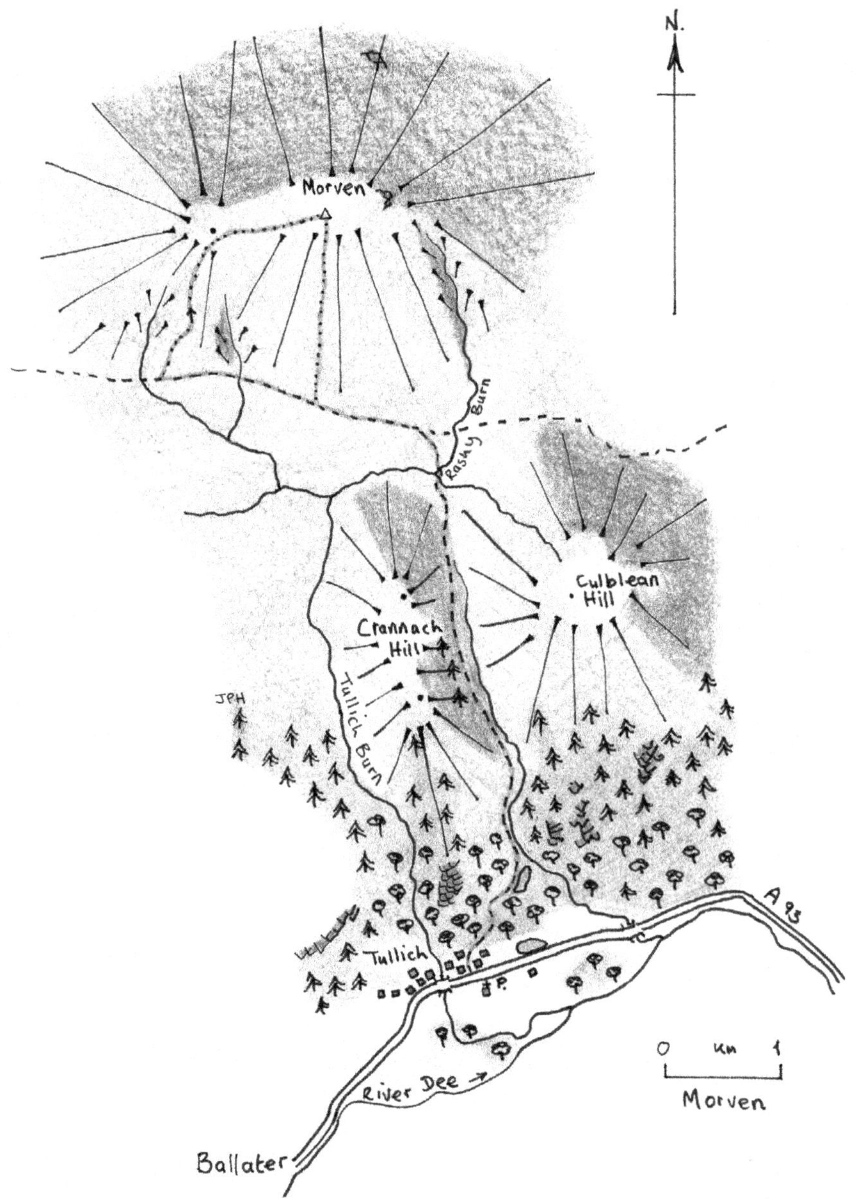

We left the car at the old church and found the gate where a faded sign pointed to the path to Morven. The first section of the walk was along the steep-sided, narrow glen between Crannach Hill and Culblean Hill, providing shelter from the bitter WNW wind. Crannach Wood was charming, an open, natural woodland dominated by birches. On the surface of a frozen lochan the pale seed heads of the marsh grass, trapped in the ice, shivered in the wind. A mature Scots pine had been snapped in half in one of the storms and we had to clamber over its fallen limbs.

As we climbed higher the birches gave way to young Scots pines, the temperature dropped and the snow on the path became deeper. I turned to look back to the south. Mount Keen, a white pyramid, rose into a pearl grey sky streaked with pale yellow and dark orange. At the northern end of the glen we came to the Rashy Burn and an open, bleak expanse of snow-covered moorland. After a tricky crossing on ice-capped boulders we trudged through deep drifts to reach an east-west track across the moor. This too was snow-covered but the going was easier. We bent our heads into the cold blast and began a two kilometre trek west. The alarm calls of red grouse were the only sounds apart from the steady hiss of the wind.

We had chosen to walk along the track to reach the western slopes of Morven, which looked a little less dauntingly steep. The top of the hill was hidden by a snow cloud.

Snow had covered all paths so we left the track at what we thought was a good enough place and began the long climb to the top. It was hard going. The tops of juniper bushes stuck out from the powdery surface on the lower slopes, they had caught the snow and great drifts had collected around and downwind of them. I made slow progress up through this, with James following in my footsteps.

After the juniper, I stopped to watch a ptarmigan in its white winter coat. It became alarmed when James came up behind me and flew off, inches above the snow. Shortly after, I saw the first mountain hare, again in a white winter coat. It took fright and sprinted off, kicking up a little cloud of fine powder snow. As I toiled up into increasingly severe conditions I saw four more white hares and marvelled at how they survive up there.

Mountain hare, Morven.
4/1/12.

The wind speed increased, the temperature dropped like a stone and the wind chill became potentially dangerous. I was glad to be wearing my Buffalo jacket but my hands, encased in thermal gloves with lined mitts over the top, were already cold.

There were no more deep drifts as the powerful wind had blown a lot of unconsolidated snow off this higher zone. Icy rocks now covered the surface. I took extra care with each step as a fall up there in those conditions could have fatal consequences.

The final section, in the snow cloud, was most extreme. I battled against the wild arctic wind, dry snow pellets rattling off my jacket and stinging my eyes. My hands were stiff and numb. At the summit cairn I stood with my back to the wind while James covered the last ground. His jacket and hat had a thick crust of ice and the drips from his nose had frozen to an icicle. We could barely make ourselves heard over the wind but, typically cheerful, James indicated that he wanted to take a photograph. I stood beside the ice-crusted cairn as instructed and struggled to remain upright while the photo was taken. Satisfied, he shouted, "I feel it would be wise not to linger up here." I did not need any convincing and turned to begin the descent.

Going down was considerably quicker than going up. The descent to the track was only 1,262 feet/372 metres but the temperature and wind chill difference was startling.

It was still very cold and exposed on the moor, however, and the wind was rising. We turned our backs to it and followed our footsteps back to the Rashy Burn. This we crossed without slipping off the boulders into the surprisingly deep brown water. Despite not having stopped at all for a rest, food and a hot drink, simply because we had not found a place out of that cruel wind, we marched on into the glen for a kilometre before halting. Crannach Hill was high enough at that point to provide shelter and we sat down in the snow.

Never have I enjoyed peanut butter and honey sandwiches, washed down with steaming mugs of tea, more. We were unusually quiet for a while, concentrating on the serious business of refuelling, until James patted his stomach and said, "Ah, that's better."

In good fettle, we set off on the last part of the walk, back down the glen. It was delightful to walk through the natural woodland in the dying light. The subdued winter tones of pale brown, pale yellow, beige and grey have a particular beauty. We saw five sheep in the trees and at the end of the glen met a shepherd looking for them, the first person we had seen all day. We told him about the sheep and he set off, crook in hand and Border collie by his side.

Big wet snowflakes began to fall as we pulled off our boots at the car. Our window in the stormy weather had been brief but had coincided with our walk to the minute. James phoned Sheena who was in Ballater and, bypassing formalities, restricted his conversation to four words, "Put the scones on."

We wished her a happy New Year and stepped from the cold, wet dusk into the light and warmth of her little flat. There we were pampered with glasses of (non-alcoholic) mulled wine, smelling of Christmas and her excellent home baking, including the requested scones. Stories were swapped of our respective Christmas activities. James professed to hate it all, echoing the 'bah, humbug' sentiment expressed in the card he had sent us. Then he waxed lyrical about the five festive meals to which he had been invited. He did, of course, see the irony. His cracker jokes are unprintable.

It was dark when we left, the icy wind throwing sheets of sleet at the car. James settled into the passenger seat, sighed contentedly and said, "What a grand day."

28/1/12

Brown Cow Hill

Finding the Well of Don

Outside my warm house the air was still, there had been a hard frost and the constellations were clear in the black sky. I drove along the silent streets, onto the old arched bridge and looked over to where the Don runs into the sea. The waters were calm, which was a good omen for the day. The hillwalkers' weather forecast came onto the radio: cold; minus 5° Celsius on the tops; very little wind; sunshine; snow showers later.

I left my car at James's house and he drove us west up Donside. With the dawn came a blood red sky, turning the white fields pink. The bare black branches of the trees were thick with hoar frost.

We parked at Corgarff Castle, a stark and grim English garrison built to control the road. James said, "I visited the castle many years ago. I expect that you won't be able to do that any more as it will have been turned into an interactive, real-time, virtual experience."

In minutes we were away from the road and following a track up into the wintry hills. James stopped to point out the growing area of blue sky and ended up flat on his back, there was sheet ice beneath the powdery covering of snow.

The track ended and we headed across rough ground upwards towards the Brown Cow Hill ridge. The ground was iron hard. Pools in the peat bog, streams and small waterfalls had all turned into big lobes of ice, some pale green and some identical to Kendal Mint Cake.

The red grouse did not seem to be as panic-stricken by us as usual, perhaps it was the cold making them torpid. One fine bird even struck a pose on a rock and we were able to walk quite close before his nerve broke. Higher up was a ptarmigan which we had not seen against the snow until it moved.

There were mountain hares in very good condition and we had some interesting close encounters. They would sit erect and watch us until we crossed a critical point and then off they shot.

The top of the ridge turned out to be an undulating frozen plateau. We sat down to enjoy a hot drink. The views were wide indeed, with a great feeling of space and of being in wild land. Snow lay on Lochnagar in the south. The sky above that mountain was apricot in colour and a pale green band stretched from its summit to the sea in the east. The sun was low and the light intense, producing strong shadows and a metallic, polished effect on the western hills. Ben Avon rose above all, massive, brilliant white, with a tor like a dark spike against a pale blue sky.

Walking along the ridge we came to the highest point[10] where we sat to eat our lunch. The air barely moved, it was hushed, deserted and subtly beautiful. We were reluctant to leave.

10 Brown Cow Hill is a Corbett, 829 metres above sea level.

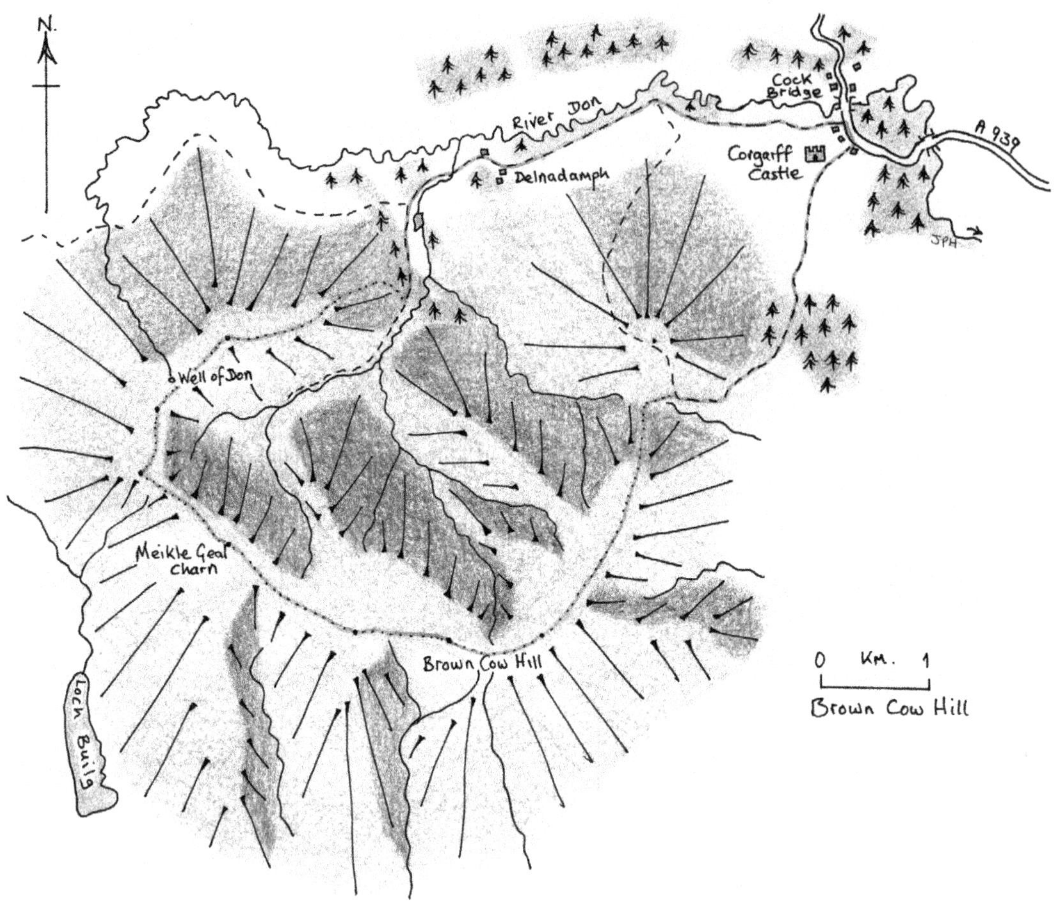

We followed the crests of the hills in a great circular route back to the castle. The walk was on granite until Meikle Geal Charn, which is made of quartzite. Its top was a pile of quartzite blocks, each iced with pristine snow. Later we came across some old, rusty fence posts. A new, electrified deer fence began to follow both the old posts and the crest of the ridge. We used a stile to cross it and search for the Well of Don. The area marked on the map was a gently sloping place of frozen peat hags with colossal icicles and columns of ice falling to solid pools, in warmer months a giant sponge to feed the headwaters of the river. I explored the network of channels and ended at the highest frozen pool, the Well of Don, the very beginning of one of the most beautiful rivers of the British Isles.

The views had now opened up to the snow-covered mountains of the north-east Cairngorms and the shapely hills to the north. We began to feel weary as we continued along the ridge, our route was a high-level circuit of 19 kilometres and looking back we could see that we had covered a lot of ground.

Coming down from the heights we stopped by a large pool created by an old dam built across the Meoir Veannaich, a tributary of the Don. Downing our last hot drinks we looked at the perfect reflections of the winter trees in the mirror glass of the pool's surface.

3/3/12

Carn Mor

Navigating in the Ladder Hills

Given the weather forecast, we knew that we were in for a wild day. Wind buffeted the car as I drove in low gear up the notorious Cock Bridge to Tomintoul road. I stopped at the Lecht Ski Centre, the highest point on that road and parked in the deserted car park.

Well wrapped up, we crossed the road and followed an old fence uphill. At the top of this first slope, ski tows marked the end of the land given over to winter sports. Ahead lay the lonely and bleak Ladder Hills. The highest summit is the Corbett of Carn Mor, our objective for the day. I made moves to use map and compass to work out the direction in which we had to walk but James, with a knowing look, announced that there was no need. He had climbed the hill before and we had simply to follow the old fence which marked the county boundary and it would lead us all the way to the top.

A continuous stream of low cloud was being blown over the hills which made visibility poor and the line of weathered fence posts welcome. The south-easterly wind was cold and powerful, 40 miles per hour with gusts much stronger. I felt the right side of my face go numb, despite my winter cap and pulled up my hood. Hail rattled off my waterproofs.

As conversation required so much effort in that wind we walked in Indian file, each locked in his or her own thoughts. I began to focus on the world at my feet and in the limited distance I could see ahead. The terrain was of two types. One was peat bog with

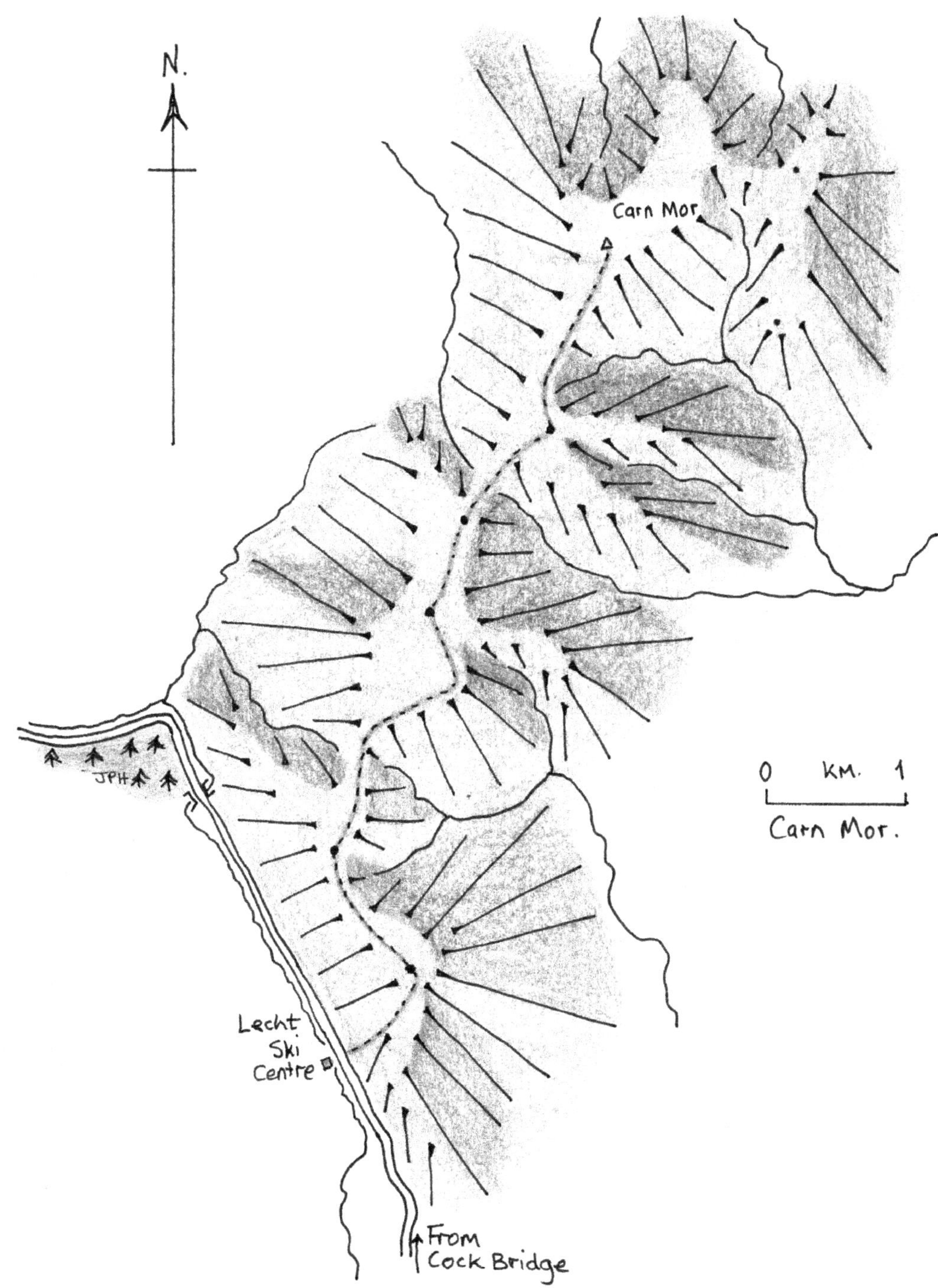
N.
Carn Mor
0 KM. 1
Carn Mor.
JPH
Lecht
Ski
Centre
From
Cock Bridge

pools which forced us to detour away from the fence posts. Some pools were crystal clear and others had bright green algae on their surface. In some places the bog had been eroded and we had to climb down the sticky black sides of peat hags and back up again. As we emerged we disturbed pairs of red grouse which rose and clattered away into the mist. The second type of terrain was a thin stony surface carpeted with mosses and lichens. This was hard and dry and walking was much easier over the short plant cover.

I began to notice detail. There were many types of moss and lichen, each one different and together forming a patchwork of contrasting colour and texture. The tallest was reindeer moss, a pale metallic grey branching lichen which covered extensive areas of ground. Other patches were of maroon, deep red, pale yellow, jade green and a luminous pale green. I wondered why the reindeer moss stood taller in some areas, producing branched stems, but was a low carpet in others. I then saw that the short areas had been nibbled down systematically and I wondered by what. A mountain hare appeared, mottled white with blue-grey spots and that answered my question.

The lichens in particular impressed me, growing on bare rock and obviously thriving in this extreme environment. An off-white clump made of delicate fronds looked like it would blow away with the next gust of wind but when I bent down to examine this strange plant it was firmly anchored to its slab of rock.

Even the fence posts were interesting, each weathered into a different shape, all bleached by exposure to sun, rain and snow and all old enough to be colonised by crusty rosettes of lichen.

I was happy. The land rose and fell as we climbed each eminence on the main axis of the hills. Warm and dry, I was content with my restricted view, absorbed in the minutia of marvellous things I would barely notice on a clear day when my attention would be on the wide prospect and the way ahead.

I came to a cairn and stood, buffeted by the wind, waiting for the others to join me. "Just follow the fence," said James. The fence dropped quite steeply down to the left and we dropped down with it. The wind roared over the ridge top and cold, sleety drops smacked onto my waterproofs. There were more bogs, further stony patches carpeted with lichens and mosses and I remained locked in my private world.

It was the wind that snapped me out of my reverie. It no longer blew on my right side but blew on my back instead. I carried a mental picture of the route we should be following on the map and knew that it was just about a straight line. I also knew that the wind direction was forecast to remain constant during the day. We had clearly taken a wrong turn and dropped off the crest line to walk to the north-west. The fence did not lead to Carn Mor.

I waited for the others and expressed my concern. James used his GPS to give us a fix on our location but said, “Oh, I don’t like that grid reference at all, I’ll do it again.” The second fix was no different. We looked at the map and found that we had come down a branching spur at the cairn and my friend’s memory of following the fence to the Corbett top was clearly inaccurate. Having abdicated responsibility for the navigation, I could hardly complain, so it was heads down into the teeth of the cold wind and a rather tiring climb back up onto the ridge. Our diversion was little more than two kilometres but it felt a lot more. It was a painful lesson but, I suppose, that made it all the better.

At the cairn again, James checked our grid reference and, given what had happened and the continued poor visibility, I suggested that we walk on a bearing, which we did.

The last section was only two kilometres and the walking was on fairly good ground but I had been working my body hard for hours without a rest and my energy reserves were low. This high ridge was very exposed, however, and I could see no potential lunch spot out of that cruel wind. We trudged up the last slope to the top, over bare, gritty ground and reached the old triangulation pillar. It was no place to linger and soon we were retracing our steps.

Lunch on Carn Mor, 3/3/12.

I spotted a peat hag just off the line of our reverse bearing and declared that it was as good a lunch spot as we were going to get. The others agreed. We slipped down the black, sticky side and found places to sit, our boots in the dark pool that filled the bottom of our shelter. The sleet had now turned to snow which whistled over our heads. As unlikely as it may seem, lunch was a cheerful affair. None of us have it in our nature to complain and instead we laughed in the face of adversity. My honey and peanut butter pieces yet again proved a perfect hillwalker's lunch as I felt almost instantly revitalised. Mugs of steaming hot tea provided some comfort and helped keep the cold at bay.

It was not wise to linger in those conditions and we were soon climbing back up, my fingers numb with cold as I had removed my mitts to eat. At the cairn we were surprised to see a landscape of sunlit hills to the south and west, the cloud was breaking up.

The walk back was a delight. Although still assailed by the wind, the snow had stopped falling and we were warmed by the bright sun. The path dipped below the crest of the ridge and this provided some shelter so I suggested another stop to finish our hurried lunch and enjoy a hot drink. The sun had changed the whole character of the walk, no longer were we engaged in a grim struggle, instead we felt relaxed for the first time and with that feeling came a wave of warm tiredness. We looked at the faded tans and beiges of the late winter hills with their patches of old snow. "What a shame," said Morag, "that the sun hadn't come out earlier."

"Yes," replied James, "but I think that we need to be tested sometimes and not get too complacent."

It was hard to get up again.

We pulled off our waterproofs and boots when back at the ski centre then got in the car. The doors slammed shut and we sat for a moment appreciating the quiet after a day of roaring wind.

Donside was beautiful in the late afternoon sun, a charming place of meadows, woods and steep hills. A pair of buzzards played in the wind above the road, perfectly complementing the landscape.

7/4/12

Ben Starav and Beinn nan Aighenan

An Easter walk in the Glen Etive mountains

Morag drove slowly down Glen Etive. The early morning sun lit up the snow-streaked peaks that rose like towers from the narrow river flats. She stopped to look at a group of hinds with a calf just beside the road and again a little further on for a group of stags, most still with antlers. Two youngsters from the group walked, unconcerned, beside the car. She had to stop just before the parking place for a stag in his prime who took his time crossing just inches from the car bonnet then stood looking at us.

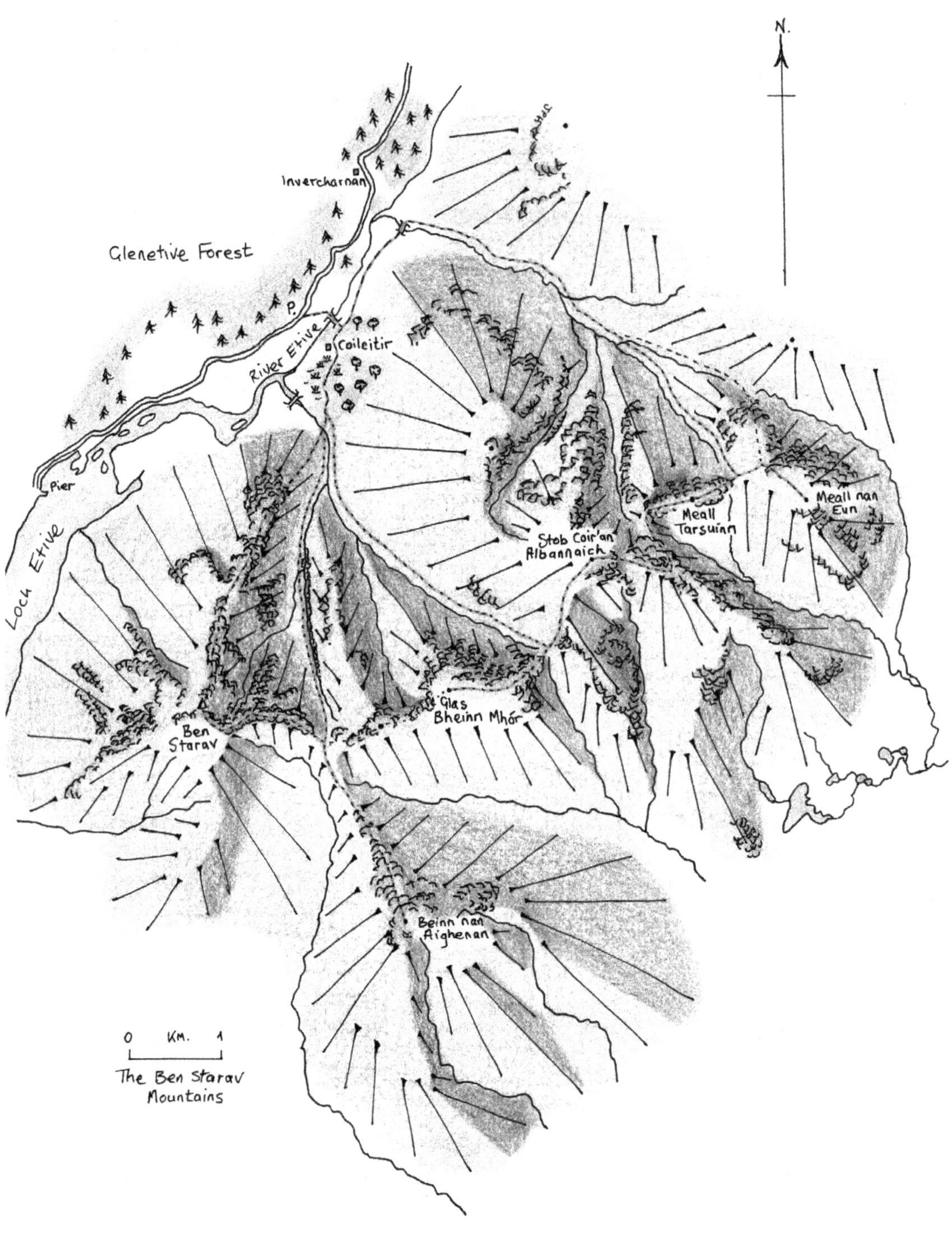
N.
Invercharnan
Glenetive Forest
P.
Coileitir
River Etive
Pier
Loch Etive
Meall nan Eun
Meall Tarsuinn
Stob Coir'an Albannaich
Glas Bheinn Mhór
Ben Starav
Beinn nan Aighenan
0 KM. 1
The Ben Starav Mountains

We walked down to the bridge and I looked into the dark pool beneath. Morag remarked that it would be perfect for a cool off swim after a walk on a hot and sticky day.

A new fence had been built around the cottage at Coileitir. Its gate displayed a sign which directed walkers to the left so we obediently followed the instruction. It led us to an unpleasant path across a peat bog which, I am sure, has claimed a number of unfortunate walkers. Two mature stags stood watching us, obviously anticipating the amusement of more of those peculiar humans walking straight into the same patch that swallowed the others.

We survived, however, and ended up on the smooth, polished rock bed of the Allt Mheuran. There had been heavy snow during the week followed by a thaw so there was plenty of water roaring down to join the Etive. "Should there not be a bridge?" I asked. James consulted his map.

"We should have gone right at that gate," he replied, "We've ended up too far upstream."

Wading was tricky, even though the water only surged up to calf level, because the polished rock has a growth of slippery algae. Morag suffered a wet boot but otherwise we got across without disaster. Readers beware, there is often a lot more water in this fast flowing stream, so I advise using the bridge.

7/4/12 Two mature stags stood watching us.

On the west bank we stood for a few minutes to consider our route. Ben Starav was the first objective, its long north-eastern spur ending abruptly at our feet. A high bealach, no more than a notch in the mountain ridge to the south, separates Ben Starav from Glas Bheinn Mhor, another of our targets. Beinn nan Aighenan (pronounced yanan), the hill of the hinds, lay out of sight over five kilometres to the south. This elusive Munro was the third in our sights. I wondered whether I would have the stamina to climb all three. It was certainly going to be a major undertaking.

We started a few metres above sea level and I set the pace as we steadily climbed the 1,000 metres of the long, steep spur. When we stopped to catch our breath the views to the north and west were worth all the effort. Bidean nam Bian, with a cap of dazzling snow, rose majestically above the sharp peaks of Glen Coe. Down below on Loch Etive, a coaster with a bright blue hull, trimmed with red below the Plimsoll line and with a white wheelhouse, had just taken on a load of timber at the little pier. Grey smoke came from its funnel as it gently moved away into the main channel. I found it reassuring that in an age where technological innovation changes the world with bewildering speed, I was watching a scene that would have been familiar to Para Handy.

900 metres up the ridge we stopped for a hot drink and a snack. There had been very little wind so the morning's weather was only changing slowly, but changing it was. Cloud and rain was due to cover the area in the afternoon and already the peaks of Glen Coe were capped with white cloud. We turned to admire the summit of Ben Starav, a serrated granite chisel blade which appeared black above the snowfields. "Positively Alpine," remarked James.

We needed to use our hands as we climbed the granite boulders and stepped pinnacles to get to the high ridge. Soon we were walking across patches of snow and, as expected, the first wisps of cloud came streaming up the western side of the mountain just as we reached the top.

The narrow path followed the very edge of a wall made of vertical columns of granite. The columns were made aeons ago as the granite cooled and shrank, leaving massive organ pipes that today rise up from the high corrie far below. We came to a cornice capping a colossal slab of snow sticking to the organ pipe wall. An ominous crack ran parallel to our path where the slab would break away, causing an avalanche into the snow-filled corrie.

Then we began a steep descent onto a narrow ridge of granite castellations. We needed handholds again and took care. This led to a part of the mountain with monumental granite ribs ending in sharp points, tilted just off the vertical. One long seam of white quartz followed the dark granite ribs. I felt a compelling desire to return to this place to explore and sketch and absorb the curious atmosphere. Would it feel as strange without the thin, slowly moving ghosts of mist?

At the bealach we were just under the descending cloud and could see down the lonely glen of the Allt Haliater to Beinn nan Lus. The slopes of Beinn nan Aighenan made the eastern wall of the glen but the top of this Munro was shrouded in cloud. We fortified ourselves with lunch and set off towards it. The west wind picked up and the rain started, so we stopped to put on our waterproofs.

The path, disappearing at times, led through a rock wilderness. There were extensive granite slabs littered with huge boulders, some perched on what looked like unstable pedestals. Once more I felt the desire to return on a fine day to explore the slopes of this remote mountain.

The going was heavy on our return journey from the summit, with a big climb up to the bealach. There we sat down for a hot drink as all three of us were shattered. We peered through the fine rain but could see nothing of Glas Bheinn Mor and decided to save it for another day.

North from the bealach down into a steep, confined gully was the most direct route back. We were brought to an abrupt stop at the head of a deep, perfectly straight, very narrow gorge. It was a fault line filled with orange/pink felsite which, being less resistant than the granite, had been eroded out by fast-flowing water. The little stream running along its floor was not the culprit. I pictured a roaring stream coming from a decaying ice sheet. The path ran along the very rim of the gorge and was no place for anyone with vertigo. Morag suggested that it was made to be a film set for The Lord of the Rings.

We followed the felsite down to the junction with the Allt Mheuran and came back to the place where we had crossed the river. There was a little more water but we got safely across.

It was a slog across the bog. I was very weary. The dark pool under the bridge could have tempted me on another day but I had no energy left to peel off my boots and clothes, never mind cope with the cold water. We got back to the car 9½ hours after we had left it.

Morag drove up the glen. She stopped again to look at a young stag that walked alongside the car but I was wet and chilled and wished she would drive on. I changed into dry clothes at Tyndrum and we drove to the Clachan Cottage Hotel at Lochearnhead. It took a bowl of hot soup, a pot of tea, chicken, black pudding, mashed potato and gravy to get life seeping back into my cold, tired limbs.

7/5/12

Carn Liath

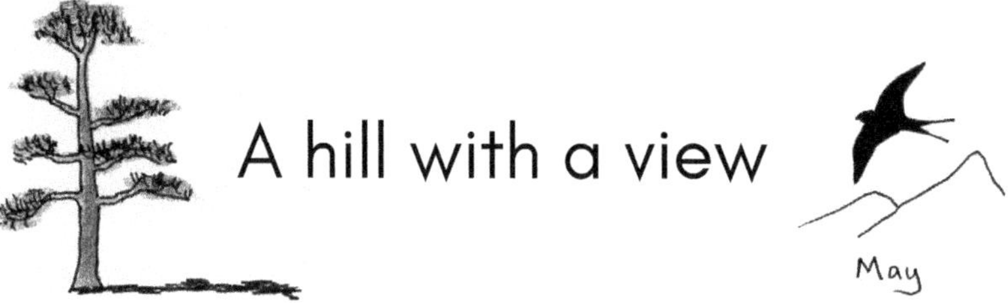

I drove slowly as we approached Inverey to give us a better chance to spot the Hanging Tree but, as on previous occasions, we arrived at the car park by the memorial having failed to do so.

Walking over the bridge and then along the track on the west side of the Ey Burn we were, predictably, discussing the weather forecast. It was to be a cold, still morning but the warm front of an Atlantic depression was to roll over this part of the Highlands around lunchtime, bringing snow to the tops and rain to lower areas. With this in mind, James and I had planned a modest walk of 10 kilometres or so. Our objective was Carn Liath, neither a Munro nor a Corbett. My companion had assured me, however, that I would be impressed when we reached the top.

Following the track along the Allt Cristie Mor, we stopped to watch the water rush through the channel of a little gorge cut into banded quartzite and then slow abruptly in a still, perfectly clear pool. Leaving the noise of the water, the silence of the hills closed around us. The smart plumage of a pair of goosanders caught our eye as they flew low down the stream and landed with a splash. Then all was silent again.

There was a small cairn on the bealach at the head of the glen, marking the start of the path that leads north to the top of Carn Liath. The ground became a litter of angular fragments of the banded quartzite cap of the hill with only the tips of these rocks protruding from the summit snowfield.

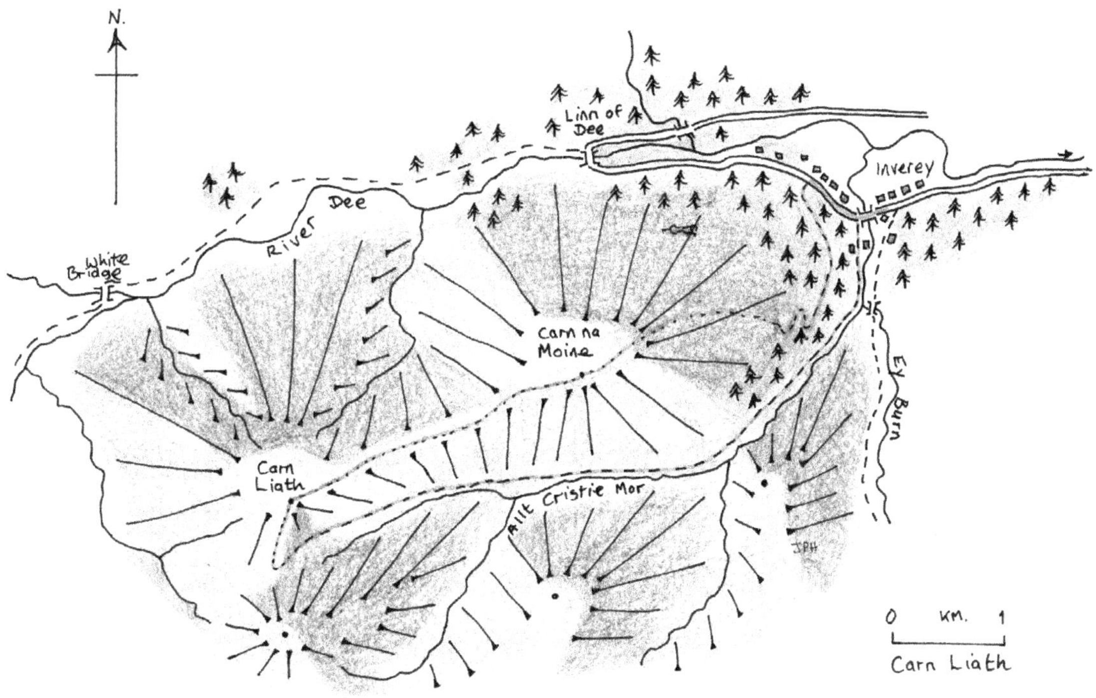

As we approached the cairn I told James that I was indeed impressed by the panorama. To the north the dark cleft of the Lairig Ghru is surrounded by the Cairngorm giants of Cairn Toul, Braeriach and Ben Macdui, all snow-covered on that May day. The snows of Lochnagar and the Mounth caught a shaft of sun in the east. To the south and west rose the ridges of the wild and lonely country which stretches to Beinn a' Ghlo, snow-capped like its northern and eastern neighbours. Above all this were fantastic cloud shapes, their swirling greys punctuated by little patches of blue. There were flat rocks at the cairn so we brushed the snow off them and sat down to enjoy lunch amid all this splendour.

We lingered there but when a fine, dry snow began to fall it was time to pack up and go. We headed north-east towards Carn na Moine, a three kilometre ridge walk as fine in its way as any I've done. The sun winked out but we watched snow showers over the mountains to the north, white vertical lines coming from dark clouds.

We stopped at a cairn shaped like a stone seat and were charmed by a snow bunting that shot out from the slabs. Time stood still for a while as we sipped hot drinks and watched the light change on gleaming Lochnagar. A raven spotted us and wheeled gracefully high above, waiting for us to go so it could land for crumbs.

The end of the ridge dips down into resin-scented forest. We disturbed a red deer which ran into the trees, then all was still again. We could smell the wood smoke from the

cottages at Inverey before we emerged from the trees. The first raindrops quickened our stride back to the car where we pulled off our boots. The doors were slammed shut and the rain, with perfect timing, began to fall heavily.

Soon we were stretching our legs in front of the log fire in the Fife Arms enjoying a pot of tea and scones, watching the rain run down the windows.

26/5/12

Meall nan Eun, Stob Coir' an Albannaich and Glas Bheinn Mhor

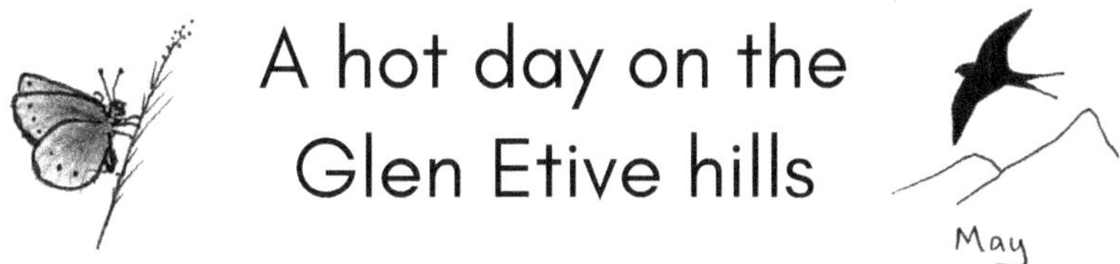

I had been a fortnight without my car while the garage waited for a part. It arrived and was fitted at the last moment on Friday afternoon. I told the mechanic that I was driving across country to the West Highlands that same evening and he suggested, "Best not take it out of mobile phone reception."

It turned out to be a lovely drive on that spring evening with the westering sun back-lighting the translucent new leaves of the trees.

We joined Morag at Crianlarich Youth Hostel where we intended to spend the night. Inside, we joined an eccentric mix of people. There were three groups of West Highland Way walkers, the first well-spoken student girls, the second made up of young men and the third a lively crowd of young women. The latter two groups were clearly from Glasgow. One of the young men wore nothing but swimming shorts and sported large tattoos. Whatever he said to impress the young women was met with merciless put-downs, the

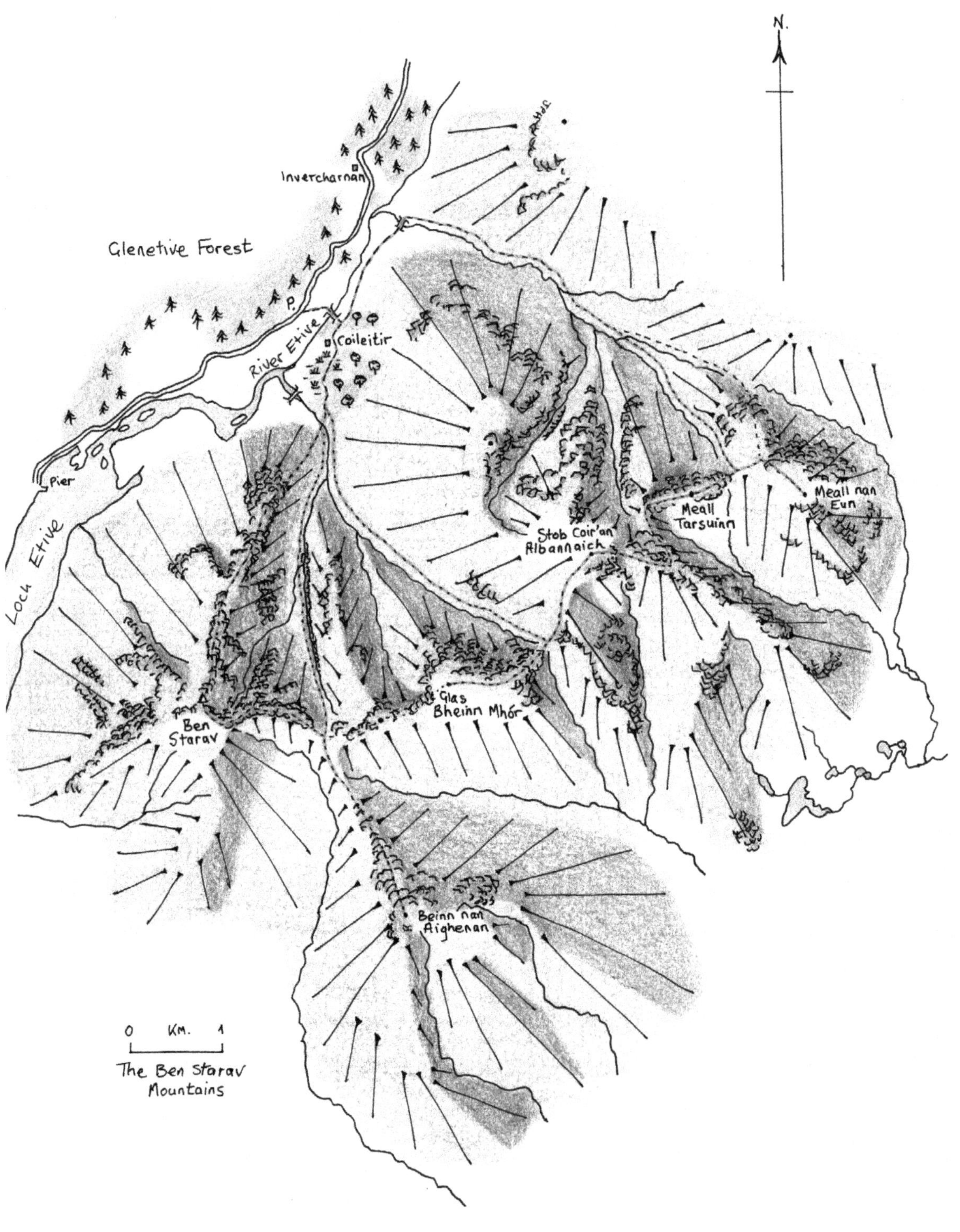
N.
Invercharnan
Glenetive Forest
P.
Coileitir
River Etive
Pier
Loch Etive
Stob Coir'an Albannaich
Meall Tarsuinn
Meall nan Eun
Ben Starav
Glas Bheinn Mhór
Beinn nan Aighenan
0 KM. 1
The Ben Starav Mountains

women being quick to retort, "We've seen better." Three much older hillwalkers looked on, silent and disapproving. The warden came to join our little group and she was good company.

Early next morning Morag, having heard the tale of my car, elected to drive us to Glen Etive, just in case. We passed cars parked on the few level areas by the single track road, their owners still asleep in the little brightly coloured tents down by the river. Morag found a space and we stepped down from her car into a warm morning with a perfectly blue sky overhead. It was most unusual.

We walked to the bridge and stood peering down into the deep, dark water of the gorge. It was 8.30 a.m. On the east bank we turned left to follow the track.

Our steps raised pale dust. I stopped to look at a little green hairstreak butterfly, its wings like emeralds in the bright sun. It performed a curious dance and then settled among the bright new spring leaves where it was so well camouflaged that I had to wait for it to move before I could see it again. A cuckoo called, proclaiming his territory to possible mates and rival males.

I stopped at the bridge over the Allt Ceitlein to enjoy the spectacle of the surrounding mountains, each lit by strong sunlight. On the far bank I turned east to follow my companions who were striding ahead into a side glen that would give us access to the ridge line ahead. It seemed a long way on that warm morning as we gradually climbed the gentle gradient. A second cuckoo and later a third called as we walked, a clear signal that spring was soon to be overtaken by early summer.

Stepping over the bleached bones of old pine stumps I pictured the glen as it was, a place filled with ancient Caledonian forest. Now all was bare. The only trees were the birches in the steep, narrow gullies that divided the crags of the side walls.

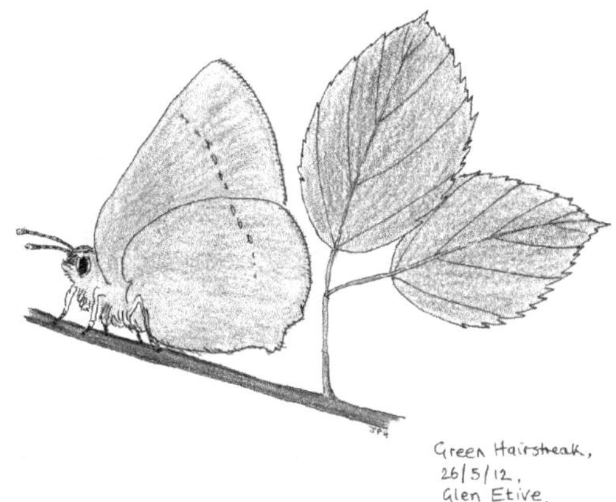

We climbed up onto granite. The Allt Ceitlein tumbled over the pink rock in a series of waterfalls with clear pools at their base. We began to see dark frogs, many of them quite small. The air shimmered in the heat above the exposed rock. Large blue-green dragonflies performed their extraordinary aerial manoeuvres.

It felt like my legs were made of lead on the final climb up to the bealach between Meall nan Eun and Meall Tarsuinn. The strong, warm wind was funnelled through this depression between the two hills, drying my shirt. James and I were having a drink when a tired Morag plodded up to where we had flopped down. She announced that she was struggling and had decided to go back and rest by her car while waiting for us. Once assured that she was safe enough to return down the glen alone, we said farewell. I felt exhausted and suggested that we rest and eat some early lunch, hoping that I would revive after a couple of honey and peanut butter sandwiches and a mug of tea.

Packed up again, I got back onto my feet and slowly led the way east up the gentle slope of Meall nan Eun. It was rather like the Cairngorms with its exposed granite and sparse, low vegetation growing in the granite grit. The climb was easy and I began to feel more optimistic about completing the planned route.

At the cairn, James used his GPS to make quite sure that we were, indeed, on the summit of our first Munro. There was a 360° sweep of mountains around us, Schiehallion, Ben Lui, Ben Cruachan, Bidean nam Bian and Ben Nevis distinctive among the many others. As we were going down towards the bealach where we had parted from Morag a dotterel rose in front of our feet. Its chestnut breast looked red in the intense sunlight, the strong colour making it likely that this was a female. The cuckoos as we climbed and this handsome bird as we descended seemed appropriate for a hill named hill of the birds.

By the time we were climbing up the other side onto Meall Tarsuinn I was back into my stride. As we began to descend to the next bealach we faced the grand granite cliffs of Stob Coir' an Albannaich, the peak of the Scotsman's corrie, which were covered by large snowfields. One of the reasons we had decided to approach from the east was to enjoy this aspect of what is an impressive mountain.

On the floor of the bealach were tiny lochans with jewel-bodied dragonflies hovering over them and then darting away on their strange missions. Looking up at the granite cliffs, we decided to use a grass floored gully to get up onto Stob Coir' an Albannaich's narrow south-east ridge. We stopped to sit on rocks a little way up the gully to eat the rest of our lunch. It was sheltered and the sun was hot on our backs. The view was straight down to the floor of Glen Etive and the mountains beyond. The only sound was that made by a waterfall.

James feeling the heat on Stob Coir'an Albannaich, 26/5/12.

We climbed up to the ridge and stopped for a cup of tea. Lying down on the carpet of warm, bone-dry mosses, James closed his eyes. I could have slept but the thought of our friend waiting down below spurred us on and we were soon walking up the narrow ridge that leads to the summit. We were overtaken by a solitary young fell runner, the first person we had seen that day.

After visiting the large cairn on the edge of the granite cliffs we set off down the crispy, cushioned cover of desiccated mosses, lichens and liverworts. The steady, warm wind did little to keep us cool. The convex slope got much steeper as we approached the next bealach and we had to traverse across.

The bealach was another funnel for the unusual warm wind. We climbed steeply up the granite crags beyond and then the slope levelled off until near the summit of Glas Bheinn Mhor, where there was a final steep haul up the ridge. On top, I enjoyed the views while James did his familiar check with his GPS. I was particularly interested in Beinn nan Aighenan to the south, having climbed it in the previous month but, as the weather had closed in, seeing nothing of it. The mountain turned out to be steep, rocky and lonely. We discussed the merits of going west over a top to the bealach between it and Ben Starav and then down by the narrow gorge or backtracking. Our main consideration was to get back to Morag as quickly as we could, so we started back down the path we had just climbed.

Our walk out down the Allt Mheuran seemed endless. It was sheltered from the wind and the air was still. There was much exposed rock which was too hot to touch. It reminded me of a walk around the old walls of the City of Rhodes in throbbing heat. I dropped the brim of my hat as I was being burned by the westering sun and decided that, despite cuckoos being tropical birds, it was too hot for them to call.

Back at the bridge we met a team of divers. One was keen to tell me that the water beneath was 10½ metres deep and that he had seen a salmon. He seemed very lively compared to me which was not difficult to understand as I was hot, dusty and exhausted and he had just emerged from the dark, cold water.

Morag looked concerned as she watched us struggle up the last bank. She gave us bottles of water and while we drank told us that she had met the husband of a seventy year old triathlete who was still competing all over the world. He had provided our friend with a comfy chair and cups of tea so she had enjoyed good company and a rest and was feeling much better than she had felt on the ridge line.

I took off my sunspecs and could see nothing but blurred outlines. I was glad that I was not driving. I got into the car, closed my eyes and went to sleep. Give me a nice, normal, cold day any time.

At Crianlarich, my car started first time. In the Clachan Cottage Hotel, Lochearnside, a big pot of tea, vegetable broth, roast lamb, mint sauce, mashed potatoes and a second big pot of tea were consumed.

"You look like you needed that," said the waitress.

5/6/12

Clachnaben

A hill with a crown on Diamond Jubilee Day

Union Street was strung with red, white and blue bunting and union flags from end to end. I drove its length to pick up James as we were going to celebrate the Diamond Jubilee holiday by climbing Clachnaben. We picked up James's old friend, Peter and before long were driving through the forest that grows on the lower slopes of the hill on its eastern side.

The sun shone and we had the prospect of a good day. A buck roe deer grazed peacefully in a clearing in the forest, just before we crossed the Bridge of Dye. We parked at the next bridge, crossed the Dye and walked north along its bank. We soon had our first view of the hill, clach-na-beinne, the stone on the hill, although James and Peter pronounced it the local way, clochnaben. There was a fair bit to go but, even from our viewpoint, the large granite tor on the summit showed why it was given this name.

We walked over Miller's Bog, which was dry and through a larch wood, its elegant trees wearing translucent new needle leaves. Ahead were Clachnaben's steep slopes, its distinctive tor rising abruptly in a cliff wall, like a rock crown on the summit. As I looked, a gap in the clouds allowed the sun to illuminate this crown, turning it to gold, an appropriate image for a diamond jubilee.

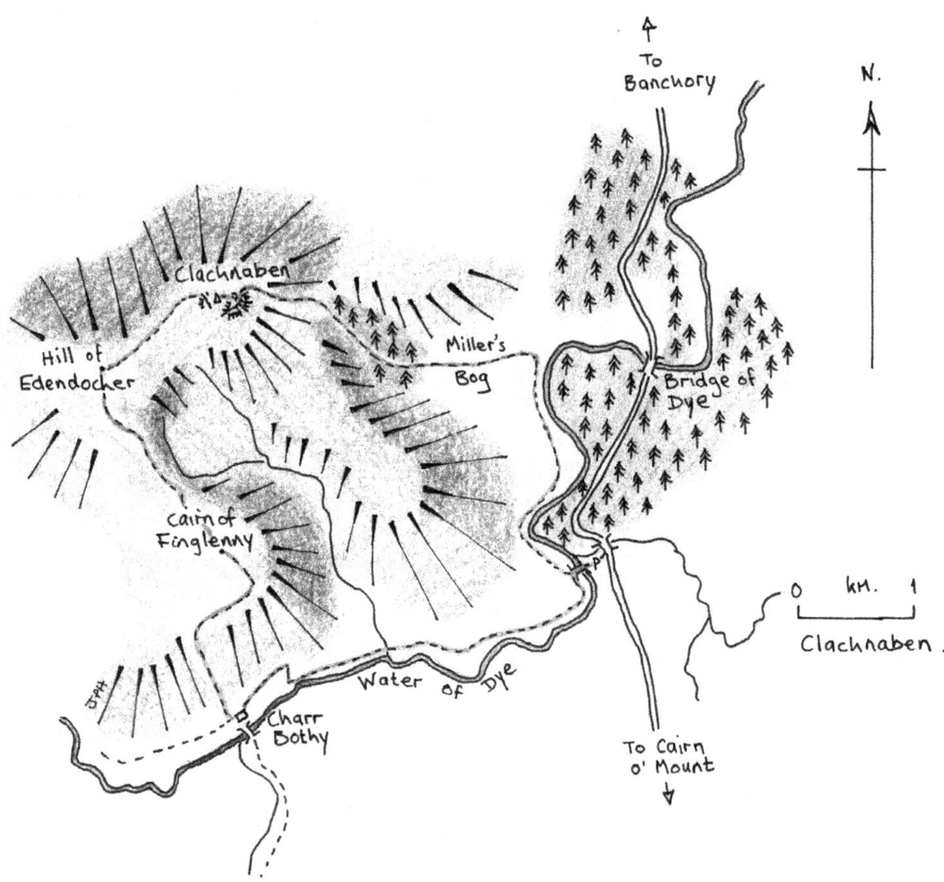

A well-made path led to the top where we climbed up the granite outcrop to a narrow summit with steep drops on three sides. The tor is the eroded stump of a volcanic plug. Eroded but still resistant enough to provide the high ground for fine views. Bennachie stood out clearly to the north and Mount Battock to the west, with the high, snow-capped Cairngorms beyond. It had become windy and cool so we left this handsome hill and walked on.

We crossed high, exposed moor on our way to the Hill of Edendocher, the hiss of the wind across the heather disturbed at intervals by the clatter of red grouse. At the hill we turned south and came down to Charr bothy. It seemed a good idea to eat our lunch inside, out of the wind.

I asked James whether he had hung up any bunting to mark the day and he replied, "I have, indeed, done so. It's the same bunting used for the Silver Jubilee, the Coronation and George V's Silver Jubilee in 1935. It's red, white and blue plus yellow and green."

"Why the yellow and green?"

"I think it's my family's Aberdonian frugalness because that colour combination would also cover Indian and Irish public events."

Lunch eaten and outside again we discovered that the Inverbervie Walking Club had arrived. The sun had broken through and its warmth encouraged us to stay and chat for a while. We learned that they were all retired and had quite an adventurous programme.

On the brisk walk back to the car, Peter talked about salmon fishing with his father in the high pools of the River Kirkaig in Sutherland.

James and I returned to Clachnaben for our post Christmas walk that year. It was a fine winter's day and we sat on the tor watching skeins of geese against a pale lilac and pink sky. Deep snow drifts covered the moor. We ate lunch in Charr bothy again and laughed when a cloud of steam was released from James's waterproof trousers as he peeled them off.

2/7/12 - 6/7/12

Torridon

It rained and it rained and it rained. The Met Office confirmed that it had been the wettest June on record. We left the downpours behind when we turned into Glen Torridon but were prepared for the worst.

I smiled at the geraniums growing in the old boots at the door of the hostel and at the warden who gave us a warm welcome. James had taken charge of the planning and shopping for our dinners, so I knew that we'd eat well. After leek and potato soup and the best Aberdeen Angus sirloin steak we sat on the sofa looking out of the enormous window at the rugged mountain landscape to the south. A stag with fine antlers strolled across the meadow on the far side of the road. Our reverie was interrupted by the warden who invited us to the quiet room. From there we watched a pine marten raiding the bird table. It was an athlete, jumping up to snatch its choice then dropping down to eat its fill on the grass. The last leap secured large items and it loped away carrying them, probably to a den with kits.

3/7/12

Beinn Liath Mhor and Sgorr Ruadh

A bright day in the Coulin Mountains

I got out of bed and went anxiously to the window but, mercifully, it was not raining. We made an early start and ours was the first car in the car park for the path that leads north-west between Liathach and Beinn Eighe. This was not to be our route, however, and we crossed the road to go south past the SMC's Ling Hut. We climbed the path up the side of the waterfall with its pink rocks and golden pool. It was difficult to get into my stride as there were so many interesting things to see. There were common spotted orchids and frogs everywhere, mostly this year's batch but some much bigger. There were red and purple-blue damselflies, various bees and a dozen or so leopard-spotted magpie moths.

The path ended at a large, flat-topped boulder with three rocks on top. From there we made our way across rough ground and up into Coire Grannda, a huge, glacier-carved bowl with near vertical side walls and headwall of Torridonian sandstone. We climbed a steep path that zig zags up to a notch in the headwall and came to the bealach between Beinn Liath Mhor and Sgorr Ruadh. There, above a small lochan, we sat down for a late

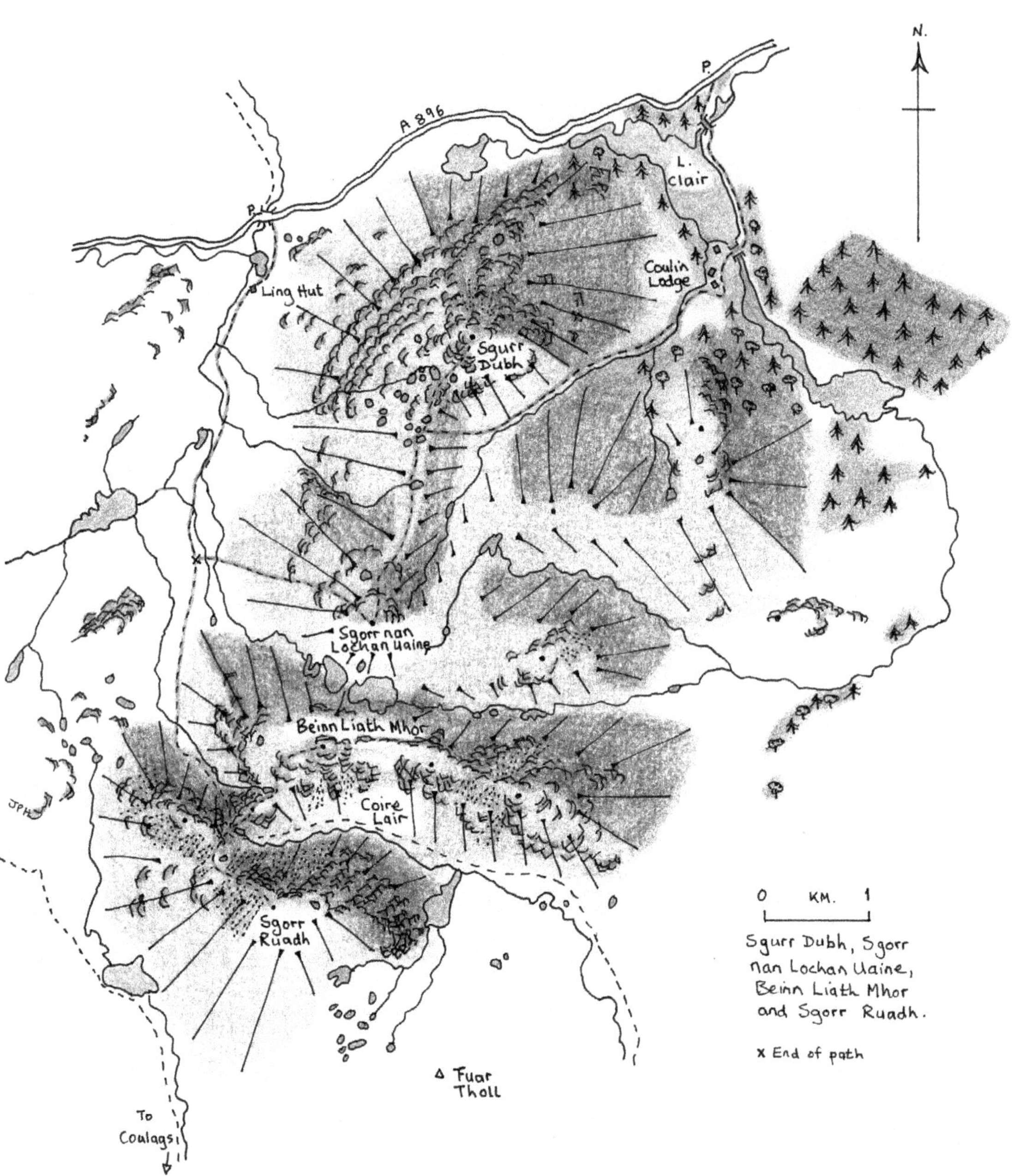
N.
A 896
P.
P.
L.
Clair
Coulin
Lodge
Ling Hut
Sgurr
Dubh
Sgorr nan
Lochan Uaine
Beinn Liath Mhor
Coire
Lair
Sgorr
Ruadh
Fuar
Tholl
To
Coulags
0 KM. 1
Sgurr Dubh, Sgorr
nan Lochan Uaine,
Beinn Liath Mhor
and Sgorr Ruadh.
x End of path
JPH

breakfast. It had stayed dry on our walk in, getting brighter all the time. Now, as I drank tea, the cloud lifted from the mountain tops and the sun came out. Looking down into Coire Làir it seemed that the last glacier had only just melted. The glen below the corrie is a classic U-shape on a grand scale, with steep, cliff-lined walls, raw screes and a litter of dumped boulders.

Rested, we began the climb up to Beinn Liath Mhor. At first we walked on Torridonian sandstone slabs and pavements, scrambling from one level to the next. We needed our hands to get safely up a particularly steep chimney. Sitting on the last pavement is the mountain's white quartzite cap. This is broken into a scree of sharp-edged blocks, unstable, smooth and potentially dangerous. We stopped half way up and thought of Pixie Scott, one of the leaders of a West Highland expedition for Bridge of Don Academy pupils, who had slipped and died at this very spot as she descended from the summit.

On top is a well-made, tall cairn which stood out against the bright blue sky. A ptarmigan appeared from behind a block, grey patches on top and white underneath, invisible among the quartzite whenever it stopped moving. The views on that clear, sunny day were excellent. The Beinn Liath Mhor ridge looked perfect for a high-level walk but that was for another day. Liathach and Beinn Eighe were cloud free, the former looming above a sparkling Loch Torridon. Beyond was the cobalt sea with its mountainous islands.

Beinn Liath Mhor (left),
Sgorr Ruadh (right),
Looking East.
3/7/12.

Of more immediate interest, Sgorr Ruadh, our next challenge, was revealed as a shattered old tower. The summit on a day like that was a place to linger, so we sat down to eat some lunch.

On the move again, we went carefully down the screes and returned to the bealach. From there we began to climb Sgorr Ruadh, once more finding ourselves on quartzite blocks. The bedrock of the mountain is breaking up and sheer white screes fall hundreds of metres to the corrie below. The path goes along the very brink of the drop. James passed a one word comment, "Airy." Once at the shelter cairn we collapsed onto the flat slabs used by hillwalkers as seats and finished our lunch. I enjoyed my corned beef and pickle sandwiches and had a second mug of strong, reviving tea. By contrast, James appears to fuel himself with a large number of chocolate bars when on the hills.

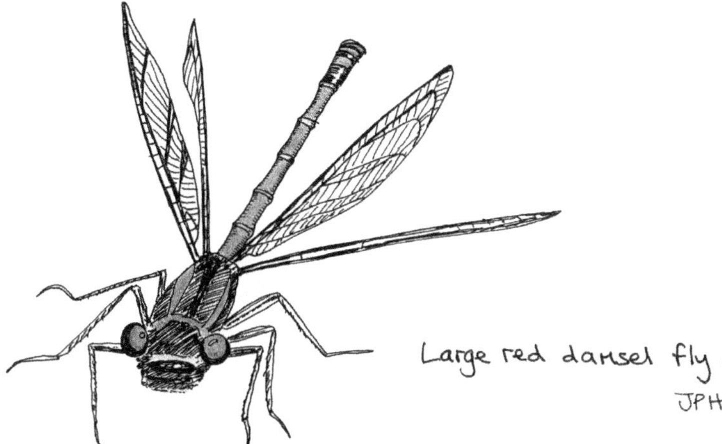

It was still bright and it was interesting to see Fuar Tholl so clearly. That, however, was also for another day. Looking across to the Beinn Liath Mhor ridge, I pointed out a white cat on a scale comparable to that of the white horses of the English Downs.

On the return journey there is a path across the floor of the corrie but we had to leave it and find a route across rough ground to regain the long path from the Ling Hut. We were pleased that the line we chose took us precisely to the boulder with three rocks on top. Then it was a hot walk back to the starting point, distracted by red grouse, many more frogs, red damselflies and dragonflies. The golden pool under the waterfall looked tempting but we marched on. We got into the car, shut the doors and, with lucky timing, there was a heavy shower, the only one of the day.

Back at the hostel we welcomed Morag when she arrived then worked as a team to prepare a dinner of pea and ham soup, lasagne, cheesecake and Italian red wine. The evening was spent relaxing on sofas with shoes off and feet up.

4/7/12

Slioch

Coarse language on the 'dark mountain'

Early next morning we embarked on a long, hard walk to climb Slioch. This started at Incheril and the path followed the east bank of the Kinlochewe River. We walked under hoary, aged oaks scattered through an open wood of ancient rowans and alders, some hollow, some rotten. It was warm and sunny and full of birdsong. As we approached the bridge over the Abhainn an Fhasaigh, Slioch stood ahead, its top clear of cloud. I tried to point this out to James but he marched on with his head down, muttering, "I don't trust this mountain."

The bridge carried us over a deep, polished gorge through which the water thundered. We climbed the path to a junction marked by a small cairn. James, who had done this walk three times before, led us straight ahead, which was to prove a mistake.

The path was a delight. The air was pungent with the smell of bog myrtle and there was a beautiful array of flowers. White cotton grass bobbed in the breeze. I counted four types of orchid, the common spotted orchid and others with plain leaves and flower heads lilac, dark pink, spotted or marked with 'eyes'. There were more of the red damselflies, frogs, hairy caterpillars, dragonflies and a half dozen pearl-bordered fritillaries. I photographed this attractively marked butterfly so that I could determine which of the fritillaries I had

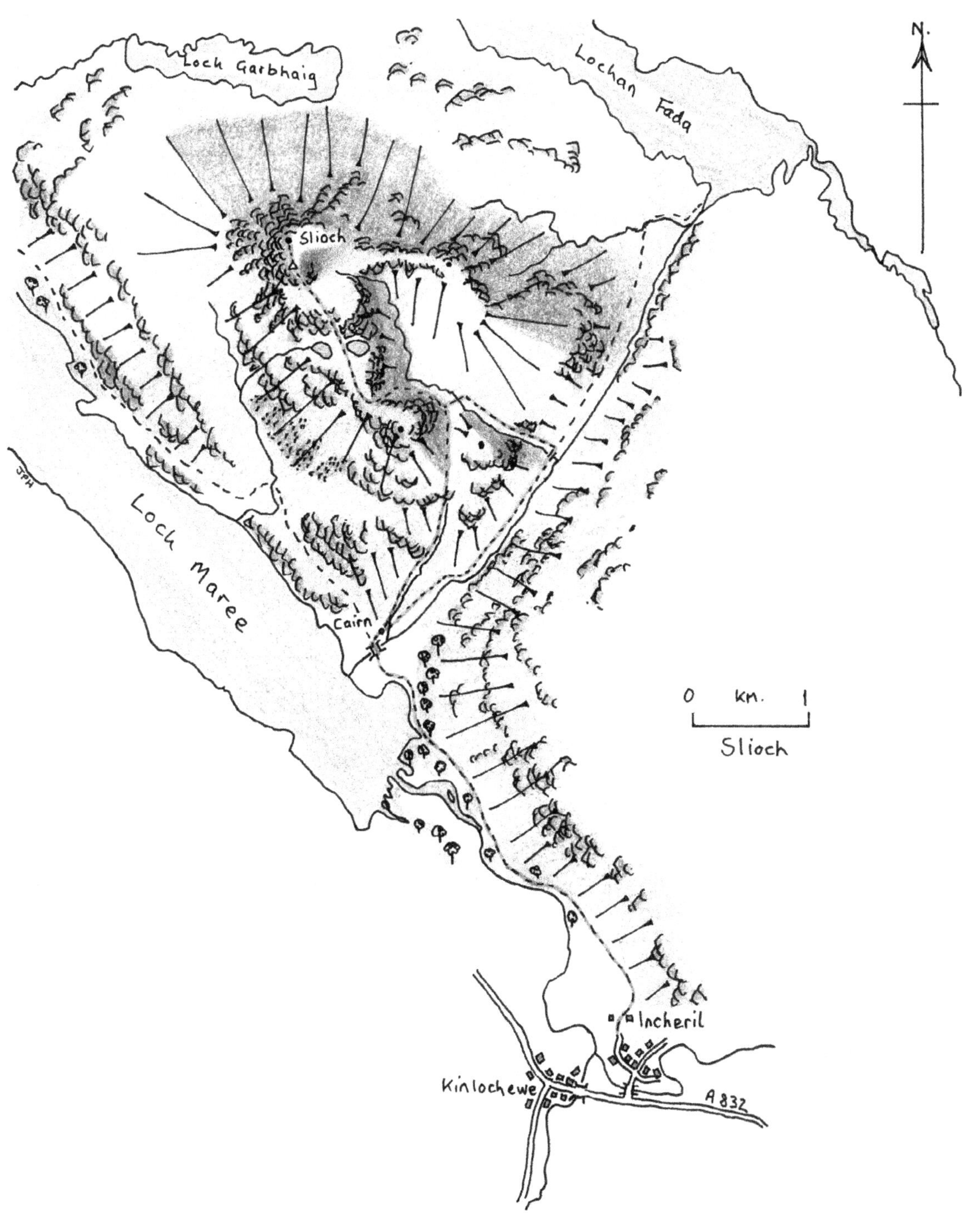

N.
Loch Garbhaig
Lochan Fada
Slioch
Loch Maree
Cairn
0 km. 1
Slioch
Incheril
Kinlochewe
A 832
JPH

Pearl-bordered Fritillary,
Slioch
4/7/12.
JPH

seen and discovered that they are in serious decline elsewhere in the UK. Whatever is killing them off is absent in the pristine environment of the Highlands and it made me think, yet again, about how precious this area is and how important it is to protect it.

We arrived at the place where the stream from Slioch's great corrie is crossed by a little bridge. A waterfall caught the sun further up the slope. Realising that a mistake had been made, James switched on his GPS and I, for the first time, got out my map and saw that the route I had marked on it started back at that little cairn. We should have turned left. Having made similar mistakes before, I should have known better.

Our way of rectifying the error was to follow the line of the stream up to the waterfall and beyond. This was heavy work with the sun on our backs and we were soon drenched with sweat. Past the waterfall we found ourselves in a gorge and had to climb out. This route is not recommended.

By the time we reached the impressive Coire na Sleaghaich we were exhausted and had to sit down or, in Morag's case, lie down. After a drink and some food we got up to survey the corrie floor and walls. I looked at the map and suggested a line which would take us back to the path. Once on it, it was simply a matter of following it as it climbed the corrie wall and led us to the two lochans which mark the start of the final climb to Slioch's summit.

We looked up from the lochans and were disappointed to see that a cap of cloud covered the highest part of this most unpredictable of mountains. Toiling up into the cloud mist, we arrived at the triangulation pillar. "I once climbed to this point on an awful day and, when safely down, was told that it was not the true summit," said James, "I admit to using some coarse language but repeated the climb the next day, again in awful conditions." Having told us this sad tale, we trudged off in the direction of the North Top, peering in the thick mist to see a path. It was so thick, however, that we had to walk on a bearing. It started to rain and as we sat down to pull on our waterproof trousers James muttered, "I'm considering using some more coarse language."

Once at the cairn I suggested that, despite the conditions, we should find some shelter and eat lunch. We needed the energy. I led us down under a sandstone crag where we could sit in the lee of the wind. I ate my sandwiches and warmed my hands on a mug of tea. Morag suggested that the cloud might clear but James remained resolutely pessimistic, telling us, "This is my fourth time up here but I've yet to see a view. And," he added, "my last."

We set off to retrace our steps but realised that we were walking towards Sgurr an Tuill Bhain and had to backtrack. For the second time on this mountain three experienced hillwalkers had made a rudimentary mistake. Back at the cairn we set a bearing and discovered that the path we wanted began after a stony patch slightly to the right of the one we had taken. In the thick mist we had to check the bearing again on the way back to the triangulation pillar. Once we had passed it Morag said, "That's good, it should be straightforward now." Before she got to the end of that sentence I had slipped on the stones of the badly eroded path and torn the knee of my waterproof trousers. It was a relief to come out of the cloud cap and see the two lochans again.

After a rest and some tea we set off down to the corrie. To our surprise, the sun was shining in a blue sky and I soon had to remove my shredded waterproofs. It was hot work walking down the steep path. This went over Torridonian conglomerate with pebbles of jasper and other minerals. I added stones to the little cairn and, should I return, will not make the same mistake again.

Looking back from the bridge, Slioch had cleared. James narrowed his eyes, "It's a dark mountain and I think it delights in teasing people."

The walk back through the trees was hot and seemed much longer than on the way in. Two snow buntings kept us company for a while before posing on a fallen tree then suddenly deciding they had something important to do and flitting off.

Back at the hostel we enjoyed another retro meal of Scotch broth followed by Aberdeen Angus steaks with red wine. In the quiet room afterwards, James was praised for his good taste.

5/7/12

Sgorr nan Lochan Uaine and Sgurr Dubh

A grand view of the Torridon giants

In the morning, Torridon was clammy in its thick blanket of mist. We parked a car at the turn off for Coulin Lodge then drove back to the Coire Dubh Mor car park. Our walk took us past the Ling Hut and right to the end of the path. Ever optimistic, I suggested that the mist might be part of a temperature inversion and the peaks might be standing in bright sunlight, a suggestion dismissed out of hand by James in one word, "Fanciful." I used the flat surface of the boulder (with three rocks on top) that marks the end of the path as a table on which to lay down my map and set a bearing for Lochan Uaine.

Morag interrupted me to say, "No need, it's breaking up."

We had climbed up to the very top of the thick layer of mist and now could see our way ahead up Sgorr nan Lochan Uaine's north-western spur. Progress was slow because we kept stopping to look at the extraordinary views. To the east and south we were walled in by mountains but to the north and west was a vast white sea of mist above which the peaks rose like fantastic fortresses. Liathach was particularly spectacular.

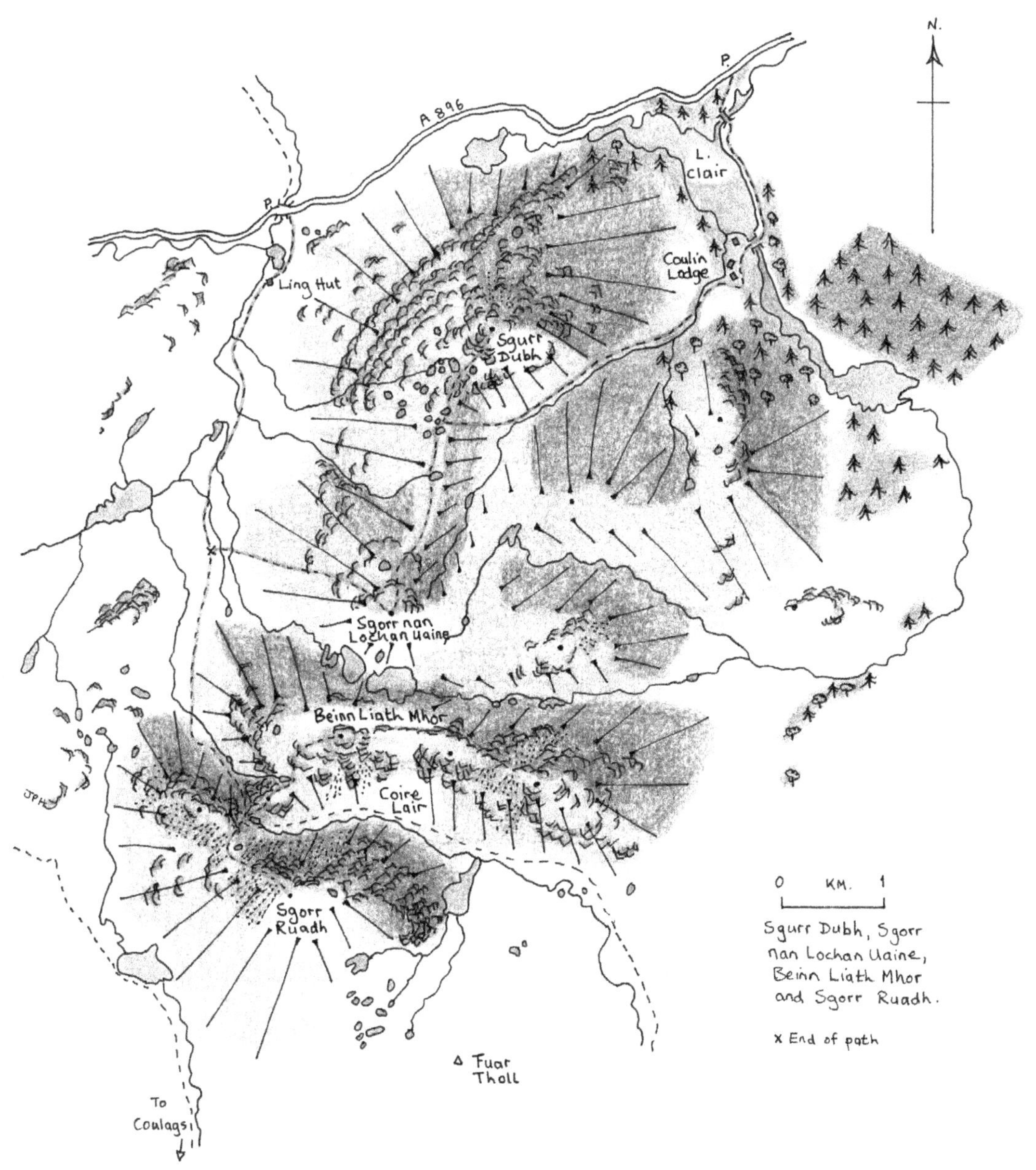

Once again, I enjoyed the abundance of wild flowers, butterflies and dragonflies. Frogs were everywhere. Sometimes five or six would jump out of the way with one using my boot as a springboard. I began to notice fine dwarf junipers, the original bonsai trees and these were common along the whole of the ridge, firmly rooted in narrow cracks in the rocks.

Higher up, we left the ancient sandstone and climbed onto an unstable slope of razor-edged white quartzite blocks. The views from the top were worth all the effort we had put into getting there. The sea of mist persisted to the north and west, Liathach and Beinn Eighe rising majestically from its white shore, both perfectly sharp against a deep blue sky. To the south we had an excellent view of the impressive ridge of Beinn Liath Mhor, on which James and I had stood two days before. We sat down in the shelter cairn for a snack and a cup of tea and noticed a little frog on one of the blocks. "How on earth did it get all the way up here?" asked James.

After a delicate descent on the sliding scree we slowly made our way north along a wild and beautiful ridge. Our route was mostly on a succession of outcropping sandstone ribs garnished with piles of weathered stone pancakes. I stopped at one place to point out the unconformity between the Torridonian sandstone and the Cambrian quartzite, a surface representing many millions of years of erosion of the Precambrian landscape. We passed little lochans, each reflecting the bright blue of the sky. It was hot and silent. On the shore of one of these picturesque lochans we stopped to look at the white walls of our second Corbett. "I have no desire to climb up all that dangerous loose rock," announced James, "I'll wait for you at this spot."

Morag and I put away our walking poles and scrambled along the last of the sandstone ribs. We crossed a high bealach and picked a steep gully up the quartzite wall we faced. Hands were needed as we climbed carefully to the top. Then we made our way across a wasteland of shattered white blocks to the summit cairn. There were fabulous views in a 360° Torridonian panorama. I could understand why my guidebook had described this Corbett as providing the best views in this part of the Highlands. Liathach and Beinn Eighe, just across the glen, were superb in the strong sunshine.

We chose a different gully for our descent and found James stretched out on a warm slab of sandstone. As we settled down beside him I said, "I wonder if anyone has ever before enjoyed a picnic and sunbathed on the shore of this mountain lochan?"

"Probably not," he replied, "even on such a perfect day as today we have not seen another human being."

After a leisurely and most enjoyable lunch I stood up to look into the lochan. A newt swam away from my boots using a breast stroke with front and back legs synchronised.

We made our way down to the east and joined the Coulin path. Along it were lots of sundews. I stopped to look at the husk of a little insect that had become trapped in the sticky 'hairs'. Soon we were in a picturesque glen with grand old Scots pines. We crossed the bridge then, on the shore of Loch Clair, dark clouds rolled over and thunder boomed ominously. We hurried. Back at the car, we shut the doors and for the second time in three days, the heavens opened.

From the summit of Sgurr Dubh, "the best view in Torridon".
(Liathach on the left, Beinn Eighe on the right). 5/7/12

Dinner included ham and pea soup, red or white wine, honey roast salmon with vegetables and cheesecake. Three very full hillwalkers sat in the quiet room later and agreed that the day's walk was to be recommended. The warden told us that the weather gods had been smiling on the North-west, which seemed to be the only patch of the British Isles with sun. We told him that we were driving home in the morning and he warned us to take care as the forecast was for heavy thunderstorms and flooded roads to the south.

18/8/12

Sgurr Eilde Mor and Binnein Mor

The Garden of Eden

James and I arrived in the evening at the Blackwater Hostel Lodge, an old wooden chalet perched high above Kinlochleven. We did not have a second to admire the wonderful views across Loch Leven because the air was a thick soup of midges and we had to run for the door. Each guest that evening arrived in a similar fashion, a rush to the door, a frantic scramble to punch the security code, a crash into the hall and horrified exclamations, "They're just vicious little vampires!" being the only printable one.

Morag staggered in with her bags, "I've lost pints of blood! Are all the ****** windows shut?"

Early next morning we drove over the bridge, through Kinlochmore and up the road leading to Mamore Lodge. A new gate was open but a forbidding sign announced that it was liable to be shut and locked at any time. If it had not been for the good advice of our host at the hostel to ignore the sign we would have been put off using this traditional starting point for Mamores walks.

I was glad that James and Morag never spend long putting on their boots as the "little vampires" soon realised that breakfast had arrived. It was a perfect morning for these creatures, warm and cloudy with light rain. There is always a balance in nature between predator and prey, however, and in this case a reasonably fit human can move faster than its tormentors.

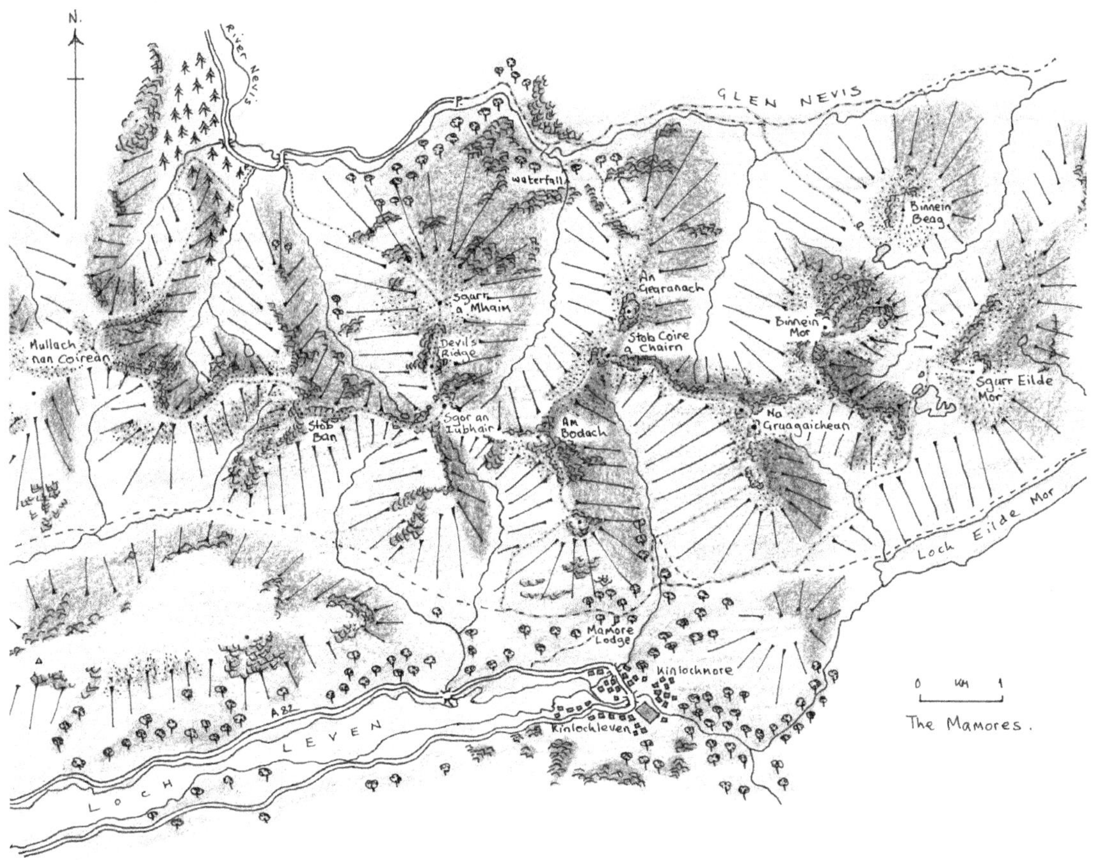

We walked briskly through the dripping woods, James setting the pace. As the trees began to thin I spotted a group of three mountain ringlets. I normally stop to watch butterflies settle on particular flowers but not that morning.

At 700 metres, where a small cairn marked the start of a path which zig zags up onto Sgor Eilde Beag, there was enough wind to ensure that we could stop for a cup of tea without being attacked. It had been misty and drizzly, the heather was in bloom and the hills beyond Loch Eilde Mor were rich browns, beige and russet, tinged with a purple blush. Autumn, we agreed, had begun.

We walked round to Coire an Lochain, stepping over rocks in two places where the path had been swept away by landslides. The cloud stripped from the perfect sharp cone of Sgurr Eilde Mor and the sun came out, flooding the mountain and the corrie with brilliant light. The path led us across a natural causeway between the main sheet of water and a lochan on its north-west side. Then we began the difficult ascent of Sgurr Eilde Mor's north-west ridge. The quartzite screes were unstable and the uppermost section was both slippery and extremely steep. It was no place to stumble.

I was relieved to climb up onto the final rib of exposed rock that led to the tall summit cairn, despite being hit by a powerful wind as I did so. Icy drops of rain began to smack onto my clothing. It got much worse when at the cairn and we retreated to a low wind shelter that had been fashioned from the litter of quartzite blocks. I pulled on my waterproof trousers, placed my rucksack at my head and lay flat among the rocks, head facing the wind direction. Morag did likewise but James produced a 1950s vintage long raincoat and fought to put this on over his mountain jacket. The wind intensity increased and the icy drops of rain transformed into snow and then into large hailstones. We had no option but to lie still and weather the storm. "Winter now." shouted Morag above the racket.

As soon as it subsided we got onto our feet and struggled against the wind back down the ice-slicked rocks. I turned and began descending the steep screes, taking a sweeping zig zag line but not able to stop myself glissading down the most unstable sections. As soon as I arrived at a place I felt was tentatively secure I stopped and looked back. Morag was just behind me and James, much further up, was slowing his descent as much as he could. We were now in the lee of the fierce wind.

At the foot of the ridge I suggested to Morag that we should stop to rest and eat lunch. The view to the north of Binnein Beag and Binnein Mor with the Grey Corries beyond was of a mountain wilderness. Curiously, the autumn colours we had observed not long before when looking south were replaced by a palette of greys, tired browns and malachite greens. The sky was blue again with racing white clouds and the sun hot on our backs. "What season is it now?" I asked and we both declared, "Spring!"

"It's Mallory!"
Sgurr Eilde Mor
18/8/12.

James came swaying down the track, his pale trousers had tucked themselves into his boots, his raincoat flapped about his calves and his old brimmed hat completed the picture. "It's Mallory!" exclaimed Morag.

Lunch was a convivial affair. We talked about the recently ended London Olympics, discovering that we had all been gripped by the performances of our athletes and felt proud to be British.

Our rest over, we walked to the shore of the lochan and surveyed our next challenge, Binnein Mor. Encouragingly, the summit was clear against the blue sky. We spotted a narrow path going up Sgor Eilde Beag's north-east spur and then traversing west to a point where we could see faint zig zags going up onto the ridge. Cloud had covered the highest ground again but, full of hope, we followed James.

At Binnein Mor's South Top we were in the cloud mist but James surged on. After descending 50 metres or so he came to an abrupt halt, declaring, "This doesn't feel right. I think we've turned down the wrong ridge again." A quick check using a GPS and my 1:25,000 scale map showed that his gut instinct was spot on, we were on our way to Na Gruagaichean. Back at the South Top I took a bearing (as I should have done at the start) which, when followed a little way, revealed the correct path. As I walked along it I wondered why three people with so much collective experience kept making the same error. I vowed (again) to always take a bearing in such situations.

Binnein Mor's main top felt dramatic as we clambered over its exposed rock teeth but the cloud denied us any views. We went the whole length of the chisel blade summit and when we checked the GPS found that we had overshot the highest point.

We returned the way we had come, keeping to the highest ground. "A pity," remarked James, "that we couldn't see anything." By the time we were on top of Sgor Eilde Beag, however, the cloud was breaking up and streaming away to the north-east. We looked across to the pointed cone of Sgurr Eilde Mor where, on its narrow summit, we had been pinned down by the violent hailstorm. Now the mountain was lit by the westering sun and all was at peace. The lochan below was the deepest blue.

We stopped near the main track below Sgor Eilde Beag's southern spur for a last cup of tea. It was warm in the strong sun and there was a pleasant breeze, each condition welcome for the comfort it provided and because it kept the midges at bay. Around my feet were plump blaeberries. These had carpeted the sides of the track on the way up, along with a scatter of red cowberries and little black crowberries. This must be the very best time for the mountain creatures like grouse and red deer to fatten up.

It became hotter and hotter as we walked back along the track. We left it at one point to climb onto a little mound on top of which had been placed a pale marble bench, a

18/8/12
The Garden of Eden.

memorial to someone who had loved both laughter and this beautiful place. We sat on the bench and looked at the wooded shores of Loch Leven with its sheltering mountain walls. All was flooded with late afternoon sunlight and appeared so luxuriant that I felt we must be about to walk down into the Garden of Eden.

Summer in the Garden of Eden. The picture was completed by a handful of mountain ringlets flashing the bright orange 'eyes' on their wings. As we got nearer to the woods there were dozens of these colourful butterflies on either side. By the time we were in the trees we had seen hundreds. James asked what the collective noun is for them. I remembered a flight of butterflies but, on looking it up at home, discovered that one can use rabble or kaleidoscope, both of which would have been particularly apt for this colourful, disordered spectacle.

I fell behind as I was taking photographs of the mountain ringlets, some sharing flowers with bees. As I approached the car park at Mamore Lodge it felt like the end of a marathon. Remembering athletes like Jessica Ennis and Mo Farah, I ran the last section while my companions cheered and made a finish line with their poles.

22/9/12

Sgurr a' Mhaim, Sgor an Iubhair, Stob Ban and Mullach nan Coirean

An autumn day on the Mamores

The shortest way from Aberdeen to Glen Nevis is by The Lecht but I wondered whether I had chosen the best route when driving through snow on the summit. Coming down to Grantown-on-Spey, however, I was rewarded by an incredible sight. Torrential showers were tracking across the flat expanse of Strathspey, each backlit by a red westering sun. It looked like tall columns of intense flame topped with black smoke were destroying the peaceful pastures.

Waiting for me at the Glen Nevis Youth Hostel were my son, Tom and his young Kiwi wife, K. Morag arrived shortly after. Once we had eaten and made our plans it was time for Tom and K to go back to their tent and Morag and me to retire to our dorms as we had an early start. At the hostel door we looked up into the black night and saw a long, straggling line of torches coming down the path from the top of Ben Nevis. "Why," K asked, "are all these people up there in the pitch dark?" It was disturbingly apocalyptic,

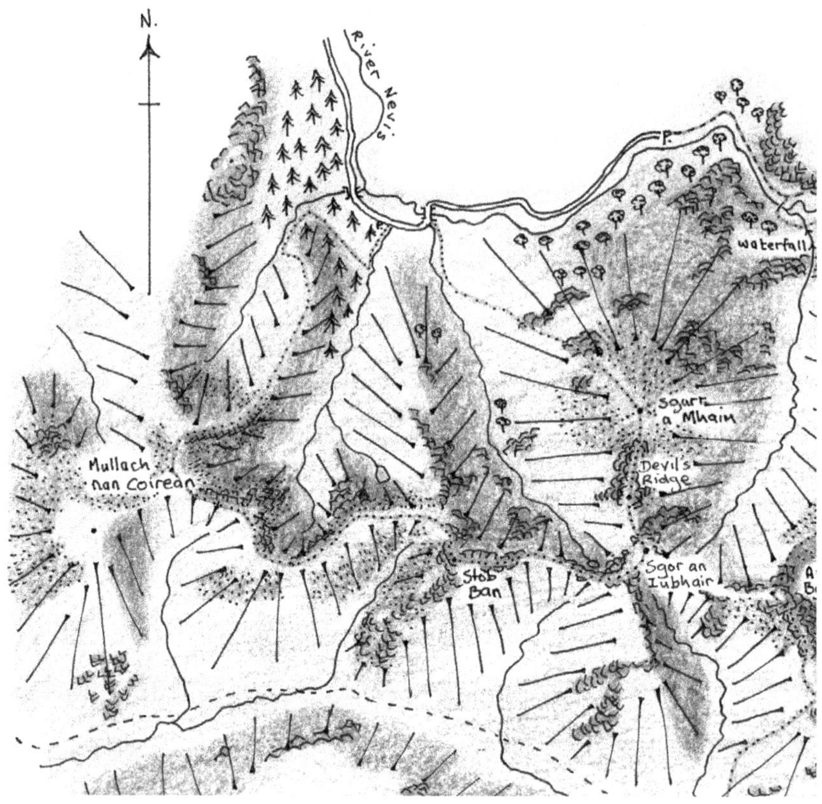

Extract from the map of the Mamores on page 289

and all the more so later when we were kept awake by the sound of rescue helicopters. We discovered that a person descending the path in darkness had died at 10.00 pm as a result of tripping and falling into a gully.

In the frosty morning we drove to Achriabhach, Tom blearily sipping from a mug of coffee and K wrapped up like the Michelin Man following night temperatures of minus two degrees. A herd of Highland cattle, most ginger but some black, were purposefully striding north along the road and we had to stop while they passed. At the stile which marked the start of the path up to Sgurr a' Mhaim a notice attached to a post was headed, 'Mamores grazing'. K looked puzzled then asked, "What sort of creature is a mamore?"

The ascent was unrelentingly steep for over 1,000 metres. We climbed out of the clammy mist and saw how it filled the floor of Glen Nevis like a white sheet. Ben Nevis and the surrounding peaks were sharply etched in dazzling light and dense shade. Sadly, our path was in the shade so we toiled up the frozen ground with not a pause until we emerged into the welcome sunlight of the rocky summit. The mountain has a cap of hard white quartzite which has been shattered by frost to form blocky screes. This makes the upper part look as if it is snow-covered, especially when seen from the west. Across the glen to the north Ben Nevis actually had a cap of fresh snow. It had never looked so bright and inviting but in my mind was its darker side and the tragedy of the previous night.

We rested at the cairn and ate some early lunch. The roaring of stags drifted up from the side glens and a glossy raven hung on the gentle breeze. The Aonachs, the Grey Corries, the Mamores and the mountains of Glen Coe were crystal clear and beautifully lit by the low autumn sun but it was the prospect of our next stage that interested us most. We stood in a row, warming our hands on mugs of tea and looked down at the Devil's Ridge. There was a long, abrupt drop from our viewpoint and then a particularly narrow, rocky ridge led steeply up to the pointed summit of Stob Choire a' Mhail.

Once packed up and embarked on this adventurous section I was glad that the rocks were dry and that the wind was negligible. At the start of the climb onto the ridge there were two sections where hands were needed, the holds were rather small and some care was required, but in those conditions it was quite straightforward. The ridge quickly became very narrow, with steep drops on either side but again not too worrying as long as care was taken with each step. An interesting feature which would be a serious challenge in the ice and snow of deep winter.

The Devil's Ridge from Sgurr a' Mhaim. 22/9/12.

We climbed down to a high bealach with a small frozen pool. Tom and K decided to go down to the bright green Lochan Coire nam Miseach and then up onto Stob Ban's east ridge. Morag and I climbed up onto Sgor an Iubhair first.

Sgor an Iubhair, the peak of the yew tree, is an interesting mountain. Four huge corries have eaten into its sides and narrow arêtes divide them; one we had just walked along from the north, another led east to Am Bodach, a third south to Stob Coire na h Eirghe and the last our route to the west. At one time it was classified as a Munro but today is a humble Top. We stood on the broken quartzite which covers the surface of the summit and were surprised to see three small blocks a couple of metres from our boots slowly begin to move. They were ptarmigan, so perfectly camouflaged that we had been unaware of their presence. Their grey and brown was mottled with winter white, perfectly matching the white, lichen-encrusted rock. In seconds they were invisible again.

On Stob Ban's steep and rocky east ridge we could see Tom and K high above, making slow progress. This mountain's east face is a series of precipitous buttresses and gullies, eroded from a giant fold of quartzite beds. Pale screes tumbled into the corrie far below. The sharp angle of the ridge made the climb hard work and we needed to use our hands again on the last section.

Mullach nan Coirean from the East. 22/9/12.

On that wonderful day, Stob Ban's narrow rocky summit was a place to sit down and savour. It had warmed up so we sprawled comfortably in the sun and enjoyed a relaxed lunch. The sinuous ridge leading west to Mullach nan Coirean, the height of the corries, looked like a perfect high-level route. I counted five of the corries which give the Munro its name, three on the north side and two on the south side. There was a clear change in geology, with the quartzite giving way to a dark red rock which turned out to be granite.

Lunch over, we stood on the very edge of the precipice which falls down to Coire Mhusgain. It was a perfect viewpoint from which to look back to the ground we had already covered which was, by mutual agreement, impressive.

The ridge walk to our final Munro was perfect, with wide views over the Glen Coe mountains, Loch Linnhe and the empty country beyond. We stopped to photograph granite pinnacles and again on the final ascent where our viewpoint provided a dark red granite foreground with Stob Ban, white peak, rising behind. The strong afternoon sun illuminated the white cone of Stob Ban and it was clear how it got its name.

Sgurr a' Mhaim (L.) and
Stob Ban (R.) from
Mullach nan Coirean.
22/9/12.

After a brief pause for a drink we began the long descent by the north-east ridge. The only boggy ground we encountered that day was on the lower part of this ridge, before we entered the forest. Just before the final stile Tom announced that he had been sure that he was going to slip and fall and then did precisely that. The last section down through the trees and along the bank of the Allt a' Choire Dheirg was dusky and cool. The path passes a fine waterfall, full of energy that day after the week's heavy rain.

We met up later at the busy pub between the hostel and the campsite. Broccoli soup with crispy warm rolls, venison casserole and South African red wine were ordered. The service was excellent, all was piping hot and delicious and the portions were suitable for diners who had just completed a ten hour mountain walk.

10/11/12

Ben Rinnes and Corryhabbie Hill

In the heart of malt whisky's 'Golden Triangle'

Tom, K, James and I drove north in the red dawn of a frosty November day. We left the car in the car park below the prosaically named Round Hill and began the steady climb up to the summit of Ben Rinnes.

The air was clear and views soon opened up. To the north, the unmistakable hills of Sutherland rose beyond the deep blue of the Moray Firth. To the west lay the snow-capped mountains of the Cairngorms and to the south and east fine hill country rolled on down to the low sun over the sea.

North of the track a thick layer of peat had been dug to fire the local whisky stills.

As we got higher the cold south-westerly wind grew stronger and I was glad of my warm mitts and jacket. The ground was frozen hard and the granite rocks slicked with ice.

Above, we could see one of the hill's granite tors or scurrans. These probably gave Ben Rinnes its name, 'rinn' in Gaelic meaning a sharp point. The highest point is on top of the wonderfully named Scurran of Lochterlandoch. As I was taking out my camera to photograph the others on top of this feature I was disappointed to see thin cloud blow over it. My disappointment was short lived, however, as my companions shouted for me to climb up quickly. I turned to where they pointed to see a perfect Brocken spectre. I was

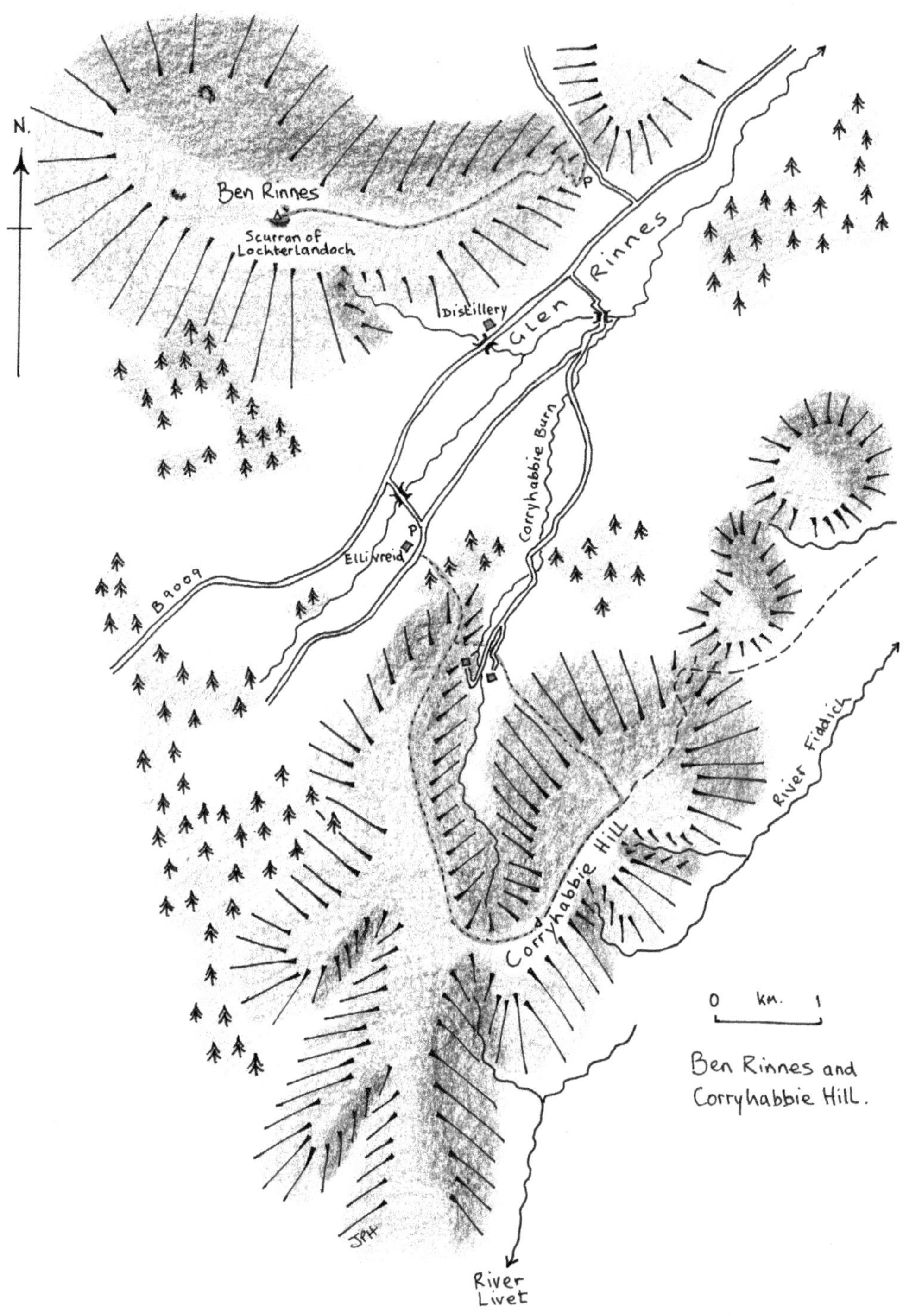
N.
Ben Rinnes
Scurran of Lochterlandoch
Distillery
Glen Rinnes
Corryhabbie Burn
Ellivreid
B9009
Corryhabbie Hill
River Fiddich
0 km. 1
Ben Rinnes and Corryhabbie Hill.
River Livet

glad that I was holding my camera as this magical spectacle is so ephemeral. This time, obligingly, it stayed long enough for K to walk down into it and I was able to photograph her standing in the centre of the spectre's double rainbow rings. My own shadow replaced K in the centre of the rings and the Cloud Appreciation Society's description of the Brocken spectre as 'a ghost from the Sixties' came into my mind, it being surrounded by rainbow colours and having very flared trousers. Given that I was the spectre, a ghost from the Sixties seemed particularly apt.

The wind, blowing from the Cairngorm snowfields, did not invite us to linger up there and we were soon descending the granite rocks of the summit. We paused to look at a pair of ptarmigan. One flew off, skimming the ground, to hide behind a boulder. Its partner stood its ground and posed, a study in irony with its white winter plumage making it so easy to see against the dark pink rock.

We rested at the car and ate an early lunch. I was enjoying a cup of tea when Tom sidled up to my rucksack and, to my surprise, removed a can of Guinness from the top pocket, saying, "Thanks for carrying this to the top and back for me, it's a shame it was too cold up there to sit and drink it." Sometimes one has to re-learn old lessons. It was my friend Fionn's trick appearing in a younger generation.

We drove past the distillery and parked just before Ellivreid Farm. My Ordnance Survey map showed Corryhabbie Hill as the highest point on a massive, flat topped ridge, eaten into by a north-facing corrie from which flows the Corryhabbie Burn. At the end of a track which runs south-east from the farm rises a long spur which steps up to the Hill of Achmore, then Little Lapprach and, finally, Muckle Lapprach. The spur forms the steep western wall of the corrie and seemed the best way to climb up to the heights which dominated the horizon to the south.

An overgrown track through the deer grass and brown heather came to a stop on the Hill of Achmore and we had to make our way up over rough ground. Only on the final steep ascent did we find a narrow, little-used path which helped us up to the crest. As I stood with James waiting for the others to join us I commented that, had this been a Munro rather than a Corbett, there would be a wide, probably badly eroded path up to the summit.

As we walked together over the easy ground of the summit ridge I thought about the significance of this rather unassuming hill. The water running off in little burns to the south becomes the River Livet and that running off to the east becomes the River Fiddich, each name known across the globe. This finest of hill water, like that emerging from the granite springs of Ben Rinnes, combined with local barley, is transformed into some of the very best malt whiskies. Peat from these hills also played its part, firing the kilns in the distilleries. To the south-west The Glenlivet and Tamnavulin are produced; to the north Benrinnes and Glenfarclas; to the east Pittyvaich, The Dufftown, The Balvenie and Glenfiddich. These are perhaps the best known but there are as many again much loved by connoisseurs.

The old triangulation pillar had a shelter cairn built around it but the low sun still shone and we were able to sit outside, in the lee of the cold wind. We rested there and finished our lunches and hot drinks, enjoying the wide panorama which ended in the distant curved horizon of the North Sea.

It was too cold to linger so we were soon marching along Morton's Way, a wide track which runs along the crest of the ridge. After a kilometre we turned north to descend the short heather of a broad spur named The Saddling on the Ordnance Survey map. We curved to the north-west and jumped across the Corryhabbie Burn below the house named Shean Dhu on my map and Sheandow on James's map. Climbing up onto the spur that we had walked up earlier we disturbed a roe buck and doe. They looked down the slope at us, froze for one second, then sprang into the air and bounced down to disappear in the bushes lining the burn.

Back on the track leading down to Ellivreid Farm we walked slowly. The sky was turning pink, a winter flock of birds settled in a coppice and I felt the peace of this lovely glen.

9/1/13

St Colm's Well and The Hill of Cat

Well Beloved

It was a perfect winter morning, the ground was white with frost and there was not a cloud in the sky. James and I drove slowly along the long, single-track road that follows the Water of Feugh through the hoary old birches and twisted Scots pines of the Forest of Birse. We parked at the road end beside the chapel and set off along the track which leads to the castle.

A heron had been fishing in the clear pool underneath the little bridge. It was clearly not expecting the stamp of our heavy boots above its head and it tried to make a rapid escape upstream, not an easy thing for a bird with such big, broad wings. It bounced off a gorse bush, recovered, then was well away in three slow-motion flaps.

Heron, Birse Castle, 9/1/13

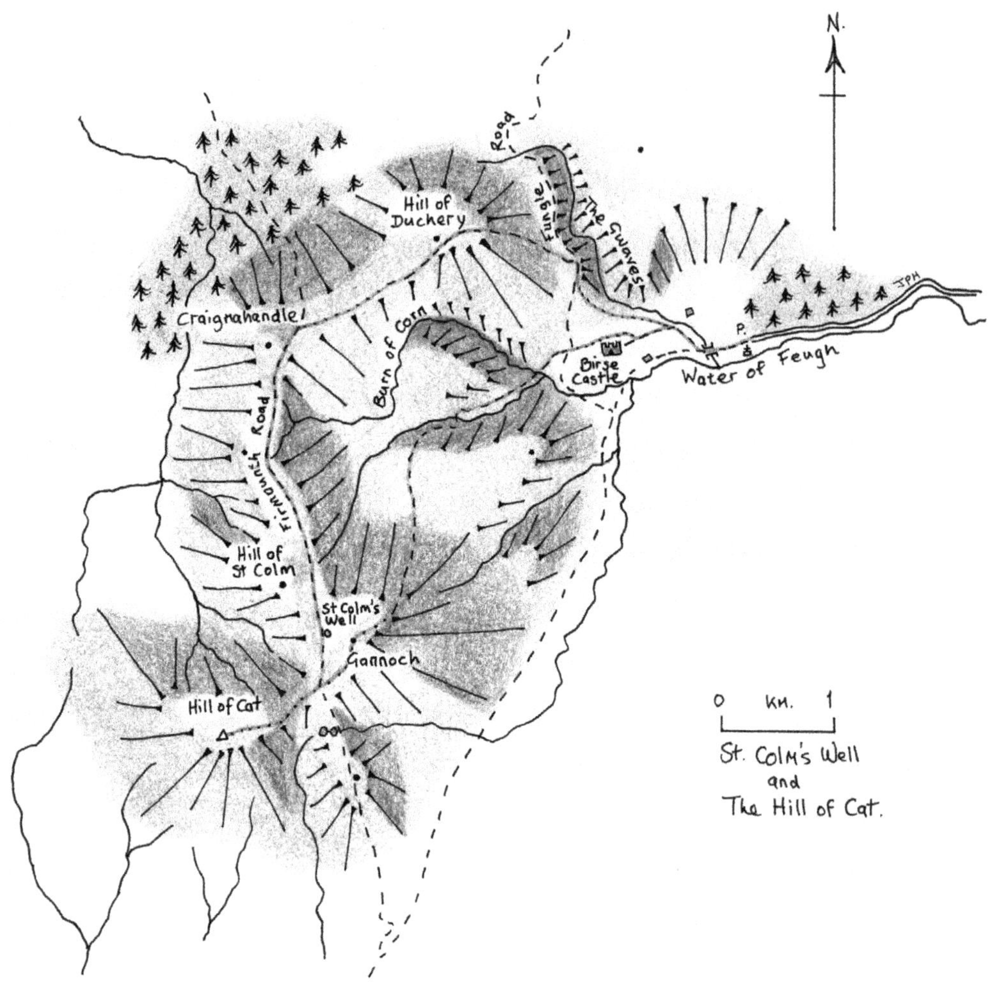

We followed a sheep track up the spur behind Birse Castle and stopped when out of the shadow of the lower ground. With the low sun on our backs we looked into The Gwaves, a dramatic gully with steep walls a hundred metres high. James asked if it was a corrie but I thought it more likely to have been carved by a torrent of glacial meltwater from a decaying ice sheet above.

On the historic Fungle Road, no more than a track to contemporary eyes, we met the estate keeper. He was emptying his traps, throwing the stiff rabbits into a large bucket. He explained that he tries to keep the numbers down because they attract weasels and stoats from the lower ground and these predators attack the grouse. We told him that we planned to walk up onto another ancient track, the Firmounth Road and follow it to St Colm's Well. He pointed out the line of hilltops to the west that we would follow then wished us a good day and went back to his traps. The keeper was the sole person we saw on that peaceful day.

We followed the track to the Hill of Duchery and tramped across the heather to visit its cairn. Under that clear blue sky visibility was perfect and we could see Bennachie to the north-east, the snow-covered Cairngorms to the north and west and the wide, empty country of rounded hills to the south.

On Craigmahandle we joined the Firmounth Road. A cairn had been constructed here to display a metal plaque which gave details of the National Nature Reserve in the Forest of Glen Tanar to the north. It was a welcome sight as there is little shelter on these hilltops and it provided a windbreak against a north-west wind so cold it was burning our cheeks. Our backs to the stone and faces to the sun, we enjoyed a hot drink and a snack.

The walk along the Firmounth Road was full of interest. We stopped before the long, steady climb up onto the Hill of St Colm to look at the colours in the landscape. In the foreground were vivid green pools, each with a skin of ice as clear as glass. Beyond was an expanse of dry, bleached yellow grass, each tussock throwing an almost black shadow in the low winter sunlight. Further up were the rich browns and burnt reds of the old heather sweeping to a sharp horizon with a pale blue sky. These were not the bright colours found on the shores of the Mediterranean and other southern lands but no less beautiful in their subtlety.

As we neared the top of the Hill of St Colm, snowfields lined the old track, each patterned with shadowed hollows separated by sculpted, sparkling ridges. We stopped at a small cairn of lichen-encrusted granite boulders, noting that the face of the central slab was carved with the inscription W.F. 1814. Neither of us could offer an explanation but the pause to consider it led to us looking across to the Hill of Cat, checking the map and concluding that we had walked past our main objective, St Colm's Well.

St. Colm's Well

9/1/13

JPH

We discovered the old well about 500 metres back down the track. The cap stone and marker stone were covered in moss and lichens and partly hidden by tufts of dry deer grass so it was easy to miss. The spring flowed from under the cap stone and fell into a clear green pool. This was the source of a fast little burn which flowed under the old road and downhill to the west. The marker stone had the inscription Well Beloved, carved around a Celtic cross. St Colm was the person who came to Deeside in the Dark Ages and brought Christianity to the area.

The nearby Hill of Cat had the prospect of being an excellent viewpoint so we decided to make its summit the furthest point of our walk. A fence marks the line of the county boundary between Aberdeenshire and Angus and we followed this across pools turned to solid ice, hard frozen peat hags and dimpled snowdrifts to the weathered triangulation pillar on the top. From there the prospect was magnificent, with hills stretching to the horizon in every direction. I felt very small and insignificant in that big, lonely landscape.

There was also beauty above our heads. High clouds had begun to creep across from the west and were getting nearer to the sun. They were small, smooth and fleecy in a repeating pattern known as a mackerel sky. The lower clouds were tinged with pink, with lilac clouds above and then brilliant white. The north-west wind, however, did not encourage us to stay and we walked down to find a sheltered place behind a peat hag and facing the sun. This island in the snowfields was a perfect place to eat lunch and we lingered there, watching the light change as the pink clouds crossed the sky.

Content, we walked back to the Firmounth Road, crossed it and climbed Gannoch, the hill above St Colm's Well. Here we found a track which led down to Birse Castle. It was a good walk back, with the winter sky to the north and east still clear of cloud and a line of purple and pink appearing along the horizon. We stopped to look into the deep gully cut by the Burn of Corn, filled with boulders and gnarled deciduous trees all thickly covered in green moss, a perfect fairy dell. There did not appear to be anyone in residence at the castle, but we skirted the grim old building then cut through the wooded grounds and were soon back at the car.

When driving back through the forest a roe deer ran across the road in front of the car. Most drivers would have just missed hitting it but would have collided with the second, James avoided both. Emerging from that section of the road with steep forested slopes on either side we were surprised to see that the sky was blood red, it seemed a fitting end to a fine winter day. I was pleased that the blood was in the sky rather than on the car.

10/6/13

Ben Vorlich (Arrochar Alps)

A glimpse of the underworld

As I walked from the car park at Inveruglas I felt like a young dog let off his leash. My winter and spring had been intensely busy, I had retired, sold my house in Aberdeen and moved to Dundee. There had been very little time for the hills. The heavy falls of snow which had continued until the end of April had given me some consolation, especially when I listened to reports of friends turning back after attempts to struggle up through the drifts and of avalanche deaths. It probably was a good time to be getting the jobs done.

A hawthorn was just starting to blossom, a good four weeks late after the coldest spring in fifty years. I remembered my Grandmother's, "Never cast a clout until the may's out," and smiled to think I'd got my timing right.

I scanned the southern spur of Ben Vorlich and decided to go straight up. The ground was dry and I wanted part of my walk at least to be away from the eroded Munro path. It was hard work but a good choice. The slopes were carpeted with bluebells and new bracken with tightly curled tops, like the hawthorn a month late. These are plants of the woodland floor, a relic of a time when the mountain's skirts would have been completely forested. The only surviving trees were a scatter of birch and rowan, growing out of crags and boulders where it had been difficult to browse them. Growing next to the drifts of bluebells were many other spring flowers and these were visited by an army of bees and small white butterflies up to a height of 750 metres.

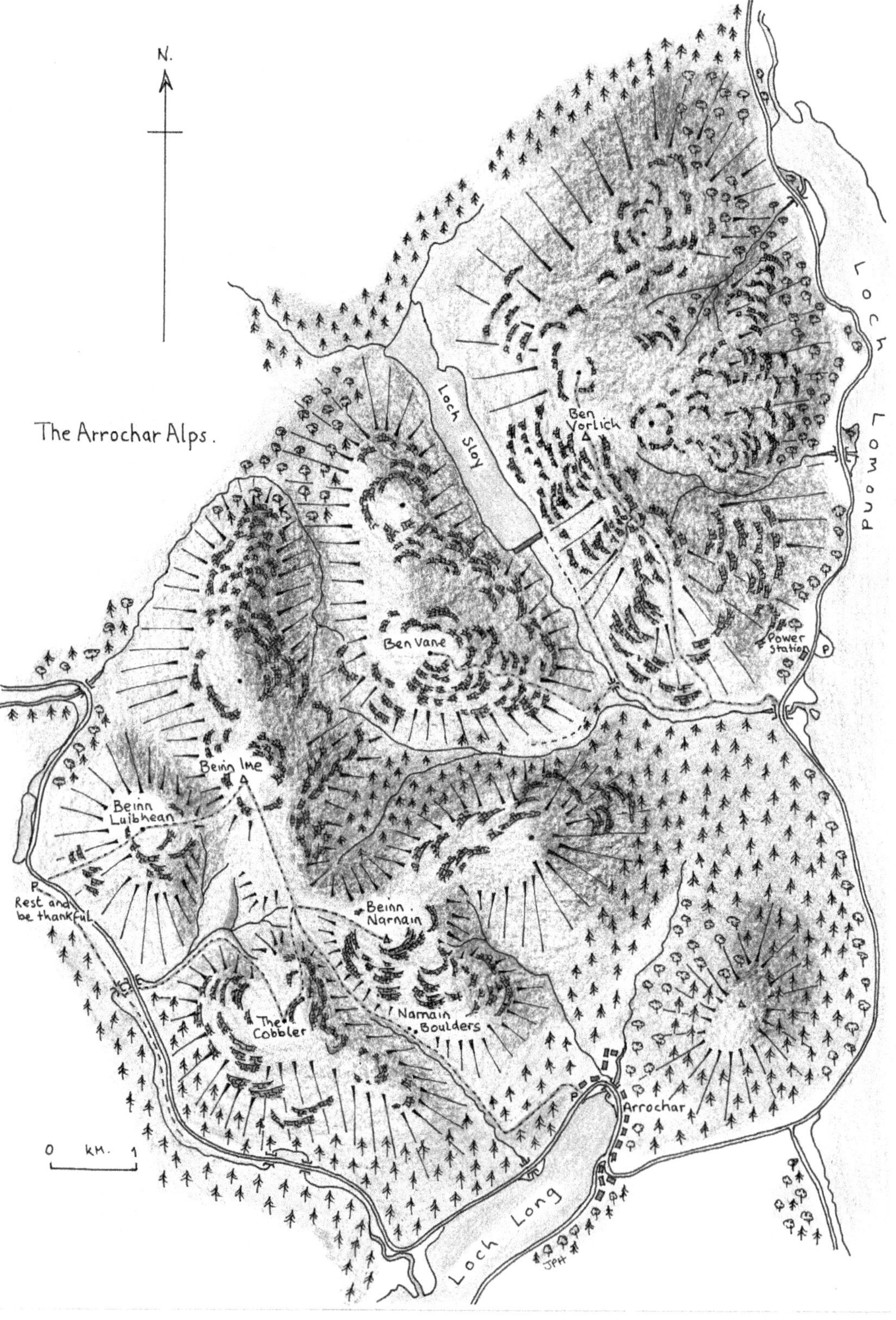
N.
The Arrochar Alps.
Loch Sloy
Ben Vorlich
Loch Lomond
Power station
P
Ben Vane
Beinn Ime
Beinn Luibhean
P
Rest and be thankful
Beinn Narnain
The Cobbler
Narnain Boulders
Arrochar
P
0 KM. 1
Loch Long
JPH

I walked up to the cloud base and sat on a crag to have some lunch while I could still enjoy the view. It was a perfect vantage point for Loch Lomond and was high enough to see Arrochar on the shore of Loch Long to the south and Loch Arklet to the east.

Packed up again, I continued up through the crags and was soon in the cloud. There was little wind and it was a real pea souper. I took a bearing and set off into a strange world of distorted outcrops, ghostly shapes and silence. At the base of looming rock towers I came across deep fissures and chasms. These plunged down into the dark heart of the mountain and I would not have been at all surprised to see in them a flash of the red eyes of some underworld creature.

The exposed rock and fractures continued for well over a kilometre and then I came upon the Munro path, twisting up the western slopes of the ridge. I began to make better time but was sad to leave the wild, pathless section of my walk. The mist continued to play its tricks, however and I nearly lost the path on two occasions. The "tap, tap" of my walking poles was the only sound and as I approached the highest part of the ridge the sensation that I was being watched made me turn around.

I passed the triangulation pillar and walked on to the North Top. As the wind had risen I dropped down the western side of the ridge a short distance, sheltered in a cleft in a massive outcrop and unpacked my flask and sandwiches. I could only see things a few metres away but found that I was drawn to detail. The undulations of the intense folding in the schist; the bands of quartz running parallel to these folds; the dripping moss where there was some shelter and higher up the many coloured lichens, clinging to life where weathering had given them a tenuous hold.

On the way back I decided to descend by the Munro path. There were more fissures and caves, some quite complex with entrances at different levels. I left the path to look more closely at one of these caves, drawn by the sheep's skull near the entrance. It was quite fresh, with the teeth all intact and fine curved horns. I clambered up and peered into the darkness of the cave, wondering what might live in the heart of this mountain.

The steep path was hard on my knees but I was quickly out of the cloud and back into a warm summer day. I could see the way down to the vehicle track I would follow back to the car. Turning around, I looked back and up one last time at the blanket of mist that hid such an extraordinary world.

21/6/13

Auchnafree

On a warm Midsummer Day

I sat in the warmth of hazy sunshine beside the Loch Turret dam, waiting for Morag to join me. On this longest day of the year it had been light for seven hours and the bees had already done a hard day's work gathering pollen from the carpets of wild flowers. Dozens of green-veined white butterflies danced together in the still air, stopping only to refuel on nectar. They were unusual in having pronounced dark veins on their wings. A curlew's haunting cry came from over the water. I dozed off and was woken by the rattle of my friend's car over the cattle grid.

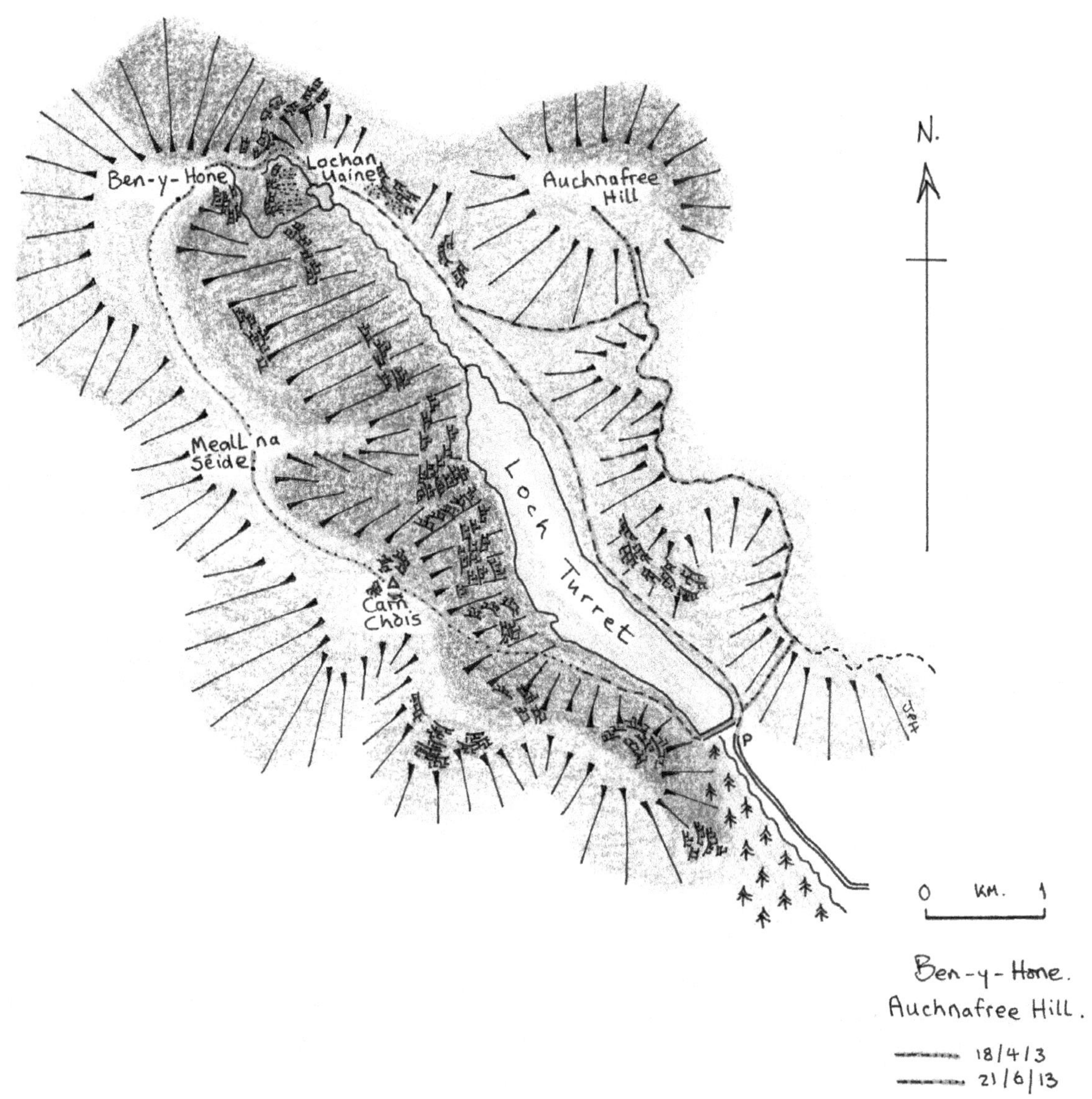

We took a line north-east and climbed up through the dry grasses and rock outcrops onto the ridge. There we found the track that wound north-west most of the way to Auchnafree Hill, our objective for the day. Larks rose and sang their strident song, making claim to their patch of inhospitable ground. The track took us along the rim of a deep corrie drained by the Barvick Burn, the Blue Craigs at its headwall. We stopped for a cup of tea at Choinneachain Hill's western cairn and enjoyed the silence and the views.

A couple of kilometres further on we left the track and followed a stream up onto Auchnafree. Underfoot was a rich carpet of blaeberry and cloudberry, the latter in bloom with splendid white flowers framed by its distinctive leaves. The hill has two cairns and we decided to lunch at the lower one as it had the best views.

Fuelled up like the butterflies, we joined the track again and followed it down into Glen Turret. The floor is a mass of humps and big rocks marking the ablation moraine dumped when the last ice melted in this old glacial trough. A scatter of rowans grew from the rocks and I remarked on the fact that they were in blossom so late in the season, a consequence of a winter which lasted until April. Lochan Uaine lived up to its name, being covered by a floating mat of bright green algae. We stopped there for a last cup of tea in a sun trap sheltered by the rock walls of the corrie, listening to the feet-feet-feet of the meadow pipits and watching the white butterflies flit between flowers. Morag pointed to the path we had taken ten years before up to Ben-y-Hone.

The walk back along the loch shore was splendid, with the sun bringing out the best of the landscape's colours. We stopped twice to watch golden eagles spiralling up on thermals. The sad call of the curlew told us that we were nearly back to the dam. It was strange to think that we were only a few kilometres north of Crieff but had not seen another person all day.

26/6/13

Beinn Bhuidhe

At the heart of our culture

At the walkers' car park at the head of Loch Fyne, James and I examined the map. I suggested using the road on the east side of the River Fyne as the cartographer had made it look more substantial than that on the west side, shown only with broken lines. James, however, declared that his guidebook indicated that the western route should be used and so we mounted our cycles and set off that way. It proved to be a bit of a challenge on a rough, stony track which took us through a gravel pit, around heavy plant moving on caterpillar tracks, through the middle of a large herd of Highland cattle and across a small lake of slurry. This last left its mark on James who had to dismount in its centre to let a lorry go past. We stopped at the bridge where our track met the road we should have taken and I asked, knowing the answer, how many decades old the guidebook was.

A couple of kilometres of uneventful cycling brought us to a gate with a sign stating that no bikes could be ridden past this point. We must have failed to read it as we rode on to the house at Inverchorachan and left the bikes there.

The first stage of our walk was up a steep-sided gully. A lively stream rushed down it over a series of waterfalls, some with deep, clear pools at their base. The sheltering walls gave this delightful place a microclimate which supported a lush vegetation. The upper storey was made up of birch, rowan and alder, then there were tall plants dominated by

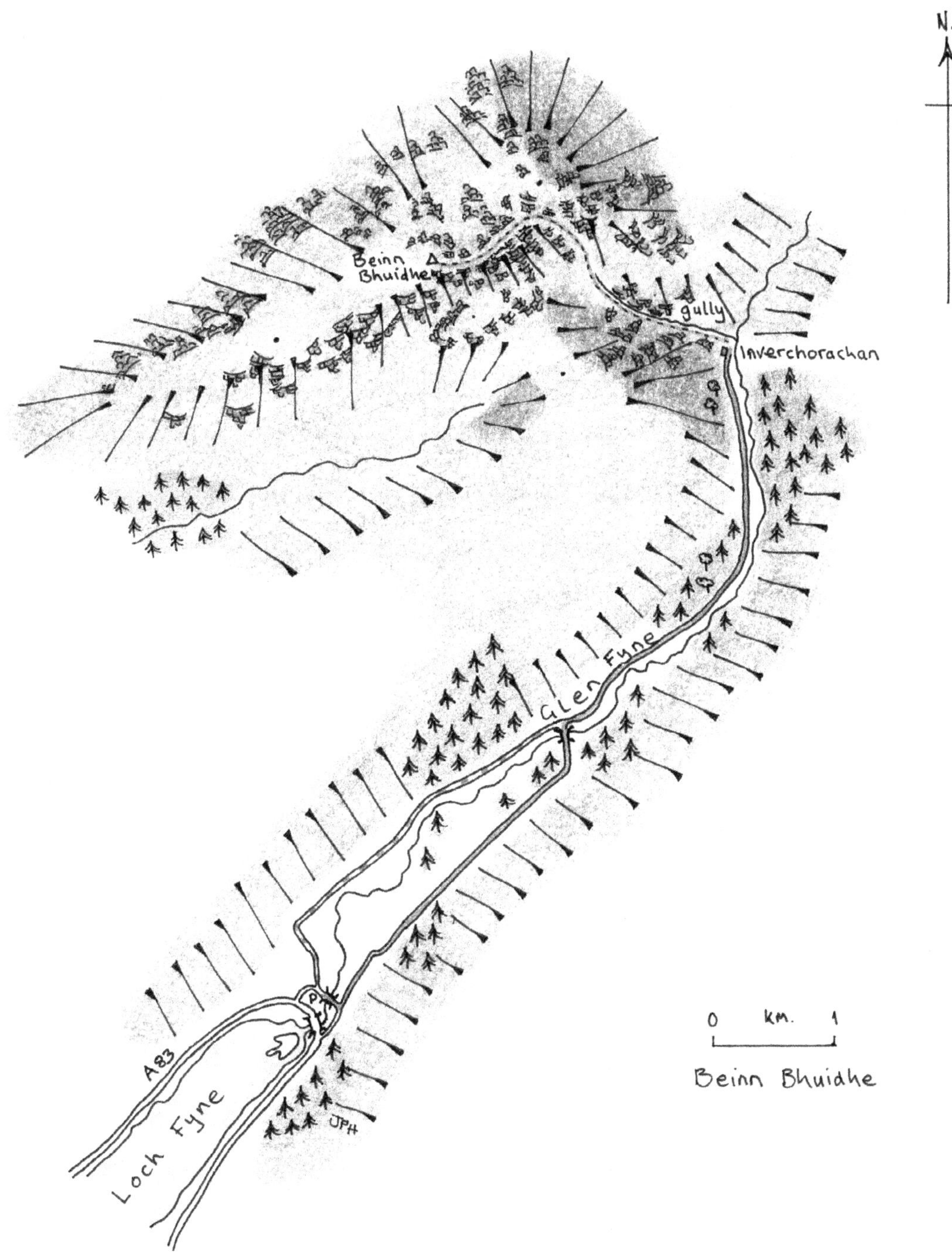
N.
Beinn Bhuidhe
gully
Inverchorachan
Glen Fyne
A83
Loch Fyne
P
JPH
0 KM. 1
Beinn Bhuidhe

bracken but including swathes of yellow irises and pink foxgloves. Wherever the light could get through there was a multitude of shorter wild flowers like tormentil and forget-me-not. The path is steep and our hands were needed at some awkward sections with sharp drops to the boulders far below. The sun had shone since dawn and it was warm and humid.

The jungle,
Beinn Bhuidhe.

We were hot and sticky when we climbed above the last waterfall and caught the welcome breeze of the open hill. Resting on a rock to drink a cup of tea we enjoyed great views over the rocky Crianlarich hills and the Arrochar Alps, picking out the distinctive shapes of Ben Vane and The Cobbler.

A short walk across the hummocky floor of one of Beinn Bhuidhe's corries brought us to the foot of the tall rocky wall of the mountain's main ridge. A very steep path zig zagged up to a notch high above on the knobbly skyline, it had worn down to the rock in places, exposing sheets of muscovite mica, silky and golden in the sun. Once up that we turned south-west to follow the path to the summit.

This path follows the edge of the sheer cliff and needs concentration. It is not the place to get distracted by the views and make a wrong step. We came to the last pull up to the summit, our steps quickened with expectation, only to be disappointed. There, directly below on the prow of Clachan Hill, was a wind farm. James was furious. At the fallen triangulation pillar we looked at the landscape, starting at the wind turbines and covering the full 360°. To the west was the Isle of Mull, its mountains seeming to float on the Hebridean sea. To the north, range after range of blue mountains stretched to the distant horizon. We could pick out Bidean nam Bian and the whaleback of Ben Nevis, the only peak with a cloud cap. To the east our eyes swept over the craggy peaks clustered around the northern banks of Loch Lomond. "This is matchless and so rare," declared James, a statement given more weight as it came from a person who has travelled to most parts of the world.

Carefully selecting a spot where our backs were toward the turbines, we settled to eat our lunch, discussing the way these colossal white machines, out of scale with our modest hills, are increasingly eroding our precious wild landscapes. Neither of us disagree with the use of wind turbines but some sites are completely inappropriate. The Highlands are known worldwide for their scenic beauty and Scots are intensely proud of their rugged wildness, so much so that it is not too much to say that they are at the heart of our culture. This alone should be enough for the Scottish Government to protect the mountains from industrialisation.

On the way down we met a young couple. The girl was having difficulty breathing after climbing up through the tall bracken that filled the gully. It was much hotter in there than on the way up and we took plenty of time to descend. I made a number of forays into the lush vegetation which included drifts of knapweed and orchids, being careful where I placed each footstep as there were young frogs everywhere. It was good to see so many bumble bees (Bombus lucorum) and fittingly for a jungle, huge dragonflies. The pools beneath the waterfalls tempted us but we had to consider our drive back to the east coast.

As I cycled back down the glen, threading through another herd of Highland cattle, I thought of those who had to walk out along that long road, a tough prospect.

21/7/13

Beinn Sgulaird

Hot work

James and I drove across the country in that rarest of occurrences, a Highland heat-wave. It had been 29° Celsius in the campsite at Tyndrum and the campers, nearly all West Highland Way walkers, were lying by their tents exhausted. We had taken a wooden hut for the night so we left our sleeping bags there and went to the kitchen to make some tea. Two Danish girls with burnt cheeks were interested in the map we spread out on the table and they stayed to chat to the two old-timers, providing most agreeable company.

We were up at 5.00 a.m. so that we could make an early start and avoid some of the heat. The car was left on the lovely shore of Loch Creran and we quickly gained height on a raw bulldozed track. The slopes are grassy and provide grazing for hill cattle. We threaded through two groups drinking from shallow, muddy pools, the only water sources we saw on the parched hillsides.

It was hot work getting to the bealach as we were in the lee of the easterly breeze. Once there we enjoyed the wind on our faces as we rested and drank from our bottles. There was a steep scramble ahead up the south spur of the ridge so we climbed at a gentle pace under the fierce sun. The rock had changed to pink granite and we passed many perched blocks, giant boulders left by the melting ice, some precariously balanced on three or four small rocks. The low ground between Beinn Sgulaird and its eastern neighbours was littered with them.

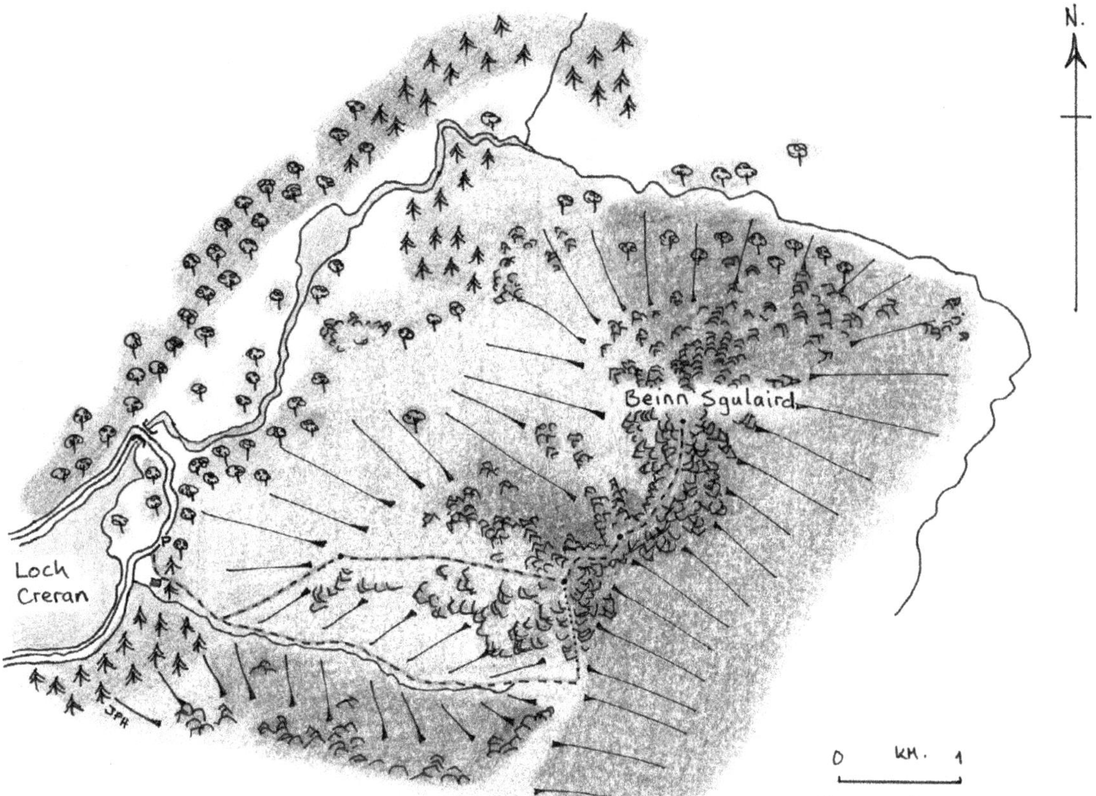

Beinn Sgulaird

At a particularly steep section I looked up to see a big old ram. He looked like he had evaded recent round-ups as his fleece was matted and trailed to the ground. I climbed nearer and nearer and only at the last moment, when I could have reached out to touch him, did he proudly and slowly step out of my way. He was the king of the mountain but it was a lonely job as we saw no other sheep that day.

Just past the ram I pulled myself up and onto a granite outcrop and surprised a herd of 40 to 50 hinds. They poured gracefully down the eastern side of the mountain and despite being on such open ground performed a miracle of disappearance in under 30 seconds.

Large Heath.

The slope began to ease and we came across small pools with wonderful dragonflies, one blue and the rest brown. I stood and watched their aerial manoeuvres, marvelling at flying skills and acceleration I have not seen matched by any other animal. The hot, dry weather seemed to have benefitted butterflies as we had seen many on the way up and here were mountain ringlets, some nearly black, dark orange coppers and pale orange heaths.

The plants did not appear to have suffered from the heat-wave either. Purple bell heather and bright yellow bog asphodel were like jewels in the bright light and delicate pink orchids stood among the nodding cotton grass.

We rested on the south top, grateful for the breeze and looked at Beinn Sgulaird's rocky ridge. It is a giant, elongated granite tor and a fine ridge walk from our viewpoint to the summit. There were sections where we needed to use our hands but the rock was bone dry and its rough surface provided good grip. Our progress was slow as we kept stopping to enjoy the views on such a perfect day.

At the summit we halted for lunch and looked at the surrounding mountains. To the north, Beinn a' Bheithir looked splendid. I thought of those walking its sinuous ridge and could picture the fine views they would have of the Glen Coe mountains. Beyond, Ben Nevis was completely clear of cloud and surrounded by mountains with quartzite caps looking like snow in that strong light. These included the Grey Corries to the north

21/7/13
Beinn Sgulaird

of the Water of Nevis and Sgurr a' Mhaim and Stob Ban to the south, contrasting with the red screes of Mullach nan Coirean. Our gaze swept past Ben Starav, Ben Lui and Ben Cruachan and then across the shimmering sea to Mull and Ben More. A golden yellow band above the western mountains faded through pale green into the deep blue sky. I lay back on the dry moss and looked up at the fine white brush strokes of wispy cirrus clouds which made the blue even more intense.

James woke me to say it was time to walk down. I felt guilty as he had been picking up litter around the summit cairn while I slept.

We retraced our steps, meeting other walkers as we expected on such a fine Sunday. Some were in shorts, some hatless and even shirtless and all had a combination of burnt legs, shoulders and faces.

Our descent from the south top was down the west spur among more dragonflies and dancing butterflies. There was a wonderful smoky smell of hot earth mixed with drifts of sweet perfumes from the bell heather and mountain herbs.

The views were down onto Loch Creran with its attractive new bridge at the narrows. Near the shore, we stopped to watch an eagle circling overhead. Here, the air smelled of warm resin from a stand of old pines and it was good to end our day walking in their blissful shade.

13/8/13 - 14/8/13

Seana Bhraigh • Sgurr Breac

Good fortune and a great prize

Just past Braemore Junction is Iain Kay's little bunkhouse, which I was surprised to discover is in his tidy back garden. Rain began to fall as I arrived.

James, Morag and I were joined by Julia, a young German girl who had travelled here alone to see the Highlands. We enjoyed a good, home-cooked meal and a companionable evening. That night I was awoken by heavy rain drumming on the metal roof. The sound grew faint and was replaced by a pair of tawny owls calling to each other, "tu-whit, tu-whoo".

Early next morning we left the cars at Inverlael and cycled through the forestry, leaving our bikes at the gate in the deer fence. It was a fine day and ahead lay a long walk to the remote Seana Bhraigh.

All went well until we came to the ford and discovered that the overnight rain had turned the river into a roaring torrent. All we could do was tramp over the rough ground on the south bank until we found a better place to cross. Even there, however, the boulders we used as stepping stones were well submerged and water swirled over our boots.

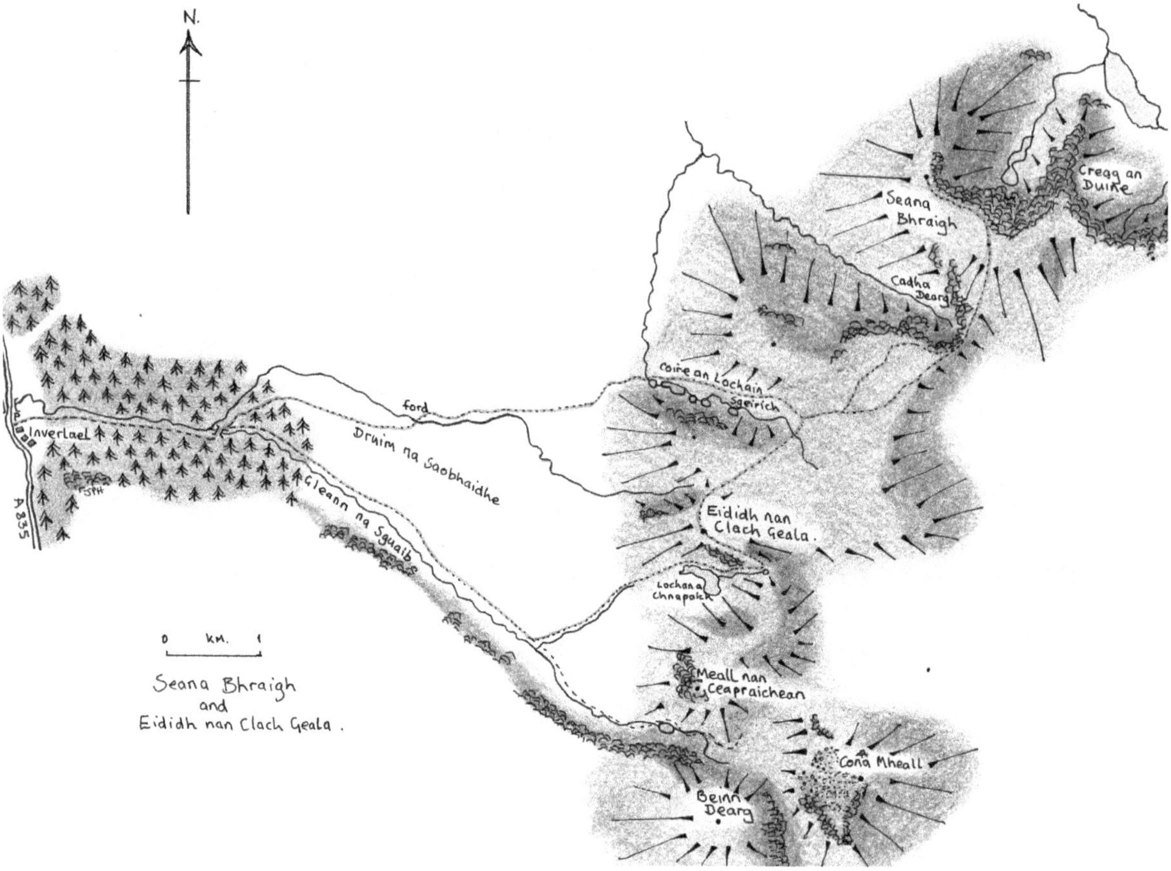

Seana Bhraigh and Eididh nan Clach Geala.

We stopped at a line of little lochans for tea and a rest and shortly after setting off again came to the end of the path. Agreeing on a line through the crags and outcrops, we set off into a wilder landscape. At one point we stopped to watch a hind and her calf just ahead who had not caught our scent. They looked in first class condition after the lovely summer.

Hind and calf, Seana Bhraigh.

Our next stop was on the edge of the cliff which is the headwall of the massive Cadha Dearg. We looked down into a classic corrie with a wide glaciated U-shaped valley beyond. Grazing peacefully on the floor was a large herd of hinds, tiny red-brown specks at that distance. We looked up to Seana Bhraigh and were disappointed to see it covered in cloud.

On the south top, the wind began to tear holes in the cloud and we crossed our fingers that it would be swept away.

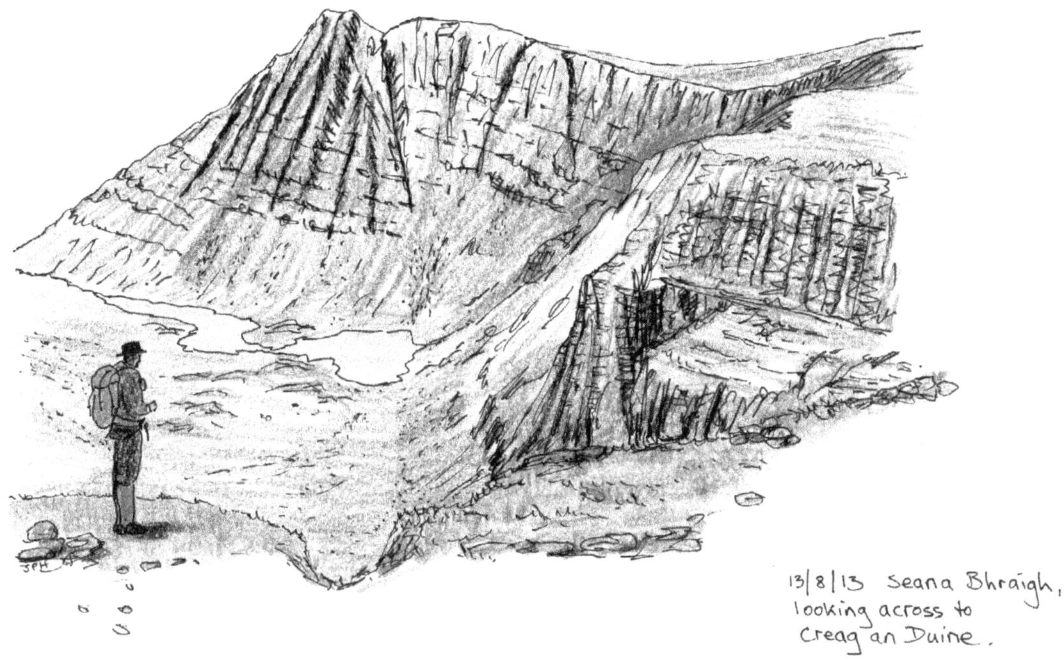

13/8/13 Seana Bhraigh, looking across to Creag an Duine.

At the summit, which we agreed was a great capture, we sat behind the shelter cairn as the wind was in the north-west. There was enough visibility to let us see that we were perched on the very edge of the sheer cliff which forms the headwall of Seana Bhraigh's vast northern corrie. We ate our lunch, packed up and then, like a miracle, the cloud blew away to the south-east. Revealed was the spectacle of this iconic mountain's northern cliffs. We followed the cliff edge for an hour onto the Creag an Duine ridge, enjoying the view across to the outlandish and unique silhouettes of the Inverpolly mountains.

Our way back began on an intermittent path that followed the headwall of Cadha Dearg. We met a male and a female ptarmigan who were not too concerned about our arrival. They wore their late summer mottled plumage but when they did fly off, making their wooden rattle sound, they showed us their brilliant white wings.

Another hind was grazing just ahead of us. She moved over the skyline and when we got there we saw that she had joined a group of 40 to 50.

We had tea at the lochans to fortify ourselves for the long walk out. When we got to the ford we were relieved to see that the water had dropped considerably and we crossed with no difficulty.

The bikes provided the perfect end to our expedition, giving us a fast run back to the cars and allowing us to complete our walk in under 10 hours.

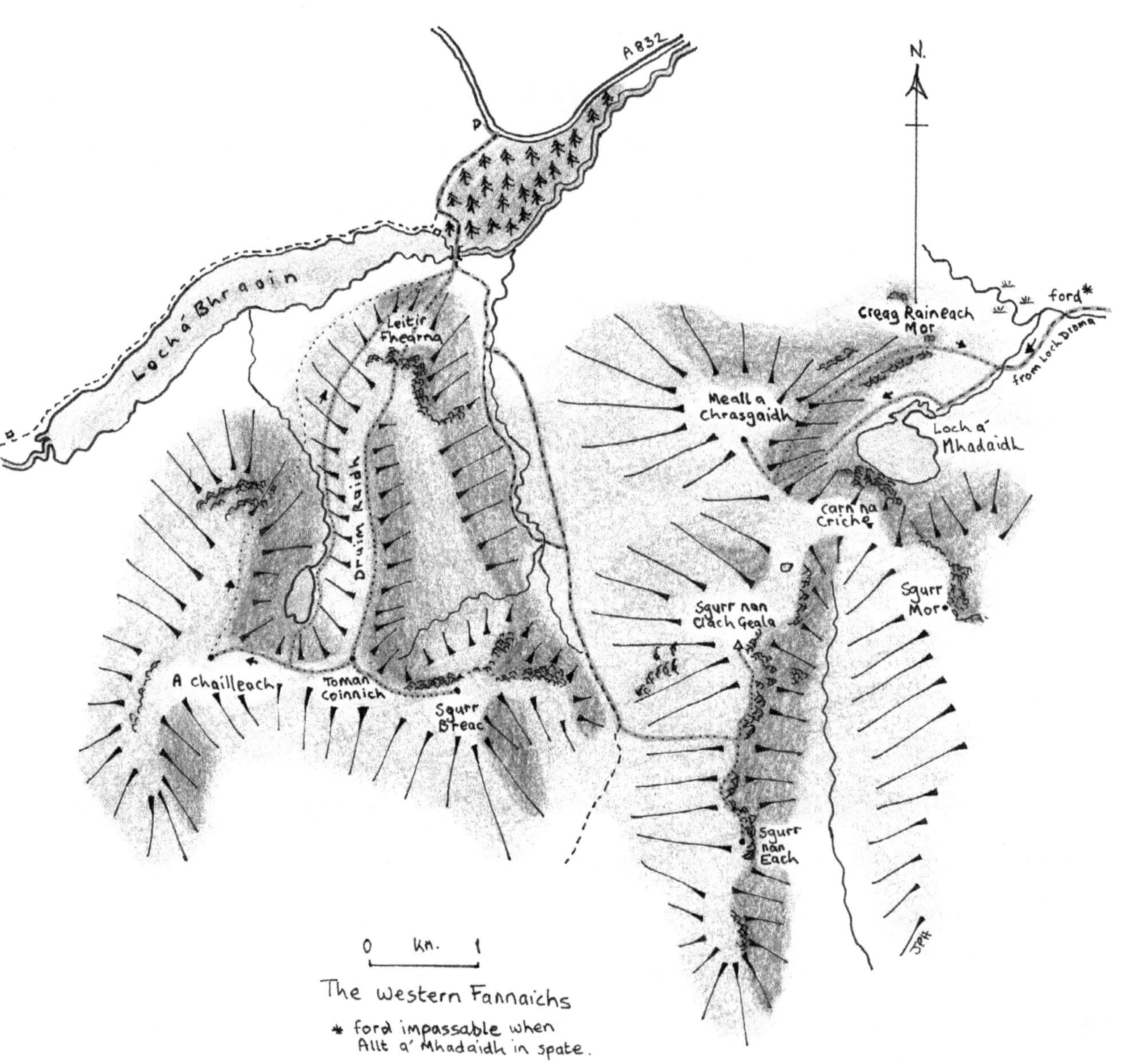

The following day, Morag and I rose at 5.00 a.m. James stirred to say, "I wish you a good day," adding, "I'll rise at a more acceptable time and take a civilised breakfast at the Aultguish Inn."

We parked above Loch a' Bhraoin and discovered that the public right of way had been diverted from the old boathouse through the forest.

Our route was up the Leitir Fhearna, which meant a hard climb but a remarkably quick way to gain height. It was a fine walk along the crest of the Druim Rèidh, there was cloud on the summits but we hoped that it would lift as it had done on the previous day. We stopped to watch over 50 hinds walk across our path in a long line.

14/8/13
On the bridge over the Abhainn Cuileig, Sgurr Breac in the distance.

On Toman Coinnich we entered the cloud. There was a strong wind and it was cold enough for us to need jackets and gloves.

We climbed up onto Sgurr Breac in the clammy mist. I was using my GPS to check that we were at the true summit cairn when holes began to tear in the cloud and we could see that we were indeed on the very top. It was too cold to linger so we turned back. We had only taken a few steps when the cloud cleared, revealing the grand scale of the mountain.

Back on Toman Coinnich, we turned to admire Sgurr Breac and then enjoyed a fine walk back along the Druim Rèidh. The sky was now blue and the sun hot so we stopped to pack away our warm gear. It was a crystal-clear morning and the best views were to the north and west. An Teallach was the most striking, looking like a mountain from a fantasy film. We marvelled that once we had climbed those remarkably steep slopes.

Sun-warmed rocks in the lee of the wind provided a perch for a perfect breakfast spent quietly watching a large herd of hinds grazing far below on the floor of Coire Breac.

20/8/13

Beinn a' Chlachair

The stonemason's mountain

I was on the road by 6.00 a.m., partly because an Atlantic depression was due to sweep across later in the day. It was a golden morning in the Carse of Gowrie and over the Highland Line the low sun beautifully illuminated the late summer colours of the Drumochter Hills.

I parked at the western end of Loch Laggan and was watched by a buzzard sitting on a pole as I took my bike out of the car. I cycled over the bridge and two buzzards rather ponderously flapped down from the trees. One kept me company for a while, a couple of metres above.

The cycle ride to Lochan na h-Earba is to be recommended. I left my bike on the beach then cut across the rough ground under Sgurr an t-Saighdeir to the track, making a small pile of stones to show where to leave it on the way back.

Beinn a' Chlachair, hill of the stonemason (the name reflecting the sound of that ancient trade), has two north-west spurs embracing its big corrie and I decided to climb up the nearest one. It was rough ground again, but dry underfoot. The heather was in bloom and there were ripe blaeberries, cowberries and cloudberries all the way up the slope. I thought of the deer eating their fill and putting on fat for the winter. Meadow pipits were everywhere and I stopped to look at a particularly large, pale coloured frog.

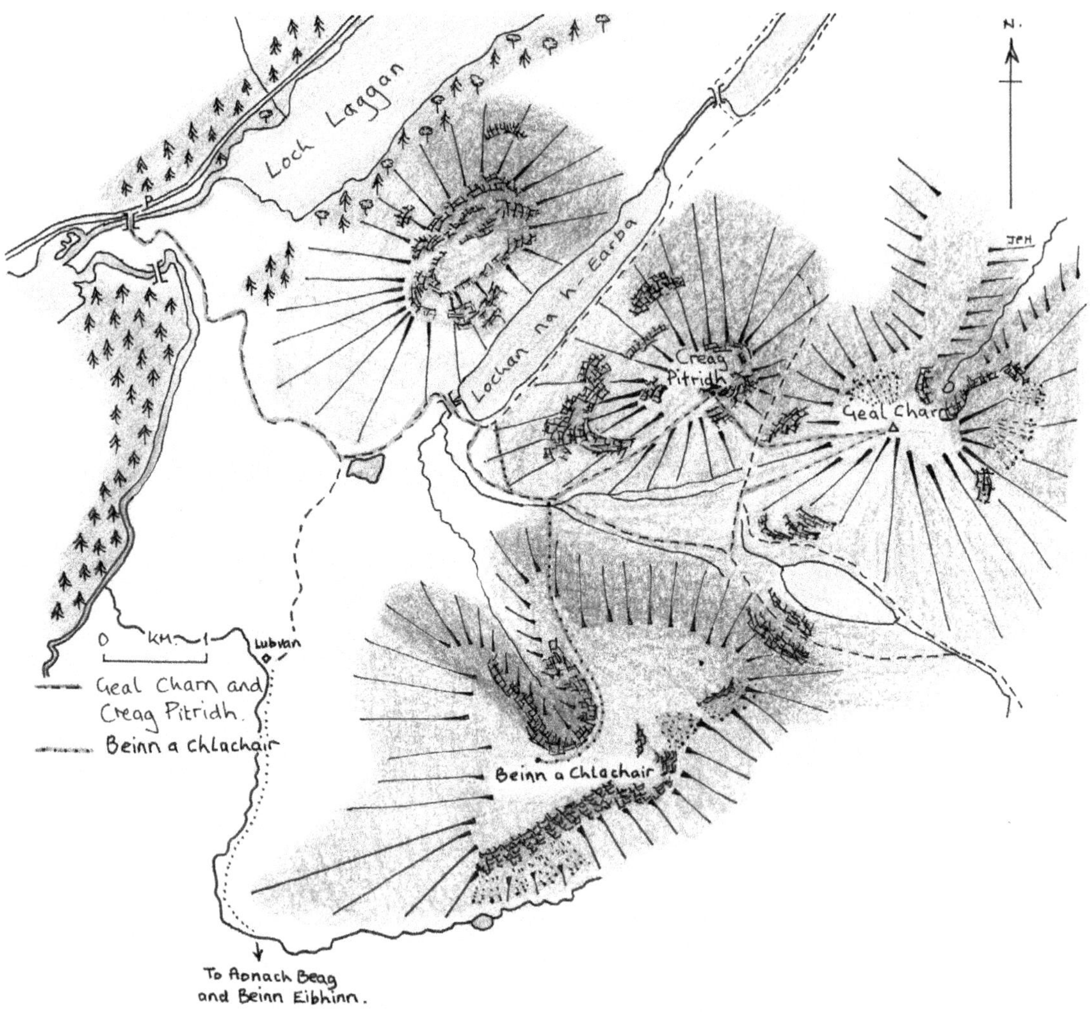

On the crest of the ridge I stepped onto stony ground and caught the strong westerly wind. It was surprisingly cold so I made for a rock outcrop topped with large boulders as it was the only shelter I could see up there. I found a pleasant alcove in the lee of that wind, put on a warm jacket and enjoyed a late breakfast with a clear view across to Creag Pitridh and Geal Charn with its large pointed summit cairn.

Warmed up by mugs of tea and with my energy levels topped up, I continued around the rim of the corrie, enjoying the spectacle of the mountain's plunging cliffs.

I clambered up onto the summit cairn, looking forward to the views to the west but met with a hurtling wall of cloud which smothered the summit in two seconds. Consoling myself with the clear views I had experienced on the way up, I turned round and made

my way down the stony slope. I stopped after 100 metres or so and wondered whether I was going the right way. There was no sign of a path among the rocks and I could see no landmarks. One voice in my head said, "Don't be silly, of course you're going the right way," but the other, more experienced, voice said, "*Better be safe than sorry. Set a bearing.*" So I did and was surprised to see that, in that short distance, I had managed to veer round to face south-west when I should have been walking north-east. At that moment the cloud blew off the top of the mountain and revealed all. I turned 180° and began to walk down the same spur I had come up.

Back at the outcrop, I sat on the same rock, sheltered from the wind and ate a pleasant, unhurried lunch with a panorama of mountains before me. I thought about the deep litter of angular rock pieces on the summit of Beinn a' Chlachair and understood why the mountain got its name.

On my way again, I found a bit of a path but left it to go down rough ground to the track far below. This was marked by the shoes of a ghillie's pony, led up to collect a red deer carcass. I turned off the track at my little pile of stones and was soon on the beach beside the lovely lochan. Patches of sunlight lit the steep crags on each side and made the water sparkle. I was sad to leave.

My bike ride back to the road was a boon as I barely had to pedal. A buzzard on the same pole watched me take off my boots. I shut the car door and fat raindrops slapped onto the windscreen, the depression had arrived.

26/8/13

Aonach Beag and Beinn Eibhinn

The challenge of the Munros

Early morning fog is not uncommon along the Carse of Gowrie but I could not switch off my fog lights until Drumochter. There I was treated to the wonderful sight of a temperature inversion. The mountains were like islands in a foamy white sea. As I drove down to Loch Lagan, however, I plunged back into the eerie world of the fog.

I cycled to Lubvan in fog. I walked to the end of the Ghillies' path in fog. The one redeeming feature of it is that one is more aware of what is immediately underfoot. The hill ponies had left their shoe prints going out and back, kept busy in this stalking season. A newt, going in my direction, swam breast stroke in a puddle.

Crossing the Allt Cam at the ford, I climbed up Meall Nathrach on a bearing to the west of the crags. I did not expect a path on this little-used approach to the hill and there was none. As I approached the top I climbed out of the fog and it was a strange sensation to look down on the surrounding billowy ocean. Did it stretch all the way back to the starting point of my journey on the Firth of Tay? Looking across to Beinn a' Chlachair, I thought of standing on its tall cairn six days before. I would not have known the mountain well at all had I not had this view of the dramatic cliffs of its south face. Turning to look south, there was still a lot of Aonach Beag to climb.

At the point where the steep, rocky slope began to ease a little, I came upon a group of hinds. The wind was in the south-west so they had not caught my scent and I came

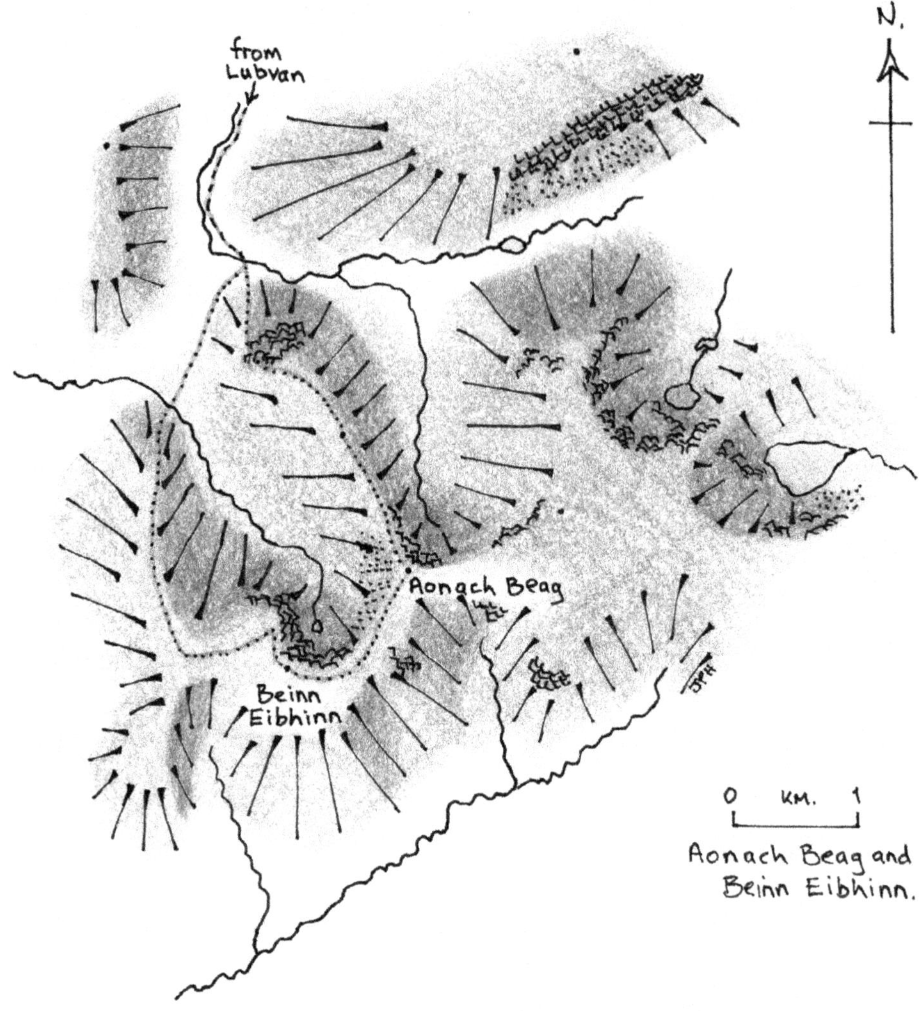

remarkably close to them. Once they had seen me they performed their disappearing trick, heading down to Coire na Coichille.

It was still early, the cloud was blowing off the summit and the wind was cool. I clambered down from the cairn onto a rock which stuck out like a pulpit from the sheer crags of the north-east face. There I ate an early lunch, drank mugs of hot tea and had a much needed rest. I was watching the fog being blown up and over the bealach below, then melting like smoke in the dark blue sky when I heard a male voice in intense discussion with somebody but by the time I had packed up and returned to the cairn there was no one. Then I spotted a person in a red jacket going fast up the narrow curved ridge to Beinn Eibhinn. Why only one person?

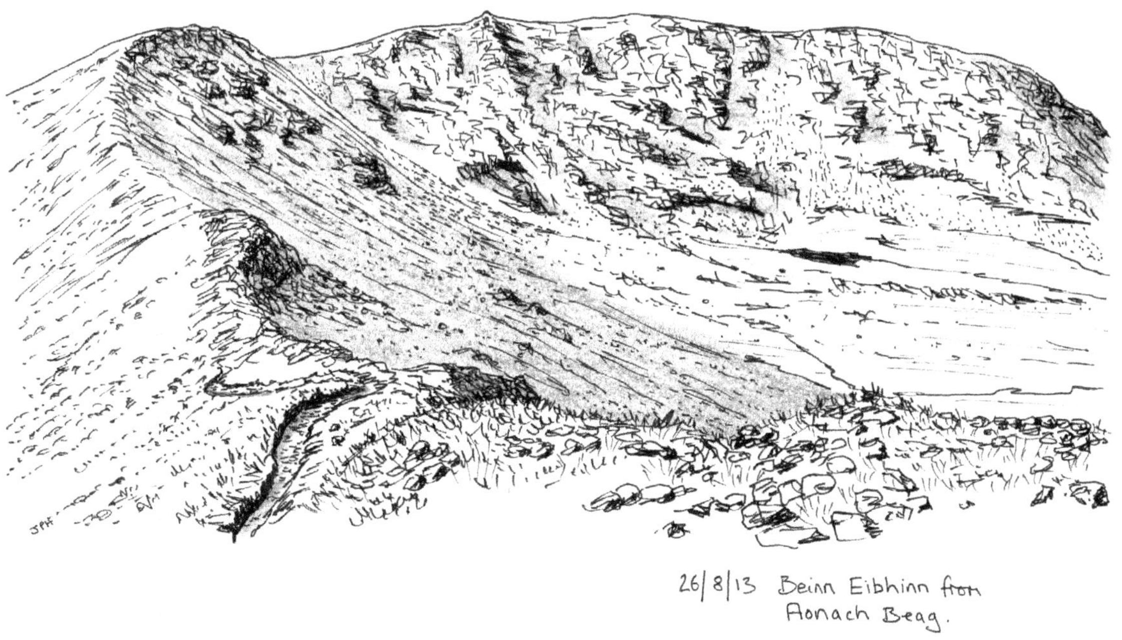

26/8/13 Beinn Eibhinn from Aonach Beag.

I followed the well-worn Munro path, stopping often to enjoy the form of this mountain, pronounced byn ayveen, which means delightful hill. Far below, a herd of about a hundred hinds grazed in a pool of sunlight on the corrie floor. The person ahead was a fit looking young man and he met me as he returned down the ridge. He had come from Culra bothy and had seen no one but me. I asked about the voice on Aonach Beag. "My wife called on my mobile, heard the wind and told me to get straight down."

"She must worry about you."

"That's an understatement. I would love to climb the Munros but she hates me going, so I probably never will."

"I feel sorry for you both!" We parted with a smile.

After the cairn, I left the path and walked around the corrie rim. Beinn Eibhinn lived up to its name, particularly for the view across the grand corrie to the shapely Aonach Beag. I then headed west into pathless country again, intending to turn north and go down the Sron an Fhuaran ridge. It was dry, the sun was hot and it was good walking.

I stopped behind a perched boulder as big as a lorry to shelter from the breeze and finish my lunch. I was at peace and far away from cares. It is this that calls me to these wild mountain places and I saw something of it in the eyes of the young man in the red jacket. I hope that he has managed to return. Does it matter that he may never climb the Munros? Would I be able to climb them all? I have talked to hillwalkers who have hung up their boots (or planted flowers in them) after climbing their last Munro, a reaction that I find most odd. I would like to become a Munroist, to achieve this mountaineering feat, but afterwards would like to wear out many more pairs of boots in the Highlands.

My memory of the walk down will be of the wide prospect over Glen Spean with its backdrop of the Creag Meagaidh mountains. On the corrie floor I crossed three twinkling burns with little silvery waterfalls and dark pools. There were frogs everywhere. I startled a red grouse, intent on fattening up for the winter. The heather was blooming, the slopes were carpeted with berries and various bizarre species of fungus poked up through the deer grass. Now that I was down from the ridges it was hot. I crossed back over the ford, made fast progress along the path and was soon back at the ruin. A Land Rover and horse box for the hill ponies was parked there.

It was a joy to cycle back. Four glossy blackcock flew over me in formation and I stopped to watch them. They tilted a little sideways, showing off their brilliant white wing bars and long tails. I twisted round to look back at the mountains, a little sad that I was leaving that elemental world. I would return home more relaxed, with a feeling of well-being which lasts several days, then I begin to crave the next adventure and reach for my maps.

I love the free breath of the broad-wing'd breeze,
I love the eye's free sweep from craggy rim,
I love the free bird poised at lofty ease,
And the free torrent's far-upsounding hymm;
I love to leave my littleness behind
In the low vale where little cares are great,
And in the mighty map of things to find
A sober measure of my scanty state

John Stuart Blackie
From *'Lays of the Highlands and Islands'*, 1872

The author was a professor of Greek
at Edinburgh University
and lived from 1809 to 1895

Acknowledgements

Thanks to my wife, Jane, for understanding that I need my days of peace and freedom, and for the proofing and critical reading of this book. To my sister, Helen, for her support and suggestions.

To the Jolly Boys for their friendship and the memorable days.

I am a stubborn and determined man and my companions can suffer as a consequence, so I thank three people in particular who have suffered at times beyond the call of duty. My son, Tom, who pulls us back from potentially dark moments with his humour. Morag, a trusty mountaineer to her bones. And James, who can soldier on through the toughest days and never lose his mischievous wit.

I am grateful to the Scottish Mountaineering Club for their excellent guides and the Ordnance Survey for their world-leading maps.

Finally, a techno-dinosaur like me needs technical support when writing a book and that was provided by my patient son-in-law, Chris.

Index of mountains and hills featured in Book 2

Munros in bold text

Also by Jack P. Harland

HIGHLAND JOURNAL

1. THE MAKING OF A HILLWALKER

J P Harland

JACK P. HARLAND

'This is a remarkable achievement.'

George Douglas

ISBN: 9781789013252
Paperback: £15.99
Ebook: £6.99